Satan's Silence

Satan's Silence

RITUAL ABUSE AND THE MAKING OF A MODERN AMERICAN WITCH HUNT

Debbie Nathan *and* Michael Snedeker

BasicBooks
A Division of HarperCollinsPublishers

Designed by Elliott Beard

Library of Congress Cataloging-in-Publication Data
Nathan, Debbie.
    Satan's silence : ritual abuse and the making of a modern American witch hunt /
  Debbie Nathan & Michael Snedeker.
        p.   cm.
    Includes bibliographical references and index.
    ISBN 0-465-07180-5 (cloth)
    ISBN 0-465-07181-3 (paper)
    1. Ritual abuse—United States.   2. Ritual abuse victims—United States.
  3. Satanism—United States.   I. Snedeker, Michael R.   II. Title.
  HV6626.52.N379   1995
  346.1'5554'0973—dc20   95–22288
                                                                            CIP

96 97 98 99 ❖/RRD 9 8 7 6 5 4 3 2 1

To the memory of Eric Henrikson and Morton Stavis
and to the men and women still incarcerated,
including those whose names we know:

Gerald Amirault (Malden, Mass.)

Bernard Baran, Jr. (Lanesborough, Mass.)

Jeanie Bendt (Wenatchee, Wash.)

Lawrence Catcheway (Wenatchee, Wash.)

Anthony Cox (Kern County, Calif.)

George Cox (Kern County, Calif.)

Carol Doggett (Wentachee, Wash.)

Mark Doggett (Wentachee, Wash.)

Harold Everett (Wenatchee, Wash.)

Idella Everett (Wenatchee, Wash.)

Patrick Figured (Smithville, N.C.)

Gary Filbeck (Wenatchee, Wash.)

Abel Fonseca (Lopez) (Wenatchee, Wash.)

Jessie Friedman (Great Neck, N.Y.)

Francisco Fuster (Dade County, Fla.)

Barb Garaas (Wenatchee, Wash.)

Dorris Green (Wenatchee, Wash.)

Ralph Gusvik (Wenatchee, Wash.)

Robert Halsey (Lanesborough, Mass.)

Manuel Hidalgo (Wenatchee, Wash.)

Sonja Hill (Smithville, N.C.)

Laura Holt (Wenatchee, Wash.)

Sadie Hughes (Wenatchee, Wash.)

Paul Ingram (Olympia, Wash.)

Daniel Keller (Austin, Tex.)

Francis Keller (Austin, Tex.)

Robert Kelly (Edenton, N.C.)

Brenda Kniffen (Kern County, Calif.)

Scott Kniffen (Kern County, Calif.)

Alvin McCuan (Kern County, Calif.)

Debbie McCuan (Kern County, Calif.)

Marilynn Malcom (Vancouver, Wash.)

Linda Miller (Wenatchee, Wash.)

Jeffrey Modahl (Kern County, Calif.)

Alan Parker (Hendersonville, N.C.)

Mildred Parker (Hendersonville, N.C.)

Kenneth Bruce Perkins (Houston, Tex.)

Randall Reed (Wenatchee, Wash.)

Michael Rose (Wenatchee, Wash.)

Debbie Runyon (Bainbridge Island, Wash.)

Michael Joseph Schildmeyer (Edgewood, Iowa)

Grant Self (Kern County, Calif.)

Nancy Smith (Lorain, Ohio)

Ray Souza (Lowell, Mass.)

Shirley Souza (Lowell, Mass.)

Larry Steinborn (Wenatchee, Wash.)

John Stoll (Kern County, Calif.)

James Toward (Stuart, Fla.)

James Watt (White Plains, N.Y.)

Jenny Wilcox (Dayton, Ohio)

Kathryn Dawn Wilson (Edenton, N.C.)

Contents

Preface

Writing this book has been hard for us. There was a time when publicly expressing skepticism about small children being ceremonially raped and tortured by organized groups was, as one journalist put it, practically an indictable stance. We can testify to this: in the late 1980s, one of us had the police at her door, on a maliciously false report of child maltreatment, after publishing an article suggesting the innocence of a day-care teacher convicted of ritual abuse.

Several years later, the national mood has changed. Doubting is easy now and, for many of the people we know—especially lawyers and journalists—even fashionable. Both of us have been lauded for our early skepticism, praised for helping free innocent prisoners, and asked how we were able to remain clearheaded when so many others didn't.

For people not caught up in a hysteria, it is easy to demonstrate its absurdity. What is hard is to appreciate its sense, to recognize how a social panic "works" for people—people who may not be very different from the skeptics who deride them. Because our backgrounds have pushed us toward this understanding but also repelled us from it, readers should know how each author developed an interest in the issue of ritual child abuse.

One of us, Debbie Nathan, is a freelance journalist who first learned of ritual sex-abuse accusations in 1984 while holding her two-year-old daughter in a rocking chair. A radio newscaster announced that elderly women at a prestigious preschool in Los Angeles had spent years making pornographic pictures of their students while terrorizing them into silence by mutilating their pets. As I listened, I looked at my napping child and felt the kind of twinge you get when you hear about a serial killing in another state, or an act of terrorism in a foreign country. I shook my head at the world's perversity, rocked the chair harder, and put the news out of my mind.

Two years later, I took it up again. A case had just broken in El Paso, Texas, where I live. There, two women had been judged guilty of the same grotesque crimes the McMartin teachers had been charged with. The Texas women were the first female workers at a public child-care institution to be convicted, and parents all over the city had grown terrified of day care. I had followed the trials only superficially, but decided to look into them now.

With a preschooler in my life, and plenty of time to interact with her and her friends thanks to my husband's well-paying job, I had an idea of how young children act when they are hurt, what their faces look like when they are anxious and frightened, the way they act when they try to keep secrets, the delight they take in talking scatologically, the disconcerting phobias they suddenly develop about foods they formerly loved, beds they once thought safe from monsters, and habits—such as naps—that they used to indulge in happily. At the same time, I was painfully aware of my own feelings about leaving my child in public care so that I could write: the guilt I experienced when she would occasionally grab me as I left the preschool and beg me not to leave, the vertigo when she complained one day that the male owner of her day-care center had "hurt" her. It turned out that he had too enthusiastically hoisted her up by her underarms, inadvertently pinching them. But until I got these details, I felt completely off-balance, ready to believe the worst.

My experience with my daughter and my perspective on my conflicts about working guided me during the eight months I investigated the case in El Paso. Poring through records, I found no evidence to support the accusations, except for parents' and professionals' panicked ruminations on youngsters' behavior that sounded normal to me—and kids' halting, confused answers given during interviews to questions that were so leading that they were bound to produce frightening fantasies and even serious emotional disturbance in the children.

It dawned on me that the convicted teachers were completely innocent, and I was horror-struck to think that they were in prison and that no one, least of all the local media, seemed to think there was anything irregular about the situation. The women's fate seemed to me a serious issue, not just for civil libertarians but also for feminists concerned with fears about public day care, female labor-force participation, children's normal sexuality, and, perhaps most dramatically, the tendency to demonize women for these social anxieties.

Belief in ritual abuse was so esconced that one could hardly discuss its cultural and political implications, since to do so, one first had to show that the accused were innocent. This was the task I faced in the late 1980s as I tried to publicize the criminological and legal truths of the cases. That, and freeing people from prison, became the practical and moral center of my writing about several other cases, including those of Kelly Michaels in New Jersey, Francisco Fuster in the Miami area, and a group of Puerto Rican and African-American day-care personnel convicted in the Bronx.

The other author, Michael Snedeker, is a lawyer who represents convicted felons on appeal. In 1986, after taking two years off to travel and write, I called around to the courts in California and asked for cases. The Court of Appeal in Fresno mailed me a truckload of transcripts, the bulk of which were records of two Kern County cases. While appellate attorneys customarily defend felons who are guilty of at least some of the offenses for which they were judged guilty, in the cases that comprise the heart of this book, the defendants were accused—and often convicted—of crimes that never happened at all. Working on their cases has given me ample opportunity to demonstrate this. But even while I tried to free my clients from prison, I was troubled by questions that carried me beyond my role as a defense lawyer.

In particular, I wondered how and why children could come to make the foulest of accusations when the charges are not true. As my work proceeded, it became clear to me that youngsters were not the sources of the accusations, or even of much of the testimony. My question then became, Why was confirmation of these horrible narratives so avidly sought, not only by professionals whose careers came to include the task of unearthing satanic ritual abuse but even by the children's parents? And why were so many people—including me, when my only acquaintance with these cases was via the media—so quick to overlook the improbabilities, so ready to believe?

The legal work and journalism we did before we wrote this book helped overturn convictions in several ritual-abuse cases, including those in El Paso and Kern County. We became the confidants of a population who emerged from prisons anguished and mystified about the wreckage made of their lives. We could have written a book about these twentieth-century Jobs, but we were not as interested in the accused as in their accusers. What reasons did they have for doing what they did? What did they share with those of us who like to think we could never fall prey to moral panic?

For the parents and professionals who have built ritual-abuse cases, the slightest skepticism represents ultimate betrayal, not only of children but of the accusing adults' very identity as saviors of young victims. In such a polarized atmosphere, to be identified as a doubter is to be excoriated as part of the patriarchal backlash against children's and women's attempts to fight sexual violence, and to be banished from the offices, homes, and confidences of the accusers.

We thus found the usual research avenues blocked. A few nationally known child-protection professionals, such as child-trauma researcher Anthony Urquiza and the FBI's Kenneth Lanning, responded to our requests for interviews and information. But most of this country's prominent child protectionists, including long-time leaders of the American Professional Society on the Abuse of Children, did not respond to our letters and calls, or they declined to speak with us. We got the same reaction from the director and board members of Believe the Children, the leading organization in the United States proclaiming the existence of ritual abuse.

Faced with this virtually monolithic cold shoulder, we devised another way to reconstruct the professionals' and families' involvement with ritual-abuse cases. We began a far-reaching and exhaustive review of the artifacts they left behind: their speeches at conferences; the findings of faux-scientific studies that professionals who believe in ritual abuse have done on children and their parents; the notes therapists kept of their sessions with young "victims"; the depositions and trial testimony of expert witnesses talking about how they entered the child-abuse field; and the anguished diaries that prosecutors instructed mothers to write about their sons' and daughters' behavior—chronicles that would be handed over to defense lawyers.

These documents are revealing, but like potsherds and hieroglyphs, they have an archaeological feel to them, one that clashes with the fact that the ritual-abuse panic is only a decade old. The people involved in it are very much alive and the tensions they articulate far from resolved. We hope that our work will inspire other researchers to talk with them and take up where we left off. Much still needs to be done. More can surely be learned about the role religion has played in the enthusiasm for ritual-abuse accusations. Questions also remain about how belief in the charges functions for mothers, and for other women who become proponents. The latter issue is still difficult to pose. After all, women and children are subject to a tremendous amount of real sexual violence, and when feminists express even the slightest doubt about some claims, they risk having their uncertainties seized on by those who would deny the rest.

Talking about sex-abuse panic thus immediately situates one in clichés of betweenness: between a rock and a hard place, or perhaps more to the point, between the devil and the deep blue sea. It is a tricky space to be in, but one that needs to be held and expanded if we are to navigate toward women's and children's welfare.

For researchers wishing to use our sources, we have archived several thousand pages of discovery material obtained from the McMartin case (including several dozen of the investigative interviews done with children) at the Psychology Department of McGill University in Montreal. In the same collection are also child interviews and other materials from the Country Walk (*Florida v. Francisco Escalona Fuster*), El Paso (*Texas v. Michelle Elaine Noble*), and Wee Care (*New Jersey v. Margaret Kelly Michaels*) cases. All references cited in the endnotes as "author's possession" can be accessed at McGill. In the text of this book, we have changed the names of accusing children and parents who have not appeared in the media under their own names. To facilitate locating documents pertaining to these individuals, however, we have assigned them the same initials as their real names.

Acknowledgments

O ver the two years that we worked on this book, dozens of scholars, independent researchers, reporters, editors, attorneys, librarians, child-protection professionals, and defendants in ritual-abuse cases helped us gather documents, establish contact with sources, and make sense of what we were reading, hearing, and writing about ritual-abuse accusations. Almost unfailingly, the people we asked for help responded with tremendous generosity and good humor. Many labor on the cutting edges of anthropology, sexology, psychology, journalism, and the law.

In particular, we want to thank (in alphabetical order), Bill Andriette, Anita Beckenstein, Madeline Beckman, Maggie Bruck, Peggy McMartin Buckey, Diane Campbell, Holly Capello, Stephen Ceci, Tom Charlier, George Csicsery, Shirley Downing, John Earl, Bill Ellis, Dan Finneran, Christine Fuentes, Kristine Fuster, Marty Gottlieb, Teresa Gray, Jan Haaken, Diana Halbrooks, Evan Harrington, Robert Hicks, the Interlibrary Loan Department of the El Paso Public Library (Elaine Berg, Debbie Ciafre, and Barbara Stephens), Suzanne Patricia Johnson, David Kemp, Michael Kenny, Kay Larson, Amy Liebman, Elizabeth Loftus, Matt Love, Sarah Maitre, Roy Malpass, Kelly Michaels, Sherrill Mulhern, Luiz Natalicio,

Roy Nokes, Paul Okami, Jim Okerblom, Eileen Ridge, Robert Rosenthal, James F. Smith, Steve Squire, Lawrence Stanley, Jackie Starmer, Ralph Underwager, Carole Vance, Jeffrey Victor, Hollida Wakefield, Ellen Willis, and J. M. Wood.

We also want to thank our agents, Ling Lucas and Ed Vesneske, and our editors at Basic Books, Steve Fraser and Linda Carbone, for taking an interest in our work and encouraging us through the long, tedious process of producing a book. Then there are our families. The company and support of our partners, Morten Naess and Lisa Short, made it all possible. And when we got tired, our children, Sophy, Willy, Beckett, and Zoe, kept us conscious that what we were writing needed to be said.

Satan's Silence

Introduction

According to a claim that has been promoted for more than a decade by preachers, police, prosecutors, psychotherapists, child-protection workers, and antipornography activists, there exists in this country—and, indeed, around the world—a massive conspiracy of secret satanist cults that have infiltrated everywhere into society, from the CIA to police stations to judges' chambers and churches. The devil worshipers have even secreted themselves in day-care centers and preschools, the story goes, where they pose as teachers. This prospect has been particularly frightening, for it is said that satanists consider youngsters attractive prey for rape and torture and easy recruits for their faith.

In late 1994, as the last chapters of this book were being written, a research team under contract with the federal government announced, after studying the matter for almost five years, that they had made a determination about this claim, which has terrified many people in America. The study, which cost taxpayers $750,000, determined that the rumor of satanic conspiracies was unfounded and that there was no evidence of any organized incursions into public child care.[1] Even so, during the same year the research findings were publicized, it was possible to go to the juvenile section of the public library in many U.S. cities and find colorfully illustrated copies of *Don't Make Me Go Back, Mommy: A Child's Book About Satanic Ritual*

Abuse.[2] It was also possible to turn on the radio and hear Joan Baez performing "Play Me Backwards," her song about a youngster who witnesses a diabolic ceremony in which adults dressed as Mexicans slaughter a baby, remove its organs, and make other children play with them. One could stand in a supermarket checkout line and read the women's magazine *Redbook*, with its survey indicating that 70 percent of Americans believed in the existence of sexually abusive satanic cults, and almost a third thought the groups were being deliberately ignored by the FBI and police.[3] If one sought out a psychotherapist, the chances were good that he or she believed these cults were organized into a vast conspiracy whose crimes were responsible for many patients' emotional problems.[4] And if one were to examine the files of district attorneys' offices throughout the country, there was a considerable likelihood that some would contain allegations of ritual sex abuse.[5]

When these cases proceeded to indictment, the accusers were often young children and the accused preschool teachers or the youngsters' own parents. The trials that resulted were lurid, yet tedious in their similarity. As the defendants, many of them women, sat looking dazed, distraught, or scornful, children—or adults speaking for children—recited litanies about brutal and grotesque assaults committed against them. Testimony typically included accounts of being raped and sodomized with weapons and other sharp objects while camera shutters clicked and videotape machines rolled, of participating in the slaughter of animals and human infants, of being kidnaped in vans, boats, and airplanes, of hearing threats that their parents would be killed if the abuse were disclosed, and of suffering these tortures while the perpetrators engaged in devil-worshiping rituals.

Defense lawyers would protest that there was no evidence to support these claims: no adult witnesses, no pornography, no lacerations on youngsters' genitals, no blood, no dead babies—and virtually no talk of abuse from the children until investigators and their parents pressured them relentlessly to disclose.

To this, prosecutors would inevitably counter that the defendants had terrorized the children to keep them quiet. Expert witnesses would take the stand and explain that the youngsters' silence was a sign of abuse. So were many behaviors that common sense might suggest were benign, but which child-protection workers understood as signs of trauma: bed-wetting, nightmares, and masturbating, for instance. Sometimes an expert would explain that organized satanists look like nice people but are geniuses at concealing evidence, and have been doing so for hundreds of years. In fact, as one prosecution witness was wont to point out, the Caribbean servant Tituba, who cared for the girls who were responsible for the seventeenth-century Salem witch trials, was herself a ritual child abuser.

After this kind of testimony, some trials resulted in acquittals, but others produced guilty verdicts. In El Paso, Texas, in 1985, Gayle Dove, a popular middle-aged preschool teacher and community volunteer, was charged with sexually molesting both boy and girl students, inserting sharp objects into their genitals, making pornography, and threatening the children with masks, wild animals, and vows to kill their parents if they disclosed the crimes. A fellow teacher, also a seemingly well-adjusted woman, was also charged. Both were convicted and sentenced to life in prison. In a case that surfaced in New Jersey during the same year, bright, outgoing Kelly Michaels, a woman in her early twenties, was accused of similar crimes and found guilty, even though there was no record of illegal sexual activity or of psychopathology in her past.

In North Carolina in 1993, day-care operator Robert Kelly was convicted on ninety-nine counts of sexual abuse and punished with twelve consecutive life terms.[6] The cook at Kelly's center, twenty-seven-year-old Kathryn Dawn Wilson, was found guilty on five counts and sentenced to life in prison. In Austin, Texas, a middle-aged couple named Daniel and Frances Keller got forty-eight years apiece. They joined a growing population, which may now number in the thousands, of people whose lives were shattered by allegations of "ritual sex abuse." The lucky ones were tried and acquitted or, if not indicted, only bankrupted by legal fees. Others were fired from their jobs, run out of their communities, or had their children taken away from them. Dozens more, including the El Paso, North Carolina, and Austin defendants, were convicted and imprisoned for crimes whose only substantiation was words.

Those words seemed to come from children, and they were first uttered in the early 1980s, when cases like Los Angeles's McMartin Preschool scandal erupted. McMartin dragged through the courts during most of that decade, and when it ended, it had transmogrified into the longest and costliest trial in American history. By then, the mass media was publishing skeptical reports about copycat cases that had left dozens of men and women languishing in prisons. Most of these accounts criticized the unreliability of small children's words. "Out of the Mouths of Babes," one article was titled. "Do Children Lie?" asked another.

Downplayed in this work was that at the beginning of each ritual-abuse case, the children had been eminently reliable, but what they communicated was that they had *not* been molested by satanists. Indeed, it was only *after* an investigation started, after intense and relentless insistence by adults, that youngsters produced criminal charges. By then, their utterances had nothing to do with their own feelings or experiences. Rather, what came from the mouths of babes were juvenile renderings of grownups' anxieties. For the young accusers in ritual-abuse cases, the acts of speaking constituted a profound irony, because the more they said, the more their efforts to describe their reality were silenced by adult projections and fantasies.

Those fantasies exercised an irresistible hold on American society during the 1980s and 1990s. Belief in ritual-sex-abuse conspiracies was the stuff of moral panic, not unlike the crusades of the McCarthy era. During the conservative Reagan and Bush administrations, there was another eruption of tension, over changes in gender relations that had been brewing for a generation. Between the early 1960s and the early 1980s, many middle-class adolescents stopped keeping their premarital sexual experimentation a secret from adults, abortion was legalized, the proportion of unwed teenage mothers more than quadrupled, the divorce rate tripled, women with young children streamed into the workforce, and day-care centers proliferated. The swiftness of these changes unsettled many Americans, and society's new villain became the satanic child molester.

This image cast a wide swath of fear over the political and cultural landscape. To right-wing Christian fundamentalists steeped in lore about devils and stewing with hostility toward public child care, it was not hard to embrace the notion of satanists infiltrating day-care centers. Indeed, in the early 1980s, belief in ritual sex-abuse conspiracies extended from a host of concurrent rumors that were promoted by law-and-order conservatives and the Christian media: satanist livestock killers, devil-worshiping corporate executives, and rock musicians who dubbed their songs with subliminal, demoniacal messages.

To secular-minded, educated American liberals, claims about satanism sounded as ludicrous as a Mark Twain or an H. L. Mencken spoof on holy rollers, and commentators clucked in bemusement. There was no smiling, though, at other, related rumors: about rashes of stranger-abducted children, countrywide kiddie porn mafias, or, later, satanist connivance in day-care centers. Although these apocryphal stories were also promoted by conservatives, they struck as deep a chord in people who watch public television as they did among Geraldo Rivera's and Oprah Winfrey's audiences.

Feminists were particularly susceptible to sex-abuse conspiracy theories. Indeed, the alliances women's activists struck with conservatives around these claims often turned bizarre: as when Gloria Steinem contributed money and public support to a ritual-abuse proponents' group whose coordinator later claimed that it was the U.S. government, and not an ultraright militia movement devotee, who bombed Oklahoma City's federal building in 1995.[7]

This book examines how such alliances coalesced and how belief in ritual abuse subjected hundreds of people to state-mandated persecutions that in many ways compare with the Salem witch trials. It attempts to explain how a public library could offer little children a picture book about torture in day-care centers, how the airwaves could reverberate with the voice of former antiwar activist Joan Baez now intimating that immigrants are satanic, how dozens of blameless people are still languishing in prison on such charges—and, above all, how this irrationality could endure for more than a decade and provoke only a murmur of protest. In a culture as heterogeneous as ours, so extensive a moral panic can be achieved only by concerted efforts at institutionalizing it.

Indeed, this is the way belief in ritual abuse spread: via an impassioned, nationwide crusade conducted by social workers, therapists, physicians, victimology researchers, police, criminal prosecutors, fundamentalist Christians, ambitious politicians, antipornography activists, feminists, and the media. It was a powerful effort that did not come together overnight. But as it took shape, a veritable industry developed around the effort to demonstrate the existence of ritual abuse. In the absence of conventional evidence, the proof became words obtained via suggestion and coercion and the most ambiguous of behaviors, from both youngsters and the accused. Verbal "disclosures" about events that never happened were obtained from children using interviewing techniques that cognitive psychologists have subsequently discredited as dangerously coercive and suggestive. Additionally, prosecutors introduced new forms of therapeutically induced "evidence"—such as preschool-age children's play with toys and with dolls that have genitals, their vague scribbles and drawings, and parents' retrospective accounts of their children's nightmares and masturbation—to show that the youngsters had been traumatized by abuse.

In the name of saving children, meanwhile, prosecutors exploited popular anxieties about sex to perform character assassinations on defendants. Testimony was given and innuendo spread about the promiscuity of the accused, about their purchases of *Playboy* magazine, their homosexuality, even their fondness for 1960s counterculture music. Bolstering these appeals to the public's worst prejudices, prosecutors such as Miami's Janet Reno, a self-styled women's advocate who would later become head of the Justice Department under the Clinton administration, encouraged the use of sophisticated psychotherapeutic methods, such as hypnosis and "guided imagery" exercises to obtain confessions from defendants. In other cases, the venerable tradition of the jailhouse snitch was revived as informants were trotted out to offer perjured testimony about defendants' confessions in their cells.

Although these efforts convinced many jurors that children in ritual-abuse cases had been violated, there were still skeptics in the courts, the media, and the public who were suspicious of the evidence and who demanded harder proof. Often they were convinced by novel medical evidence, produced with recently developed examination techniques that appeared reliable. Actually, they were technologically updated versions of the medieval preoccupation with scrutinizing female genitalia for signs of sin and witchcraft, and of nineteenth-century forensic medical campaigns to detect promiscuity and homosexuality by examining the shapes of lips and penises. The fact that modern physicians' diagnoses in ritual-abuse cases were invalid was not revealed until the late 1980s; in the meantime, the word of these doctors sent many defendants to prison.

While the new medical findings bore at least a superficial resemblance to evidence traditionally allowed into criminal trials, there was little or no precedent for admitting videotaped interviews, closed-circuit television testimony, hearsay accounts of abuse by adults speaking for children in court, or expert testimony about children's play with dolls, their drawings, and sexual-abuse behavioral syndromes.

Attempting to overcome this problem, child-protection advocates borrowed from earlier feminist efforts to reform rape law as they successfully introduced the new sex-abuse evidence into courts. Their triumph, however, was highly problematic, not just for defendants but also for the integrity of the justice system and for the children in sex-abuse cases. Claims about the validity of the new evidence were based on political and prosecutorial passions rather than empirical research, and they undermined judicial efforts to arrive at justice through fact finding rather than emotion and influence. The new evidence also communicated romantic assumptions about children's inherent "innocence" that echoed traditional ideas about "good" women—and counterposed them to images of evil-doing females like the accused in day-care abuse cases.

Meanwhile, feminists who espoused the existence of satanist sex conspiracies characterized their belief as a political attempt to give children a civic voice, analogous to the effort to gain one for women. The irony of this rhetoric is that the youngsters in ritual-abuse cases were indeed silenced, but by prosecutors rather than perpetrators. Videotaped interviews made during the early cases show that when children were allowed to speak freely, either they had nothing to say about abuse or they denied that it ever happened to them. Once it became obvious that these records would prevent guilty verdicts, prosecutors began advising investigators not to keep tapes or detailed notes of their work. This silencing of youngsters was reinforced by the practice of hiding exculpatory evidence from defense lawyers and sealing records from the press—in the name of protecting the child victims.

Given the fact that belief in ritual abuse became so quickly and monolithically institutionalized, it is not surprising that the first skeptics were friends and family of the accused who were easily dismissed as disreputable, and who sometimes themselves were charged with being child molesters. By the mid-1980s, a few child-protection professionals, journalists, and prosecutors also began entertaining doubts, but when they aired them, many were censured by their colleagues and discouraged from publicizing their concerns. Doubt gradually coalesced, however, and just as belief in the validity of the cases had a moral conservative tenor, so did much disbelief. By the late 1980s, opponents of state involvement in family life were using

ritual-abuse accusations as a warning about the dangers of child protection and therapy, and issuing across-the-board condemnations of feminism and feminists as
predatory wreckers of happy homes. Ritual-abuse proponents responded by dis-
missing every criticism as antifeminist and antichild backlash, all the while ignoring
their own complicity in discrediting child protection and the women's movement.

Believers also mounted their own backlash, by developing ever more reticulated
arguments to make the incredible sound reasonable. Their latest effort involves
resurrecting "dissociation theory," a body of psychological thought dating from
nineteenth-century theories of female hysteria positing that victims of sexual abuse
shield themselves psychologically by banishing their traumatic memories from consciousness. With dissociation theory, ritual-abuse proponents explain children's
silence as the result of amnesia, and this, they claim, further proves that the youngsters were horribly abused. The diagnosis used to advance this rationalization is
post-traumatic stress disorder (PTSD), a relatively new psychiatric label whose origins lie in the 1960s-era protest movement against U.S. involvement in the Vietnam
war. With its implicit condemnation of violence—particularly male violence—
PTSD has become an attractive illness for feminists and child-protection advocates,
and claims that ritually abused children suffer from the malady have provided fresh
ammunition with which to justify their obsession with the devil.

What follows is a history of that obsession, and an analysis of what has been
said—and not said—to promote it. Our aim is to explore what the children in ritual-abuse cases were actually communicating before their utterances, behaviors,
and bodies were reinterpreted through the language of cultural panic. We restore
the voices of defendants before they were transmuted by false confessions and
guilty verdicts. By examining the ways in which many child-protection leaders and
organizations profited by building and justifying ritual-abuse cases, we reveal the
real message behind their current warnings that skepticism will hurt women and
children.

There are many silences to be broken here. Perhaps the biggest one emanates
from thoughtful women's advocates and child protectionists who doubt the logic of
ritual-abuse claims but hesitate to speak out because they lack an analysis with
which to articulate their skepticism. In offering them words, we hope to open
avenues for rational discussion about a terrible episode in our country's history.
Such discussion is sorely needed, because during a time when it has become fashionable to speak of evil, if there is anything that can be called satanic about ritual
abuse, it is the cacophony of media and scholarly prurience that has silenced
thoughtful exploration of its roots and meanings. By challenging that silence, we
give voice to our culture's deepest fears and yearnings. By listening, perhaps we can
find real ways to protect our children and empower ourselves.

PART I
Rumors of Evil

ONE

The Best of Intentions

W hen Americans turned on their radios and televisions in the spring of 1984 and first heard how satanist teachers at the McMartin Preschool in Los Angeles had slaughtered pet rabbits in front of children, it seemed that a horrible new pathology of perversion and cruelty had suddenly struck from nowhere. The idea that elderly and middle-aged women could spend twenty years secretly raping and torturing hundreds of preschoolers in their charge was at once utterly absurd and, strangely, not surprising. In the national mind, wide-eyed disbelief coexisted with a cynical (if fear-struck) matter-of-factness as ritual-abuse cases spread across the country.

But, like any grand social panic, the ritual child-abuse scare of the 1980s and 1990s did not spring full-blown from one incident. Its roots go back a decade, when feminists made sexual abuse a public issue and when the victims were understood to be mainly daughters violated by incestuous fathers. Incest, many child-protection advocates believed then, could be ameliorated only by promoting gender parity in the workplace and family. Equality would enable girls to resist male relatives' sexual demands, and would give mothers the economic wherewithal to protect daughters by taking the children and leaving home.

These feminist visions were obscured, however, by an intransigent, societywide insistence that the problem lay merely in the minds of a few troubled men. Accordingly, the cure for sex abuse was psychotherapy, coupled with family counseling.

And if treatment was all that was necessary, sex abuse was not so much a crime as an illness. Hence, rather than calling for careful, impartial investigation by the police, accusations demanded intervention by psychotherapists prepared to take the side of the aggrieved daughter, and to "heal" the perpetrator—even if he insisted the charges were false.

The idea of sex abuse as illness inspired social workers, psychologists, and others who, in the 1970s, were flocking to the newly emerging child-protection profession. Within a decade, their new theory—that the accusing children are always to be believed and that adults who demur are always lying—had become the typical U.S. law-enforcement response to reports of sex abuse. During this period, mental health workers with virtually no training in forensics supplanted the police as investigators of these allegations, and the stage was set for the wave of false charges and panic that erupted in the 1980s. To understand how this happened, one must return to the early days, when child protection was in its infancy and all seemed well.

Sixties Idealism

The Arizona Children's Home hardly seems a likely place to begin a history of ritual-abuse allegations. A rambling institution in Tucson, it looks very different from the homey neighborhoods and prosperous suburban preschools where such cases have surfaced. Originally established for orphans and children from destitute families, the Home opened at the turn of the twentieth century in a stately Spanish-style mansion. By 1970, the main building was in terrible disrepair and its young residents were housed in dreary, barrackslike dormitories.[1]

Most children were in residence then because their parents had been judged neglectful or abusive. Most were also very poor. And without exception, they were severely emotionally disturbed. Their behavior was so aberrant and disruptive that they needed constant monitoring by psychiatrists and social workers. The children were also supervised twenty-four hours a day by a crew of paraprofessionals who earned minimum wage and made themselves available on the weekend, at night, and for overtime. Traditionally, the people who did this work had been blue-collar and poorly educated. But in the late 1960s, the Children's Home got a new director who began recruiting among the college-educated and conscientious objectors to the Vietnam War. These young people were fired up by social activist urges and willing to devote long, poorly paid hours to helping troubled children. Many had liberal education or fine arts backgrounds, and virtually all had led sheltered middle-class lives.

They were unprepared for what they saw at the Home. One woman, a college sophomore when she started working there in 1970, was shocked to find bruises and burns on some of the children that, she learned, had been inflicted by their parents. Other workers were shaken by the youngsters' mental illness. According to one account, there was a boy who refused to interact with people but instead spent all his time aping the sounds of a refrigerator. One young girl set fires, and another delighted a male counselor by rocking on his knee. Only later did he realize with dismay that she had been masturbating on his leg.

Amid the tragedy and chaos at the Arizona Children's Home, employment there took on an almost missionary aura and fostered an intense camaraderie. The paraprofessionals spent their leisure time at the same bars, and as a group took the children on long camping trips. They spoke about stopping the war, about opposing Richard Nixon, and about the problems of the youngsters in their care. A strong sense existed among them that helping troubled children could change the world, and they took their jobs so seriously that many changed their college majors and entered the helping professions.

Kathleen "Kee" MacFarlane was one of these young workers who found herself transformed by the Arizona Children's Home. She was twenty-three years old when she started working there in 1970 and had just earned a bachelor's degree in fine arts from a small Ohio college. Before that, she had attended a Catholic girls' high school in New York State that was run by a convent of nuns. Newly married when she lived in Tucson, MacFarlane was taking art courses at the University of Arizona. Her ambition was to be a sculptor.[2]

But soon after taking the job she became totally absorbed, particularly with its girl residents, including the little girl who masturbated on the counselor's knee. Counselors like MacFarlane were only dimly aware that this child and others might have been molested. They were seldom told exactly why their charges were at the Home. And in the early 1970s, psychologists and social workers hardly discussed sexual abuse. One former paraprofessional remembers a child who visited her parents occasionally. Over many months, the staff realized that she was being battered and fondled by her father.

These revelations apparently had a profound effect on MacFarlane, and after several months at the Children's Home she abandoned her plans of becoming an artist and applied for a federal scholarship to attend the University of Maryland's School for Social Work. There, before she had anything to do with child welfare, she became involved in feminist efforts to raise women's wages and combat domestic and sexual violence.[3] In 1972 she wrote a pamphlet, "What to Do If You Have Been Raped," for a women's counseling center in Baltimore.[4] The following year, as a lobbyist for the National Organization for Women, she argued at congressional hearings for the minimum wage to be extended to cleaning women.[5]

The same year, America entered an economic watershed as its standard of living began a long, steady decline.[6] Concurrently with this downward slide, the Nixon administration established Title XX of the Social Security Act, which capped previously open-ended social services spending. Thereafter, most entitlement programs had to petition for money from a single federal source whose funds were limited. Title XX's aim was to shrink projects that already existed and to discourage new ones.[7] It was interpreted as an expression of fiscal stinginess, reflecting the growing social and political hostility toward the poor and minorities like blacks and women.

In 1973, Walter Mondale, angling for the Democratic party's presidential nomination, took up a new and promising legislation called CAPTA, the Child Abuse Prevention and Treatment Act.[8] It was the perfect bill for a politician searching for a safe, caring issue. Under its provisions, a modest $20 million a year would be given to researchers studying child abuse and neglect and to states so that they could set up intervention and treatment programs. Even so, Mondale knew that President Nixon and other conservatives would oppose CAPTA if they thought it addressed poverty, inequality, controversies about the use of corporal punishment, or anything else that challenged parents' traditional authority in families. Accordingly, the senator and his supporters stringently avoided the topic of physical discipline. They also ignored child neglect and its clear connections with poverty. Instead, they concentrated on physical abuse, and promoted the idea that parents who afflicted their offspring with what doctors called Battered Child Syndrome were themselves suffering from a psychological malady, one that could strike any mother or father.[9]

By the time Senate hearings for CAPTA convened, this medicalized interpretation of child abuse was so firmly established that experts like Brandeis University professor of Social Policy David Gil found it impossible to promote a different analysis to the politicians. After doing a groundbreaking national survey of child abuse in the 1960s, Gil had concluded that neglect and battering were intimately tied to poverty, and that the federal government's reluctance to correct social and economic inequality made Uncle Sam the country's worst child mistreater. But Mondale interrupted Gil and reminded the audience during the hearing that "this is not a poverty problem, it is a national problem."

The dismissive treatment Gil received contrasted with the admiring attention the senators gave another witness, Maureen Barton Litflin, a Southern California woman who went by the pseudonym "Jolly K." She recounted a story of how her mother had demeaned her when she was a youngster. After she had her own children, she verbally abused her daughter and once tried to strangle her. Another time she threw a kitchen knife at the girl.

Jolly K. talked about how she desperately sought treatment for her abusive impulses, and how even private counseling didn't cure her of her abusive urges. Finally, her therapist, a psychiatric social worker, urged Jolly K. to start her own self-help group. She took his advice, and eventually named the group Parents Anonymous. Jolly K. told the congressional hearing how the group had helped her and other parents nationwide to stop maltreating their children, and she stressed that Parents Anonymous was "realistic." It was also very inexpensive, she added, since its success depended on "inner resources," and on people who donated their time. Jolly K. lamented how the government gave more priority to funding abortions than it did to saving battered children. She beseeched the legislators to approve CAPTA so that Parents Anonymous could receive federal support.[10]

Congress heeded her plea, and in 1974 CAPTA was enacted. Almost immediately, it became clear that by not emphasizing poverty or family and gender issues, Mondale had medicalized not just battering but also neglect, emotional maltreatment, and sexual abuse. All these areas were now covered under CAPTA, and the states were mandated to intervene in case of violations. Before the law, only doctors were legally obligated to report abuse. Now, any state wanting CAPTA money had to require therapists, teachers, and school administrators to report abuse as well.

There was an explosion of these reports following the reforms, and soon there were not enough personnel to handle all the complaints. The shortage was especially acute when it came to experts in sexual abuse, which in the early 1970s was child protection's newest subspeciality. The gap was at first filled by a pioneering group of feminist-minded social workers who addressed the problem of incest and molestation in their work to reduce violence against women. MacFarlane was one of them.

By the mid-1970s she was working in Maryland and New Jersey, running a sex-abuse treatment group for children and conducting therapy sessions for incestuous families. She also had achieved impressive feminist credentials with her battered women's project and rape victims' pamphlet. In addition, she was developing abuse-intervention policy for New Jersey's Division of Youth and Family Services, helping social planners in the state of Maryland formulate similar programs, and writing grants to fund them.[11] In the newly emerging and as yet underpopulated protection field, she had plunged in and made a name for herself.

Thus, in 1976, while still in her twenties and with only a master's degree in social work, MacFarlane was hired as a sex abuse specialist by the National Center for Child Abuse and Neglect (NCCAN). One of MacFarlane's jobs was to review grant applications and decide which child-abuse research and demonstration proposals deserved funding.[12] She thus played a major role in deciding which programs and theories would fade and which would become public policy. MacFarlane's decisions also influenced whether the career of a child-abuse researcher or administrator failed or flourished.

Young, personable, and now divorced, MacFarlane had no family responsibilities to conflict with her work. If she influenced the efforts of her grant applicants, it is equally true that they affected her thinking about what child abuse was and how to combat it. By considering two major projects that she sponsored during her tenure at NCCAN, it is possible to see how the cadre of a new profession defined child maltreatment reports and, ultimately, sex-abuse accusations, as claims that should always be believed, no matter how questionable they might seem later.

Politicking with Parents Anonymous

To begin our review, it is necessary to go back to the days when battering was a much more visible public issue than sex abuse, for it is during this period that child protectionists defined maltreatment as a symptom of psychopathology needing intervention by mental health professionals instead of the police. At Walter Mondale's 1973 CAPTA hearings, the Democratic senator and other legislators had been captivated by Jolly K.'s portrait of Parents Anonymous, and Kee MacFarlane—who had just received her social work degree—was equally impressed. While still studying in Maryland, she had acted as the coordinator for that state's first Parents Anonymous chapter and for one in New Jersey.[13] Parents Anonymous later received some of CAPTA's first funding, and after MacFarlane was hired by NCCAN, she shepherded a major grant proposal through the agency for additional monies for the group. Thanks to her efforts, by 1977 the federal government was underwriting new Parents Anonymous chapters throughout the country.[14] MacFarlane played a major role in nationalizing the idea that child battering was a not a problem of poverty or inequality, but a psychological disease that could be cured, much like alcoholism, by attending meetings with one's fellow sufferers.

Hence, even before incest became an issue, the federal model for child-abuse intervention was the self-help therapy group, where parents—especially mothers—tried to defuse the daily frustrations and anger that led them to beat, shake, curse, and scream at their children. Attributing such behavior to female psychopathology runs counter to feminist analysis, of course, and also goes against the grain of leftist thinking. But most child-protection activitist who were progressive or women's advocates embraced the therapy model for various reasons. Besides the fact that Parents Anonymous appealed to conservative politicians as well as liberals, it also advanced the democratic idea that ordinary people could help each other by sharing their problems and by pooling resources, such as baby-sitting. Parents Anonymous did make family life easier for parents and safer for children. Meetings also gave prosecutors and other child-protection authorities an opportunity to listen to and sympathize with troubled mothers and fathers.[15]

The Prosecution Problem

Sex abuse surfaced as a public issue a few years after child physical abuse did. By then, child protectionists understood that the most effective way to gain resources to fight sex abuse was to cast it as they had battering: as a problem that knew no socioeconomic boundaries. Later research, however, would show that, just as with physical abuse and neglect, sex abuse was linked to poverty.[16] Women's and children's advocates downplayed this work, but they still found that their efforts to punish offenders were stymied by several perplexing dilemmas. One was the fact that the state had always winked at the problem. Indeed, in her classic study, *Father-Daughter Incest,* psychiatrist Judith Herman noted that legal sanctions for people convicted of having sex with children looked harsh: according to several states' statutes, a man could get life in prison for having intercourse with his prepubertal child, and some mandated the death penalty. Yet such draconian sentences were extremely rare, Herman noted, and most cases were never tried at all.

Failure to prosecute was not due merely to state indifference. Incest defendants usually pleaded innocent, and district attorneys knew that putting these men on trial hardly ever won a guilty verdict. The biggest obstacle to successful prosecution was the lack of corroborating evidence, since even abusive sex rarely leaves medical evidence. Further, there are seldom witnesses besides the two people involved, leaving only the accuser's word versus the defendant's. Traditionally, a swearing match between two people gives juries insufficient information to find guilt. And in the courtrooms of the 1970s, even when there was additional evidence, the basis of the case—a child's testimony—was often viewed with suspicion.[17]

For girls who did successfully prosecute before the late 1970s, the workings of the justice system often felt more damaging than the incest. After making a report, the victim was often subjected to embarassing genital examinations, to the police visiting her at her school to interrogate her, and to being sent to a juvenile home or foster care. Pending trial, the father usually remained at home, where he often convinced the family to withdraw their accusations. Even then, the charges still made the evening news, jeopardizing his reputation and job.

Things could get far worse in the event of a successful prosecution. A guilty verdict could leave the wife and children in dire economic straits, with the sudden loss of the father's income. In families with much to lose, mothers could put intense pressure on their daughters to retract accusations.

What could be changed to allow these children to tell the truth? Some prosecutors tried circumventing problems, such as the lack of evidence and girls' tendency to recant, by doing everything possible to avoid trials. In order to stay out of court, district attorneys tried to elicit a guilty plea from the defendant by offering him a generous bargain: confess to the incest, agree to see a therapist, and you'll be placed on probation. The deal seemed sweet for fathers, but it was not so attractive for the family. Few therapists were trained to counsel child molesters, and when a clinician was available, only the offender got treatment—even though the daughter and wife surely needed therapy too. Further, few therapists were willing to work with probation officers, so they seldom told authorities when a father had stopped attending therapy. Even if he showed up regularly, that was no guarantee that he wasn't molesting his daughter again.[18]

Silicon Valley

The first efforts to confront the difficulties in combating incest were born in California's famed Silicon Valley. By the early 1970s, this area south of San Francisco had become a hub for the electronics, aerospace, and data-processing industries. Many of the first employees in these enterprises were well-educated white men whose wives did not work.

But, as sociologist Judith Stacey has noted in *Brave New Families*, her account of Silicon Valley families in the 1980s, many marriages in the Valley had begun disintegrating a decade earlier, amid the domestic and gender upheavals that were rocking middle-class homes throughout the country. Women in particular were questioning their housewife roles and returning to college or to the workforce. Their newfound independence often precipitated divorces, but even when marriages remained intact, the buffeting they suffered from the political change rattled these families.[19] Sex-abuse researchers have suggested that such upsets can bring to light domestic secrets, including revelations about incest.[20]

While these transformations were occurring in Silicon Valley, the Santa Clara County Juvenile Probation Department, the Valley's agency in charge of child-abuse complaints, was following national trends by urging the public to report suspected incest. The authorities did not expect much response, however. According to common wisdom and the old statistics, for every million people, which was the approximate population of Santa Clara County, only about one incest case a year could be expected. This notion was quickly revised by a torrent of reports—some thirty annually by 1971. The county did not know what to do with all of them. In response, officials handled the cases the same way they dealt with other crimes: through the police department and district attorney's office. This status-quo approach shamed daughters by removing them to juvenile homes, left fathers at home to silence witnesses, and dragged domestic scandals through the media. Formerly prosperous and respectable men were jailed, their marriages destroyed, careers ruined, and families consigned to the welfare rolls.[21]

All this was particularly unsettling in a pristine community like Silicon Valley. Heretofore, incest reports nationally had usually involved lower-class families.[22] The prospect of ruining thirty computer wizards a year was deeply discomfiting. Putting their wives and children on the dole was also troubling, not to mention expensive.

In 1971, a psychiatrist consultant for the Santa Clara County Probation Department began wondering whether therapy might be an alternative to incarcerating these fathers. He hired a local psychologist, Henry Giarretto, to develop a pilot project.[23] Giarretto was a marriage and family counselor who believed that incest arose from poor self-esteem. Giarretto believed that by neglecting "the inner need of its citizens,"[24] American society contributed to the self-esteem problem. And in an echo of Battered Child Syndrome thinking, he also blamed psychological problems caused by the offender's unhappy childhood in a dysfunctional family.

At the same time Giarretto and his wife, Anna, also a marriage and family counselor, were characterizing incest as a symptom of bad families, feminists were blaming even "good" families for the problem. In patriarchal families, feminist psychiatrist Judith Herman wrote, "fathers rule but do not nurture . . . [and] mothers nurture but do not rule."[25] This dichotomy, she believed, made men insecure about their sexuality, uncomfortable around children, and thus apt to see daughters as private property that they could enjoy sexually. Above all, incest was an exercise in power that fathers played out in their homes. In order to eradicate incest, power in families needed to be redistributed. Some radical feminists believed this could be accomplished only by banishing men from the family altogether.[26] Others, like Herman, wanted to transform home and workplace relations so that fathers would share child-care tasks equally and become nurturers.

Nevertheless, Herman believed that democratizing parenthood would take generations.[27] Meanwhile, the idea of prosecuting and imprisoning incest offenders appealed neither to her nor to others across the political spectrum. Although feminists were hardly worried about ruining male reputations or dunning the government for welfare for women and children, many had come to political age in the antistate New Left, and they were leery of law-and-order approaches to crime. Conservatives, meanwhile, abhorred the idea of putting more families on welfare, and liberals favored rehabilitating criminals rather than simply punishing them. In addition, many longtime mental health workers retained a residue of Freudian, psy-chodynamic theory, which, at its best, tried to address the emotional complexities within incestuous families. At its most superficial, though, it tended to encourage the maintenance of traditional families and to sympathize with incest offenders at their wives' and daughters' expense.

Blaming Women, Saving Families

Dr. Roland Summit exemplifies this attitude. He would become one of the major architects of ritual-abuse panic and its tendency to demonize people charged with sex abuse, but ironically, when he began working in child protection, Summit was so sympathetic to incestuous fathers that he implicitly faulted their wives for their crimes. This is not surprising, considering that he studied psychiatry in the early 1960s, before feminists challenged the Freudian tendency to attribute men's mis-behavior to bad mothers and mother figures.[28]

Summit had become interested in sex abuse early in the 1970s, as part of his job as head physician with the Los Angeles County Community Consultation Service. He was a sort of municipal psychiatrist who advised citizens' groups, police depart-ments, and other organizations about mental health issues. In this capacity, he was contacted in the early 1970s by Jolly K., of Parents Anonymous, to organize the group's first board of directors. He agreed, and through his involvement with Par-ents Anonymous, he heard accounts of sexual abuse both from people recalling childhood victimization and from offenders seeking help.[29]

Initially, Summit considered considered incest offenders deviants who should not be allowed into Parents Anonymous. Jolly K. disagreed. Molesting one's offspring, she insisted, was a type of child abuse, so offenders deserved the same considera-tion from her group that it offered to mothers who threw toys at toddlers.[30] Eventu-ally Summit came to describe these offenders as normal and redeemable, but he framed their behavior within a conservative, psychodynamic model that he called the "family romance." It was a romance whose protagonist any man supposedly could identify with: the hapless father who "would never approach a child on a play-ground," but who, now that he had his own children, naturally felt a certain erotic attraction for the "delicious little creatures" he had spawned.[31]

Summit, married, in his forties, and the father of daughters, implied that viewing one's children as "delicious" was a common impulse, but one that sometimes evolved into incestuous compulsion. This might happen when a man approached middle age and started realizing that the "horizons and dreams" of his youth were contracting. Then, Summit noted, as the man grappled with his midlife crisis, his wife was not home to lend support. Instead, she was "absorbing herself in a job, church, or social commitments."[32] According to Summit, this turn from domesticity had no connection to the era's changing economy, or to social commitments inspired by sixties political upheaval, or even to the lure of women's liberation. Instead, the seventies mother who took a job or did volunteer community work did so because she felt "depressed at the loss of her youth and the weakening of her girlish attraction," and she was no longer "invested in endorsing her husband's ego needs." She was, in other words, a bad wife.[33]

Enter the daughter. As a toddler she had merely enchanted her father on the playground, but now Summit feverishly described her as an adolescent who was "learning to transmit the magical vibrations our society requires of the emergent woman." She was "mercurial, kittenish, provocative, enigmatic"[34] and radiated "the fragile innocence of a child mixed with the vaguely destructive allure of the temptress."[35]

At the same time, Summit saw this domestic Lolita as a reincarnation of the good, traditional wife. While her mother engaged in neurotic job and community pursuits, the daughter greeted her father fondly when he returned after a miserable day at work. As she cheerfully laid his food on the table and entertained him at dinner, she became "an uncanny likeness of the girl who once spurred him to greater accomplishments, who made him feel loved and strong, and who excited in him an unquestioned virility and potency."[36] Under the circumstances, the poor father could hardly help being aroused, and there was no one around to save him from his lust. His wife, after all, acted "remarkably oblivious" to the developing incest since it promised to free her from her husband's unwanted demands.[37]

In synopsizing this romance, Summit dutifully blamed the father, but his implicit accomplice was the modern, self-absorbed wife who triggered in her husband a "natural human frailty" that made him cross the "invisible border between loving and leching."[38] That border needed reinforcing, Summit thought, but not by imprisoning the beleaguered father. Far better, he thought, to strengthen the family by putting all its members into therapy.

The Giarrettos embodied this idea in their Child Sex Abuse Treatment Program (CSATP), which aimed to prevent recurrences of incest by helping offenders achieve "personal awareness" and "self-management."[39] As dedicated marriage and family counselors, they predicated this goal on the traditional two-parent family. For them and for most of their colleagues, the foundation of a good domestic system was a husband and a wife who got along well. If they did, incest was unlikely. If, however, their relationship was defective, sexual misdeeds might erupt, and they would not cease until the marriage and family underwent therapeutic "reconstruction."[40] Part of the repair work involved getting the mother to apologize to her daughter. "You are not to blame," she was supposed to say. "Daddy and I did not have a good marriage. That is why Daddy turned to you."[41]

Feminist Bargains

The Giarrettos had a strong bias for preserving marriages, and when they promoted their program they claimed that one cause of incest was the ever-weakening nuclear family.[42] Many feminists believed just the opposite—that far from minimizing incest, nuclear families encouraged it.

While the marriage-preservation policy undoubtedly appealed to moral conservatives, one would have expected feminists to frown on an organization that not only blamed mothers but also idealized matrimony. They were willing to excuse these gaffes for various reasons. For one, they knew they could not get the government to support antidomestic violence efforts if they talked about skewed power, whether it derived from maldistribution of wealth or, even more unmentionably, from patriarchal inequality. The ban on raising these subjects was even stronger in the late 1970s, when the Giarrettos sought federal funding, than it had been a few years earlier when Walter Mondale was trying to do something about child neglect and battering. In Washington, MacFarlane was as aware as anyone of how pointless it was to use class-conscious or feminist talk when one went lobbying for funds.

But feminists did not back the the Giarretto's pro-family program simply as a compromise with moral conservatism. On the contrary, many women's advocates found much to like about the Silicon Valley approach to incest intervention. Most appealing was that it included a self-help component, Parents United, in which veteran women members helped newcomers locate community resources such as housing, jobs, and lawyers. CSATP women also attended sex education classes where they learned to explore and assert their erotic needs. Self-expression was further promoted via encounter sessions featuring gestalt, psychodrama, and Games People Play exercises. At a typical meeting, members did group exercises that involved talking about sex and expressing emotions such as anger and aggression.[43]

Feminists who were making peace with the continued presence of fathers in families were also excited by the Giarretto program's efforts to control men's private behavior and, in so doing, to make them "more submissive and nurturant" toward their wives and children.[44] Herman approvingly noted how this retooling was accomplished, amid a totalistic climate of ascetic discipline, intense religiosity, zealous group cohesion, twelve-step rituals, confessions, and expiations of sin. The offender father had to maintain perfect attendance and punctuality at the CSATP meetings, and while present he was not allowed to smoke. For homework he had to keep a diary describing his every sexual impulse, write an autobiography detailing how his incestuous desires developed, and then publicize this material before fellow group members. They might praise him warmly for his efforts, but they might also viciously denounce him for his misbehavior and urge him to do the same to himself. He was also made to think about what would happen if he ever abused a child again, and to do this so often that if he fantasized about incestuous sex, he would sweat, tremble, and retch. In exchange for submitting to these humiliations, offender fathers were rewarded with fervent group support, including profound expressions of emotion and affection from other men.

Deeply impressed with how this group process sensitized men to their abusive impulses, Herman overlooked its simultaneous authoritarianism. She approvingly compared the Giarretto men's meetings with forced political reeducation programs in revolutionary societies, and seemed little concerned that the students in such classes are political prisoners under threat of death if they do not learn their lessons. She applauded the use of mind control to "rehabilitate" men who have "used their power to oppress and exploit others but who are judged not to be irremediably depraved." Likewise, she wrote, CSATP and Parents United–style incest programs were also fashioning a 'new man.' "[45]

As far as the Giarrettos were concerned, a new family was also being made, one that (as a Parents United spokeswoman put it) reflected how parents and children could be organized via group therapy to break society's "network of alienation."[46] Parents United families were "winner families," Henry Giarretto said, and if the government would fund what he called National Family Resource Centers, "loser families" could learn from the winners.[47] So enamored was Giarretto with his idea that the country's moral economy could be redistributed, even if its material wealth couldn't, that he christened his organization the Institute for the Community as Extended Family.

Social Workers as Police

The catch to all this idealism was that the typical father at the CSATP and Parents United sessions was not participating of his own free will. He went, as a San Jose police officer put it, because if he didn't he would "hear the sound of the slammer."[48] In addition to going to the meetings, he was expected eventually to confess to his sexually abusive behavior; if not, he could also expect to go to prison. Or if he avoided prison with a trial that ended in acquittal, he would still probably lose his family, his good name, and his job. If, however, the accused father enrolled in CSATP and Parents United, he would not even have to miss work to be arrested. He could come to the police station at his own convenience, be booked and released without paying bail, and the police would not contact the press. Finally, if he confessed before his preliminary hearing a few months later, child-protection authorities would advise the judge that he was a Giarretto program regular. They would recommend probation, a fine, and community service with Parents United. If the judge suggested incarceration, it was usually far milder than state prison. Instead, the usual recommendation for a CSATP client was that he spend a few months in the local jail, with ample time off to go to work, and to attend more CSATP and Parents United meetings.[49]

Kee MacFarlane and other child-protection professionals dubbed the arrangement a Godfather Offer because, they said, it was one the defendant could hardly refuse.[50] They were right. Before the Giarretto program began, most of Silicon Valley's accused incest offenders pleaded innocent. Afterward, the confession rate skyrocketed to 90 percent.[51]

This stunning increase was due not merely to the fathers' cooperation. With the Godfather Offer, investigators found they could also involve the rest of the family, including daughters. San Jose police officer Eugene Brown explained how this was accomplished. Before the CSATP, he and his colleagues used to question the daughter before arresting the accused offender. Now, in order not to traumatize the child, police did not interview her. Instead, they talked to her teacher, mother, or another adult who had made the abuse report. Then they treated this secondhand account as though it had come straight from the young accuser. Only later would she be questioned, but at that point, the interviewer usually was a woman social worker instead of a policeman, since it was felt that girls would tell women things they would be ashamed to reveal to a man.[52]

So entrenched did this belief become that soon it was common for the whole investigative interview to be conducted by a social worker, with no exposure to proper methods of forensic questioning and no police present to monitor her. This was a dramatic departure from traditional criminological practice, which requires that interviews be done by law-enforcement personnel trained in how to avoid suggestive and leading questions and in the principle that not all accusations are true. For the authorities, though, abandoning forensic practices was worth it if it could resolve incest cases without subjecting children to intrusive interrogations and genital exams, or their fathers to embarrassing arrests, trials, and imprisonment.

Even with the new interviewing methods, many girls refused to accuse their fathers. In response, the Santa Clara County investigators devised another way to open the girls up—they would appeal to their feminine sense of dutiful nurturing by casting them as junior Florence Nightingales to their fathers. As the police officers explained:

We approach them with, "Daddy may have a sickness. Now if Daddy had a broken leg, we would want him to go to the orthopedic doctor and get his leg fixed. An orthopedic doctor is one who fixes broken bones. You'd want him to go to the doctor for his broken leg, wouldn't you? . . . And if Daddy had appendicitis, we would take him to a surgeon who specializes in people with sick stomachs, and you'd want him to get to that doctor as soon as possible, wouldn't you? . . . And if Daddy has something wrong with his head, with how he thinks, we would take him to a psychiatrist to get him help. You would want him to get help for any of these things that are wrong, wouldn't you?"

The victim usually will concur by now. So we say, "Okay, I've been told that maybe Daddy has a little sickness in his head and we're here to try to help Daddy get better. . . . If he does go to jail, he'll be gone for a little while, only a few months."[53]

Once the girl heard that she was responsible for helping cure Daddy and that he would not go to prison, she usually revealed what he had done to her. Her account was recorded on audio- or videotape. Then, if the defendant still denied the abuse, authorities made him review this damning document. It was a final, dramatic confrontation that made most offenders "fall apart and admit," according to police.[54]

For those men who still insisted they were innocent, another program supplemented the Giarrettos' inducements with legal threats that made a guilty verdict and imprisonment seem so imminent that defendants frequently threw in the towel and plea-bargained. Seattle's Harborview Sexual Assault Center, which had started out as a feminist rape-treatment center, took this approach. Staff there urged therapy and light sentences on incest defendants in exchange for confessions. But they also worked closely with the district attorney's office to prepare trials. To ensure guilty verdicts, the Sexual Assault Center also promoted legal reforms that would make it easier for children to testify and boost their credibility as witnesses.[55] Though the constitutionality of many of these innovations was questionable, civil libertarians had little to say about them because in the late 1970s they were hardly ever used. The reforms' main function was as bluffs. Harborview social worker and center director Lucy Berliner explained:

A lot of times a mother will say to me, "I'm not going to let my kid go in to trial, that's just too much." I say, "O.K., fine, but don't tell people that right now. Let's just see if by filing the charges and letting him know you're serious, see if he'll admit to it and plead guilty." And in fact very few cases go to trial. . . . There's always a trial set, but they'll plead that morning or any time from the point they're charged to the trial date itself.[56]

A report on Berliner's center claimed that three-fourths of Seattle's accused incest offenders did confess, and most were then signed up for Giarretto-style therapy. In the other communities the proportion of plea bargainers was even higher.[57]

With success rates like this, it was no wonder that the Silicon Valley approach to incest dazzled nearly everyone working in child protection. Neither is it surprising that among social workers and therapists attached to investigations—and even to police who later picked up their theories—the word *denial* came to mean something quite different from how law-enforcement authorities had traditionally understood it. For most crimes, when the accused insists he is innocent, his disavowal of guilt is taken as negative evidence. Detectives who hear, "I didn't do it," know they will have to find other evidence to make their case.

With the new approach, a man's protestation of innocence was deemed *positive* evidence that he was guilty. This logic flowed from the fact that in the 1970s, incest was still such a hush-hush, shameful topic that for a child to make a false accusation was almost inconceivable. Because she could not be lying, her father's "denial" took on a new meaning, one lifted from the lexicon of therapy, where to be "in denial" means to refuse to own up to one's problems.[58] Transported into social worker–run incest investigations, the father who denied the charges was especially despicable, since not only was he shrugging off his problem but he was also betraying his obligations to his daughter. This was something that child-protection professionals, particularly social workers and therapists, would not tolerate. As a federal publication that MacFarlane assisted in producing put it, regardless of how much a father might deny abusing her, the girl making accusations *must* be believed if she is to "overcome feelings of powerlessness" and "shake off the effects of sustained manipulation."[59]

The Triumph of Therapy

By 1975, the psychotherapeutic approach to investigating sex abuse was in place in the Silicon Valley and ready to spread elsewhere as the California legislature that year awarded the Giarrettos some $200,000 to establish a training center for every child-protection worker in the state. There they would learn how to "hasten . . . the process of reconstitution of the family and marriage."[60] They would also learn that it was now considered acceptable—indeed, advisable—for social workers and therapists in lieu of the police to do criminal investigations, and that if an accused offender denied having committed the abuse, this was a sign of his guilt. The Godfather Offer was institutionalized throughout California, and by the late 1970s, virtually every sex-abuse worker in the state had traveled to Silicon Valley for CSATP training and to meet their colleagues.

Roland Summit was one who made the trip. He did not have any children as patients, but his job as Los Angeles County mental health consultant had propelled him into full-time writing and lecturing about child sexual abuse. He came to see himself as an authority on the subject and a romantic, idealistic sounding board for the community's darkest secrets. He compared himself to the hero of *Kings Row*— a 1940 novel (later made into a movie co-starring Ronald Reagan) he had read as an adolescent—which deals with small-town passions; a deviant physician; his beautiful teenaged daughter, whom he kills after she prepares to reveal he is molesting her; and her lover, a sensitive medical student who learns of the incest too late to prevent the murder.[61] As the self-styled incarnation of this fictional student, Summit also acted as an adviser about sexual abuse to several private and public agencies, including the Los Angeles District Attorney's Office, its police department, a local television station, and the city council.[62]

In 1978, he went to San Jose[63] and was so impressed with the Institute for the Community as Extended Family that he soon joined its board of directors. At the same time, he wrote "The Child Sexual Abuse Accommodation Syndrome," a manifesto that poignantly describes how daughters victimized by incest often falsely recant in order to maintain family equilibrium.[64] Summit also promoted the idea that "children never fabricate the kinds of explicit sexual manipulations they divulge in complaints or interrogations,"[65] and that they should therefore always be believed, no matter how illogical and incredible their accusations sound.[66] Such belief was a moral imperative for child-abuse specialists, Summit wrote, and essential for the well-being of the entire society. The paper and its missionary appeals was not published for another five years, but meanwhile, it was widely circulated in manuscript form and eventually hailed as one of the child-protection field's most salient works.[67]

Shortly after Summit finished his CSATP training, MacFarlane invited the country's most influential child sex abuse experts to a meeting in Washington to form networks. Summit attended, along with other CSATP and Parents United supporters.[68] By now, MacFarlane was also an avid enthusiast of the Giarrettos' program (she would later serve as president on Parents United's national board of directors),[69] and not simply because of its humane attitude toward punishment or concern for women's and girls' welfare. As a federal bureaucrat, she had a keen sense for which child programs could win support from morally and fiscally conservative politicians. She knew CSATP's promise to save marriages and families was bound to humor even the most hidebound fundamentalist. Even more appealing, the Giarretto method was inexpensive, since the program's therapists and group leaders were already working in and being paid by their states' child-protection agencies. Additional no-cost labor was provided by graduate psychology and social work students doing internships, and by veteran Parents United members acting as counselors. More significantly, CSATP's high confession rate freed the government from having to pay for trials, maintain men in prison, keep their children in foster care or to put their families on welfare.

With MacFarlane's help, NCCAN in 1979 gave the Giarrettos $200,000 to train child-protection workers nationally.[70] With that, social workers and therapists throughout the country began descending on San Jose for training, then they returned to their communities and started new programs. The results were dramatic. The year before the federal grant went into effect, MacFarlane had conducted a national survey of sex abuse intervention programs and found fewer than a handful. Three years later, she counted three hundred. Sixty were direct offshoots of the Giarretto model and many others were variations.[71]

Thus, by the beginning of the 1980s, incest was no longer the dark secret it had been a decade earlier, when Kee MacFarlane started her job at the Arizona Children's Home. Now, thanks to an alliance among feminists, therapists, and law-enforcement officials, it was becoming possible for daughters to disclose their victimization and for fathers to admit their guilt. In national media from the *New York Times* to *Playboy*, *The Ann Landers Encyclopedia*, and *Donahue*, testimonials abounded from repentant fathers, newly assertive wives, and girls regaining their dignity.[72]

Yet later research would reveal that many incest offenders also molest children outside their families (and they rape grown women as well).[73] Further, there is evidence that regardless of what kind of treatment sex abusers get, as many as one in seven goes on to offend again.[74] Ironically, then, politicians' and child protectionists' fervor to keep fathers in families left many youngsters and women at risk for further abuse. And by pushing Godfather Offer confessions, the therapy model of sex-abuse intervention replaced skilled forensics personnel with social workers and others who knew nothing about how to test the validity of criminal sex-abuse charges and who unstintingly believed all of them.

Such credulity was hardly a problem in the 1970s, when the vast majority of the accusations and confessions were truthful. But if national consciousness about sex abuse was rising in new and heartening ways during that decade, it was also descending into primeval depths of fear and irrationality that soon would produce a wave of false charges and a panic over ritual abuse.

TWO

Demonology

In 1970, the same year that Kee MacFarlane dedicated her life to helping youngsters abused by their relatives, America began pulsing with rumors about
threats to children that sounded even darker and more frightening than incest.
Throughout the decade, a rash of claims would spread, in the popular culture and
later among local and national policing agencies, that America's youngsters were
gravely threatened by psychopathic murderers, kidnappers, occultists, pornographers, and child molesters. These stories were either baseless or grossly exaggerated, but the media, politicians, feminists, psychotherapists, and child-protection
professionals helped promote and spread them. Then, in the 1980s, a Republican
presidential administration turned its back on the incest-intervention efforts of
child protectionists like Kee McFarlane, propelling her and her colleagues into theory and practice that would ignite mass panic over ritual abuse.

Subversion Scares

"That plump red apple that junior gets from the kindly old lady down the block
may have a razor blade hidden inside," the *New York Times* warned during Halloween season, 1970.[1] For the next few years, the media repeated this admonition
and reported that hundreds of trick-or-treaters had been murdered or injured by
deadly objects purposefully put into their candy by adults.[2]

Yet, strangely, the culprits never seemed to have identities. Attempting to track down Halloween sadists, sociologist Joel Best reviewed decades of newspapers from all over the country and found only two deaths caused during the 1970s and 1980s by trick-or-treat candy tampering—both by a member of the child's own family. Only a handful of other incidents were documented. None resulted in serious harm, and many turned out to be attention-getting hoaxes perpetrated by children.[3]

Halloween sadist stories are apocryphal, and so are many other popular warnings about children in danger. They bear the hallmarks of "urban legends"—modern myths that are passed on as true and believed by almost everyone who hears them. One typical story warns about drug dealers who loiter around grade-school playgrounds, offering children Mickey Mouse stickers that are laced with LSD. Another concerns a girl who went to the bathroom by herself at a mall restroom and vanished. Authorities quickly sealed off the building and found the kidnaper and the child—but her hair had been cut and dyed and her clothes changed so she would not be recognized.[4]

Though these stories are not true, they sound as though they are. This is so, in part, because the typical urban legend is spread not through the mass media but by word of mouth or on school and workplace bulletin boards. The tale is always told as though it just took place, and if communicated orally, it is said to have happened to the narrator's friend, or to a friend of a friend.[5] These details and credibility reinforce a sense of community. At the same time, they rework ages-old folktales that are so venerable and culturally ingrained that when people with good imaginations hear only the barest outline of a new legend, they can generate details that conform remarkably with stories already circulating.

Related to the concept of urban legend is the *memorate*, a term folklorists use to describe the process by which an individual uses popular legends to explain an ambiguous or puzzling experience—such as a perceived contact with the supernatural. People who describe "close encounters" with UFOs appear to be using memorates, as do those who claim to have seen Elvis Presley after he died. These stories allow the tellers to share enigmatic feelings in socially acceptable ways, without stigmatizing themselves as deviant.[6]

Memorates and urban legends are credible partly because they draw on a rich stock of old folk material, updated with Elvis, toy stores, or other details from current popular culture. A deeper reason the stories are believable, though, is that they communicate anxieties about perceived social emergencies and often express grassroots desires to transform political and social structures.[7] The first UFO encounters stories, for instance, emerged at the start of the cold war, concurrently with Western preoccupations about invasion and control by the Soviet Union.[8] Likewise, the LSD-sticker legend and the mall-restroom story reflect fears about drug use and con-temporary social anomie and issue a veiled call for more policing of children.[9] Like-wise, the Halloween sadist legend, with its themes of children leaving home at night and accepting lethal candy from strangers, is both an expression of angst about chil-dren's increasing socialization away from the family and a nod to candy companies' desire to commercialize Halloween further by abolishing homemade treats.

The deep social anxieties, yearnings, and political projects disguised in these narratives are incarnated in contemporary bogeymen like aliens, mall kidnapers, and trick-or-treat psychopaths, with their faddish spaceships and candy bars. But the new villains have venerable ancestors. In the West, rumors of evil done to inno-cents date back to the ancient Greeks, and comprise part of what anthropologists call a subversion myth—a story that attaches blame for complicated problems to scapegoats. Subversion myths appear in times of acute social stress, and typically contain several elements. Most basic is a conspiracy narrative, in which the plotters are usually racial and cultural outsiders. Or they may be members of the culture's powerful elites, such as aristocrats, politicians, priests, or the police.[10]

The crimes these culprits are charged with constitute the most evil, loathsome behavior imaginable, perpetrated against society's ultimate symbol of its own purity and self-renewal: its children. In many subversion myths, the young victims are said to be destroyed by draining their blood, excising their vital organs, ampu-tating their limbs, and cannibalizing their flesh. If all this were not terrible enough, the perpetrators in these stories often wreak their atrocities amid rituals of public promiscuity calculated to violate the culture's strongest sexual taboos, including incest.

These terrible accusations first appeared in Western culture before the Christian era, when Greeks leveled them against Jews. Later, in the Roman Empire, members of Christian sects were said to ritually sacrifice infants and conduct incestuous orgies. Historian Norman Cohn recounts the impact of such accusations in Lyons in A.D. 177. There, the entire Christian community, including its pagan slaves, were hounded by mobs, stoned, imprisoned, and tortured until the slaves declared that their masters had cannibalized children and held incestuous bacchanals. Following these "confessions," the Christians were killed.[11]

As Christianity's popularity increased, earlier persecutions were forgotten as sects accused each other of incest, cannibalism, and child murder.[12] Centuries later, believers elaborated the "blood libel" myth that Jews ritually murder young Chris-tian children. The rumor originated in twelfth-century England and quickly spread to Europe. In France, dozens of Jews were executed and burned at the stake. Simi-lar atrocities occurred in Germany, Spain, Czechoslovakia, Russia, and Italy.

During the Reformation, blood libel stories were eclipsed by Protestant and Catholic scapegoating of suspected witches and minority Christian sects. But in the mid-nineteenth century, anti-Semitic rumors returned with a vengeance in Europe, Russia, and Egypt, and were formalized in the *Protocols of the Elders of Zion*, a phony document fabricated in Russia that outlined a Jewish conspiracy to conquer the world. Ritual-murder trials occurred in Eastern Europe until the eve of World War I, and were accompanied by brutal pogroms that fueled massive Jewish emigration to the West. But even in the United States, blood libel rumors persisted in communities, such as Chicago and Fall River, Massachusetts, where Eastern European Jews and Christians lived in the same neighborhoods.[13]

Variants of the blood libel myth still exist. After the 1968 student uprisings in France, rumors flew in provincial cities that the Jewish owners of trendy boutiques were trapping and abducting teenage girls in their stores' dressing rooms. Recently, hundreds of French parents insisted that several children had been kidnaped, photographed, raped, and eviscerated. Even though there were no missing children and no evidence, the sadistic child kidnapers were said to be Turkish and Northern African immigrants—whom many French blame for sabotaging their nation's economy and culture.[14]

In poor Asian and Latin American countries that supply children to adoptive parents from rich nations, popular resentment of growing economic inequality between the First and Third Worlds has lately been expressed through rumors that these babies are being slaughtered and their organs used for pediatric transplant operations. In 1994, three foreign women were severely beaten in rural Guatemala by crowds incited by these stories.[15]

The United States has also supplied fertile ground for subversion myths about children. During the height of antipapist hysteria, in the 1830s and 1840s, several books were written by women claiming to be ex-nuns who had escaped from convents where they witnessed orgies, torture, witchcraft, and the slaughter of infants. One account was so popular that in the years before the Civil War, its sales were surpassed only by *Uncle Tom's Cabin*. During this same period, ex-nuns and priests, real or feigned, made a handsome living touring the country and testifying about the slaughter of innocents at the hands of mothers superior and bishops.[16]

Fear of ritual child killing still exists in the United States, but these days the culprit has changed—as illustrated by events in eastern Kentucky. In 1988, thousands of terrified residents from several counties there called police to report rumors that blond, blue-eyed children were being targeted for sacrifice. This time, though, the predators were not said to be of any particular ethnicity or race. Now they were supposed to be satanists.[17]

Demonology

Why satanists? This latest scapegoat is explainable via the anthropological concept of the *demonology:* the narrative, specific to every culture, that identifies the ultimate evil threatening the group. During periods of social turmoil and moral crisis, societal preoccupation with its demonology intensifies.[18]

In Christian cultures, the demonology is based on the concept of a threat from Satan and his mortal agents.[19] Normally, this idea is ridiculed by the state and its intelligentsia. Confined to folk belief, its main function is to explain disease, ostracize village deviants, and reinforce community mores. But when demonology has been taken up by entire societies, the results have been devastating. During the Middle Ages, for instance, the Church was challenged by political competitors and by the Black Plague, which wiped out a third of Europe's population during a time when epidemics were considered divine vengeance for lack of faith. Confronted with these threats, medieval intellectual elites appropriated ordinarily harmless witchcraft beliefs and warned that the world was menaced by a devil so mighty that he could be controlled only by new nation-states of the devout, joined with each other through kings and the Church. This unity must be maintained, the intellectuals insisted, even if it meant burning everyone who supported Satan. Such was the logic that drove the medieval witch trials, as well as the legends and literature describing their obscene sabbats and ritual child murder.[20]

By the twentieth century, intellectuals had abandoned the idea of Satan battling with God and replaced it with materialist explanations for problems such as disease. Yet deep within the culture, the demonology prevails in times of crisis. When it is promoted by powerful social institutions and mixed with subversion myth, scapegoats are persecuted, often with deadly results. In the United States after the Russian Revolution, Communists were ferociously condemned as sexual deviants, rapists, anti-Christs, devils, and foreigners. In Nazi Germany, the government used the same imagery against both Communists and Jews, and rationalized ancient fears with the cooperation of social science, medicine, and the mass media.[21]

Half a century later in the United States, these institutions have also helped foment satanist subversion myths, though not as consciously as the Nazis did with Jews. Hollywood, for instance, is much less interested in attacking devil worship than in filling movie theaters, and beginning in the late 1960s and early 1970s, the industry realized that Satan sells tickets. During this period, *Rosemary's Baby* and *The Exorcist* were adapted from novels into blockbuster movies. Their phenomenal success was due, in part, to the way they employed ancient demonological imagery to communicate contemporary social anxieties.

In the movie version of *Rosemary's Baby*, released in 1968, the heroine is a pregnant young Manhattanite who gradually realizes that her baby is not her husband's, but the Devil's. Five years later, *The Exorcist* depicted a twelve-year-old girl possessed by Satan. Following that film's success, a rash of copycat movies featured youngsters colonized by the Devil.[22]

This cinematic casting of children as Ultimate Evil resonated with the times. By the late 1960s, women were regulating their fertility in unprecedented ways, through birth control pills and abortions that in some states were already legalized. They were also postponing maternity, bearing fewer children, and leaving them in other people's care as they entered the workforce.

Much of the increase in women holding jobs came from married mothers,[23] but contrary to the expectations of upper-middle-class feminists, many of these women did not feel liberated by their new jobs. They went to work because they had to, in order to keep their families afloat economically. Between 1973 and 1990, the median income of young families with a head younger than age thirty plummeted by almost a third, and even when wives went to work, family income hardly rose.[24]

The institutionalization of the two-worker family created massive social speedup as parents juggled responsibilities between work and home. Most of the extra labor fell to women, who still did the bulk of child care, cooking, and household chores.[25] Single mothers had a worse time than wives. With the decline of the breadwinner-husband ethic, many men reneged on child-support payments after divorce, or avoided marriage entirely. And while it was often women who chose to shun matrimony or leave it, single motherhood was a terrible deal, given that women still earned far less than men.

Under these circumstances, child rearing seemed more arduous, draining, and conflictual, and the tensions women felt were vented through the devil-child movies' use of increasingly resonant symbolism. In 1964, a national poll found that 37 percent of Americans believed in Satan as a literal entity. By 1973 the figure had risen to half the population, and it continued climbing during the next two decades.[26]

Growing belief in the Devil and his works is part of a general shift from rationality to mysticism in contemporary American culture that is independent of any particular religious ideology. At the same time, preoccupation with Satan reflects the growing popularity during the last generation of fundamentalist Christianity, with its belief that Lucifer is at war with God for the souls of mankind, and that the final battle will be taking place soon. While this belief is long-standing among fundamentalists, millenarian excitement grows stronger when thousand-year periods turn—as one is soon scheduled to do.

American intellectuals have long ignored or mocked these preoccupations, but that has not discouraged fundamentalism's survival, nor its recent resurgence. For the past generation, much of the growth has occurred among people in declining sectors of the economy, who have turned to small churches for solace and companionship.

Traditionally, fundamentalists lived in rural areas, and were poor and politically marginal. But this is no longer the case. As the 1970s unfolded, poverty spread in the cities and suburbs, along with massive changes in relations between men and women, parents and children. These changes unsettled people across the economic spectrum, and fundamentalist Christian churches reaped the benefits. As their membership exploded, the churches established an economic and political power base, acquiring radio and television networks and broadcasting their beliefs nationally via Reverends Jerry Falwell and Pat Robertson and other media celebrities.[27]

By the end of the decade, many fundamentalists were middle class and even wealthy, and could no longer be written off as ineffectual bumpkins. Falwell's establishment of the Moral Majority in 1979 marked their active entry into conservative politics, as they registered tens of thousands of voters and promoted candidates at all levels, from municipal to federal. Protestant churches often allied themselves with Catholic and Mormon fundamentalists, and the publications and television and radio networks these groups developed comprised an infrastructure that could provide members with instant information and marching orders about political issues.[28] As a powerful force on the New Right, fundamentalists organized campaigns against sex education in schools, legal abortion, and the Equal Rights Amendment. Attacks were typically posed in demonological language: sex education was said to encourage fornication, abortion was state-sanctioned murder, and the ERA violated biblical injunctions about the proper relations between women and men.

Cult Fears

The 1960s counterculture, meanwhile, engendered many new religious groups. Some were variants on Protestant fundamentalism, while others took their beliefs from ancient occult-magical traditions, from the human potential movement, and from non-Christian, Asian theologies.[29] The United States has a long tradition of demonizing unconventional religions by condemning them as politically subversive, brutal, authoritarian, sexually immoral, and endowed with supernatural powers.[30] These suspicions erupted again in the 1960s and 1970s. They were fueled by several interest groups, including distraught parents who claimed that their (usually adult) children were being "stolen" from them. Leaders of established fundamentalist religions also resented New Age religions, fearing competition for members. Disgruntled defectors from the new groups criticized them; so did some therapists and academics.[31]

Out of these forces, organizations such as the Cult Awareness Network and the American Family Foundation formed to discredit the new groups and "rescue" young people from them.[32] The Unification Church (the Moonies) and the International Society for Krishna Consciousness (Hare Krishnas) came in for particularly fierce attacks and sensationalist publicity. The claim that they were brainwashing their devotees was widely disseminated and generally accepted, even though studies indicate that people who join such groups seldom remain members for more than two years. Nevertheless, the brainwashing epithet became a powerful weapon justifying illegal acts, including kidnaping members and forcibly "deprogramming" them.[33]

By the early 1970s, critics were also calling organizations such as the Unification Church "cults," and comparing them to the Californians who murdered movie star Sharon Tate at Charles Manson's bidding. The word *cult* conjures up visions of a fanatical group subversive of Judeo-Christian values and led by a manipulative zealot commandeering mind-controlled acolytes. Any popular skepticism about this image evaporated after 1978, when hundreds of followers of the Reverend Jim Jones committed mass suicide at the People's Temple in Jonestown, Guyana. After that, to be labeled a cult was to be automatically demonized.[34]

With that connection established, anticult activists went on to address Americans' increasing obsession with the Devil. By the early 1980s, they had much material to work with. The previous two decades had witnessed a plethora of new religions, such as Wicca and neo-Paganism, whose members claim roots in the shamanistic practices of ancient Europeans and call themselves witches. Sociological research indicates that although wiccans and pagans are organized into "covens," believers do not typically follow charismatic leaders. Instead, they practice their rituals alone and avoid proselytizing. In the 1970s, there were some three hundred such groups in the United States.[35]

Other witchcraft groups were self-proclaimed satanists. The biggest was Anton LaVey's Church of Satan, founded in San Francisco in 1966. A former circus musician, LaVey enjoyed pointing out that movie stars such as Sammy Davis Jr. and Jayne Mansfield had been members of his church, and he performed satanic baptisms and weddings for celebrities that were heavily publicized. Many sociologists speculate that the Church of Satan functions mainly as a social spoof, much as professing allegiance to Lucifer during the nineteenth century was a way for leftists and aristocrats to mock bourgeois conventions.[36] For whatever reasons it attracts people, though, the Church of Satan has, at most, only five thousand active members. A spinoff organization, the Temple of Set, is far smaller.[37] Despite these tiny numbers, and the fact that neither group has ever been implicated in any criminal activity, by the early 1980s both had become lightning rods for anticult and antisatanist fears.

After becoming preoccupied with adult satanists, anticult organizations also began worrying about children being recruited to devil worship. The stretch of imagination needed to make such a claim was slight. By the early 1970s, some teenagers were calling themselves satanists, and a few were committing acts of serious violence. In 1971 in Vineland, New Jersey, two teenaged boys tied up a twenty-year-old and drowned him in a pond. The local newspapers described the killers as satanists and characterized the homicide as part of a ritual. As it turned out, the victim had a history of mental illness and had asked the youths to help him commit suicide.[38]

Most criminologists believe that blaming satanism is an after-the-fact rationalization for law-breaking, not its cause. Speculation about the relationship between teenage occultism and felonious misbehavior is somewhat academic, though, since most self-styled teenage satanists are white, upper-middle-class suburban boys whose main activity as devil worshipers consists of gathering in small groups and practicing black magic, which they do not learn from the Church of Satan or any other adult-oriented group. Instead, they improvise rituals with chants and routines picked up from friends, heavy-metal rock lyrics, popular movies, magazines, and books.[39]

Occasionally, they commit illegal mischief, such as writing graffiti, overturning gravestones, and assaulting animals. Although the outcome of such behavior can be disturbing, often it has no connection with satanism. America has a long history of church desecrations, cemetery vandalism, and animal mutilation, and there has not been a significant increase in these crimes in recent years. Folklorists and criminologists therefore speculate that much of what currently is being called teenage satanism is merely the latest enactment of "legend trips"—visits adolescents enjoy making to supposedly supernatural sites in their communities, such as haunted houses or cemeteries. Typical activities during legend trips include lighting bonfires, vandalizing property, telling ghost stories, and chanting spells.[40]

Starting in the late 1960s, some police and other adults who happened upon legend-trip sites interpreted them as evidence that the local youth were involved in organized satanism.[41] These perceptions were echoed by small-town newspapers and by a growing number of police officers who represented themselves as experts on satanism, as well as by Christian preachers, revivalists, and parents in the anticult movement.[42]

Their dire warnings were soon buttressed by a spate of rumors and urban legends about mysterious killings in the countryside and Faustian bargains in the city. In 1974, the nation's press began reporting that ranchers were finding cattle dead in the fields, their bodies drained of blood and their sex organs removed "with surgical precision." Shortly after these stories emerged, an inmate at Leavenworth Federal Penitentiary told an official from the U.S. Treasury's Bureau of Alcohol, Tobacco and Firearms that the killings were being committed by a supremacist cult who used animal genitals during black mass orgies, and who planned to kill prominent liberal and black politicians, including Edward Kennedy and Barbara Jordan. In response, the federal government began a nationwide investigation of satanist organizations, and a Treasury Department report about the racist, cattle-mutilating cult was distributed to police throughout the country and leaked to the press. The inmate's claims were eventually discredited as fabrications, but it was too late: the government report had taken on a life of its own.

On its heels, satanic livestock-killing rumors spread through the Southwest and Midwest, but investigating officials found that the animals' death and mutilation had been caused by snakebites, coyote attacks, common diseases, and rodents or other small scavengers. The ranchland cult legend died for a while, only to be reborn in other satanic myths.[43]

One, widespread in 1977, had it that Ray Kroc, chief executive officer of the McDonald's fast-food enterprise, had appeared on a television talk show and bragged that his business was thriving because he was tithing his profits to the Church of Satan.[44] Kroc had said nothing of the sort, but the rumor was a perfect example of populist hostilities that often emerge in urban legends and that the McDonald's story embodied, as many Americans during the 1970s were forced into minimum-wage service work like the kind offered at hamburger franchises. The Ray Kroc rumor barely surfaced in the world of respectable discourse, but other urban legends did, and they caused a whirl of confusion.

The Procter & Gamble legend was one. For decades, all the company's products, including such homemaker staples as Tide laundry detergent, sported a trademark man-in-the-moon face flanked by thirteen stars. According to rumors that began in the early 1980s, the venerable logo was actually a secret satanist symbol. The media played no part in spreading this story. In urban-legend fashion, it traveled through word of mouth, church sermons, chain letters, and bulletin board postings. The message always included urgings to boycott the company's products until it rescinded its evil pact.

By mid-1982, Procter & Gamble was being bombarded with mail, phone calls, and threats against employees and celebrities who promoted its products. Executives attempted to quell the rumor by persuading fundamentalist Christian leaders and the national media to assure the public that the company had nothing to do with satanism. In a few months, publicity was favorable and sales were up. But then the satanic soap company legend began spreading anew. In 1985, Procter & Gamble admitted defeat and removed the moon and stars from all its products.[45]

The Kiddie Porn Crusade

Grassroots rumors and small-town media hype were not the only sources of worries about threatened youngsters and cultists in the 1970s. Child-protection experts, feminists, and the government also played a major role in adding a sexual component to the national fear.

In 1977, Congress considered the problem of child abuse from a different angle than the one it had focused on during the CAPTA hearings three years earlier (see chapter 1). Now it concentrated on child pornography, which had recently made its first appearance in "adult" bookstores. Almost immediately, there was a public outcry against kiddie porn. One leader of the campaign was psychiatrist-lawyer Judianne Densen-Gerber, the flamboyant founder of an international drug-rehabilitation program that would later be exposed as coercive and cultlike under her authoritarian leadership.[46]

In 1976 Densen-Gerber happened upon some child pornography, and the discovery transformed her, in her words, into "a raving banshee."[47] She mailed the material to legislators and began touring the country, warning about widespread forced child prostitution, kidnaping, and murder. As a result, major newspapers and national television programs began denouncing child pornography and demanding that it be outlawed. The flood of concern led to congressional hearings. At one, Densen-Gerber dragged in a trunk filled with material, waved it before shocked legislators, and angrily claimed that in her travels she had counted 264 child pornography magazines published each month. She also claimed that children were being routinely sold for "snuff" films—movies recording actual murders. Further, she said, as many as 1.2 million American children were victims of child pornography and prostitution.[48]

Densen-Gerber was followed by Lloyd Martin, a sergeant with the Los Angeles Police Department and former member of its vice squad. Martin was head of the department's new Sexually Exploited Child Unit, a group of detectives who investigated juvenile prostitution, kiddie porn, and sex between children and adults who were not related to each other. The Sexually Exploited Child Unit was the first of its kind in the United States, and, as its head, Martin considered himself a pioneering expert on child sex abuse.[49]

The use of youngsters in commercial sex materials, he told Congress in 1977, was a multimillion-dollar enterprise and a large part of the pornography industry. Speaking at the same hearing, Densen-Gerber claimed that production and distribution were highly organized and controlled by sophisticated crime syndicates. Martin warned of vast networks of pedophiles. One, he said, was the Rene Guyon Society, whose slogan was "Sex before eight or then it's too late" and whose membership numbered five thousand.[50]

Densen-Gerber warned that making pornographic images of children was the most heinous crime imaginable, one that led to their "mutilation." Martin agreed: sexually exploiting a child, he said, was "worse than homicide." Further, Densen-Gerber contended, incest was "on the rise" because of child pornography.[51] The press demonstrated no skepticism about these declarations, nor did it question the witnesses' improbable claim that as many as one in twenty-five American children were being sold for sex and posed in obscene pictures.[52]

The media's credulity was hardly challenged, because it assuaged deeper fears. For a public confounded about incest and child molestation, it was reassuring to think that these seemingly intractable and ubiquituous evils could be blamed on something as deviant yet concrete as kiddie porn. On the other hand, many people suspected that sex abuse was caused by more than dirty magazines but had other reasons for embracing Densen-Gerber's and Martin's logic. Some feminists were troubled by pornographic depictions of women and, when Congress held its hearings, had already begun a moral crusade around the issue. In 1976, Diana Russell, a feminist sociologist who later would win government funding to study the prevalence of incest, co-founded the San Francisco–based Women Against Violence in Pornography and the Media.[53] Nominally, the group opposed violent portrayals of women on television, record album covers, and other mass media. But in practice, members concentrated their efforts against pornography, even those genres that they defined as nonviolent. Their focus was codified when a New York branch of the group dropped the word *violence* and shortened its name to Women Against Pornography.[54]

The new organization's emphasis on stamping out pornographic images of women mobilized broad-based support, during a time when the women's movement in general was experiencing increasing disarray and disorganization. By the mid-1970s, feminism's strength had peaked in America: the ERA, which had passed in several states by 1973, was stalled under right-wing, grassroots assaults, and newly legalized abortion was also under attack. The backlash did not come only from men. Feminism during the 1960s had questioned family roles, undermined traditional assumptions about sexuality, and envisioned women as public beings—all of which contradicted long-standing notions about gender identities and posed unsettling questions about selfhood for women. Amid the anxieties provoked by these transformations, domestic life remained difficult and sexual violence persisted. But instead of these problems being attributed to the failure of government or community, feminists were blamed for contradicting biological destiny. In defensive response, many began to embrace romantic, essentialist views of women's sexual purity and their superiority as the caretakers of children.[55]

By the mid-1970s, the trend was to blame patriarchy not on male social roles but on males themselves. According to this essentialist view, biology was destiny, or, as Susan Brownmiller put it in *Against Our Will,* her popular 1975 treatise on rape: "By anatomical fiat—the inescapable construction of their genital organs—the human male was a predator and the human female served as his natural prey."[56] Sexism, racism, hunger, war, and ecological disaster, *Ms.* magazine founder Robin Morgan wrote three years later, were all due to "the Man's competitiveness and greed."[57]

Antipornography feminists pandered to the idea and dramatized it by demonizing male sexuality. Writer Andrea Dworkin, for instance, warned women that sex with men was unremittingly exploitive and dangerous: "the stuff of murder, not love."[58] Her view of intercourse was equally bleak: "Fucking," Dworkin wrote in 1976, "is the means by which the male colonializes the female."[59] "Man fucks woman; subject verb object," echoed her theoretical collaborator, Catharine MacKinnon, in 1982. MacKinnon also suggested that women have no sexuality apart from what men desire from them, and she equated pornography with rape, incest, and other sexual coercions.[60]

Dworkin's and MacKinnon's views are contradicted by the fact that much pornography caters to gay men and has no females in it; that some is produced by women; and that many pornography consumers are women (a 1989 survey, for instance, found that 47 percent of the adult-video rental market was comprised of women, who rented the materials by themselves or as members of couples).[61] Despite all this, and despite the fact that to date no research has found a causal connection between pornography and violence—and much work has found none[62]—antiporn feminists claim that there is a causal connection and that pornography is not protected speech.

The cultural feminist insistence on a direct link between dirty pictures and violence was seized on by moral conservatives, whose priggishness about sex often seemed archaic to the larger culture. Antipornography feminists rescued the conservatives, however, by coupling violent sexual depictions to concrete, measurable harm. This equation allowed fundamentalists to modernize their rhetoric by replacing embarrassing terms like *sin* and *lust* with more respectable ones such as *women's degradation,*[63] even as it offered women the chance to rage against persistent patriarchal inequalities. As Victorian feminists had done a century earlier, women's advocates allied with conservative men who had no interest in gender equality—indeed, who staunchly opposed it.

Many people, including many feminists, who found pornography distasteful were torn by their belief in the First Amendment right to produce and view it. On the other hand, sexual depictions of children seemed incontrovertibly wrong, and for free-speech advocates, Densen-Gerber's and Martin's horrifying claims were cathartic. Columnist Ellen Goodman communicated this response as she described her disgust at "being force-fed the 'heroics'" of adult pornographers like Larry Flynt, publisher of *Hustler* magazine, who recently had been charged under obscenity statutes and cleared on First Amendment grounds. But now, as the congressional witnesses paraded their dire statistics and pictures of nude children, Goodman felt a "sense of relief." Now, she wrote, Americans could register their disapproval of pornography in a "refreshingly uncomplicated" way—by denouncing the child sexual exploitation industry as an "unequivocal villain."[64] Congress, too, was unequivocal. In 1978, the Child Protection Act had been enacted to eliminate commercial child pornography by forbidding the sale of material depicting subjects younger than sixteen, and by funding law-enforcement efforts to eliminate production.

But when officials swung into action, they found almost nothing to destroy. Shortly after the new law was passed, the Federal Bureau of Investigation began an extensive sting operation in which agents raided major pornography warehouses across the United States. They found no material involving children. Illinois' Legislative Investigations Commission (ILIC) initiated an even more searching inquiry with identical results. The commission concluded that by the time the Child Protection Act went into effect, kiddie porn had already disappeared completely from the commercial chain of distribution; there was little evidence of its existence underground, either.[65]

The frightening claims of Densen-Gerber, Martin, and other "experts" were thus grossly exaggerated, not only in the ILIC's and FBI's estimation, but also according to subsequent congressional investigations. Organized crime has never been involved in juvenile prostitution. At its height, kiddie porn grossed far less than $1 million per year (compared with billions of dollars for the adult industry).[66] And during the 1970s and 1980s, the total number of people affiliated with pedophile-support groups in the United States was probably fewer than 2,400 (the Rene Guyon Society, with its infamous slogan, most likely had one member).[67] Most of this information was publicly available by 1980, but during the next few years, officials and much of the media continued to claim that commercial child pornography involved millions of children and a vast underground network of pedophiles engaged in a multibillion-dollar business.[68]

Social paranoia about malevolent molesters was aggravated during this period by an emerging school of victimologist researchers who used social science rhetoric to advance moral claims about child sexual abuse.[69] Investigators like Diana Russell found that by age eighteen, 54 percent of all women had been sexually abused.[70] Another study concluded that 62 percent were victims.[71] The new numbers were published by the mass media, and they were terrifying.

What popular audiences did not realize was that the new research vastly broad-ened the definitions of sexual abuse.[72] A child, for instance, could be anyone from a toddler to an older teenager (including one who was married). Whereas abuse ear-lier had meant fondling or penetration, now it included acts such as exhibitionism and verbal propositions by age-peers.[73] Given these revisions, sexual abuse could now mean anything from a father anally raping his three-year-old daughter to a seventeen-year-old girl cat-called by a boy her age. Further, a large body of research suggests that minors, especially girls, who have sexual contact with adults generally suffer negative reactions and continuing problems later in life;[74] at the same time, many people show no ill effects, and a small proportion report that they enjoy or benefit from the experience.[75] Nevertheless, many victimologists regarded every incident as inevitably traumatic, even devastating.

Their research did help focus attention on the unwanted and often traumatic sex-ual attentions that children (again, particularly girls) routinely endure. But it also became difficult to distinguish different types of experiences and children's varying responses to them. Incidents such as father-daughter incest almost always involved patently skewed, coercive relationships. Others were far more ambiguous. One gray area was "hustling," or boy prostitution with men clients. In the 1970s, child-protection officials began conjecturing that hustlers were Mafia-controlled and often prepubescent.[76] Neither assumption was true, and subsequent studies revealed that hustlers tend to come from low-income families. Or they are gay, but their families and friends are so homophobic that they feel compelled to seek sex and sociability with adult men.[77]

Yet child protectionists and politicians were reluctant to discuss hustling as a poverty problem, and even more loath to condemn homophobia aggressively. In fact, just the opposite happened in the late 1970s, when moral conservatives accused gays of "stealing" straight children and turning them into homosexuals. An influential promoter of this paranoia was the singer and Florida orange juice–industry representative, Anita Bryant. In 1977 Bryant launched "Save the Children," a drive to revoke a Miami-area ordinance barring discrimination against gays. Her campaign denounced gay men as child molesters, and it received national attention.[78]

At the same time that homosexual men were being denounced as child molesters, sex-abuse researchers and law-enforcement officials were promoting the idea of rampant, conspiratorial cabals of men bent on sexually abusing youngsters. Boston psychiatric nurse Ann Burgess, who earlier had studied women's emotional reac-tions to rape, was the main proponent of this new idea. In the late 1970s, she stud-ied men convicted of having sex with groups of children. Although some were girls or young boys, most were male adolescents similar to the youths involved in hustling.[79] Burgess called their group activities with men "sex rings,"[80] and soon law-enforcement personnel were making baseless claims about giant rings, linked through computer and transportation networks, to move children around the nation and the world in order to molest them and make pornography. At a federally funded conference Burgess organized in 1981, a detective from Indiana called these apocryphal rings "cults" and speculated about ways to ferret them from the "underground."[81]

By the early 1980s, even professionals and the government were fomenting panic-laden images of children as helpless prey for secretive, organized evildoers. If musings about cults and billion-dollar pornography mafias were not enough to feed the fear, the missing children panic added more fuel. One morning in 1979, a six-year-old named Etan Patz vanished near his home in lower Manhattan and was never seen again. Two years later, Adam Walsh, also six years old, disappeared from a Florida department store and was later found with his head severed.

These chilling and highly publicized cases set off a tidal wave of concern for missing children. Soon milk cartons and shopping bags were covered with photographs of American youngsters whose parents did not know where they were. The situation was said to be grave: politicians and journalists estimated at least 50,000 kidnappings annually, most committed by strangers.[82] If even the low estimate had been correct, it would have meant that practically every U.S. school would have at least one pupil missing—yet no one seemed to know of a case personally. Still, few doubted the numbers. The media published them, and the government repeated them. Much of the rhetoric linked the missing children problem to sexual abuse and pedophiles.[83]

Later research would reveal that, in fact, the vast majority of abducted children are snatched by divorced, noncustodial parents, and that annually, only a few hundred are taken by strangers for more than a few hours.[84] This information would not be publicized until the latter part of the 1980s, however. In the meantime, frightened parents flocked to police stations to have their children fingerprinted. Pedophile kidnapper fears burgeoned and spawned urban legends about small children snatched in malls and castrated in public restrooms.

There are, of course, violent crimes committed by sexual psychopaths against children. Such offenders are extremely rare, but during the missing-children scare, they became the focus of intense grassroots organizing by a group emerging from the new "victim's rights" movement—a national effort that had begun by demanding more sympathetic treatment of people who had been raped and assaulted, but which by the late 1970s was teaming up with conservative, law-and-order police and prosecutor organizations.

Panic in the Clinic

It was only a matter of time before "satanists" would be blamed for the missing children phenomenon. The first public charges came in the 1980 book *Michelle Remembers,* co-authored by Michelle Smith and her psychiatrist, Dr. Lawrence Pazder.

Michelle Remembers is a first-person testimonial in which Smith claims she was tormented during her childhood by a satanic cult whose members imprisoned her for several months during 1955, when she was five years old. The book is filled with graphic descriptions of little Michelle being tortured in houses, mausoleums, and cemeteries, being raped and sodomized with candles, being forced to defecate on a Bible and crucifix, witnessing babies and adults butchered, spending hours naked in a snake-filled cage, and having a devil's tail and horns surgically attached to her. There is also an account of a cult attempt to kill the child and make it look like an accident, by placing her in a car with a corpse, then deliberately crashing the vehicle. These grotesque abuses are said to have gone on for almost a year, until Michelle's indomitable Christian faith discouraged the satanists, and they set her free. She then completely forgot the experiences for more than twenty years, until she entered therapy with Dr. Pazder.[85]

The problem with Smith's "memories" is that there is no independent verification for them; indeed, there is much to contradict them. Smith is from Victoria, British Columbia, and residents of the neighborhood where she was raised say her father was alcoholic, but that otherwise, there was nothing remarkable about her family. A neighbor and a former teacher recall that Smith started first grade in 1955, attended school regularly, and was photographed for the yearbook—at a time when *Michelle Remembers* has her locked in a basement for months.[86]

Further, Smith has no records of childhood hospitalizations, and, while Pazder has documentation that she was treated for dental and dermatological problems as an adult, neither condition has any particular relationship to the tortures she claims she suffered. Pazder also claims to have interviewed an elderly pediatrician who said he could "vaguely recall" treating Smith for injuries she might have gotten in a car collision. But there are no newspaper accounts during late 1954 and early 1955 of any fatal traffic accidents resembling the one in the book—and the local newspapers from that time gave detailed coverage to even the most minor mishaps.[87]

A more likely explanation for Smith's "memories" is that they resulted from therapeutic suggestion. During the 1990s, a new term, "false memory syndrome," entered the popular and mental health field lexicon, to describe the phenomenon whereby patients—primarily women—in psychotherapy for common problems such as depression emerge with previously unremembered recollections of brutal childhood sexual abuse. Dating as they do from the late 1970s, Smith's stories are early examples of the false memory process, but they are not the first ones. Therapeutically induced confabulations about childhood sexual abuse have a long history, going back the late nineteenth century, when Sigmund Freud and other European clinicians were treating female hysterics.[88]

Dissociation Theory

Freud's French mentors, Jean-Martin Charcot and Pierre Janet, believed that hysteria occurred when a child suffered a trauma so unbearable that the mind developed amnesia by "dissociating" the terrible event into another psychic compartment, separate from consciousness. The memory was thereafter forgotten to the conscious mind, but intruded itself in somatic ways: through the paralyses, tics, bleeding, and fits, for example, that caused patients to seek treatment. The cure for hysteria, according to dissociation theory, was to access that memory and bring it into consciousness. The method of choice for this procedure was hypnosis. During trance, patients produced impassioned and detailed stories about all kinds of childhood traumas, including incest and molestation.[89]

Freud took these stories of abuse seriously. Based on his work with thirteen female patients, in early 1896 he announced his "seduction theory" of neurosis, which claimed that hysteria and similar psychopathologies were invariably caused by the trauma of childhood sexual violation. In formulating this notion, it is clear that Freud pressured the women who entered therapy with him to produce abuse narratives that he interpreted as memories, and that he contributed his own sexual preoccupations to their stories.

According to Freud's own accounts, before patients began analysis, they knew nothing about the scenes he wanted them to remember. Many were indignant at his suggestion that they had been abused as children, and produced "memories"only after being virtually forced to. As Freud wrote, "One only succeeds in awakening the psychical trace of a precocious sexual event under the most energetic pressure of the analytic procedure, and against an enormous resistance. Moreover, the memory must be extracted from them piece by piece."[90] Indeed, his efforts to elicit abuse memories were so intense, and his refusal to take no for an answer so intransigent, that he complained to a colleague that he was "almost hoarse" from pressuring patients for ten to eleven hours a day.[91]

Freud eventually gave up the seduction theory of neurosis, as well as the use of hypnosis, partly because he recognized that many of his patients' "memories" seemed illogical, impossibly bizarre, or otherwise untrue. In formulating a new explanation—that the stories were actually fantasied symbols of unresolved oedipal drives—Freud opened the door to a psychopolitical critique of patriarchy and the phallic obsessions masculine domination creates in children of both sexes, but particularly in girls. At the same time, the fact that the mental health professions were male-dominated meant that, until recently, clinicians overwhelmingly used the Oedipus complex to dismiss most girls' and women's reports of sexual violation as nothing more than obscene imaginings.[92]

By the late 1970s, however, the seduction theory of neurosis and the dissociation model of psychic trauma were being rehabilitated, partly because of feminist influence, but for other reasons as well. Hypnosis, for instance, which fell out of favor during the rise of Freudianism, had been revived during the 1950s by the federal government, out of fear that Chinese Communists in Korea were using sophisticated techniques to induce captured American soldiers to make hostile public declarations about capitalism and the United States. The government began calling this practice "brainwashing," and, though research has since discredited the concept, the idea that Manchurian candidate–style manipulations and subliminal messages can create human robots has remained popular in American culture.[93]

During the McCarthy era, when the brainwashing concept was widespread, the federal government provided more than $5 million to researchers to study the uses and effects of hypnosis. Findings replicated what had been well known among clinicians in the previous century: some people are highly hypnotizable and can produce dramatic bodily changes in response to suggestion; and, while memories elicited under trance can be richly textured and feel like real experience, many are actually fantasies.[94]

Though forensic psychiatrists of the 1970s generally knew about these research findings, many therapists did not. One reason for their ignorance was that the mental health field during this period was undergoing profound changes, producing increasing numbers of therapists who were less trained than their predecessors and more apt to accept at face value patients' accounts of their pasts.

Since then, the number of people entering the psychotherapy professions has skyrocketed, and the field has changed from a primarily male-dominated one to mainly female. Many were graduates of new, freestanding professional schools that proliferated to train them. These institutions had no affiliation with universities, their admission standards were low, and their commitment to scientific standards of inquiry was far from rigorous.[95] In Freud's time, people seeking psychological help tended to be female, and the same was true in the 1970s. But by then, the therapeutic relation between patient and healer had changed. Earlier, a woman typically saw a male clinician who acted emotionally distant and analyzed her problems through the lens of Freudian drive theory and its emphasis on inner impulses in conflict with the external world (the notorious Oedipus complex is one example). With the feminization of psychotherapy, today's patient is likely to see a therapist who has rejected drive theory for object-relations approaches. According to object-relations theorists, psychopathology results from bad parenting and other external trauma. Bad feelings and behavior are dignified as normal coping responses to these terrible events, and clinicians typically "re-mother" their patients by acting warm and empathic toward them.[96]

As more women entered therapy, the eating disorders, depression, anger, and unpleasant dreams they brought with them were increasingly framed as caused by severe childhood trauma. Therapists focused on recovering memories, using hypnosis and other consciousness-altering techniques. When patients began telling stories of sexual abuse that they had not recalled before treatment, feminist-oriented clinicians did not question their credibility. Instead, theoreticians such as Jeffrey Masson and Judith Herman revived the old concepts of dissociation and repression to explain how traumatic memories could have been isolated so long from consciousness before finally returning in therapy.[97]

Multiple Personality Disorder

Swayed by the increasing popularity of repression and dissociation models of neurosis, both among mental health workers and in the culture generally, patients began to produce previously unremembered stories of childhood sexual abuse. Many of these were accounts of fondling by fathers, cousins, and uncles; others, like the accounts of Michelle Smith, described grotesque scenarios of sadomasochism committed by hooded and robed figures of both sexes.

The most bizarre tales often came from patients who had been diagnosed as schizophrenics or borderline personalities, but who now were labeled as suffering from multiple personality disorder (MPD)—a condition in which, proponents believe, one or more "alter" personalities emerge from a traumatized child to manage the dissociated memories.[98] Before 1970, fewer than 200 people worldwide had ever been assigned medical labels reminiscent of today's MPD, and a mere handful of them came from the United States. After that date, the number of cases mushroomed—to at least 1,000 in 1984,[99] then several times that number by 1989.[100] The vast majority were located in North America, and they were overwhelmingly female.

Skeptics contend that unlike disorders such as schizophrenia and mental retardation, MPD has no medical validity, and that it is more properly viewed as a social identity, often constructed as a joint effort of patients and their therapists. Chris Sizemore's multiplicity was described in 1957 in *The Three Faces of Eve*, written by her psychiatrists, Corbett Thigpen and Hervey Cleckley. In this best-selling book, which was made into a movie, the authors disapprovingly described "Eve White" as a quiet, mousy wife and mother. They could barely conceal their awe and excitement, however, at the emergence of a throaty-voiced, cigarette-smoking, bachelorette alter personality whom, in the classic mother/whore tradition, the therapists christened "Eve Black."[101] After the Eves (and a third personality) were presented to the world in print and at the movies, Thigpen and Cleckly were shocked when they were contacted by thousands of women who were diagnosing themselves as multiple personalities.[102]

In 1973 a book called *Sybil* appeared, in which a woman was said to have developed sixteen personalities after being chronically raped and tortured by her mentally ill mother. Although Sybil also became a best-seller and later a television film, revelations have lately emerged that suggest the patient had been diagnosed as schizophrenic, but was encouraged by her therapist, Dr. Cornelia Wilbur, to produce multiple personalities as a strategy to market the book.[103]

Sybil was read by millions of teenage girls and adult women, and a rash of copycat books soon followed. Meanwhile, Wilbur joined the psychiatry department at the University of Kentucky, where she collaborated with faculty studying patients diagnosed as suffering from multiple personalities. Under hypnosis, many produced stories about sadomasochistic sexual abuse, including details about gang rape and being buried alive, mutilated, and forced to murder infants.[104]

Many early MPD therapists noticed that large percentages of their patients came from fundamentalist Christian families. This was probably no coincidence, considering that as early as the 1960s, Pentecostal Christians had been promoting a diabolic theory of mental illness that later integrated ideas about devil possession with secular theories about MPD.

As Pentecostalism made inroads into mainstream Christianity during the 1970s, so did belief in demons, who were considered embodiments of sin. Demons could invade people, Pentecostals claimed, and the most susceptible individuals were those who practiced folk healing, spiritism, card reading, New Age rituals, and similar blasphemies. Children whose parents engaged in these activities could also be Devil-possessed, and become physically and mentally ill. Once the youngsters were stricken, the only cure was to cast out the devils.

The ancient ritual of exorcism became a model for this healing. Christian counselors used it in the 1970s to cure emotional afflictions, and they likened it to therapy for multiple personality disorder. Growing numbers of these clinicians combined demonological concepts with secular psychology,[105] and some women went back and forth between the two kinds of treatment providers.

In hindsight, it seems clear that, like UFO and Elvis encounter stories, the tales of cultic abomination that emerged from these sessions were attempts by troubled women and their therapists to mediate anxieties and emotional disorganization through the cultural formulations of subversion myth and demonology. Such story making was particularly compelling for patients and clinicians from devout Christian backgrounds, and the authors of *Michelle Remembers* were no exceptions. A dedicated Catholic, Pazder had a long-standing interest in possession states and exorcism. (He had also studied Western African witchcraft rituals, and some of the details Michelle remembered, such as being buried in a pit, echo these rites.) For her part, Smith had attended high school in a Catholic convent and thus was familiar with the religion and its symbols.[106]

Much of the book, including photographs the authors say depict visitations by the Virgin Mary, places it as inspirational allegory for pious Catholics. It became a mass-market success because it combined sacred motifs with the same therapeutic themes that had made *Sybil* a best-seller. In 1980, when *Michelle Remembers* was first published, it did not occur to book reviewers or the media to investigate the authors' claims. The next year, Pazder presented a paper at the American Psychiatric Association's annual meeting, where he coined the term "ritual abuse."[107]

Soon other women were revealing to the media, the police, and their therapists that they, too, had been assaulted as children by members of satanic cults. In the wake of their stories, a group of prominent American psychiatrists who specialized in hypnotherapy began organizing the International Society for the Study of Multiple Personality & Dissociation (ISSMP&D). They elaborated and formalized treatment techniques, including methods for communicating nonverbally with alter selves by having them wag the host personality's fingers to answer yes or no to therapists' questions.

While Pazder and Smith made headlines, Ronald Reagan was also dominating the media. His new administration immediately began to gut the National Center for Child Abuse and Neglect, dramatically slashing its funding. As a result of the cuts, NCCAN laid off much of its staff, including Kee MacFarlane.

Unemployed, she left Washington and took a job with a beleaguered community sex abuse treatment program in Los Angeles. There, shortly after she arrived, a decade's preoccupation with moral conservatism, subversion myth, and demonology would come full circle with the frustrations of feminists, child-protection activists, and parents who watched helplessly as the government turned its back on youngsters' well-being. The country was ripe for a drama to enact this angst.

It made its debut in California.

PART II
Satan Speaks

THREE

Beginnings: Mary Ann Barbour

Three waves of ritual-abuse panic rose in Southern California in the 1980s and were felt all across the country: the nation's first "sex-ring" scandal, the bold accusations against teachers at the McMartin Preschool, and a firestorm of cases triggered by McMartin. Taken together, they trace an arc in which the psychotic delusions of a few individuals were translated into public policy. Through these cases, officials would hone a flawless system, with methods for promoting criminal charges, a patina of science to lend authority, and a rhetoric for explaining away the lack of evidence. The three chapters in part II will take up each of these cases in turn.

Bakersfield

California's Great Central Valley, stretching from north of Redding to south of Bakersfield, is an immense trough, at most sixty miles wide but over four hundred miles long. A flat, featureless place, normally shrouded by a brown haze or low-lying fog, it holds little interest for tourists. The Valley has long drawn immigrants looking for work, though, because its oil-based and agricultural economy is prodigiously productive.

Bakersfield, the Kern County seat, resembles all the other Valley towns strung like beads along the north-south thread of Highway 99. These communities are suffused with an "implacable insularity," Sacramento native Joan Didion has written, and the locals are proud of their small-town, non–Los Angeles values.[1] At the same time, the small-business owners, government workers, and branch office employees of the agricultural corporations that dominate the area are plagued by an inferiority complex. Though Kern County's middle class values propriety and strives for respectability, it must cope with an unruly, multiracial underclass that keeps labor cheap and the criminal justice system busy. Kern County sends a greater proportion of its residents to the gas chamber than any other county in California. The poor live in the southeast part of Bakersfield and in small towns outside the city limits. In these communities, within the jurisdiction of the Kern County sheriff, lived the accused members of eight child sex rings. The largest ring would eventually be known as the Satanic Church case, and would implicate more than sixty adults and seventy-seven children. In the 1980s, Kern County seemed more deeply infected with moral panic and fear for its children than any other part of the United States.

Early on a Tuesday evening in January 1980, an electrical contractor named Gene Barbour telephoned the sheriff's office and asked for help. His wife, Mary Ann, had not been sleeping well for months and had become increasingly distraught. Gene reported that three days earlier, Mary Ann had taken off in the car; when she returned, he removed a tire so she couldn't leave again. Now she was tearing up all the family snapshots and threatening to stab him.[2]

A sheriff's deputy who answered the call found Gene restraining a tall, heavyset, disheveled woman. Gene showed the deputy a knife he said Mary Ann had threatened him and herself with, and added that she had a gun hidden in her car. When the deputy asked Mary Ann what was wrong, she spent forty-five minutes talking frantically about how her six-year-old step-granddaughter, Bobbie, had been molested, and how everyone was now out to get Mary Ann. She became so agitated that the deputy took her to the psychiatric ward of Kern Medical Center.[3]

Once there, she, took up her story again, and explained how the man who molested Bobbie had also killed people and about the terrible nightmares she had lately been suffering. A doctor noted that Mary Ann seemed delusional and paranoid. He diagnosed her as suffering from a form of schizophrenia and prescribed two antipsychotic medications. That done, he never saw her again.[4]

Mary Ann Barbour, now thirty-seven years old, had lost her father in a truck-train collision when she was a preschooler. She once fell from a moving car when she was young, and as a result, had a plate in her head. She also had terrible scarring on her arm from where a relative had thrown her through a window. Her mother was a domineering woman, Mary Ann told a hospital therapist, and as a child she had preferred spending time with her grandmother. These visits took her away from a household populated by a series of stepfathers—after her father's death, her mother had remarried, divorced, and married again. When asked how these men had treated her, Mary Ann would not respond.[5]

All the therapists learned was that when she was fourteen, Mary Ann ran away from home and married, then separated, had a child out of wedlock, married again, had two more children, and spent years on welfare.[6] Finally, in the mid-1970s, she met Gene Barbour, who earned a good enough living with the Southern Pacific Railroad to own a five-bedroom house.

Mary Ann was Gene's third wife. His first was Linda, with whom he had had two daughters: Debbie and Cindy. In the late 1960s, Linda began an affair with a man named Rod Phelps. Gene left, Linda and Rod married, and Debbie, who was twelve, stayed with her mother and her new stepfather. Soon, though, she asked to live with Gene again. The reason, she said, was that Rod Phelps had tried to molest her.[7]

Less than three years later, Debbie married, at age fifteen. Her groom was eighteen-year-old Alvin McCuan. Like Debbie, he was a high school dropout, but he held a steady job as a sheet metal worker for Southern Pacific. Their first daughter, Bobbie, was born a few weeks after the wedding. Another girl, Darla, came two years later. By the late 1970s, Debbie and Alvin were well into adulthood, marriage, and family life. Alvin continued working with the railroad, and Debbie ran a day-care center in her home. She still visited her mother and stepfather, who now lived in Atascadero, west of Bakersfield. Bobbie and Darla went along on these visits. They also spent several weeks each year visiting Gene and Mary Ann and traveling with them on vacations.

Mary Ann doted on the girls, and part of the attention she paid them was a frequent, close scrutiny of their genitals. This had started in 1977, when Darla was only two years old and Bobbie was four. Mary Ann had examined them then and thought both girls' vaginas looked bruised and large. She began to suspect that Rod Phelps was molesting his step-granddaughters, and she started having "conversations" about this with Bobbie.[8] Bobbie had nothing to say about it and neither did Darla. Over two years passed while Mary Ann nursed her suspicions and continued to study the girls' genitals.

In January 1980, Mary Ann called a pediatrician friend of the family and reported that her thirteen-year-old daughter, Maggie, said that Bobbie had said Rod Phelps molested her. The pediatrician examined Bobbie and found that her genitals indeed were red and bruised, and that the vaginal opening looked too big. Bobbie would not say what had happened. The doctor was unaware of Mary Ann's anatomical inspections, and of the possibility that these examinations might be the cause of the trauma. Instead, she concluded that the abnormalities probably were due to penile penetration by Rod Phelps.[9] Kern County's Child Protective Services was called, and two days later, Bobbie and her parents were interviewed by social worker Velda Murillo.

Murillo was one of the county's most respected interviewers of suspected sex-abuse victims. In 1984, she would be featured in an instructional videotape used in the San Joaquin Valley to teach child-protection workers how to obtain disclosures. On the tape, she tells how important it is that only the investigator and the child be present. The room must be locked and Murillo also recommends that interviewers allow themselves "plenty of time with the child"—a whole day, if necessary—because "you never know what you're going to get into." She stresses the need to talk about what *might* have happened, then to seek a yes or no answer from the child.[10]

Murillo used all these techniques on Bobbie but, just as the pediatrician had been unable to achieve a disclosure, she had trouble, too. "Bobbie denied anything had happened," Murillo's report indicates. "I told her I knew someone had been messing with her and I wanted to help stop it. . . . She began sobbing, but still could not tell me anything." Eventually, Murillo called a sheriff's investigator and the two of them continued interrogating Bobbie. Finally, the child told them that "one time last summer, her grandpa Phelps had put his hand in her panties and put a finger inside her vagina." Authorities proceeded to Atascadero to question Rod Phelps.[11]

Mary Ann insisted that Bobbie and Darla be removed from their parents' home, since Phelps had access to it and to the children who attended Debbie's day-care center. But the McCuans had already promised authorities they would keep Phelps away, and they also offered to put the girls into therapy. When Murillo explained all this to Mary Ann, she became "extremely excitable"—even "irrational," as Murillo's colleague put it.[12] Mary Ann phoned the sheriff's office, demanding that he remove the children. She also contacted her congressional representative and the state attorney general, but received no response.[13] Rod Phelps, meanwhile, was vehemently denying that he had abused Bobbie.[14] To Mary Ann Barbour, it seemed there was no justice in the world. Only after she got a gun and pulled a knife on her husband did the authorities take notice.

Following that outburst, she spent six days under psychiatric observation. Antipsychotic drugs eventually calmed her, and after two days she was transferred to a cheaper hospital. The psychiatrist and social worker who evaluated her there apparently believed her story that Bobbie had been molested, and that this was the cause of Mary Ann's mental state. When she was discharged, her diagnosis read simply "anxiety" and "marital maladjustment." She left with no medication except sleeping pills, and was told to return for outpatient counseling with a social worker.[15]

At home, Mary Ann's obsession did not abate. She telephoned Betty Palko, a Welfare Department social worker whom she had met years earlier while attending a job-training program, and now she asked Palko to help get Debbie McCuan's day-care license revoked. Palko notified the licensing department, but representatives found nothing amiss at the center and refused to close it. Hearing this, Mary Ann concluded that Palko had plotted to thwart the investigation.[16]

She then found another avenue for her obsession. Mary Ann called Jill Haddad, leader of the Bakersfield chapter of the national victims' rights organization SLAM, or Stronger Legislation Against Molesters.[17] A woman in her thirties and the co-owner of a mortgage company, Haddad came from a local family who had gained prominence because many of its men had made careers in the sheriff's department and other law-enforcement agencies. Haddad helped found the local chapter of SLAM in 1980, and it soon became a major component in Kern County's criminal justice system. The organization was given a copy of all sex-crime arrest reports, and the DA's office consulted with SLAM leaders about which cases should be tried.[18] Haddad would later join the board of directors of Lloyd Martin's Foundation for America's Sexually Exploited Children (FASEC).[19] As head of the Los Angeles Police Department's Sexually Exploited Child Unit, Martin was one of the "experts" who had testified, at congressional hearings in 1977 about the dangers of wide-spread child pornography.

Soon he was running FASEC out of his garage and traveling the country giving lectures on the dangers and prevalence of pedophilia and kiddie porn. Martin had antagonized the local gay community by leading warrantless vice raids on its gatherings in the 1970s. He then alienated powerful Southern Californians by making public statements about the Boy Scouts of America and Boys' Town harboring pedophile adult volunteers. Eventually, his superiors decided that Martin's involvement with FASEC had crossed the line into obsession, and he was removed from the Sexually Exploited Child Unit. He then quit the police department and devoted all his time to FASEC.[20] Haddad joined him in lobbying for changes in the criminal law regarding sex-abuse prosecutions, and the two became very close—so close that they eventually divorced their spouses, married each other, and shared leadership of FASEC. As a court-qualified expert witness in child sex-abuse cases, Haddad also created the new Sex Abuse Coordinator position in the DA's office, which the American Bar Association praised as "innovative." The person assigned this new job was supposed to "help the victim and communicate with other agencies involved in child sexual abuse investigations."[21] The first hiree was social worker Carol Darling, wife of Sergeant Brad Darling, the head of the sheriff's Child Sex Abuse Unit.

When Haddad met Mary Ann Barbour, she listened to her story sympathetically and sent her literature about child sex abuse.[22] Mary Ann had become less agitated, but was still keenly interested in whether the girls were still being molested. When they came to visit, she continued to peer at their genitals.

In October 1981, eighteen months after her hospitalization, Mary Ann contacted a Kern County probation officer and told him that she was afraid Darla and Bobbie were still being molested by Phelps. The McCuans had agreed to keep the girls away from their step-grandfather, but Mary Ann claimed they had seen him two months earlier, and that after the visit, she had found bruises around their genitals.[23]

The probation officer referred Mary Ann's complaint to the child-protection authorities, and when Velda Murillo received it, she teamed up with Kern County Sheriff's Deputy Betty Shaneyfelt and visited the girls' grade school to interview them. Afterward, the two women wrote that the girls claimed they had been molested—not just by Phelps but also by Alvin McCuan, their father. According to Murillo, Bobbie said that Alvin had touched her between her legs, that he sometimes put his tongue in her mouth and his fingers in her vagina, and that he rubbed his penis between her legs. All this was supposed to have been going on for two years, and had happened most recently the previous week. Darla, Murillo reported, made the same claims. Additionally, Darla said that her father had ejaculated on her. Both girls reported that their step-grandfather had done the same things to them earlier.[24]

Alvin McCuan was promptly arrested, and Bobbie and Darla were taken from their family and booked into Shalimar, a Kern County juvenile home. During their first few days there, they were not allowed visitors, except for social worker Betty Palko, who dropped in to comfort them and reassure them they would be well cared for.

Hearing that Palko had been allowed to visit when she wasn't, Mary Ann became extremely upset. She, Deputy Shaneyfelt, Carol Darling, and various juvenile court officials vehemently complained that the social worker assigned to the two little girls was not sympathetic to their complaints of sexual abuse and wanted to "lose the case." But the social worker assigned to the case was, in fact, not Betty Palko, and a supervisor who investigated concluded that although Mary Ann was "understandably distraught," her charges were groundless.[25]

While the girls were in the juvenile home, Mary Ann was becoming close friends with Jill Haddad. The relationship soon spilled into the legal arena: when Child Protective Services sought to remove the children from their parents permanently, Haddad gave expert testimony in support of the action.[26] At the hearing where the custody decision was made, Bobbie testified that her father and step-grandfather had both "kissed me down there" and "touched me down there" with their hands. Alvin had done the same to Darla, she said. But, Bobbie reported, contrary to what Murillo had written, her father had never put his fingers up her vagina, nor had he licked her vagina, or stuck his penis between her legs or anywhere else. She also said that the only time her father had touched her "down there" was when he was bathing her. When questioned again by the prosecutor, she agreed that her father "kissed and touched" her in her "private parts," but she denied that he had done anything else with his lips or mouth, or that she had ever seen his penis.[27]

After both girls were legally separated from their parents, Mary Ann and Gene petitioned for permanent custody. Bobbie's and Darla's social worker—the same one who had been excoriated by Mary Ann and her supporters—was aware of Mary Ann's psychiatric hospitalization in 1980. Even so, she felt Mary Ann no longer suffered from emotional problems, and she recommended that the girls be placed with the Barbours. In February 1982, Bobbie and Darla become official members of Mary Ann's and Gene's household.[28]

Days and Nights in the Barbour Home

Before they moved in with the Barbours, the girls had seemed happy and cooperative, and records from the juvenile home show no evidence that they acted in unusual or sexual ways while there. But within a few weeks after they started living with Mary Ann, she began calling the girls' caseworker, as well as their therapist, every few days and reporting that Bobbie and Darla were having nightmares, throwing tantrums, and masturbating. According to Mary Ann, these behaviors were especially pronounced after the girls' mother visited them; and Debbie's continued access to her daughters displeased Mary Ann. Her calls continued, and now she said, the girls were doing sexual things to her, like asking to suck her breasts and waking her up by rubbing her breasts and lower body. They were also coming up with "interesting and shocking statements."[29]

Meanwhile, Alvin McCuan was searching for a respectable character witness for his upcoming trial. He chose his friend Scott Kniffen, who made a good living as an inventory manager for a diesel company. His wife, Brenda, stayed home and cared for their two boys, six-year-old Billy and nine-year-old Byron. They were a close family. Scott coached wrestling and soccer, and Brenda taught Bible school. They knew the McCuans because Brenda's brother had gone to high school with Alvin. Occasionally, they socialized at the Kniffens' house and played canasta.

By the end of March 1982, when Alvin's preliminary hearing started, the Barbour home was in chaos. Mary Ann had stopped sleeping again, as she had in 1980 before being hospitalized, and she was keeping Bobbie and Darla up all night with her. After one of these sleepless nights, the girls took the stand in court and spoke about their father molesting them. But they did not stop there. Now they were saying that their mother sexually abused them as well. Debbie McCuan was read her rights and advised to get an attorney.[30]

The sun was barely up the next morning when the caseworker got another call from Mary Ann. The girls, she claimed, had told her "a lot of new things," about orgies, and money changing hands. But when Deputy Shaneyfelt interviewed Darla and Bobbie, they said they had never mentioned these events. And Bobbie told her therapist she had never been molested at all.[31]

Nevertheless, a day later, their therapist described both girls as "eager to discuss the molest with anyone who will listen." And that night, a night after several others without sleep, a distressed Mary Ann called the caseworker again. Bobbie and Darla were terrified, she said. Someone was at their window, and when they checked outside, the gate was open. Mary Ann was sure that her family was in danger, especially because two men in a brown car had been following her lately. She also claimed that Betty Palko, the social worker she had spoken with two years ago about getting Debbie McCuan's day-care license pulled, had come with her boyfriend to the girls' school. There, Palko had threatened them with rape, and told them they would be "wiped out" if they didn't keep quiet. Another time, Mary Ann said, Palko came to the girls' school with someone dressed in a Halloween costume. She and her boyfriend had threatened the girls because they, too, had molested them. There were a lot more people involved, Mary Ann added, and some had warned that they would burn the Barbours' home down. "This thing is big," she concluded before hanging up the phone.[32]

There would be no sleep after that call, for Mary Ann or the girls. Again they stayed awake throughout the night and into the early morning hours of April 2, 1982. It was a Friday, and even before the child-protection people had left home for their offices, Mary Ann was on the phone again. She reported that the girls were revealing that they had been tied up, chained, beaten, and taken to motels and sold for sex "to anyone that wanted them." Photographs and movies had also been made of them, and other caseworkers besides Betty Palko were involved.[33]

Later that morning, Mary Ann, Darla, and Bobbie met with Murillo, Shaneyfelt, and Deputy District Attorney Medelyian Grady. They described orgies in which Scott and Brenda Kniffen were key participants, along with their two young sons, Alvin's cousins Larry and Tommy McCuan, and Larry's children, Lynette and Tricia. Murillo spent all that day with Darla and Bobbie.[34]

On Monday, Mary Ann went to the district attorney's office and recounted horrific details of mass molestations that she claimed the girls had described to her, including the placing in their vaginas of cat and dog food, which animals would then be summoned to eat. As perpetrators, she listed Scott and Brenda Kniffen, Betty Palko, Palko's boyfriend, a Welfare Department worker named Daphne and another named Scott, and Alvin McCuan's elderly grandparents. Mary Ann also noted that the girls had watched snuff films depicting murders, and that at the end, a voice warned that, "This is what happens to little girls that talk."[35]

That afternoon, the children's caseworker went to the Barbours' home. As Darla and Bobbie watched cartoons on television, Mary Ann told the social worker that one snuff film showed a "little girl who told" having her arms and legs cut off. The girls had seen themselves in such movies, Mary Ann said. Their lives were in danger, along with the entire Barbour family's. Palko had visited the girls at the juvenile home, she said, and had threatened them, calling them "sow sluts."[36]

The DA's office accepted Mary Ann's charges, and the next day moved to gain custody of Bobbie and Darla. A confidential affidavit drafted by Deputy District Attorney Don McGillivray and signed by Shaneyfelt repeated Mary Ann's charges, even those implicating employees of the Welfare Department in child torture, snuff films, death threats, and pornography production. Two days after the affidavit was signed, on April 8, 1982, all the people Mary Ann named who could be found were arrested at dawn. Their homes were searched and their children taken to the juvenile home. Billy Kniffen was six years old at the time. "I remember my last day with my parents," he recalled recently. "My mom woke me up. She was crying, and at the same time saying that everything would be all right. Police were all over, going through every drawer, every part of the house."[37]

At the McCuan home, Bobbie directed the deputies to places where she said pornography was hidden, but none was found. She and Darla were also taken to the Kniffens' to direct the search, and once again, there was no pornography. At the Kniffens' Bobbie said she had been raped while hanging from hooks. No holes were ever found in the ceiling where hooks could have been, but a police photographer snapped pictures of Bobbie with her hands clasped over her head. Other shots were taken of her posed in attitudes of sadistic victimization. That afternoon, Mary Ann Barbour assured the girls' caseworker that there was "much more to come."[38]

Scott Kniffen remembers the authorities coming for him at the diesel service where he worked. They were in plain clothes, and "when they said they were going to arrest me, I thought it was a joke, like a singing telegram. It seemed unreal."[39]

Eager to profess their innocence, Brenda and Scott both agreed to talk to the authorities, and were interviewed separately by Sergeant Don Fredenburg. Brenda said she was confident that once officials talked to her sons, they would see that the charges were ridiculous. Scott sat listening as Fredenburg read him police reports replete with allegations of abuse made by Darla and Bobbie. Scott politely but firmly denied each charge. Fredenburg asked what he knew about the McCuans. Scott told him the families had been friendly, had sometimes played cards together, but had seen little of each other during the past year.

Late that morning Fredenburg took a momentary break, then returned to tell Scott that his sons were "telling us a lot of the same stuff" about pornography making and sex abuse that the McCuan girls had talked about. "That's absurd!" Scott exploded.

"Nothing of that nature ever happened. Completely absurd." "Why would your son say that?" asked Fredenburg. "I have no idea," answered Scott, mystified.[40]

When Billy and Byron Kniffen arrived at the county children's home, they were greeted with cookies and milk supplied by Velda Murillo and Carol Darling. The two women were assigned to interview the boys, and spent much of the day with them. When they said the children were claiming the same things as Bobbie and Darla, the extended Kniffen family was incredulous, but the district attorney's office would not allow any of them to see Billy and Byron. The DA's office also told the Welfare Department to ignore a court order specifying that the boys be interviewed by Betty Palko's accused boyfriend's attorney.[41]

Meanwhile, because of Mary Ann's warnings about threats to their lives, Bobbie and Darla were moved to a foster home in the mountains east of Kern County, under guard—and away from their step-grandmother. Almost as soon as the children were separated from Mary Ann, Bobbie's story of molestation started falling apart. On April 15, she told a sheriff's investigator that Mary Ann had forced her to invent the accusations against her uncle, Tom McCuan. Bobbie's story had first developed when Mary Ann told her that Darla said Uncle Tom had molested her. Bobbie knew nothing about this. But, as she later described in court testimony, Mary Ann questioned her relentlessly, and refused to take no for an answer. When she said nothing had happened, Bobbie recalled later, Mary Ann "wouldn't believe me . . . so I had to go my sister's way. . . . She kept on asking me and asking me and I told her that he did not molest me, but she kept on saying, he did, he did, he did, and I said no, he didn't, and so I had no choice. . . . She kept on talking about it . . . [asking] 'Is it the truth? Is it the truth? Is it the truth?' "[42]

This went on for "a whole day," according to Bobbie, and the ordeal was one that she apparently did not want to suffer again. When Mary Ann began accusing Betty Palko of being a molester, Bobbie agreed almost immediately. Later, in describing how she came to make her charges against the social worker, Bobbie remembered that one day she was playing croquet outside. She passed by a window and heard Mary Ann asking Darla about Palko. Mary Ann then called Bobbie in and told her that Darla said Palko abused Bobbie. She asked Bobbie if that was true. Bobbie quickly answered yes. Then she "went on out and played another game of croquet."[43]

When authorities learned that Bobbie was recanting her allegations against her uncle, the DA's office promptly took the girls from their foster family and moved them back to the county children's home. There, they received visits from Mary Ann almost daily. In a few weeks, the Barbours regained custody and took the girls home.[44]

The Kniffen boys were also carefully monitored for any signs of recantation. When a preliminary hearing began for the Kniffens and the McCuans, in June 1982,

Billy and Byron were the first witnesses. Tearfully and in monosyllables, the boys agreed that they had participated in mass molestations, and that films had been made of the assaults.[45] When they left the stand, their caseworker took them to a local park to visit their two grandmothers. One of them, Corene Oliver, told the Kniffens' lawyer the next day that while she was pushing Byron on a swing, she asked whether his testimony against his parents were true, and Byron said it wasn't. Why, then, had he given it? Oliver said that when she put this question to her grandson, he replied that he was scared of the lawyers and wanted to talk to the judge by himself.

Instead of granting Byron's request, the judge advised Corene Oliver to hire a lawyer. Byron's attorney then sued her for inflicting emotional distress on the boy, since his foster mother reported that Oliver told the child that if his parents went to prison, they would kill themselves. Based on this accusation, the judge declined to call Byron as a witness and refused to see him privately. Oliver, meanwhile, was arrested and charged with witness tampering and perjury.[46]*

Bobbie and Darla followed Billy and Byron to the witness stand. They, too, answered in affirmative monosyllables as the prosecutor described rococo scenes of group sex activity.[47] By now, their lives, both in their families and in the courtroom, were so saturated with talk of perversity that perhaps alleging abuse was the only way the girls could express their feelings about anything unpleasant. Bobbie got irritated with her grandfather, Gene Barbour, during the preliminary hearing, then told the deputy district attorney that Gene had molested her—and withdrew the accusation only after extensive conversation and counseling.[48]

Nevertheless, her accusations unnerved officials involved with the case. The girls had picked up Mary Ann's paranoia of social workers—or, as Bobbie confusedly put it, "of anybody that works for adoption." Betty Palko posed special horror: Bobbie was even more frightened of her than of her grandfather Phelps or her sex-ring offender parents.[49] But if the girls were terrified of state officials, the feeling was mutual among people like veteran social worker Georgia Herald. Asked to chaperone Bobbie and Darla through Palko's trial, Herald demurred because she was "concerned about being alone with those girls" and with the possibility that she herself would end up accused.[50]

The apparent source of all this anxiety, Mary Ann Barbour, took the stand in August 1982, as the last witness at the preliminary hearing. Oddly, she did not remember telling authorities five months earlier that Darla had asked to suck her breasts. Neither did she recall seeing the girls masturbate, Darla telling her that "Mommy watched while Daddy fucked me," or hearing from daughter Maggie that

---

*Eighteen months later at trial, Byron testified that he had indeed told Oliver that he had lied at the preliminary hearing about his parents molesting him.

Bobbie had said, while watching the television program *Soul Train*, that she would like to "suck" a black man. Mary Ann also did not recall saying that someone came to the girls' school and threatened them with a Halloween mask, that they had been frightened by a prowler at their window, or that they had told her about seeing themselves in porn films. She denied ever telling a social worker that there was "much more to come" or that others from the Welfare Department were involved. "I guess it's easy to forget things that have been bothering me," Mary Ann said as she tried to explain her amnesia. "I would rather forget them."[51]*

After the preliminary hearing found probable cause to try all four defendants on dozens of counts of sex abuse, Debbie McCuan's attorney tried to get Mary Ann's hospital records from 1980. But the judge refused to examine the documents or give them to the defense.

Judgment

The trial would begin in the fall of 1983. During the year of preparations for it, the Kern County prosecution effort attracted the attention and support of Los Angeles child-protection professionals. Officials from the two regions were already acquainted with each other, because Los Angeles since the early 1980s had been a training mecca for sex-abuse workers. Brad Darling, head of the Kern County sheriff's Child Sex Abuse Unit, had attended classes there in sex-crimes investigation and how to interview children, taught by Dr. Roland Summit.[53] Darling's chief assistant, Fredenburg, had also been to lectures by Summit, and by Lloyd Martin, on pedophiles and sex rings.[54] For its part, Los Angeles began looking to Kern County as a place where an ominous kind of sex crime was emerging—a new type of offense, calling for new methods of intervention. And the Los Angeles professionals were eager to help: Summit, for instance, helped Kern County prosecutors prepare a declaration advising that putting the McCuan and Kniffen proceedings on television would retraumatize the young victims.[55]

The trial was a replay of the earlier hearing, as the four child witnesses gave mostly "yes" answers to a flood of leading questions about their parents molesting them, selling them for sex in motels, and abusing them while the children hung from hooks.[56] The prosecution presented nothing to support these claims—no hooks, no pornography, no telltale bank accounts, no receipts, no evidence of any trauma to the children, and no adults who had seen anything suspicious.

The Kniffens and McCuans, on the other hand, desperately presented evidence that they were good parents. The Kniffens showed that their days were filled with

---

*At the 1984 trial, however, Mary Ann acknowledged having made most of these statements.[52]

public, child-centered activities, and their weekends with organized sports or visits to the boys' grandparents, where Billy and Byron motored around the large backyard on scooters. Other children often spent the night with them, or they stayed over with friends. The boys had good academic records and regular attendance at school. No one in either boy's world had noticed anything suspicious.

Even so, the scales were tipped against the defendants by one witness—physician Bruce Woodling, who presented himself as a sex-abuse diagnostic expert.[57] Although Dr. Woodling had examined the Kniffen boys five days after they were taken from their parents, and although he found no scars, fissures, or other marks, he testified that when he stroked their anuses with a Q-tip, they gaped open rather than tightening shut. This, Woodling said, was the body's effort to accommodate to repeated penetration. He also told the jury that the boys had been chronically sodomized.[58]

In May 1984, the jury found all four defendants guilty. The McCuans and Kniffens had "stolen from their children the most precious of gifts—a child's innocence," said Judge Marvin Ferguson as he sentenced each adult to more than 240 years' imprisonment—at that time the longest terms ever imposed in California.[59] Front-page stories in the local newspaper were illustrated with photographs of a grim, impassive Scott Kniffen and of Brenda's face contorted in horror as they were led off to penitentiaries. At the end of the year, the local press deemed their trial the Story of the Year.

While the media patted itself on the back, Sex Abuse Coordinator Carol Darling was basking in the "outstanding" evaluation she received from her supervisors in the district attorney's office, praising her for her ability "to interview witnesses, especially children, in a directive manner, which immeasurably helps us in our cases," and for how she managed to "develop admissible evidence—something that is very difficult to do."[60]

Jill Haddad and Lloyd Martin, meanwhile, published the first newsletter for FASEC, their Foundation for America's Sexually Exploited Children. In it, photographs of Darla and Bobbie, smiling winsomely, were reproduced with black bars over their eyes, together with an appeal for contributions to keep them in private boarding school. With that, the two little girls became national poster children for sex-ring abuse.[61]

It was during the trial preparations of social worker Betty Palko and her boyfriend that Mary Ann's mental illness was uncovered. Palko's attorney argued that Mary Ann was the source of the accusations against his client, and that she was probably psychotic. Similar claims had been made in the Kniffen-McCuan trial, but to no effect; this time, Palko's attorney meticulously pointed out parallels between Mary Ann's disturbed behavior and sleep patterns of January 1980 and late March to early April 1982. Based on this and other information, he theorized that she was suffering from schizoaffective disorder[62] and asked the court for records of her 1980 hospitalization. The court agreed, and, reading the records, the attorney guessed that Mary Ann had probably been treated for other episodes of mental illness in Kern County. He was right, and a second judge mandated that the prosecution give him all their records. Four days after complying with this order, the district attorney dropped the case against Palko and her boyfriend on the condition that the newly revealed documentation about Mary Ann's mental health history be sealed or destroyed. These terms accepted, the case was dismissed.[63]

Charges were finally dropped against Larry McCuan as well, and his children were returned to him three years after being taken. None of the other people accused by Mary Ann, Bobbie, or Darla were tried, either. But the Kniffens and the McCuans, who to this day remain in prison, began their sentences watching the unfolding of another case that became a national symbol of child sex abuse: McMartin.

FOUR

Judy Johnson and the McMartin Preschool

Two hours south of Bakersfield is Manhattan Beach, a town that hugs several blocks of sparkling Pacific Ocean and seems a world away from blue-collar Kern County. One of a string of neatly groomed oceanfront communities along the southern part of the Santa Monica Bay, Manhattan Beach boasts an elegant promenade, a quaint, carefully restored historic pier, waves transected by lithe surfers, continuous volleyball games, rows of pastel cottages, and 32,000 residents who are overwhelmingly affluent. That they are also overwhelmingly white has always been a fact of Manhattan Beach life, even a generation ago, when it was an undistinguished little beach town where a working man from the nearby aircraft plants could pick up a summer cottage for a few thousand dollars.

In the mid-1960s, Virginia McMartin, a Manhattan Beach resident since the Depression era, opened the McMartin Preschool on the town's main boulevard. It was a mom-and-pop business. Virginia's daughter, Peggy McMartin Buckey, acted as administrator, and Peggy's husband, a test engineer at nearby Hughes Aircraft, helped build the school and make playground toys. Virginia hired several members of her Christian Scientist church to teach. Her granddaughter, Peggy Ann Buckey, a young woman who taught deaf education in the public schools, helped out during summer vacations and holidays.

During the years Virginia and her family cared for Manhattan Beach's children, the town underwent a profound transformation. In the wake of Southern California's real estate boom of the 1970s, bungalows that had cost $35,000 at the beginning of the decade shot up tenfold. The inflation was fed by wealthy new arrivals to the area: doctors, television executives, entrepreneurs, and others who were eager to escape the bustle of nearby Los Angeles, as well as its growing ethnic and class tensions. The gentrification of Manhattan Beach led to "tear-down" fever, as real estate dealers urged longtime owners to sell out so that newcomers could level the land and rebuild it with lavish homes and upscale enterprises.

Despite this money-driven commitment to demographic flux, Manhattan Beach clung to its image as a place where, as a Chamber of Commerce brochure put it, residents could find "small-town living, friendly neighbors and community spirit." Virginia McMartin embodied this attitude. Her work at the preschool had won her the town's most prestigious service award. Sending one's children to her became a status symbol for members of the Sandpipers, a social club of young matrons who did charitable work in the community.

There were many such women in Manhattan Beach. In the early 1980s, most parents there were married and relatively few mothers worked, remaining insulated from the sharp rise, early in Ronald Reagan's presidency, in the need for formal child care.[1] Manhattan Beach families seemed insulated also from the explosion of dual-income households that depended on out-of-home group care for children during the workday.[2] However, day care was still a popular institution in Manhattan Beach. Parents saw it as a way to give their children a head start on kindergarten and provide them with practice in getting along with other youngsters. Day care also freed up mothers to socialize and do charity work, which remained at the heart of the good life for South Bay women. Sending one's child to preschool for a few mornings or days a week was de rigueur.

Nevertheless, South Bay mothers and fathers, like everyone in the country, were exposed in the early 1980s to the media deluge of horror stories about bad day care: dirty facilities, incompetent workers, toddlers standing disconsolately in soiled diapers, or, worse, covered with bruises. This bleak picture tainted the national perception of public child care at the time, one spring day in 1983, when the McMartin Preschool staff came into the schoolyard to find a forlorn little boy they had never seen before. The boy could hardly talk but when they searched through a bag he was holding, they found papers bearing his name: Matthew Johnson. He was two years old, and his mother, Judy Johnson, had inquired days earlier about enrolling him but was told that the school was full. Now she had simply dropped Matthew off without telling anyone. Judy Johnson's behavior angered Virginia, but Peggy was more understanding. Judy, she thought, must have a lot on her mind.[3]

She was right. At age thirty-eight, Judy was trim and pert-looking, but at the same time she was quiet, very soft-spoken, and seemed laden with life's burdens. Born in Milwaukee in 1944 and raised in Los Angeles, she was a Lutheran minister's daughter whose mother died when she was twelve. According to Judy's father, she never grieved openly about her mother's death, even though she was devastated. Her lack of affect was typical, for Judy almost never showed emotion or confided in others. Instead, she always carried a Bible and seemed to deal with her problems through religion, which she studied at the University of Minneapolis. There she met fellow student Brent Johnson, and the two were married in 1969.[4]

The Johnsons then moved to Manhattan Beach, where Brent began work as a tax auditor, and Judy became pregnant with a son, Mitchell. By the time Mitchell was eight, the Johnsons were having severe marital problems. They separated in 1978 but reunited after learning that Mitchell had an inoperable brain tumor and would probably survive only five more years. Judy spent all her time with her son, and as he deteriorated, she grew angrier and angrier with medicine and doctors. In 1980, she became pregnant again. When she went into labor with her second child, she attempted to deliver by herself but had to be rushed, hemorrhaging, to the hospital.

The newborn, Matthew, did not improve his parents' marriage or end their intense conflicts over finances. Brent wanted Judy to work, but she wanted to stay home and care for Mitchell. In the spring of 1983, when Matthew was two years old, the couple separated permanently. While her husband resumed a bachelor's life and began dating other women, Judy got a sales job at a department store. She lived in a tiny Manhattan Beach cottage, with a dying child, on an unstable income.[5] It was during this period that Judy left Matthew at the preschool, which so disturbed Virginia McMartin that she told Peggy the child should not be admitted under any circumstances. Peggy, however, felt sorry for Judy, and she accepted Matthew for the school's upcoming summer session. He attended several times.[6]

That summer Judy Johnson became preoccupied with the condition of her younger son's anus. In June, she would later tell the authorities, Matthew complained that it hurt when he made a bowel movement. In July, she took him to a nearby hospital emergency room, where she told a doctor that her son's anus was "itchy" and that she thought she had given him her vaginal infection. The doctor did not examine Matthew, but he did treat Judy for vaginitis.[7] A few weeks later, Judy mentioned to her brother that Matthew's anus was inflamed. She began making frequent inspections of her son's rectal area.

On the morning of August 11, Judy later reported, she examined Matthew before he left for the McMartin preschool and he looked normal, but when he returned home that afternoon she found him red again. Matthew's father also saw redness on Matthew's anus that evening, but he attributed it to diarrhea and to Matthew's chronic problems with hygiene. He applied a zinc oxide ointment to the area.[8] Judy, however, was suddenly convinced that McMartin's only male teacher, Ray Buckey, had sodomized Matthew and had been doing so all summer. When she asked her son about it, he said no, nothing had happened at the preschool. Judy would not accept his denial. She questioned Matthew all evening to no avail. Then, she got the idea to try another tack.

Lately she had noticed how Matthew would run around pretending that he was giving people shots. As the popularity of toy doctor kits testifies, this behavior is common for small children, and although Judy hated medical professionals, Matthew had been exposed to them regularly that summer since his brother was getting hospital treatment for his tumor. Yet Judy Johnson believed that Matthew had no idea what an injection was, so she asked him if Ray Buckey had given him "shots." Again he said no, but she pressed. Finally, after repeated questioning, he told his mother that Ray "took his temperature." Judy concluded that the "thermometer" must have been Buckey's penis.[9]

The next day she called the police and took Matthew to the hospital. A doctor listened to Judy's story about sodomy, an act that, when perpetrated on a two-year-old, can be expected to leave horrific anal tears and bruising, and which is often performed with such violence that it maims or kills the child.[10] On Matthew, though, all the doctor found was a bit of redness. He did not definitively diagnose sodomy.[11] But instead of abandoning her complaint, Judy returned to the police a few days later. By now Matthew had diarrhea, and—although later court reports indicate that Manhattan Beach police detective and sex abuse investigator Jane Hoag was never able to get Matthew to admit anything to her—police reports from that period claim that he talked haltingly about his anus hurting and said he had seen Ray Buckey's penis and been photographed by him. The Johnsons went home, but soon returned and elaborated that when the picture was taken, Matthew was naked. This time, the reports indicate, Judy spoke for Matthew. She said he told her that Ray tied him up and covered his face with a hair dryer. She added that Ray had done this to other children, too. The police told Judy to take Matthew for another medical exam to UCLA's Marion Davies Clinic, where a recently formed group of doctors and social workers called the SCAN (Suspected Child Abuse and Neglect) Team specialized in diagnosing sexual assault.[12]

The young intern who examined Matthew was completely inexperienced at doing sexual-abuse exams,[13] but she found redness and scratches in Matthew's anal area. How had he gotten this way? Matthew would not say, but Judy repeated her story about Ray Buckey, and this time her claims were accepted by the doctor. She diagnosed penile penetration and advised Judy to take Matthew to the Richstone Center, a nonprofit counseling program near Manhattan Beach.[14] A few years earlier,

Richstone had been a meeting place for lay members of Parents Anonymous; now it was staffed with child-abuse therapists.[15] The police, meanwhile, opened an investigation of Ray Buckey.

The day Ray learned he was being accused of child sexual abuse, he cried for almost an hour. As far as his detractors were concerned, this was evidence of his guilt, but for those who supported him, his tears were righteous signs of innocence. To his friends, tall, gangly Buckey was a South Bay type: pleasant and likable, but drifting through life. In his mid-twenties, he was a college dropout with no real career direction, an occasional but sometimes conspicuous user of marijuana and liquor, and an inveterate habitué of volleyball games and the beach. So when he took a job at his family's preschool, the move was hailed as evidence that Ray was finally figuring out what to do with himself.[16]

But after Judy Johnson's charges, many started to see Ray in a different light. As police fanned through the community, they spoke with people who remembered things they had never thought much about, but which now seemed strange. Neighbors spoke of seeing Ray on his front steps, staring into space and sometimes crying. Teenaged girls recalled how he watched them intently while they played volleyball.[17] Someone noted that once he was reading a bodybuilding magazine in front of the children at the preschool, and another person remembered it as a copy of *Playboy*. Everyone seemed to know that Ray followed the custom of many South Bay volleyball players and surfers in not wearing underwear. They knew this because he usually wore baggy shorts, and often, when he was sitting carelessly, Ray Buckey's genitals fell into view.[18] Once this had seemed bemusing. In retrospect, it was ominous.

A week after Matthew's second medical exam, detectives started telephoning parents with children at McMartin's and asking them to question their sons and daughters about whether they had been molested. Although Ray's name was not mentioned, several people guessed he was the suspect. They had always thought it strange that a man would want to work with small children. Now things started making sense. When parents asked their three- and four-year-olds about Ray, however, none of the children said that anything bad had ever happened with him.[19]

Despite these denials, the police and many parents remained apprehensive and suspicious, especially as Matthew Johnson's allegations multiplied. In late August 1983, Judy Johnson reported to the police that while she was dressing, Matthew had walked in, stared at her underwear, and said, "Matthew wear bra." Maybe Ray had given him this idea, Judy thought. She questioned the child, and sure enough, she said, Matthew told her that Ray had put a bra on him. Later, when he saw a picture of a little boy made up as a clown and said "Matt wears makeup," Judy asked if Ray had put makeup on him. Again, she said, he concurred. The next day, she told police not only that had Ray put lipstick on Matthew but that he had tied him up with rope.[20]

On September 2, 1983, the McMartin and Buckey property was searched for pornography and other evidence of molestation. Although nothing was found, Ray was arrested. He vehemently denied the charges, and since there was no evidence to hold him, he was released. The police, however, pressed on. Using school records seized during their search, they sent a letter to two hundred families whose children currently or previously attended the preschool. The letter said that Ray was being investigated for child molesting, so parents should "[p]lease question your child to see if he or she has been a witness to any crime or if he or she had been a victim. Our investigation indicates that possible criminal acts include: oral sex, fondling of genitals, buttock or chest area, and sodomy, possibly under the pretense of 'taking the child's temperature.'"[21]

Donna Mergili, whose daughter attended the school, found out about the charges against Buckey in a phone conversation with Ruth Owen, mother of a four-year-old named Nina, who had just received the police letter. Ruth cried as she read it, and Donna, too, became distraught. Then both women hung up and began questioning their daughters. Nina denied anything bad had happened at McMartin's, but when Donna asked Tanya if she had ever played "games" there, Tanya mentioned being tied up by Ray Buckey, shut up in closets, and playing something called the horsey game with him. Donna and Ruth called the police. It was Friday afternoon, and they were told no one could take their reports until Monday. Both spent all weekend asking their children about Buckey, and Nina, too, started mentioning tie-up and horsey games. On Monday, Ruth took her to a counselor who, as Ruth later recalled, "talked to [Nina] about not letting adults touch her on her private parts . . . no touching, kissing, tickling on vagina, penis, bottoms or chest." Accompanied by Donna and Tanya, Ruth also took Nina to the police department for more interrogation about Ray Buckey.[22]

By this time, Manhattan Beach was abuzz with anxious parents questioning their children and phoning each other to compare notes. On Tuesday, the police were contacted by the mothers of two more little girls. One, age three, said Ray took photographs, but she would not elaborate. The other, five-year-old Sara Barton, told her mother, Joan, that Ray had never hurt her. The Bartons were members of the same church as Judy Johnson, and Joan did not accept Sara's denials. She continued questioning her daughter, and finally the little girl shamefacedly confessed that once she had spied Ray's genitals through his baggy shorts, and that, curious, she ran up to her teacher and touched his penis. Joan was infuriated and convinced that Ray had molested her daughter.[23] Sara, however, refused to say anything more about the matter, even though Joan broached it with her several times during the next few months.[24]

Other children, however, embellished their stories within days. Tanya Mergili talked about being sodomized, and some of her classmates said Ray had both penetrated their rectums and made them fellate him. They also named additional children as victims, but when questioned, this new group denied anything had happened.[25] The police and many parents did not believe the denials. They assumed the children were keeping quiet about the abuse, and they searched for telltale signs. One woman said she noticed that her five-year-old daughter was overly interested in her mother's genitals, and she vowed to question her further. Donna Mergili remembered that since the beginning of the year, Tanya had been plagued with vaginal irritations. Until now, Donna and Tanya's doctors had attributed the problem to poor hygiene—possibly due to the fact that Tanya had been masturbating regularly since shortly after the birth of her baby brother. Now, Tanya's vaginitis seemed to have a more sinister origin. Police detectives urged parents to take their children to UCLA for SCAN Team evaluations. These goings-on were discussed openly in Manhattan Beach's markets and churches and on its ocean-front promenade.[26]

By the end of September, a group of children who previously had denied being abused began changing their stories. Three-year-old Annie Lipson said Ray had "gone down the back of her pants when he tickled her." Bobby Vickers said Ray "kissed his pee pee." Kathy Ingram revealed that Ray had exposed himself and taken pictures of children.[27] More than a dozen children disclosed abuse—yet their stories were highly problematic. Tanya Mergili, for instance, was claiming that Ray had molested a classmate, John, and taken photos of another little boy named Teddy. Nina Owen said she saw Ray put his penis in Tanya's mouth. Another preschooler, three-year-old Mary, said Ray would put "poo" from his penis onto several children's foreheads, then take pictures. After repeated questioning by his mother, Bernie—who earlier had said nothing happened to either him or his little sister, Valerie—was saying that Ray kissed his penis in front of Teddy and a boy named Lon and sodomized Valerie. Lon said Ray took his picture and orally copulated with Teddy. Laurie, age five, said she saw Ray photograph children nude. Kathy also talked about picture taking. Mary claimed that she told teacher Babette Spitler that Ray was being "bad," and that Spitler called the police.

Yet Spitler denied knowing about any wrongdoing—and, indeed, despite the many children purportedly victimized and the long time it would have taken to undress them, tie them up, then untie and dress them again, no other adults admitted seeing such activity. Several of the children named as victims denied that anything had happened to them. And the police could not locate the pictures mentioned by the children, nor any evidence that Ray had taken them.

Nevertheless, Manhattan Beach was in an uproar as parents called and met with one another to trade stories. As children named children, mothers and fathers were contacted, told to inquire about abuse, and urged not to take no for an answer.[28]

Many parents were incredulous at the charges and disgusted with them. Sharon Walters was one. A Sandpiper member, she had two children who had graduated from McMartin's, and she had no intention of removing Trisha, her four-year-old, from the center. Walters thought the investigation was a witch hunt, but she dutifully questioned Trisha about the abuse every time the police telephoned her with more details. This began in August 1983. From the beginning, Trisha insistently denied being molested, but the calls kept coming. There were about ten of them that fall, informing Walters that Trisha's name was coming up in more and more children's abuse reports. Each time, she was urged to question her daughter again.[29]

Sharon was asked by one detective to question her daughter about a game called Naked Movie Star. During the early 1980s, this was part of a popular American children's rhyme, sometimes recited as a prelude to tag games: "What you say is what you are, you're a naked movie star."[30] Folklorists who specialize in children's material recognize this as a modern version of age-old schoolyard taunts, such as the venerable "I am rubber, you are glue / everything bad you say / bounces off me and sticks on you." But the Manhattan Beach police were not folklorists, and when McMartin children chanted about naked movie stars, the detectives concluded this meant they had been molested by Ray Buckey. They told Walters their theory, and she asked Trisha about the game. Trisha said she didn't know how to play it, and her mother was more annoyed than ever with the police. Many other parents felt the same way.[31]

By October, opinions about the McMartin case were divided between skepticism and veiled panic. The balance was about to tip, and the first nudge came from Los Angeles District Attorney Robert Philibosian.

Philibosian had been handed the job two years earlier, after predecessor John Van de Kamp had stepped down to become California's attorney general. As an appointee, Philibosian had never campaigned to be DA, but now he faced a hotly contested election for it. His opponent, City Attorney Ira Reiner, was an astute and hardened politician whom everyone seemed to know. In contrast, Philibosian was lackluster and anonymous. A poll that his campaign conducted concluded that unless he improved his image and name recognition among voters, Reiner would trounce him at the polls. The survey also revealed that a major worry among Los

Angeles residents, even bigger than drugs or drunk driving, was child abuse.[32] These findings came out less than a month after Ray Buckey's arrest.

Philibosian jumped on the McMartin case and assigned it to Assistant DA Joan Matusinka, a Los Angeles child-abuse prosecutor who in the early 1970s had helped found Parents Anonymous, along with Dr. Roland Summit. Now, in a highly unusual move, Matusinka launched her own investigation, independent of the Manhattan Beach Police Department.[33] Her motivation came not just from Philibosian's campaign effort; for Matusinka, McMartin was special because the alleged victims were preschoolers and thus particularly interesting to her and a group of Los Angeles professionals who had spent the last few years focusing on sexual abuse of very young children.

The Preschool-Age Molested Children's Professional Group

Labeling preschoolers a special sex-abuse risk group is another indication of how child-protection advocates broadened their domain of expertise in the late 1970s. This becomes more apparent when one realizes that, statistically, the younger a child is, the less likely is the chance that he or she will have sexual contact with an adult. By far the most common period for such experience is adolescence. It is rarer among prepubescent children, and significantly less common for preschoolers, toddlers, and infants. Forcible rape of preschool-aged victims is extremely infrequent.[34] As mentioned earlier, in the rare instances it does occur, the assault almost always severely injures or kills the child, as it would have if Matthew Johnson had been sodomized.

Rape cases involving children this young are so unusual that professionals wishing to specialize in preschoolers' victimization must consolidate brutal assaults with non-violent offenses, such as grandfathers fondling their four-year-old granddaughters. Even so, there are not enough cases to support full-time specialization unless one works in a large metropolis.

By the early 1980s, Los Angeles County had a population of more than seven million and an enormous child-abuse service system that involved several hundred specialists at dozens of public and private hospitals, medical centers, and health maintenance organizations. Overseeing this system was Dr. Michael Durfee, director of the county health department's child-abuse program. A Southern California native in his early thirties, Durfee had discovered sexual abuse just as Kee Mac-Farlane had, by working in the 1970s at a county home for maltreated children. As a child psychiatrist, he had served as the home's therapist and physician. A few years later, in the health department, his specialty was investigating pediatric deaths to determine whether they had been misclassified as natural when in fact they were homicides. Obviously, psychiatry could not help children who had died. Nor was counseling considered effective for the other youngsters Durfee was interested in: sexually abused infants and toddlers, who were too young to describe their experience to anyone, psychiatrists included.[35]

As medical head of the County Child-abuse System, Durfee oversaw the SCAN evaluation program at UCLA's Neuropsychiatric Institute. Besides housing the SCAN program, the Neuropsychiatric Institute in the early 1980s also boasted a group of psychiatrists and graduate students who were researching cults, dissociation, and multiple personality disorder. Some were studying women "survivors" who had begun emerging when *Michelle Remembers* was published, and who were talking about childhood abuse by satanists.

Durfee heard these stories at the same time that he did his work with child sex-abuse victims. By the time the McMartin charges surfaced, he was studying dissociation under the informal mentorship of a woman who suffered from multiple personality disorder and who claimed to have recently recovered memories of being abused during childhood in a satanic cult that sacrificed infants. Years later, she would recant her purported memories, but in the early 1980s, Durfee believed them, and he helped the woman make one of the first reports of satanic ritual murders to the FBI. The agency was unable to find evidence of the crimes; nevertheless, Durfee continued to believe that the torture and baby killing had happened. Meanwhile, he was closely associated with the Interagency Council on Child Abuse and Neglect (ICAN), a coordinating group that by the late 1970s had organized L.A.'s child-protection system so well that Durfee was able to classify very young children into a new victim group. As part of his efforts, he had recruited eighty-five social workers, doctors, therapists, and prosecutors involved in ICAN to the Preschool-Age Molested Children's Professional Group. The group, whose members were virtually all women, met every other month, under Durfee's tutelage, and vowed to make the criminal justice system more receptive to victims who were often barely old enough to talk.[36]

Indeed, one of the biggest problems with working with children this young is trying to get from them an intelligible account of what happened when they were abused. This was a special concern for psychiatrists Roland Summit and David Corwin. Corwin, in fact, was one of the first therapists to receive specialized child-abuse training at a new UCLA program organized by Summit, which paired psychiatry residents with sex-abuse victims associated with Parents United, the self-help organization for incestuous families started in California's Silicon Valley in the 1970s (see chapter 1).[37] Corwin and Summit had observed that attempts to glean forensically useful information about sex abuse from preschoolers often failed because the children became confused and cowed by multiple interviews and demands that they testify in court amid hostile defense attorney grilling.

The two men proceeded to organize some members of the Preschool-Age Molested Children's Professional Group into a task force whose aim was to devise ways of videotaping children's first interviews. The idea was that with this record-ing, no further questioning would be necessary either in or out of court; the videotape would substitute for the child in all proceedings.[38] The group members also explored ways to make the interview more child-friendly, by using toys, dolls, and other pro-jective techniques unknown to the police but long familiar to child therapists.

Matusinka was a member of the group. So was Kee MacFarlane, who had joined when she moved to Los Angeles in early 1982, after losing her National Center for Child Abuse and Neglect position to the Reagan administration's budget cuts. Mac-Farlane's plan was to stay on the West Coast a few months, write a book about sex-abuse victims' problems with the criminal justice system, then return to Washing-ton and enter law school. Once in L.A., however, she became enmeshed in the local child-protection network. By early 1983, she was co-authoring an article on mother-son incest with Roland Summit and working at the Children's Institute International (CII), a nonprofit child-abuse diagnostic and treatment facility located in a stately old house in Koreatown.[39]

Most of CII's patients were victims of physical abuse, but the center also main-tained a small, financially strapped section that interviewed and medically exam-ined one or two children a week who had been involved in sex abuse.[40] Besides writ-ing grant proposals for this department, MacFarlane also met with the children, along with a group of employees with backgrounds similar to hers. Social worker Shawn Conerly, for instance, held a bachelor's degree in history, had for several years conducted abuse interviews for the Orange County child-protection services, and was a volunteer therapist for Parents United.[41] Sandra Krebs, whose degree was in theater and journalism, had worked at a battered women's shelter and was on the national board of Parents United. Like MacFarlane and Matusinka, she belonged to the Preschool-Age Molested Children's Professional Group.[42]

In working with the task force to seek better ways to interview young victims, MacFarlane had hit upon the idea of using hand puppets, which were a venerable mainstay of play therapy and available in the offices of most clinicians who worked with children. Although the concept of using puppets during interviewing had never been tested, MacFarlane thought that fantasy figures would be both therapeutic and forensically useful because they would put the child at ease, overcome shame and secretiveness about the sexual aspects of the crime, neutralize any threats the offender had made to enforce silence, and work around immature vocabulary. The puppets became part of the CII interview protocol.[43]

The staff held their sessions with the children in a cheerily painted room overflowing with juvenile furniture and toys. To put the children at ease, the women dressed, clownlike, in mismatched clothes and multicolored stockings, and sat on the floor with the youngsters. They talked in gentle, high-pitched voices, and encouraged discussion about genitals and sexual behavior that young children hardly knew words for. And they used a new diagnostic device: "anatomically correct" dolls, which came with breasts, vaginas, penises, anuses, and pubic hair. The children were introduced to MacFarlane's collection of hand puppets and instructed that if they were too scared or embarrassed to describe their "secrets," characters like Mr. Snake or Mr. Alligator could speak for them. The CII interviewers told the children that feeding details about the abuse into a "secret machine"—a microphone connected to a videotape-recording machine—would dispose of the secrets forever and make the child feel much better.[44]

MacFarlane's Techniques at Work

By the time Matusinka took on the McMartin case, some fifteen preschoolers were listed as suspected victims of Ray Buckey. For MacFarlane, her staff, and the Preschool-Age Molested Children's Professional Group, this was the ideal population on which to test out their new techniques, and CII the perfect place to try it. Matusinka made the decision to send the children there. She told MacFarlane that having CII do the evaluations would "reduce the number of times a child is interviewed and the subsequent trauma that multiple interviews may create."[45]

Medical exams would also be provided by Astrid Heger, the institute's on-call pediatrician. Heger had little experience evaluating sexually abused children, but she planned to examine the McMartin children under the tutelage of colleague Bruce Woodling. Woodling was the doctor who had used "new techniques" to examine the Kniffen boys and the McCuan girls in Kern County. With these techniques, he had determined that the children had indeed been abused.[46] Matusinka added that to judge the strength of their allegations, instead of talking with the children herself, she would base her evaluations on the CII sessions. She called a community meeting in Manhattan Beach, introduced anxious parents to MacFarlane, and invited them to take their children to CII.[47]

One of the first families to respond was that of Tanya Mergili, the little girl who had told her mother that Ray Buckey tied her up and had played the "horsey game." By the time Tanya went to CII almost three months after that, she had been repeatedly questioned by her mother, and interviewed five times by the police (during which time she had usually said nothing), twice at UCLA, and twice more by other child-protection workers.[48] In these interrogations, the confusions and contradictions in Tanya's stories about Ray Buckey were far more extreme than the typical ambiguities and vagaries that characterize many abused children's descriptions of their experience.

At a UCLA interview for which records survive, for instance, she was not forthcoming with information, even though the SCAN physician who interviewed her used some of the new Preschool-Aged Molested Children's Professional Group techniques to try to overcome her supposed reticence and shame. When the doctor offered Tanya an anatomically correct doll, instructing her to pretend it was "Ray at the preschool" and to "show us what happened," Tanya replied: "We sing, and we, um play." "Does he ever do stuff where he plays with just you by yourself?" "Play with dolly myself," replied Tanya. "Did Ray ever pull your dress up?" asked the interviewer. Tanya nodded, but when asked to show how, she turned her attention to a stuffed puppy dog.[49]

Only after being told that she absolutely must talk about Ray pulling dresses up did the child use a male doll to lift a female's skirt, but then she only shook the male's hand at the female's stomach. The rest of the session was similar. She made tickling motions on the doll's crotch area, but not until the interviewer pointed out its urethra and urged her to show what had happened. When asked about how Ray photographed her pornographically, she replied that she was usually wearing a dress. Tanya added that when Ray removed her from McMartin's to rape her, he took her to the zoo, "and then he brings me back to the school real quick."[50]

Kee MacFarlane's technique with Tanya was much more refined. Before asking the child anything about sex abuse, MacFarlane spent several minutes engaging her in fantasy play. "Oh froggie," MacFarlane squeaked as she and Tanya manipulated a frog puppet and a toy doctor kit, "I think you have a little temperature here." The two also played with a banana puppet, Big Bird, Mr. Doggie, Mr. Dragon, Cookie Monster, Bugs Bunny, Mr. Alligator, Pac-Man, and Mr. Snake. Not until Tanya was deeply absorbed in the world of pretend did MacFarlane present her with a collection of "very special dollies in this little bag . . . they look like real people underneath . . . we can take off their clothes." Tanya then identified the dolls' "wee-wees," "chee-chees" (breasts), "butts," "wienie," and the "naugus hole," or vagina. MacFarlane proceeded to ask Tanya if she had ever seen a man's weenie. Her daddy's, Tanya answered. MacFarlane was not satisfied. "How about somebody else? . . . I know who else . . . another man." Still, Tanya insisted she had seen only her father's. "Well, I know some secrets," said MacFarlane, "that I know you know 'em, too. You know what? I know some secrets about your old school." When Tanya still didn't respond, MacFarlane added that she had seen the little girl's friends from

McMartin's, and they told her "all the bad secrets." "We can have a good time with the dolls," MacFarlane coaxed, "and, you know, we can talk about some of those bad secrets, if you wanted to. And then they could go away. Wouldn't that be a good idea?" Urging puppets on Tanya, she again asked if she knew bad secrets. "Uh-uh," Tanya shook her head. Then maybe she could figure them out, MacFarlane said. She showed off her "secret machine" and assured Tanya that she would feel better if she told it bad things about Ray. "I hate those secrets," Tanya finally said, addressing a bird puppet on MacFarlane's hand. "Ray-Ray did bad things, and I don't even like it."

Now MacFarlane took a doll with genitals, named it Ray, and told Tanya to use Mr. Animal to explain what Ray did to her. Tanya began manipulating the doll and simulating a voice for it, while MacFarlane pretended that a female doll was Tanya. "Oh, Mr. Ray—Ray-Ray, you're touching me, huh? Where are you touching me?" MacFarlane squealed. "On the wee-wee," Tanya answered, and it was not clear who she thought was making this reply. Herself? A doll? A puppet?

The session became a scene of naked dolls with genitals touching, poking and threatening each other. Cloth penises were being inserted into mouths. "Did that happen? Ooh, that must have been yucky," MacFarlane said. "It didn't happen," corrected Tanya; "I'm just playing." Puppets were eating dolls. There was talk of being spirited from the school to molesters' homes, though whether they were people's houses or dollhouses was unclear. After prompting from MacFarlane, Tanya named Peggy Buckey as a witness to abuse.

Toward the end of the interview, Tanya appeared tired of all the talk about teachers. The Ray doll was sorry for what he did, Tanya said. He promised he wouldn't do it anymore, and now he should be let out of his pretend jail. Then Tanya turned to a puppet named Mr. Squiggly Wiggly, a stuffed monkey, and a picture book about a worm. But MacFarlane wanted to return to reality. She asked Tanya, "Do you know the difference between the truth and a lie? What's a lie?" "Umm, it has big teeth, and it—and it's kind of brownish," answered the little girl. At that, MacFarlane asked whether Tanya had "told the truth to the secret machine." The little girl was mute. She only nodded, with her mouth wide open.[51]

Following the session, MacFarlane led the child out to her mother, and verified that Tanya had been molested. She urged Donna Mergili to tell her daughter how proud she was that she had told the secrets and how much she loved her. Then CII notified the DA's office that Tanya Mergili had been a victim of Ray Buckey. The process was repeated with dozens of other children. In every case, MacFarlane and her colleagues found sexual abuse.[52]

For parents like Donna Mergili, CII's verdicts only confirmed what they had suspected for months. Other mothers and fathers, though, probably would never have

believed their children had been molested had it not been for the institute's authoritative diagnosis. Although Sharon Walters, for example, believed Ray was innocent, she had questioned her four-year-old daughter, Trisha, all that autumn about
everything the police suggested, including the Naked Movie Star game. Trisha kept
denying that anything had happened to her. As time wore on, Sharon was continually
running into friends who talked about molestation at the McMartin Preschool.[53] Growing increasingly anxious, she started watching for signs of abuse in her daughter.

In mid-November, Sharon overheard Trisha ask her three-year-old sister if she
wanted to play Naked Movie Star. Alarmed, Sharon asked again about the mysterious game, but Trisha said she had only seen some of her friends playing it and had
never done so herself. Sharon was unconvinced. At a community meeting—now
being held monthly, and during which Matusinka, MacFarlane, and CII physician
Heger discussed the progress of the McMartin case—Walters approached these
three and told them what her daughter had said about Naked Movie Star. They
explained that Trisha was probably going through a stage common to sexually victimized children, in which they falsely claim that the abuse happened to someone
else because they are not emotionally ready to admit that they, in fact, were the victims. The women then suggested that Walters make an appointment at CII.[54]

Trisha's interview at CII was much like Tanya's and, similarly, MacFarlane
reported to Sharon Walters that her daughter had been molested.[55] If Walters had any
lingering hopes that MacFarlane was wrong, they were dashed when Drs. Heger and
Woodling examined Trisha and reported that her hymen was enlarged and her genital area riddled with scars, tears, and cuts. Walters was devastated. She felt utterly
betrayed by the McMartins and Buckeys. She was also guilt-ridden for having been
oblivious to her daughter's suffering.[56] She joined the growing legions of parents
walking around dazed and weeping in the checkout lines of Manhattan Beach's gro-
cery stores or collapsing in tears on its tennis courts as friends comforted them.[57]

Walters put Trisha into therapy at the Richstone Center, where Matthew Johnson,
Tanya Mergili, and many other McMartin children were already going, and where
their counselors had ample opportunity to contaminate one child's story with
another's. At the center, Trisha revealed details about how to play a sexualized Naked
Movie Star game. Soon, MacFarlane told Walters that children who had gone to
McMartin's years ago were also disclosing abuse. So in early February 1984, Sharon
also sent her older children, six-year-old Bill and seven-year-old Kristy, to CII.

Compared to Trisha, these grade-schoolers—and dozens more who were interviewed that spring—were intellectually more mature and far less prone to suggestion or fantasy than their younger siblings. If adult demands and puppet play were
inducing McMartin's current students to recount fantasies instead of real experiences, their big sisters and brothers should have been relatively immune to such

compulsions. In fact, however, the older children were subjected to a whole new set of pressures to produce abuse stories.

Kristy's experience was typical. MacFarlane began the interview by announcing that grade-schoolers like her needed to "help the little kids," because "[w]e know there were naked games" at McMartin, even though the younger children couldn't talk about them. Addressing a hand puppet Kristy was holding, MacFarlane asked her, "Do you remember that, Bear?" When Kristy shook the puppet's head no, MacFarlane berated her: "Oh, Bear, maybe you don't have a very good memory . . . your memory must not be as good as [Kristy's] friends' memories."[58]

Indeed, memories—losing, recovering, and disclosing them—became the overarching theme of CII's sessions with the older children. In an interview typical of several that survive, Conerly tells an eight-year-old girl named Alice: "So far 183 kids have been here, 183. And do you think I could put 183 kids in this room? . . . When they came here, lots of time they didn't remember very much about their preschool. Do you know why? Because when kids are real scared, you know what happens to them? They forget. That's right. . . . And so some of the kids, what we do here is we try to improve their memory and we try to unlock their brain. Sometimes when you're real scared, your brain gets locked up. . . . You honestly don't remember some stuff. It gets stored right back here in the back of your filing cabinet in your brain under 'Z.'"[59]

Although scaled down to a grade-schooler's comprehension level, Conerly's speech was an elegant exposition of the same trauma/dissociation theory that rationalized (and apparently produced) the "memories" of Sybil, Michelle Smith (in *Michelle Remembers*), and a national wave of women who claimed to have split off their recollections because of terrible sexual abuse suffered as children and forgotten until adulthood.

The McMartin students' entrance into this conceptual world was preordained, given the Los Angeles child-protection professionals' close ties to it. Dr Roland Summit, for instance, who was acting as a McMartin case liaison between the county mental health department and the South Bay area, had uncritically included in his landmark paper "The Child Sexual Abuse Accommodation Syndrome" (see chapter 1) the story of one of his patients, a woman who claimed to have recovered memories of childhood sexual abuse after many years in therapy. And in 1984, Michael Durfee—the child psychiatrist who oversaw the area's SCAN evaluation program and who was fascinated with multiple personality disorder, dissociation, and ritual abuse—operated the videocamera during interviews of two McMartin children at CII.[60] Also that year, Durfee was attending meetings of the county's Preschool Safety Task Force. This group had formed, in McMartin's wake, to deal with molestation in day care. Besides Durfee, other regular attendees included Kee

MacFarlane, Summit, and McMartin parents such as Donna Mergili.[61] As soon as these people started interacting regularly with one another, the CII interviewers began telling children that if they did not remember abuse at the preschool, it was because they had, in effect, dissociated it. Following this revelation, the children were informed that CII's job was to help them remember. As Conerly explained to Alice: "We use the puppets here and we try to figure out some stuff . . . we ask for the puppets to be detectives and see if we can find out. And we only ask the smart kids. We don't ask the not so smart kids."[62]

And to eight-year-old Keith, MacFarlane talked about how "[w]e had a big meeting the other [day] with all the mommies and daddies. They all talked, and they said, 'Boy, are our kids brave.' And some of them said, 'My kids didn't tell any secrets.' And I said, 'I know, I'm sorry.' But I think they will. . . . And they said, 'We don't know if Keith has a good enough memory, but maybe the puppets do.'"[63]

"Well, I have a good enough memory," replied Keith,[64] and although he had begun the interview saying he remembered nothing about abuse, soon he was generating stories about fondling, sodomy, and pornography making. Sharon Walters' daughter, Kristy, did the same thing, as did her six-year-old brother, Bill. Both joined four-year-old Trisha as diagnosed sex-abuse victims, and so did three-year-old Cathy Walters, who had been interviewed in April.[65] From late 1983 through 1984, about four hundred children had been interviewed at CII. The institute billed the state of California $455 for each interview and medical examination.[66]

Very early in the investigation, the idea that McMartin children could be victims had made a certain amount of sense. When MacFarlane and CII entered the case, in October 1983, the accusations were coming from younger children who actually had ongoing contact with Ray Buckey, and the crimes the preschoolers were describing were virtually all behaviors that criminologists and mental health experts recognize as typical in child-molestation cases: a man, acting alone, who played sexualized children's games, fondled them, took pictures, penetrated them with his finger, and, if he had not literally sodomized them, perhaps touched their genitals with his penis.

But Matthew Johnson, via his mother Judy, had begun describing abuse that was much less typical. In August he had spoken of being tied up and having makeup applied. By late September, his mother was reporting that Ray had worn a mask and stuck Matthew's head in a toilet. These disclosures were followed by even stranger ones, such as her claim that Ray put an air tube in her son's rectum while McMartin teacher Betty Raidor, a sixty-four-year woman, stood by and watched. Further, according to Judy, Matthew was now talking about more than having his temperature taken. Now he was saying that Ray molested him with a blood pressure cuff as well.[67]

To the therapists, detectives, and DA's office staff who maintained regular contact with Judy Johnson, her increasingly improbable accounts should have raised a suspicion that the charges were coming not from two-year-old Matthew but from her. If any of these people had stepped back from the waves of rumors, they would have realized the good possibility that Judy was delusional. Was she projecting her hostility toward the medical world onto fantasied penis thermometers and imaginary blood pressure cuffs? What did it mean when she claimed Ray molested Matthew while dressed as a minister, especially given her intense religiosity and the fact that her father was a clergyman?

The people whose job it was to listen to Judy should have made these connections and tried to help her. Instead, just as they had in Kern County with Mary Ann Barbour, the authorities took her reports literally. The DA's office expanded the investigation and continued sending children and their parents to Richstone Center, where Matthew received treatment; to other counselors associated with CII and the Preschool-Age Molested Children's Professional Group; and to South Bay Counseling Center, which employed a therapist whose own child had been diagnosed as a McMartin victim.[68] The DAs and therapists organized meetings where professionals, parents, and children elaborated on each other's accusations, and were influenced by accounts of Judy's increasingly grotesque tales.

By Christmas 1983 she claimed McMartin teacher Babette Spitler, a former social worker at the Richstone Center, had stepped on Matthew's stomach and made him vomit, and that fifty-eight-year-old Peggy Buckey had forced him to perform oral sex on her.[69] Abuse was said to have taken place away from the school, and perpetrated by people not even associated with McMartin's. A fitness club employee, for instance, was reported to have sodomized Matthew,[70] and the teachers had taken him to a beach and made him ride horses nude. Ray was accused of torturing and killing pets while dressed as a clown, fireman, policeman, Santa Claus, and clergyman.[71] No sooner had Judy revealed these details than they were echoed by a second child who talked of animals being slaughtered, and another who spoke about Ray wearing a red robe.[72]

In late January Judy added that Matthew had been abused at a "ranch" and a hotel. Other children then said the same thing. An avalanche of increasingly loathsome and absurd-sounding charges followed, often initiated by Judy speaking for Matthew, who was barely three years old and barely verbal. Following are transcriptions of Judy Johnson's statements as reported to authorities in early 1984:

Matthew feels that he left L.A. International in an airplane and flew to Palm Springs . . . Matthew went to the armory. . . . The goatman was there . . . it was a ritual type atmosphere. . . . At the church, Peggy drilled a child under the arms, armpits. Atmosphere was that of magic arts. Ray flew in the air. . . . Peggy, Babs and Betty were all dressed up as witches. The person who buried Matthew is Miss Betty. There were no holes in the coffin. Babs went with him on a train with an older girl where he was hurt by men in suits. Ray waved goodbye . . . Peggy gave Matthew an enema. . . . Staples were put in Matthew's ears, his nipples and his tongue. Babs put scissors in his eyes . . . . She chopped up animals . . . Matthew was hurt by a lion. An elephant played . . . a goat climbed up higher and higher and higher, then a bad man threw it down the stairs. . . . Lots of candles were there, they were all black. . . . Ray pricked his right pointer finger . . . put it in the goat's anus. . . . Old grandma played the piano . . . [a baby's] head was chopped off and the brains were burned. . . . Peggy had a scissors in the church and she cut Matthew's hair. Matthew had to drink the baby's blood. Ray wanted Matthew's spit.[73]

Ordinarily, this "word salad," as psychiatrists working with mentally ill patients call it, would have alerted police and therapists that the informant was delusional, but these were not ordinary times. Already, in various parts of the country, conferences were being held where law-enforcement authorities gave presentations about "sex cults." McMartin authorities like Roland Summit, who had lectured Manhattan Beach parents about their children's victimization, had gone to at least one of these conferences.[74] He had learned about the Kniffen-McCuan sex-ring case and assisted the prosecution, as had Bruce Woodling, who was now examining the McMartin children's genitals. Countless child-protection people had been exposed to the television programs, radio talk shows, and supermarket tabloids and books like *Michelle Remembers,* with their breathless accounts of satanic child-molester cults. For a culture and a profession on the cusp of panic, the more bizarre Judy Johnson sounded, the more sensible she seemed.

But why would so many young children parrot her stories? Manhattan Beach was not Bakersfield, where accuser Mary Ann Barbour was a close relative and eventually full-time caretaker of the children she spoke for. In Manhattan Beach, except for her son, Judy Johnson had no direct connection to the McMartin students. Even so, her claims rang true with the adults in the community, including parents and therapists whom the youngsters were dependent on. As this "movement" proceeded, the adults, whether consciously or unconsciously, fashioned a subculture of fanatical belief that enveloped their children and demanded their total participation. One component of this emerging subculture is illustrated in the family of McMartin pupil Sara Barton.

The Case of Sara Barton

Sara was the five-year-old who, at her mother's insistent questioning, had admitted that she ran up to Ray Buckey and touched his penis.[75] Several weeks after she made this confession, Sara was taken for evaluation to CII, where she seemed vaguely disturbed by the dolls' nakedness ("this isn't very polite," she told MacFarlane) and puzzled by the constant demand that she tell "secrets," of which she said she had none.[76] Predictably, though, Sara was diagnosed a victim. Her parents, Mike and Joan, carried out CII instructions by spending the rest of the afternoon and evening hugging her and telling her how proud they were that she had disclosed her secrets.

Sara seemed nervous and said she did not want to talk about McMartin anymore, but Joan said she had to. She gave Sara a "magic wand" to cast away "bad secrets" about Buckey's penis. The next day Mike stayed home from work and insisted that Sara tell him all about her rape. "How did Mr. Ray do it?" he asked. "Was he lying on top? On his knees?" After Sara supplied the details, Mike told her how much he loved her.

For days this cycle of insistent questioning and praise continued. When Sara said she didn't know the answers, and that she didn't know the names of children supposedly with her when the abuse was committed, her parents countered that she really did know. They insisted that she tell, "so we won't have any more secrets in our family." To help her divulge more, she was sent to Richstone Center. She also continued playing with other children involved in the case.

After a month of this, Sara was having nightmares about Ray Buckey, and her abuse stories were growing more and more bizarre. She had to suck Peggy Buckey's nipples, she said. A few days later she added that she had to suck Peggy's vagina. She also said she was forced to drink Ray's urine and to consume his feces covered with chocolate sauce. At this revelation Mike told Sara how proud he was that she was "able to talk about eating the poo-poo." He pressed her for details.[77]

By February 1984, in lockstep with the progress of Judy Johnson's phantasmagoric reports, Sara was talking about animals being slaughtered at the school and about how she was taken to a "mansion" to be molested. During this time, she also began suffering from ghastly night terrors during which she would thrash, sob, and moan, "Ooh, it's tingling, ohh, my vagina," and "Ouch—you pulled my nipples too hard." Soon she was talking about the McMartin molesters forcing her to take drugs, about fellating animals, about trips to a church and "devil land," and about being made to touch dead people.[78]

Many other children were describing the same horrible things and displaying similar chilling symptoms of psychological disturbance. Yet despite months of talk from dozens of children about rape, sodomy, feces eating, animal killing, and kidnaping, the police could find no evidence of eviscerated children or animals, no slaughtered corpses, no parent who had ever noticed a son or daughter missing from school.

Still, no one among the authorities stopped to question Judy Johnson's stories, even though as 1984 wore on, some of the assistant DAs began suspecting that she was mentally ill. By now, they were so invested in prosecuting the McMartin teachers that they avoided the implications of their realization and instead joked about Johnson. "You want to hear what Judy says happened now?" Assistant DA Glenn Stevens quipped to his colleagues, and they would all laugh. Later, when Johnson began naming as molesters school board members, strangers in cars, and models in newspaper advertisements, Stevens joked that if the assistant DAs ever needed quick sex, they should "look up Matthew," since he was the South Bay's "little town prostitute." As for the boy's mother, Stevens would complain that, "Jeez, I wish Judy would just disappear and leave us alone."[79]

Media Blitz

Meanwhile, the McMartin phenomenon snowballed. By the winter of 1984, District Attorney Philibosian took the case to the grand jury undoubtedly realizing that it would boost his vote in the upcoming election. Wayne Satz, an investigative reporter with the local ABC television affiliate, rushed to break the story. Amazingly, it was still unpublicized, even though Satz had learned of it months earlier from a co-worker whose children were involved. All that fall and winter, Satz gathered information and ingratiated himself with Kee MacFarlane (with whom he would later become intimate). Satz was the first to air a report on the McMartin case, in early February 1984.[80]

With its lurid, audience-grabber tales of innocent children sullied by sexual perversion and sadism, McMartin was every reporter's dream—perhaps especially so for Satz. According to court records filed by McMartin defense lawyers, he had a penchant for deviant and forcible sex, as evidenced by reports made about him during the notorious Hillside Strangler investigation of the mid-1970s in which ten women and girls were tortured, raped, and murdered. Attempting to find the killers, police asked local residents to notify them about men whose behavior might suggest them as the culprit. Thousands of reports flooded in, mainly from women. Though most were dead ends, they constituted a fascinating informal survey of the local male population's sadistic proclivities. One report was filed by a woman who had dated Wayne Satz. While they were seeing each other, she reported, Satz had demonstrated an intense fascination with the Hillside Strangler corpses and crime scenes. Further, the woman added, when they had sex, Satz made frightening demands on her that involved sodomy, douche bags, and practices she called "satanical."[81]

Satz's first news story on McMartin was replete with tales of rape, pornography making, and animal slaughter. He offered no information to cast doubt on the charges. Although Satz was always careful to include the word *alleged* before potentially libelous epithets like "child molester," his coverage was otherwise unrelenting in its assumption that the accused were guilty. His station boosted its ratings by running giant ads in the local newspapers, illustrated with a photograph of a ravaged teddy bear bleeding mounds of cotton stuffing.[82] Satz's approach was later so flagrantly aped by local and national reporters that years later, *Los Angeles Times* media critic David Shaw would win a Pulitzer Prize for criticizing how the press, including his own newspaper, "plunged into hysteria, sensationalism, and what one editor call[ed] a 'lynch mob syndrome'."[83]

In the spring of 1984, DA Philobosian announced that "the primary purpose of the McMartin Preschool was to solicit young children to commit lewd conduct with the proprietors of the school and also to procure young children for pornographic purposes."[84] An assistant added that "[m]illions of child pornography photographs and films" of the victims existed.[85] Of all the media people who trumpeted these claims, no one asked to see any photographic evidence—and, in fact, none has ever turned up, despite substantial reward offers and international searches by the FBI and Interpol.

In its rush to condemn the McMartin teachers, the media sided unstintingly with the prosecution. *People* magazine called McMartin "California's Nightmare Nursery." *Time* introduced its coverage with a one-word headline: "Brutalized." On ABC's *20/20* newsmagazine, host Tom Jarriel described the preschool as "a sexual house of horrors," and further inflamed viewers as co-host Hugh Downs asked, "How deeply marred are these children, Tom, and will they ever recover from it?" "Psychologically, perhaps never, Hugh," Jarriel replied.[86]

From Sex Abuse to Satanic Cult

With this kind of coverage, the South Bay became so overheated that the defendants and their property were targets of vicious attacks, even before the grand jury hearing and indictments. A stranger accosted Peggy Buckey and stabbed her in the crotch. The preschool was torched and graffitied with phrases such as "Ray Must Die." Several McMartin parents discussed hiring a hit man to bomb Peggy's car, and found one willing to do the job.[87] The situation did not improve after Peggy's arrest in March 1984, along with that of her children, Ray and Peggy Ann, her mother,

Virginia, teachers Betty Raidor (age sixty-four), Mary Ann Jackson (fifty-six), and Babette Spitler (thirty-six, with young children of her own). In jail, the prisoners lived in constant terror of being killed. One day, on a bus dispatched to a court hearing, inmates tried igniting Peggy and Peggy Ann's hair with matches, while guards looked on indifferently.[88]

The fact that the accused were behind bars did not calm the frenzy running through the South Bay, as parents and authorities pursued Judy Johnson's claims and became convinced that the McMartin staff was only one arc of a gigantic sex ring. Searching for the other accomplices, parents formed investigative squads and, armed with address lists supplied by CII, drove their sons and daughters around to find molestation sites like "the Devil House." As the children pointed their fingers at homes and businesses, mothers and fathers wrote down addresses and submitted them to the DA's office, which in turn distributed them to more parents. Housewives surveilled their neighborhoods and took down the license plates of cars that looked suspicious. A father staked out nearby commuter airports and copied registration numbers off the tails of planes, while reporting suspicious characters such as the "female pilot who may be a lesbian."[89]

The paranoia was all-encompassing. One parent, Jackie McGauley, who had a two-year-old daughter enrolled at McMartin Preschool for a short time after the investigation started, came to believe that Ray Buckey had molested her child even though the police were watching him closely at this time.[90] She also became suspicious about many other people, including a local newspaper columnist she was dating. When the two broke up, McGauley accused him of sexual abuse.[91] Later she made the same charge against a worker at the Richstone Center, where her daughter went for therapy.[92] Her allegations never went anywhere, but were lost amid a wash of outlandish claims, including rumors that the mayor's wife was ferrying corpses around town in her station wagon.[93] At times, people who spread these stories ended up accusing each other. One couple, for instance, threw a celebration party for McMartin children and their parents the day the teachers were arrested. Later there were whisperings that those two were accomplices, because, the rumor went, their business was located next to the athletic club where Matthew Johnson, and later other children, said they had been molested.[94]

Lawrence Pazder, the psychiatrist co-author of *Michelle Remembers*, visited Los Angeles in late 1984 to meet with parents and therapists to discuss his theory that the children had been molested as part of an international satanic cult conspiracy.[95] Pazder held that anybody could be involved in this plot, including teachers, doctors, movie stars, merchants, even—as some parents came to believe—members of the Anaheim Angels baseball team.[96] One McMartin parent, Bob Currie, was particularly taken with this theory. A mortgage banker and real estate investor, he had long coveted the lot where the preschool was located. Now, determined to unmask the cabal that was victimizing the South Bay's children, Currie quit working and devoted himself full-time to sleuthing. He began combing woods and beaches for satanic artifacts. Once he found a dead frog that was missing its intestines. Convinced that it was the remnant of a demonic rite, Currie brought it home and displayed it in his dining room, in full view of his frightened children.[97] Another father called a DA's investigator late one night and reported that someone from the "conspiracy" had placed a stake into his lawn. When the sun rose the next morning, the stake turned out to be a newly bloomed gladiola bulb.[98]

Parents whose children never attended McMartin's also became riddled with fear. A woman going through a nasty divorce was getting treatment, along with her children, from a therapist who had several McMartin children as patients. One day the woman saw a news report that McMartin pupils were talking about being molested in a "circus house." Immediately she suspected that the home in question was her ex-husband's, since, in happier times, when the family lived there, she had decorated a room in Barnum and Bailey–style designs for their children. Now she anxiously questioned them about molestation, as did the therapist. Soon they were talking about taking airplane rides with their former baby-sitter. When the mother drove them around town in an attempt to get more information, they pointed out a hotel where they claimed their father and his friends had sexually abused them.[99]

These youngsters' stories were hardly exceptional. Children all over the South Bay were talking about rape and rituals at day-care centers. By the end of 1984, seven area preschools had been shut down. With each new disclosure, more parents were recruited to the community meetings and burgeoning support groups. Their children were questioned by detectives who handed them checklists of occult symbols to look at during the interviews, to determine whether they had been exposed to satanic cults or rituals.[100] Then they were sent to the McMartin children's therapists, some of whom were using devil puppets during their counseling sessions.[101]

As 1985 began, hundreds of South Bay children were naming ministers, reporters, soccer coaches, aerobics instructors, grade-school teachers, and baby-sitters as abusers. They were also identifying as sites of the crimes dozens of local houses and businesses, including the Manhattan Beach Nautilus Gym, the First Baptist Church, a local car wash, a hotel, the health food store, a gourmet meat market, the airport in Torrance, and a pet cemetery. If the charges were true, one could only conclude that over the course of a decade, one-third of the children in the South Bay had been molested, raped, and then terrorized so utterly that not one had dared to tell. Not only that, but all the violations and torturous acts had been so perfectly concealed that no parent ever sensed anything amiss. And the molesters were so well organized, so serious about their enterprise, that they functioned as a Machiavellian mafia, one that would stop at nothing to avoid exposure and prosecution.

If the parents were terrified, the McMartin counselors and therapists were more so. On Friday nights, many of them could be found meeting for hours in a "support group." According to Roland Summit, a regular at these gatherings, members were "going over the edge" with fear that their phones were being tapped and that armed stalkers were targeting them for murder.[102] MacFarlane voiced this paranoia nationally in September 1984, when she testified at a packed congressional hearing in Washington that the country was grappling with organized child-molestation "conspiracies." As evidence, she noted that children attending day care hundreds of miles from the South Bay were reciting a "pornography rhyme"—apparently the Naked Movie Star taunt—as were the children in the McMartin case.[103] The rhyme, MacFarlane implied, might be the only sign of the conspiracies' existence, since their modus operandi was "designed to prevent detection, and is well insulated against legal intervention." Amid this scenario, MacFarlane added, the McMartin Preschool had become "a ruse for larger unthinkable networks of crimes against children." When pornography and prostitution were involved, the criminals would probably never be caught, since they had "greater financial, legal, and community resources than any of the agencies trying to uncover them."[104]

MacFarlane's fears were disseminated nationally in the next day's news,[105] and two weeks later Roland Summit echoed them when he told a government-sponsored sex-abuse symposium in Washington that the attendees were "privileged" to be finally hearing secrets such as those the McMartin children were revealing.[106] He seemed certain that the preschoolers were making these utterances spontaneously—perhaps because, despite his role as paid community liaison in the McMartin case, Summit never reviewed the videotapes of the CII interviews.[107]

The Demise of Judy Johnson

While authorities like MacFarlane were assembling their satanic-conspiracy theories, Judy Johnson was disintegrating. In April 1984, her husband filed for divorce. The following month she became infuriated when she learned that he had a lover, and told him that he could not see the children again. But little Matthew kept his scheduled visit with his father over Memorial Day weekend. When he returned to Judy, she promptly checked his anus and called the police, reporting that Matthew had been sodomized again. Now Matthew told her the culprit was his father. An investigation ensued, but it was inconclusive and charges were never filed.[108] Several weeks later, Judy told the police that someone had broken into her house and sodomized the family dog. She also claimed she was being followed up and down the West Coast by an AWOL marine.[109]

By the next winter, she had become reclusive, barricading herself and her children in their cottage. Concerned by her lack of response to his calls, her brother flew in from out of town. When he arrived, Judy answered the door brandishing a 12-gauge shotgun. Police and hostage negotiators rushed to the scene and found her glassy-eyed, screaming that her house was on sacred ground. Judy was taken, screaming and kicking, to a psychiatric facility, where she was diagnosed as suffering from paranoid schizophrenia. The police later searched her house and found a cache of ammunition and weapons. They also located a rifle hidden under the bed of fifteen-year-old Mitchell, who had still not died of his brain tumor, though he would shortly thereafter. When Mitchell told the police that he wanted to kill them in order to protect his mother, they sent him to the psychiatric hospital, too. The consensus was that he was experiencing delusions brought on by his dependency on his mentally ill mother—a condition that psychiatry used to call folie à deux and which is now labeled Induced Psychotic Disorder. As for Matthew Johnson, the child in whose name the case had begun, he was by now only four years old and much too young to threaten the authorities. So he was sent not to a psychiatric hospital but to stay with relatives.[110] Some two years later, his mother, who had been proclaiming that she had divine powers, died of massive liver deterioration brought on by alcoholism. She would be found lying in vomit in her house, alone.[111]

Judy Johnson was soon forgotten, but the McMartin prosecution raced on. When she died, Ira Reiner had already won the DA's election and dropped charges against five of the women defendants, calling the evidence against them "incredibly weak."[112] Peggy Buckey and Ray, however, were still accused, and Ray would languish in jail for five years before being released on $1.5 million bail. The two would finally face a jury in 1987, and their twenty-eight-month trial—the longest criminal proceeding in American history—would end in 1990 with acquittals for Peggy and a combination of not-guilty and hung verdicts for Ray. A second trial to resolve the deadlocked counts would also produce a hung jury, and charges were finally dismissed. In the end, with no one convicted and both the prosecution and defendants trying to forget seven years of tumult, quiet would eventually return to the community. But meanwhile, Judy Johnson's tortured delusions fueled a movement that spread far beyond the pastel cottages of Manhattan Beach.

FIVE

Chaos in Kern County

The social hysteria that McMartin incited upped ritual-abuse cases to another level. While at first they were products of delusional individuals, by 1984 whole social systems had been set up to justify and develop accusations and prosecutions. What happened in Kern County is an example. There, local officials assembled a remarkable apparatus for generating massive investigations and trials. It included sheriff's deputies, social workers, prosecutors, and a doctor whose methods had led to convictions in the Kniffen-McCuan case and to evidence in McMartin. But in McMartin, that evidence was not presented at trial until years later, and by then, so many doubts had developed about the defendants' guilt that they were not convicted. In contrast, the Kern County case barreled along with tremendous speed. In the summer of 1984, the local criminal justice system had constructed eight "ring" cases, each involving several people—the largest child-molestation prosecution effort in American history.

But the system was self-limiting, because in the absence of checks and balances, it generated infinitely expanding numbers of ever more grotesque charges. It eventually collapsed under its own weight when children accused a prosecutor, deputy sheriff, and a social worker themselves of being satanic molesters. In this chapter we examine that process and look at the accusers and the defendants who were carried away with it. Most of them lived in Oildale.

A Case Grows

The Kern River divides Bakersfield from the town of Oildale, where people derided as "rednecks" by the city's social climbers live in cramped, dilapidated post–World War II housing, and engage in low-intensity war with the local managerial class of deputies, probation officers, and social workers.[1] Unlike well-to-do Los Angeles, where the defense industry boomed in the early 1980s, Kern County's commodity-based economy was reeling during the same period. As interest rates rose, and agricultural and oil prices collapsed, Oildale's truck drivers, oil-field roustabouts, and fruit- and vegetable-processing workers were laid off in droves. Local businesses closed, drug use skyrocketed, and the only places people assembled were in Pentecostal churches and bars.

In June 1984, as the Kniffens and McCuans awaited sentencing, several child sex-abuse cases that had started either as classic instances of pedophilia or as contentious custody disputes suddenly transmogrified into sex-ring accusations. One of them had begun a few months earlier on a school playground. Five-year-old Bobby Martin was named as one of several kindergarten boys in a learning-disability program who "acted out sexually" toward a little girl during recess. A school supervisor who interviewed Bobby found him to be "very sophisticated in sexual matters for a kindergartner," and reported this to the boy's stepmother, Janice.[2] As the second wife of John Martin, Janice was involved in a bitter custody battle over Bobby and his two brothers, Timothy and Jimmy. Janice's archenemies in this conflict were the boys' natural mother, Marcella, nicknamed Tootie, and her new husband, Rick Pitts. Rick and Tootie had moved to Oklahoma the previous summer, but before that, the boys would spend every other weekend with them. The day she talked to Bobby's school supervisor, Janice questioned all three boys. Six years later, each would recall how their stepmother asked them if Tootie and Rick had molested them, and how when they answered no, Janice beat them, shut them in their rooms, and made them go without meals until they changed their stories. When they did, Janice called the police.[3]

The first report indicates that eleven-year-old Jimmy denied ever being molested at his natural mother's house. Timothy, age eight, said Rick had touched him once in the genital area, and Bobby said his stepfather had sodomized him. In another police report, Bobby insisted that Rick had never touched him, but added that Tootie once sucked his penis. Janice enrolled all the boys in group therapy sessions at Shalimar, Kern County's juvenile home, and repeatedly called the sheriff's office demanding that her stepsons be reinterviewed.[4]

In response, the Martin boys were questioned several times by deputies from Sergeant Brad Darling's child sex-abuse unit. The children also continued with ther-

apy, even though Jimmy still said nothing had happened. Finally, though, after several weeks of interrogation and counseling, Jimmy announced to Deputy Bob Fields
that he was "going to open up." He then proceeded to describe orgies at the Pitts's
Oildale residence, involving virtually every adult he knew. He named many more
victims, including Clarissa Pitts, eleven years old; Loreen Pitts, seven years old; and
Tootie's nieces, Amber Bloom, five, Wanda Bunch, nine, and Catherine Hogan, ten.[5]

When the girls were interviewed, Amber did not seem to understand what the
deputy was asking her. Wanda denied knowing anything, and Catherine said the
accusations were "crud" and made up by Jimmy Martin. Clarissa and Loreen also
denied being abused. Nonetheless, when they came back from Oklahoma to attend
a custody hearing for the three Martin boys in June,[6] Rick and Tootie were arrested
and charged with child molestation.

Soon Jimmy's, Timothy's, and Bobby's accusations grew more florid. They reported
that at a crowded public swimming pool on a Saturday afternoon, they had been
molested by two men named Doug and Steve, who sodomized them in an open
dressing room while other people walked by and who later fellated the boys in a car
while a woman drove. Doug and Steve, the children said, were also regulars at the
Pitts's house orgies.[7]

Janice drove the boys through Bakersfield and Oildale, urging them to look for
their abusers. Later that summer, at a gymnastics meet, the boys pointed them out.
They also fingered a teller at a bank, a woman on the street, and a passerby in a
municipal court building hallway. All of them, including the two men—whose
names turned out not to be Doug and Steve—were promptly arrested and charged
with child sex abuse. The boys expanded their descriptions of the orgies to include
handcuffs, drugs, pornographic movies, ropes, and boards to which they were tied.[8]

The girls, though, continued to insist they had not been molested, and their recal-
citrance prompted the sheriff's office to appoint a new investigator: Deputy Jack
Rutledge. He recruited Sex Abuse Coordinator Carol Darling, and the two of them
reinterviewed the girls. This time, Rutledge reported, Amber talked very briefly
about "nastys," or sexual activity between her and the suspects, and Wanda agreed
that orgies had taken place.[9]

By August 1984, as the McMartin case was burgeoning into a satanic conspiracy,
the list of defendants in the Pitts case had grown to include Rick and Tootie Pitts,
Tootie's brother, Wayne Dill, her mother, Grace Dill, her sister Colleen (Amber's and
Wanda's mother), another sister, Clovette (Catherine's mother), and Tootie's friend
Gina Miller. Two months later, Colleen's boyfriend, Wayne Forsythe, was also
arrested. According to the prosecution, these seven were only half of a group of
adults who gathered at the Pitts's home on weekends when the Martin boys were
there on custody visits. The boys claimed that they were joined by as many as ten

other children. Then, all twenty-seven people would gather in a ten-by-twelve-foot bedroom, along with movie cameras, studio lights, and video camcorders.[10] The boys, including Bobby, were made to inhale eighteen-inch lines of cocaine or heroin, forced to drink a glass of whiskey and another of beer, and were given injections with syringes that left large bruises. They claimed to have been hung from boards and, as they screamed in pain and fear, repeatedly sodomized by several grown men. These same men would also penetrate the girls, who were also screaming, and would sometimes ejaculate more than ten times. All this was memorialized on videotape, which the children had to watch. Then the Martin boys would say goodbye until their next visit.[11]

No one who saw the children after their custody visits ever noticed anything unusual about their appearance or behavior—not their teachers, their father, or their suspicious stepmother—even though they supposedly had just spent hours being raped, injected with needles, forced to drink alcohol, and dosed with potentially lethal drugs. Nor had Jimmy, Timothy and Bobby ever complained about their visits to the Pittses, or expressed unhappiness about going there. In fact, Timothy had sneaked out of his house one weekend to make his way to Rick and Tootie's when he was kept home by Janice because of a cold.[12] Again, as with the Kniffen and McCuan cases, there was no material evidence—no child pornography, no suspicious moviemaking equipment, no boards or hooks, no records of purchases or sales.

The district attorney's office had won convictions against the Kniffens and McCuans despite a similar dearth of evidence. A problem in the new case, however, was presented by ten-year-old Catherine Hogan, who continued adamantly denying that anything bad had ever happened at her Aunt Tootie's and Uncle Rick's. Deputy DA Andrew Gindes, who was assigned the case, knew that Catherine would be a valuable witness for the defense, and because she was not embroiled in a custody dispute involving the accused, she would be even more useful if he could get her on the prosecution side. He recommended that Catherine "get some counselling" and "some intensive interviewing." The person charged with these tasks was Sex Abuse Coordinator Carol Darling.[13]

Darling did not have to work very hard, because Catherine was extremely vulnerable to the manipulations of the district attorney's office. Catherine's mother had vanished upon learning of her brother's and sisters' arrests, and since then, the little girl had been living with her stepfather, Bill Hogan. "I believe that Mr. [Hogan] will cooperate in this," wrote Deputy DA Gindes[14]—and he had every reason to be optimistic. Hogan was a transsexual who had undergone surgery to change himself from female to male, and he was terrified that if this fact became public, Catherine would be taken from him. Carol Darling assured him this would not happen if he let her speak with Catherine.[15] Hogan agreed, and allowed Catherine to visit Darling well over twenty times during the fall.[16] At the end of November, just before the trial was set to start, she told Darling she was ready to talk.

With Catherine willing to claim that abuse had occurred, Gindes then turned his attention to eleven-year-old Clarissa Pitts and to her seven-year-old sister, Loreen, who were still insisting nothing had happened. He pressed their mother, Linda, and her new husband to allow the girls to be examined by Dr. Bruce Woodling. Though the couple was reluctant, Linda was reminded that her name had surfaced in some interviews as a participant in the orgies, and it was only thanks to prosecutorial grace that she was not yet on trial. The couple felt compelled to let Carol Darling take the girls to Woodling's office.[17]

Woodling's star had risen since his work for Gindes in the Kniffen-McCuan case. He had trained Astrid Heger, who examined hundreds of the McMartin children, and had helped her make diagnoses that almost all had been abused. Now he reached the same conclusion about Clarissa and Loreen.[18]

The last person arrested, Wayne Forsythe, was the latest in a long line of Colleen's boyfriends. Colleen had often left her daughters with her siblings or mother while she pursued her romantic interests, drank heavily, used drugs—and meticulously recorded these activities in her diary. Black-haired, pot-bellied Forsythe sported a tattoo, "Soledad 1981–1982," that advertised his time in state prison. He worked as an appliance stripper at a repair shop. Rick Pitts, meanwhile, worked at his father's restaurant, and it was there that he had met Tootie, who made her living waiting tables. Tootie and Colleen's mother, Grace, had a job at a local hospital as a cleaning woman. The accused were a close-knit clan with many stable personalities and some troubled ones. But, to the upper-middle-class professionals who prosecuted them, the defendants' blue-collar lives suggested that they were immoral derelicts prone to committing the crimes they were charged with.

Judge Gary Friedman, for instance, who presided over the trial, had recently been chosen president of the local Rotary Club. Each Thursday afternoon throughout the proceedings, he called a recess so he could chair the group's weekly luncheon. Friedman made no attempt to cloak his disdain for the defendants and their working-class background. When Tootie Pitts's attorney attempted to dispute the prosecution's characterization of his client as a deviant by noting that she regularly had sex with her husband, Friedman dismissed this information, comparing its relevance to "the number of chickens in the coop" in the Pitts's backyard (the family raised pigeons).

When Colleen defended herself from child-abuse charges by quoting from her diary to show that her sex life was normal and that she was not at the scene of alleged crimes, Friedman mocked her arguments as "soap opera." In a desperate attempt to show that the children had not been exposed to his genitals, Wayne Forsythe revealed the embarrassing fact that he had the words *Fuck This* tattooed on his penis—which the youngsters had not mentioned. Middle-aged Grace Dill was also compelled to describe the two cherries inscribed on her thigh, in honor of "Sweet Cherries," her citizens band radio "handle." In a further humiliation of the accused and their lifestyle, Judge Friedman complained to the courtroom that tattoos were "stupid."[19]

In contrast to Friedman's evident distaste for the adults, he made a show of doting on their accuser children, praising them before the jury and offering them sweets.[20] It was as if these children needed rescuing not only from their elders' depravity but from all of blue-collar Oildale.

The high point of the trial was Gindes's dramatic closing argument, in which he claimed that the many inconsistencies and absurdities in the children's testimony showed how terribly their elders had damaged their young psyches. In a passionate summation, he berated the defendants for their sexual "gluttony" and quoted the New Testament, warning the jury that "self-indulgence is the opposite of the spirit" and that people like Pitts clan would not "inherit the kingdom of God." Neither would the jury members, Gindes implied, if they acquitted the defendants. He finished his inflammatory peroration by waving large school portraits of each child, intoning the youngsters' names one by one, then chanting the word *victim.* Then, staring fixedly at each defendant, he recited their names, then the phrase *child molester.* The appalled defense attorneys' objections were dismissed by Judge Friedman.[21] The jury made its determinations without rereading any of the 13,000 pages of trial transcript, convicting each defendant on every one of more than 400 felony charges.[22]

Their sentences ranged from 273 to 405 years in prison; the women's time shattered previous state records. When a newspaper reporter asked Friedman why he had meted out such draconian punishments, he answered that it was because he had seen pictures of the defendants molesting the children and committing "every perversion imaginable."[23] Yet no such evidence had been presented to the jury, nor was there any found by the sheriff's office after countless searches.

From Sex Rings to Satanic Church

The judge's phantasms were shared by all of Kern County; indeed, it seemed that the whole community had plunged into a collective nightmare. By the beginning of 1985, four sex-ring trials clogged the Kern County courthouse, and a total of eight had been uncovered in an area containing about 130,000 people.[24] The Kern County media had been giving constant coverage to the topic since early 1982, when the McCuans and Kniffens were arrested. Now the local newspaper, the *Bakersfield Californian,* ran a week-long series claiming that the eight rings were only the "tip of the iceberg."[25] In the second installment, headlined "Officers Certain

Child Pornography Is Made in Kern," Brad Darling claimed that a local sex-ring network was producing child pornography and exporting it to Europe. Under the headline was a photograph of what appeared to be a pile of this material,[26] even though, to date, not one piece of pornographic evidence has ever been found.

Predictably, the series heightened local fears, and officials like Darling tried to calm them by pointing to new, improved investigative techniques based on recent research. Now, Darling said, when a sex-abuse report was received, even if the child had mentioned only incestuous activity or one perpetrator, investigators asked "if anyone else did these things." All children were questioned about rings, Darling added, "because a youngster won't volunteer. They don't even know they should tell you."[27]

Influenced by these questions, children's stories became more bizarre. In the spring of 1985, as jury members were pondering testimony in the Pitts/Dill trial, officials were engaged in an investigation that sought to link all of Bakersfield's purported rings into one huge network of devil worshipers. As the children were subjected to round after round of interviews, one cabal began to emerge as the core of a mega-organization with dozens of victims and an equally high number of molesters.

Velda Murillo, the social worker who had helped develop the McCuan and Kniffen children's accusations against their parents, was now involved in the mega-ring probe. Hired in January 1985 by the Kern County District Attorney's office to work with Carol Darling as an Assistant Sex Abuse Coordinator,[28] Murillo had a reputation as a powerful witness. She was convinced that the already uncovered rings were interconnected, and she began working with other investigators to find the evidence. One ally was Carolyn Heim, who since late 1984 had been doing therapy with children placed in Shalimar, where suspected victims of abuse were housed and treated, and at the county's foster homes.

In March, several children whom Heim was treating began talking about baby-killing during satanic rituals, and Sergeant Brad Darling got an excited report from Shalimar that a child was talking about having to worship the devil.[29] Other Shalimar children quickly echoed this disclosure, and the sheriff's department ran with their stories. Within days, it presented the Kern County DA with material to charge eleven people with child molestation,[30] and Darling and Murillo urged their superiors to proceed with prosecutions.

But some lawyers in the district attorney's office were becoming uneasy. One argued against prosecution, noting that if the new cases folded, the office would "eat it in the press" and future prosecutions would be jeopardized. As a result, the district attorney asked the sheriff to appear with more evidence.[31] Sheriff Larry Kleier and his deputies were stung and offended by this lack of confidence in their work, but they questioned the children again. They also reinterviewed the child witnesses in the other Kern County "ring" cases, and generated even more satanic stories. One, of a five-year-old named Johnny, was described thusly by interviewers Velda Murillo and a deputy sheriff:

> Johnny again told us how Demon and Big Billy would give him and Valerie shots in the arm and "butt." . . . they would have to lay on the floor sometimes and adults would "pee on them" and also "poop on them." Johnny told us that Big Billy Ray shoots animals . . . that he has seen the adults kill kittens, pigs, and cows and drain the blood out of them and dump them in trash cans . . . that they would mix blood with milk and then make them drink it . . . that the adults would make the kids eat "poop" . . . that when they would drain the blood out of these animals, they would take the blood and smear it on the crosses that they had and while the ceremonies were going on they were burning black candles. . . . He also told us, "Sometimes there were little babies there and they got hurt like the animals."[32]

Other children described similar crimes committed during satanic rituals at a "bad church" where black candles were burned. There was talk about at least twelve babies and small children murdered, and some of these victims were named.[33] Those who had no names, said therapist Heim, were "altar babies," conceived "for the purpose of sacrifice. That birth is a home birth," she explained, so "there is never a recorded birth certificate."[34]

The children's allegations of satanic ritual abuse multiplied so quickly that a task force headed by Brad Darling was created to investigate them. To keep its work secret from defendants and attorneys, the group named an imaginary suspect, and his folder served as a repository for all information about the charges. The dummy file soon contained the names of seventy-seven adults and sixty youngsters.[35]

Then the children began accusing the very officials who supposedly were rescuing them. One child said that Deputy District Attorney Sara Ryals, who had prosecuted the first defendants in the case, was herself a sex abuser, baby killer, and member of the Satanic Church. Deputy Sheriff Bill Rutledge was also named, along with social worker Cori Taylor. The new "suspects" were not arrested. Instead, the allegations against them were discarded with no significant investigation and little documentation.[36]

Doubt Arises

These claims fueled increasing doubt among district attorney personnel, doubt that was still not shared by the sheriff. In an effort to heal their differences, the heads of both offices met in mid-June. The meeting did not go well. Sheriff's employees accused the DA of dragging his feet on the cases, and the district attorney responded that the sheriff needed to provide complete information before the cases could be prosecuted. At this, the sheriff accused the district attorney of being a "ball-less son of a bitch" and swung at him. The meeting broke up, and the sheriff's deputies returned to the field seeking evidence.[37] On several occasions, they reported that children said they would take them to the Satanic Church, but "froze up" before they could find it. The sheriff ordered homes searched, backyards excavated, and the bottoms of two lakes dragged to look for bones or ritual gear. Nothing turned up.[38]

Aside from the law-enforcement officials, therapists, and foster parents, no one in Kern County was aware of this fiasco until the summer, when lawyers for two defendants acquired reams of discovery material describing the satanic church. Astounded, they took the documents to the newspapers. Headlines such as "Satanic Slayings Reported; Kern Sex Probe Launched" diverted San Joaquin Valley residents from one of the hottest summers in history. Much of the coverage turned skeptical, though, as reporters ceased relying on law-enforcement officials for information and began doing their own research.

They came up with material that debunked the accusations. Three satanic murder victims named by the children turned up alive, and a fourth, a newborn, had died a natural death years earlier in a hospital.[39] Clinical notes unearthed by the Fresno *Bee* showed that therapist Heim used "hypnotic messages" on a child who had been steadfastly denying being molested.[40] A sheriff's deputy's testimony that he introduced a seven-year-old boy to subjects such as babies dying also made the news.[41]

Stung by press insinuations and defense lawyers' assertions that the Satanic Church charges were bogus, the sheriff repeated that the children were telling the truth. As news leaked out about his argument with the district attorney, foster mothers and Darling's task force organized a letter-writing campaign urging the DA to prosecute. They spoke to service clubs, imploring them to start similar campaigns, and put even more effort into church groups, because, as Deputy Dennis Sterk put it, the members of such organizations would "believe."[42]

The tide nevertheless continued turning against the faithful. Earlier, the only people who had spoken out against the charges and convictions were members of the newly formed group Victims of Child Abuse Laws (VOCAL). Its members were largely family and friends of the accused, and in this battle, VOCAL was generally mocked and despised. By mid-summer of 1985, though, the group's concerns were picked up by influential people. The president of the Kern County Bar Association wrote a public letter warning that the children had been irreparably damaged by being torn from their families and relentlessly interrogated. The criminal justice system was also being harmed, he said.[43] Another person influential in sowing doubt was Roy Nokes, owner of a prosperous tree service, who had grand jury members as clients. Nokes' grandson had been identified as a victim by a child in a Kern County sex-ring case, and after weeks of interrogation, he named as satanic molesters his mother, his father, and an aunt.[44] The latter two were Nokes's children. In response, instead of merely joining VOCAL, Nokes also retained the most prominent criminal defense lawyer in Kern County, and he spoke to the grand jury foreman.[45] The grand jury investigated the case that summer. Appalled by what it found, the panel issued a sharply critical report and called for California's attorney general or the FBI to investigate Kern County's handling of child-abuse cases in general, and what had become known as the Satanic Church case in particular.[46]

Battered by this increasingly institutionalized skepticism, the believers stepped up their efforts. They pressed the DA to prosecute, gave more church presentations, and talked again with those who had told the most graphic stories. Among the most cooperative interviewees were Darla and Bobbie McCuan and Mary Ann Barbour. Although their relatives had been convicted and imprisoned the previous year, they now came up with new charges. They claimed that devil worship and "Satanic molestation rites," including baby killing, had taken place across the street from step-grandfather Rod Phelps's house in Atascadero.[47]

The FBI provided ground-penetrating sonar equipment and identified part of the eight-acre site as a "hot spot." In a swan song of excitement, law-enforcement officials held a press conference and announced that state and federal authorities were launching an excavation to find the bones of murdered children.[48] When the dig began in late August, bulldozers and soil sifters were surrounded by reporters. It was to be a ten-day project, but after four days, the dig sputtered to a halt. The "hot spot," said the local police chief, was apparently nothing more than a warren of rodent holes, roots, and rocks.[49]

The Satanic Church case was over, and with it all of Kern County's sex-ring cases. They had begun with unstinting belief in the delusions of Mary Ann Barbour, a terribly troubled woman. They had ended when Barbour no longer inspired belief.

The cases had not ended, however for the dozens of men and women already imprisoned—at least ten of whom remain behind bars today. Nor were matters resolved for a core of true believers. In August, California's attorney general accepted the Kern County grand jury's invitation to investigate, and sent in a team of interviewers. Carol Darling insisted to them that the satanic allegations were true and that all the accused were guilty. She told them she had reason to believe that people in the county bureaucracies, including the Child Protective Services and sheriff's office, were still involved in satanic activities.[50] Although the number of fellow believers locally had dwindled, Darling could take comfort from knowing that an expanding group of people around the country shared her beliefs.

Her husband, Brad, was promoted by the Kern County sheriff to lieutenant and invited to San Jose to lecture on ritualistic abuse cases at a Santa Clara County child sex-abuse conference where Dr. David Corwin, a psychiatrist treating children in the McMartin case, also spoke. Brad Darling reported that the symptoms of abuse presented by Corwin had been found in the satanic abuse victims of Bakersfield. He quoted from Church of Satan founder Anton LaVey, and from repentant ex-satanists. He told his listeners that he had found on the outskirts of Bakersfield a modern exemplar of ancient cults, older than Christianity, comprised of ordinary people who look and act "quite like the rest of us." He described cult infiltration of working-class Oildale, located the roots of the community's devil worship in the Ozarks, and warned of satanically poisoned watermelons dispatched from the San Joaquin Valley to supermarkets throughout the country. Among Darling's sympathetic listeners was Dr. Roland Summit, who admonished that those who openly demonstrated skepticism about such claims might be "agents" from "the other side."[51] Thus the hoary subversion myth of enemies plotting to overthrow society by sacrificing its children was institutionalized among America's most respected child-protection professionals.

And yet by the time Darling and Summit issued their warnings, Kern County's grand jury and the state's attorney general had already analyzed the Satanic Church case as a disastrous panic that disrupted the lives of hundreds of people. Why did the conference attendees reject these findings, and instead cast their lot with those who created the case? Because to accept the grand jury's skepticism, they would have had to reject McMartin. That was impossible, for, as the next chapter shows, McMartin had spurred flagging bureaucracies, propelled the Southern Californians to national prominence, and inspired copycat cases, panics, and systems throughout the country.

PART III

The Business of Ritual Abuse

SIX

A Plague and Its Healers

Depictions of child sexual abuse pervaded the American media by the time
ritual cases surfaced in the United States. In January 1984, sixty million
people watched *Something About Amelia*, an ABC-TV drama about a handsome, affluent father who sexually abuses his teenaged daughter.[1] The McMartin
case hit the nation's front pages and television sets the following month, and by the
end of the year would become a household word.[2] As tales of horrific abuse became
a cultural staple and fear for young children became pandemic, ritual-abuse scandals erupted like lesions across the country.

In the spring, twenty-four people in Jordan, Minnesota, were arrested, including a deputy sheriff and a police officer, and charged with being part of a child-
pornography and sex ring that included their own sons and daughters as victims.
Eventually, the Jordan youngsters accused their parents of murdering babies, forcing them to drink the infants' blood, and throwing the corpses into a nearby river.[3]

In April, Delorartic Parks, a janitor at the Rogers Park Day Care Center in
Chicago, was charged with sexual assault. After repeated interviews, children at the
center then accused their teachers of abusing them in satanic rituals and making
them eat boiled babies.[4]

In May, three workers at a Montessori day school in Reno, Nevada, were charged with ritually abusing twenty-six children, some of whom talked about chanting, singing, and playing the Naked Movie Star game.[5]

In June, Frances Ballard, a middle-aged woman working as a teacher's aide at the Georgian Hills Early Childhood Center in Memphis, was charged with sexually assaulting nineteen of her charges.[6] She was later joined in the dock by a Baptist minister and two other day-care employees after children began describing satanic rituals, the slaying of animals, and threats of murder.[7]

By the summer, investigators were looking at fourteen day-care centers in New York City's Bronx borough and dozens more in Southern California. Cases in which ritualistic sex abuse, pornography production, and the sacrifice of animals and humans were implicated arose in Niles, Michigan; Spencer Township, Ohio; Sacramento, California; Malden, Massachusetts; West Point, New York; and Miami, Florida.[8]

In the Miami case, Frank Fuster, a thirty-six-year-old Cuban immigrant, and his Honduran wife, Ileana, seventeen, were accused of molesting at least eight children in the home-based baby-sitting service that Ileana operated in Country Walk, an affluent suburb. Eventually, the children described a prototypical ritual-abuse case: Frank, they said, sodomized children; he and Ileana gave them mind-altering drugs; he wore monster masks; he made kiddie porn; the couple chanted prayers to Satan; and Frank slaughtered birds and threatened to kill the children's parents if they talked about the abuse.[9]

A few months later, in Pittsfield, Massachusetts, nineteen-year-old day-care teacher's aide Bernard Baran Jr. was also accused of threatening to kill parents as he molested preschoolers. Baran was quickly charged, tried, convicted, and sentenced to several life terms in prison, where he remains today.[10]

In January 1985, children described the ritual sacrifice of an infant and animals in Fort Bragg, California. In Clarkesville, Maryland, Sandra Ann Craig was accused of assaulting children with a screwdriver at her kindergarten and preschool. Craig was also accused of taking nude pictures and killing a rabbit in front of the children. Day-care workers in New Braintree, Massachusetts, were alleged to have defecated on their charges and photographed them nude.[11]

Later that year, Kelly Michaels, a young aspiring actress and worker at the Wee Care Day Nursery in Maplewood, New Jersey, was arrested shortly after she quit to take a similar job nearer her home. Wee Care children ultimately testified that Michaels had raped them on a daily basis for seven months with forks, spoons, twigs, and Lego blocks, forced them to eat and drink her feces and urine, licked peanut butter off their genitals, played the piano in the nude, made them undress and play sexual games, and terrorized them into silence by threatening to kill them or their parents.[12] In a comprehensive survey of ritual-abuse cases, Tom Charlier and Shirley Downing, reporters for the Memphis *Commercial-Appeal*, wrote that allegations triggered investigations in more than a hundred communities between late 1983 and 1987.[13]

Spreading Fear

As already noted, the first ritual-abuse cases stemmed from the fantasies of mentally disturbed women, fantasies that were taken literally by investigators primed to believe them. Doris Bell, for example, was a counterpart to Mary Ann Barbour and Judy Johnson. Bell, of Vallejo, California, became a regular attendee at meetings of incest survivors in Oakland, and soon thereafter wrote two (unpublished) manuscripts about how to obtain disclosures of child sex abuse. In these documents, Bell advised that children should be interrogated about molestation even when they do not want to talk about it.

Early in 1983, she gained custody of her two granddaughters when her son-in-law abandoned her daughter. Not surprisingly, the girls seemed unhappy and poorly behaved, but instead of attributing their problems to the recent family breakup, Bell became convinced that the children were acting out "terrible secrets." She grilled them hour after hour, day after day, for months, and did not allow them out of the house until they confirmed her increasingly horrible scenarios of abuse. After the little girls disclosed sexual molestation by their father and his friends, they did not seem as relieved as Bell thought they should be, so she "suggested that the secret had to do with cannibalism and the mutilation of bodies." In January 1984, the father and four other Sacramento men were charged with satanic rituals involving orgies with both the living and the dead and compelling children to eat human flesh.[14] The charges were eventually thrown out.

As a judge later indicated when he dropped the charges against the men, Bell was delusional. But as fear for endangered children combined with the ritual-abuse mythology, cases no longer required mental illness to trigger a prosecution. Later investigations often began when an anxious parent or caregiver became alarmed by a youngster's sexual play, or childish fears, or physical symptoms such as diaper rash—phenomena previously regarded as benign. Some of the adult anxiety around these issues was due to rapidly changing ideas about child-rearing practices. Corporal punishment became an issue when parents were against spanking but day-care workers practiced it.

Cross-cultural differences between parents and caretakers regarding displays of affection also fueled at least one ritual-abuse case. The charges against the Fusters stemmed from an incident that occurred when a three-year-old boy told his mother, as she was bathing him, to "kiss my body. Ileana kisses all the babies' bodies."

According to Ileana Fuster, she *did* "kiss the babies' bodies."[15] She was from rural Honduras, a Latino culture in which it is common for women to touch and kiss the genitals of their young children until they are about three or four years old. Such behavior is not considered sexual, but transported to the Miami suburbs, it was subject to gross misinterpretation.[16]

Likewise, changing interpretations of children's interest in sex and sexual talk triggered numerous ritual-abuse cases. In Cincinnati, camp counselors were charged with rape and pornography production when a child said the word *penis* at the dinner table.[17] In Carson City, Nevada, a middle-aged baby-sitting service operator and her nephew were charged with ritualistic sacrifice and making children drink the blood and urine of animals; the case began when a five-year-old watching models clad in bathing suits on television asked her mother if it was proper to take such pictures.[18] Recall that the Pitts case in Bakersfield began when six-year-old Bobbie Martin was found fondling a little girl behind a schoolyard bush, and an interviewer of the boy found him suspiciously "sophisticated" in sexual matters.[19]

Children's untimely discussion of sexual body parts or "excessive" touching of genitals were considered disturbing, if not deviant, by substantial segments of America in the 1980s. Overt interest in sex on the part of teenage girls was thought to be pathological, and amenable to psychotherapy, while sexual exploration by even same-age children was often defined as a problem that deserved official intervention.[20] Sexology and victimology researchers began defining "abnormal" and "inappropriate" behaviors as "abusive."[21] To many investigators, and for Americans in general in the 1980s, behavior deemed frankly abnormal for children included mutual masturbation and mock intercourse—even though these are quite common worldwide and usually tolerated. Some sexologists call these activities "sexual rehearsal play,"[22] and there is no evidence that they are abnormal, indicative of past abuse, or predictive of future maladjustment.

Currently in our culture, however, there is a suspicion that at least some of this behavior indicates past sexual abuse and potential psychological problems. The trouble with distinguishing benign from symptomatic activity, though, is that there is no empirically derived norm for what constitutes healthy child sexuality. The study most often relied on by child-protection workers for benchmarks asked mothers to fill out questionnaires counting occurrences of sexual behaviors among their children. Based on their tabulations, the authors categorized mock intercourse, oral-genital contact, and inserting objects into anus or vagina as "rare" in children younger than seven and virtually nonexistent among seven- to twelve-year-olds.[23] The conclusion was that if these behaviors are observed, sexual abuse should be suspected.

What the study completely overlooked, however, is the pitfalls of collecting data from anyone other than children themselves. Human beings generally seek privacy when they engage in sexual activity, regardless of what age they are. To think that adults would be privy to the secret play of youngsters is far-fetched. As UCLA psychology researcher Paul Okami writes: "It is difficult to imagine a potentially less accurate reporter of sexual behavior among [latency-aged children] than the children's mothers."[24]

Okami's observation is borne out by another study, which asked 128 mostly middle-class undergraduate women at a prestigious liberal arts college to describe a sexual game they had played as children that they considered normal, and how they felt when playing it. The students described kissing games, playing doctor, exhibitionism, and frank genital contact ("dry hump," as one woman put it). They also recounted the details of what the researchers called fantasy sex play, with elaborate scenarios in which they pretended to be parents, lovers, pornography stars, prostitutes, even rapists and their victims. The mean age for their games was seven and a half years old, and in half the cases, no adult ever discovered the children at their sex play. Most of the women perceived their games as normal, and many remembered feeling sexually excited by them.[25] If anything is disturbing about these reactions, it is that they show how early in life children are socialized to express their erotic impulses through the same stultified and skewed gender roles that constrain their elders. Childhood rehearsal of these roles, however, could not be more "normal." But in the 1980s, researchers were emphatically blaming it on literal sexual abuse.[26]

The First Report

Because it was adults who perceived something wrong, and not the children themselves, ritual-abuse cases are distinguished from ordinary molestation and incest scenarios in that almost all begin with reports from parents or caregivers instead of from the purported victims.[27] In family-centered cases, many charges arose during heated custody disputes—situations in which, it has since been shown, as many as half the child sex-abuse accusations are false.[28] Meanwhile, in the day-care scenarios, the accusers were generally not the kind of people whom prosecutors could easily ignore. The preschools that engendered ritual-abuse cases tended to cater to upper-middle-class professional families, and many parents had connections to—and considerable clout with—child-protection bureaucracies, politics, and the media. A remarkable percentage also had direct ties with local law enforcement, which allowed them to push successfully for prosecution.

In Miami, for instance, the mother who started the Country Walk case was a former assistant prosecutor.[29] Another mother who later lobbied for children's right to testify in sex-abuse trials over closed-circuit television was a police officer.[30] In El

Paso, one father was a border patrol agent, another was with the FBI, and a third was a retired police officer.[31] In New Jersey's Wee Care case, the boy who first accused teacher Kelly Michaels was the son of a police officer and the grandson of a superior court judge.[32] In Memphis, eight of the twenty-six children named on the indictments were related to law-enforcement workers.[33]

Parents of the accused children who were not employed in the criminal justice system often held other positions of considerable influence. A father in the McMartin case worked at the Los Angeles ABC television station; another was a city councilman in a nearby affluent beachfront community.[34] Perhaps most dramatic for the outcome of the Kelly Michaels' case was the fact that one child's mother was an editor at the Bergen County *Record,* northern New Jersey's most influential local newspaper.[35] She clearly influenced her colleague Elliot Pinsley, who covered the ten-month Michaels trial as the *Record*'s court reporter. Pinsley was in daily contact with the mother at the newspaper, and he quickly became so sympathetic to her view—which, of course, was that Michaels was guilty—that the two agreed to co-author a book about the case.[36] The plan dissolved because Pinsley had other obligations, but his coverage was consistently pro-prosecution. When a jail inmate, for instance, testified at trial that Michaels had made a confession to her, Pinsley wrote that the reason she was incarcerated with Michaels was "for fatally shooting a would-be attacker" on a Newark street. He omitted the fact that the original charge against the woman was first-degree murder, and that prosecutors had intimated to her that if she gave testimony against Michaels, she might be sentenced leniently.[37]

Pinsley was not the only journalist influenced by collegial ties with the *Record* editor, nor the most important one. Another of her friends was a senior editor at *Newsweek* who was assigned to write a story about Michaels before the trial. At the time, the case had received no critical media coverage, and virtually none at all outside New Jersey. Michaels's attorneys were inexperienced and overwhelmed by the magnitude and volatility of the charges, and would have welcomed the expertise they no doubt would have received from civil libertarians and seasoned criminal defense attorneys had a national story on the case been published, as *Newsweek* planned to do. But the article never came out; the mother saw her editor friend at a party and convinced her not to write it.[38]

Receptive Officials

One of the chief reasons why a disproportionate number of the complaining parents were law-enforcement officers was the flood of warnings and detailed information being sent to police agencies around the country. Case investigators were swimming in the same sea of media information as the average person, in addition to being deluged with a steady stream of material about sex abuse from experts, including information on specific behaviors and vocabulary that supposedly signified ritual molestation.

Congress, for instance, directed the FBI to focus on solving cases involving missing, murdered, or sexually exploited children. The agency sponsored a conference on the subject in May 1983, attended by law-enforcement officers from around the country, and devoted an entire issue of its *Law Enforcement Bulletin* a few months later to sexual abuse and sex rings. The publication opened with a message from director William Webster warning of a "clandestine subculture" of child pornographers, and advising: "Our efforts need to be coordinated—not fragmented. Information must be shared—not withheld. Every child in America is a potential victim of sexual abuse and exploitation." Some 25,000 copies of the bulletin were sent to policing entities nationwide; it was the first ever to go into a second printing.[39]

In addition, checklists of objects and practices said to be evidence of satanic cult involvement were sent to law-enforcement authorities by Sandi Gallant, of the San Francisco Police Department.[40] "Cult cops"—the low-ranking deputies and detectives who since the 1970s had been traveling the small-town lecture circuit warning of Moonies and satanist encroachments—now began describing demonolotrous cult crimes to newly respectful superiors. Throughout the Reagan and Bush years, policewoman Gallant, former FBI official Ted Gunderson, and other satanism "experts"—many of whom had spied on groups opposing racism or the Vietnam War in the late 1960s—taught colleagues, mental health professionals, child-protection workers, teachers, and concerned parents about devil-worshiping criminal conspiracies and the risks they posed to the nation's youth. The cult cops never offered proof, but they claimed that these organized cabals were active in the illegal drug market, the production of subliminal rock music lyrics, schemes to kidnap and murder children, and the kiddie-porn industry.[41]

Police figures were not the only purveyors of ritual-abuse materials to case investigators. Ken Wooden, an energetic proponent of the existence of widespread serial murder and cult maltreatment of children, was a mentor for at least one ritual-abuse prosecutor, and he co-produced an ABC-TV *20/20* segment entitled "The Devil Worshippers" in May 1985. That same year, Wooden mailed a detailed list of signs of ritual abuse to 3,500 prosecutors around the country.[42] In addition to Wooden's and Gallant's materials, the by now widely available *Michelle Remembers* guided prosecutors as they constructed their cases and supplied Gallant and other cult cops with motifs for their checklists. So popular did the book become that co-author Lawrence Pazder noted that in 1987, he was spending a third of his time consulting on ritual-abuse cases.[43]

Given all these lists and texts, it is hardly surprising that tales of satanic rituals, trips to graveyards, assaults by clowns, and injunctions to blaspheme God turned up in cases across America. Nor is it difficult to understand why children began talking about sadistic torture and satanic rituals after investigators gave parents checklists.[44] One of the most wide-ranging was a form distributed in Memphis that contained more than sixty "catchwords" said to indicate exposure to ritual abuse, including *naked, hitting, airplane, orange, secret,* and *blacks.* If children uttered these words, the list instructed, mothers and fathers were to notify the attorney general's office.[45] Behaviors common to nonabused preschoolers, like bed-wetting, nightmares, thumb-sucking, and fear of monsters, animals, blood, and the dark, also took on new meaning. No longer were they seen as predictable bumps on the road to maturity. Now, they indicated grotesque sexual violation.

The Nature of the Accusations

Children caught up in this maelstrom often reported that they had been molested by people dressed as clowns, in Halloween masks, or in uniforms. In many cases, they talked of being taken to cemeteries or funeral homes, of having to touch or eat feces and urine, and of excrement covered in chocolate. Incongruous people, like movie actor Chuck Norris, prosecutors, social workers, and television anchormen, were named as perpetrators. Abuse was said to have occurred underground or in airplanes, and animals were usually involved, occasionally as sex objects but most often as victims of sacrifices. Nude picture-taking sessions, rituals, and sex acts were almost always reported, as was blasphemous behavior and language, as well as murder, either for religious reasons or to make snuff films. All these themes—pornography, masks, rituals, uniforms, excrement, blasphemy, and murder—appeared in the checklists, guides, and questionnaires that investigators used when they questioned children.[46]

Most of these details, however, are common motifs in normal, nonabused children's fantasies. At the beginning of the 1980s, child psychology researcher Frances Ilg and her colleagues compiled a list of fears typical to children of varying ages.[47] They found that toddlers and preschoolers are afraid of clowns, Halloween masks, ambulances, monsters in the dark, animals, policemen, and burglars. Older children fear real-life dangers like escaped killers or earthquakes, because they cannot calculate the odds of being victimized by these random forces.[48] Much of the content of ritual-abuse cases is supplied by these perfectly normal fears. Scatological themes such as feces express primitive preoccupations with toilet training.

In addition, elements basic to cultural biases and contemporary folktales recur in ritual-abuse cases. In the United States, scenarios have included accusations against unknown black men who supposedly showed up at preschools to help the teachers molest children. (In the Netherlands, where prejudice against racial minorities is frowned upon but it is customary to deride the neighboring Germans,[49] preschoolers in the town of Oude Pekela told of being molested by men with German accents.)[50] Charges in the case against Kelly Michaels echoed an anti–sex education urban legend promulgated during the late 1960s by the John Birch Society and Billy Hargis's Christian Crusade. According to the legend, in some city that is always distant from where the storyteller lives, a liberal teacher eager to promote public school sex education put young children into a dark room and encouraged them to experiment erotically with one another.[51] Michaels was charged with similar behavior.

A more sensational accusation—that she placed peanut butter in her vagina and made the children lick it off—may also echo an apocryphal tale.[52] Folklorist Bill Ellis has collected numerous versions of what he and his colleagues call the Surpriser Surprised legend, a vintage fable about a woman whose friends sneak into her house to throw her a surprise party, but who are shocked to find her in the midst of having sex. Recent versions are more deviant: as the partygoers enter the home, they hear the woman calling her dog, and they find her nude, with peanut butter smeared over her genitals, waiting for the animal to lick it off.[53] The presence of peanut butter in the Michaels charges, and the earlier popularity of the sex education legend, suggest that contemporary folktales have leapt over traditional evidentiary barriers into ritual-abuse trials.

Popular anxieties about nonconventional sexuality also found their way into these cases. To turn the community and jury against defendants, prosecutors routinely denigrated their character by introducing evidence into court when they could find it, and rumors when they could not—such as that defendants were homosexuals. In some cases, for instance, those of Bernard Baran in Massachusetts and Kelly Michaels in New Jersey, there was at least a basis for the gossip: Baran was openly gay and Michaels was living in a lesbian relationship at the time of her arrest.[54] In other cases, however, the accused were older women with husbands and children, like Sandra Fabiano in Chicago and Michelle Noble and Gayle Dove in El Paso. These allegations, often salted with baseless accounts of incest and pornography, were passed on privately as the "real story" to reporters, and helped shape media coverage of the trials.

Another characteristic of ritual-abuse cases that distinguishes them from traditional scenarios is that the children began showing symptoms of abuse not before they disclosed, but only afterward.[55] Virtually no youngsters who ultimately talked about ritual violation showed behaviors that would be considered evidence of trauma until after revealing the abuse. At that point, they often became crippled with profound anxiety, night terrors, rage, sexual acting out, and other psychological problems.

Ritual-abuse cases were remarkable for their uniform lack of corroborative evidence. This was not for want of effort; law-enforcement workers went to extraordinary lengths to search for bones, bodies, pornography, burial sites, clothing—anything that would support the prosecution. The most extravagant and determined efforts were made in the McMartin case. Dozens of investigators probed numerous schools and interviewed hundreds of families in the Manhattan Beach area. Twenty-one residences, seven businesses, thirty-seven cars, three motorcycles, and one farm were thoroughly searched, and a national park in South Dakota (where Ray Buckey had gone camping one summer) were excavated. Hundreds of other buildings were photographed, and thousands of pornographic movies and photographs seized from other investigations were carefully reviewed. Investigators visited Europe in search of pictures, and enlisted both the FBI and INTERPOL to help them find evidence. Laboratory tests were conducted on every tangible item at the school in a search for blood, semen, or other incriminating fluids.

A team of archaeologists conducted meticulous digs underneath the school building and surrounding grounds, looking for tunnels the children said they had been molested in. Every sort of municipal record was scrutinized, and, in a replay of Fritz Lang's movie *M*, every known pedophile was called in for interviews. Twenty-five thousand dollars was offered, no questions asked, for even one photograph of child pornography taken at the McMartin school. Satanists, and even a psychic, were consulted by prosecutors or their investigators. All was for naught.[56] Elsewhere around the country, fields, yards, basements, and crawl spaces were excavated. Houses were searched, with and without warrants. Again, nothing was found, but this failure did little to stem the increasing conviction that ritual-abuse cases were real and widespread.

Illness by Proxy

The striking contrast between the lack of evidence for ritual abuse and the rising tide of belief in children's and prosecutors' claims can be explained only by leaving the realm of forensics and moving to the field of social psychology. Among contemporary specialists in the discipline, the older term "mass hysteria" has been replaced with "hysterical contagion" or "mass sociogenic illness." All describe a phenomenon in which large groups of people—usually in schools, factories, or small communities—are suddenly seized with the fear, unfounded as it later turns out, that an unseen danger is threatening their lives or their health. The imagined culprit may be an insect, a chemical contaminant, an individual, or a conspiratorial group. Mass illness begins when one person gets sick, then another follows, and another. Soon an entire assembly line, school, or neighborhood of people are vomiting, fainting, suffering convulsions, and calling on authorities to root out the source of their suffering. Only after investigation reveals that the offender is imaginary do symptoms subside.[57]

Using the term *mass hysteria* to describe this phenomenon reflects long-standing fears of the crowd, the mob, and rioters: the lower-class members of society whose desires are generally ignored by elites and whose eruptions are dismissed by them as disorderly and irrational, much as the expressive behavior of women has traditionally been belittled and condemned as "hysterical." Given how this feminine term has been applied to manage unfathomable and disturbing behavior, it should be no surprise that students of collective behavior have long recognized mass hysteria as more common to females than males—and particularly to grown women and teenage girls.

Recently, though, American researchers discovered that younger children, both boys and girls, can be affected. In this scenario, a group of adults becomes convinced that something or someone is threatening them; while the grownups remain healthy, their children get sick.

An outbreak of such sociogenic illness by proxy occurred in 1988 in a small town in Georgia, when several mothers became convinced that their local elementary school was harboring a dangerous gas leak. As they spread the word among themselves and to the media, they began noticing that their children had dark circles under their eyes, headaches, stomachaches, and other ailments.

Investigators from the federal government's Centers for Disease Control did exhaustive tests on the school but were unable to locate escaping gas or any other contamination. What they found, though, was that mothers convinced of the leak had communicated to each other what symptoms to expect in their children, then found them. Some of the youngsters, researchers speculated, had come down with normal illnesses, then their mothers took problems such as stomachaches out of context— and even imagined that they saw circles under the youngsters' eyes.[58] It is also possible that adults made the children ill by frightening them and by unconsciously demanding that the youngsters "prove" the existence of the gas leak by getting sick.

The same dynamic seems to operate in ritual-abuse cases, where children become proxies for parents, police, therapists, doctors, and other adult authorities. If the young "victims" in these scenarios are little more than conduits for grownup fears and desires, it is not the children's motivations that need investigating so much as it is their elders'.

How do mothers—and fathers—get involved in mass sociogenic illness by proxy?

How do they become so overwhelmed by the passions of friends and officials that their world turns upside down? Consider Jake Mrazek, who was so fond of the McMartin school that he played Santa Claus there at Christmas, yet later became a militant advocate of the theory that the teachers were satanist pornographers. When Mrazek and his wife, Margaret, first heard of the sex-abuse charges, they sent a note to Virginia McMartin and Peggy Buckey assuring them that "[o]ur thoughts, prayers and good wishes are with you" and "[w]e love you dearly!"[59] But even as they penned these kind sentiments, the Mrazeks were already infected with seeds of doubt about the teachers' innocence, since their first knowledge about the case came from a close friend who was deeply disturbed by the charges.[60]

When Jake and Margaret questioned their children, Curt and Annie, about whether they had ever been molested, both denied that anything irregular had ever happened at the preschool. Even so, Jake, a popular South Bay merchant, was drawn to the anxiety of other parents in the community. He started attending weekly group therapy sessions where mothers and fathers shared details of the crimes their sons and daughters were disclosing, and after each meeting he came home and questioned his children again. At one session, he learned about the "lookout game," in which children supposedly were posted at the top of a schoolyard slide to watch for parents and warn teachers of their arrival. After both Margaret and Jake asked Annie several times about the lookout game, she finally said yes, she had played it.[61] Later Annie added that Ray Buckey had pulled down his pants and put his hands in another girl's overalls.[62]

By late January 1984, Jake was deeply suspicious that his children had been molested, but he still wondered whether community hysteria might be fueling the charges, hysteria that even his family might be caught up in. Recognizing this possibility, he decided to follow his friends' example and take his children to CII, Kee MacFarlane's diagnostic center, for an expert opinion that would settle matters once and for all. By the day of the appointment, McMartin had already been front-page news for days, and en route to the center, the Mrazeks told Annie and Curt that their former preschool was closed because of "bad touching" and "yuckey things" happening there. They also explained that the CII interviews would be about sexual abuse.[63] The children walked into their interviews already believing, as Curt remarked, that "yucky stuff has been going on all around town." When he tried to describe particulars such as the lookout game, though, it is clear that he was fantasizing. According to Curt, a child designated as the lookout would run to warn Ray Buckey when parents arrived at the school. Buckey would then lock his victims into the bathroom while mothers frantically searched for their sons and daughters. The mothers, Curt said, would return home without the children; back at the school, Ray would inject his captives with "a poisonous shot."[64]

If Manhattan Beach had been in Georgia and McMartin's had a gas leak scare instead of a sex-abuse panic, experts listening to these stories would have diagnosed a variant of mass sociogenic illness by proxy, parents like the Mrazeks would have returned to their routines, and the case would have faded into an obscure addendum to social psychology lore. But in Manhattan Beach, the respected professionals validated the panic.

In doing so, they solidified the terror of the Mrazeks and scores of other parents, and rendered their children proxy victims. Within weeks of Annie and Curt receiving their positive diagnoses from CII, Annie was claiming that witches had visited McMartin and Curt talked of seeing a rabbit mutilated there. Jake and Margaret were driving the children through the South Bay, demanding that they point out homes of other satanic molesters and writing down addresses.[65] Other parents were making home visits and manning a "telephone tree" that informed mothers and fathers about new allegations and recruited previously skeptical families with news that their children had been named as victims.[66]

Not all families fell prey to the panic, however. Doug and Kim Wilson, for instance, never thought their children were victims even though they experienced many of the same pressures to believe that other parents did. The Wilson boys, Rob and Brett, had attended McMartin's a few years earlier but had no memories of abuse. Even so, friends whose children were describing molestation urged the Wilsons to go to CII, and they thought doing so would reassure them that nothing had happened. To this day, Rob, who was in eighth grade at the time, recalls his shame at being presented with naked, anatomically correct dolls and being ordered to name their sexual parts. Although he was embarrassed, he staunchly denied being abused. Since he had not attended the school for many years, CII personnel told his parents they were not sure whether he had been molested. They were certain about Brett, though. He was seven years old and felt frightened when the interviewer gave him a hand puppet, urged him to pretend it was talking, then insisted to the child that he had been victimized at McMartin's. Kim Wilson started crying when she heard the diagnosis, but stopped when she and her husband watched Brett's videotape and noted that he looked befuddled when the interviewer described details of the purported abuse. The Wilsons left CII as dubious as ever about the charges.[67]

The same doubt has cropped up and endured among a few families in virtually every ritual-abuse case where parents have been asked to believe that teachers or other caretakers violated their children. In El Paso, when police told one mother, Luz Garcia, that her son, Manny, had been molested, she did not believe it. Manny, Luz told the investigators, never kept secrets, and he was not ashamed to talk about sex. So why had he never mentioned anything about abuse? Because the teachers said they would kill parents if the children told, the police explained. Garcia still did not believe them. She and her family were recent immigrants from Mexico, and she pointed out that Manny didn't speak English and the teachers spoke no Spanish. Even if they had threatened the little boy, he would not have understood them.[68]

In Manhattan Beach, Kim and Doug Wilson believe they remained skeptical because Kim's grandmother had been longtime friends with Virginia McMartin. Too, the Wilsons were so involved with weekend and afterschool sports that they never had time to attend the many community meetings and quasi-social events that shaped and fueled other parents' belief in the charges. In El Paso, what divided Luz Garcia from believer parents was language and nationality. She spoke little English and, as an immigrant in the United States illegally, was hardly anxious to socialize with the border patrol and police-officer fathers who dominated the case.

Parents with close ties to credulous families, on the other hand, were more likely to conform their perceptions to those of their friends, even though believing that one's child had been raped and tortured causes tremendous shock, grief, guilt, and rage. So great was the distress of believer parents that one study of mothers and fathers involved in ritual-abuse cases has compared their reactions to the suffering of parents whose children die of cancer.[69]

Belief by Gender

Being the parent of a ritually abused child is a social role. It is one that provokes great distress but, at the same time, allows middle-class parents—particularly mothers—to vent their tensions openly, without the restraints usually imposed by a world still dominated by masculine rationality and stoicism. This implication recurs in many testimonials by believer parents, as well as in research literature about families involved in the cases.

A fascinating example of the latter is a study, popularized as the book *Behind the Playground Walls*, which was funded by the federal government's National Center on Child Abuse and Neglect (where Kee MacFarlane worked in the 1970s), and which included dozens of children and parents caught up in the McMartin panic. Mindful of the fact that none of the defendants in that case were ever convicted, researchers for *Behind the Playground Walls*, some of whom were the accusing families' therapists, claim to have studied the effects of "reported" abuse rather than abuse itself. Yet the study's authors leave no doubt that they believe their subjects were severely victimized at the preschools. That bias, in fact, is the study's basic premise.[70] Even so, because the research describes the behavior and beliefs of parents and children involved in a ritual-abuse panic, it offers a trove of information about the phenomenon and the subculture it creates among families.

The most striking thing about that subculture, according to the book, is how differently it is enacted among mothers versus fathers. This fact has been noted in other studies, and anecdotally among activist parents;[71] it suggests that being a ritual-abuse victim's parent is a feminine role. "Believing the children," in other words, is women's work. One sees this in the frequent observation that mothers usually become far more involved in the cases, doing everything from shuttling their children to therapy, to attending support groups, to trekking day after day to court. Superficially, this distaff enthusiasm derives from the fact that mothers tend to believe ritual-abuse allegations more than fathers do, and are more likely to hash and rehash the details. As a woman from North Carolina put it, her obsession to know exactly what happened to her daughter "was a drive in me that I just had to play out." Talk in her family was dominated by the case: she "pushed and pushed" her child with questions, and when she and her husband had a conversation, it unremittingly dealt with sexual abuse at the day care.[72] In Maplewood, the mother who was the Bergen County *Record* editor had the same experience. Under the pseudonym "Patricia Crowley," she writes in *Not My Child*, her account of the Kelly Michaels case, that she "needed to talk about Wee Care ad nauseam," and would stay on the phone until late at night discussing the case with other believer parents.[73] Most were women; indeed, Crowley and many other mothers have complained that their husbands grew impatient and disgusted with the wives' intense involvement with one another.

It is understandable that women would be more invested in ritual-abuse belief than men. In patriarchal culture, sexual assault is deemed the worst thing that can happen to "chaste" women or girls. Yet the far more common indignities they suffer from day to day are ignored or trivialized. Under these circumstances, rape becomes a lightning rod for the frustration and anger women feel about inequalities they continue to endure in their jobs and homes. And because sexual violation is so morally loaded, women who inveigh against it are allowed to rage against masculinity in ways that would seem threateningly unfeminine in other circumstances. This is especially true during moral crusades against child molestation, which serve as outlets for feminine rage without threatening the patriarchal status quo. During child-saving campaigns, women's traditional identities as nurturers are reinforced; yet at the same time, activist mothers are allowed to separate themselves from the family in the name of championing it.

In ritual-abuse cases, one place where separation goes on is in therapy. As *Behind the Playground Walls* found, mothers were more likely to seek counseling than fathers.[74] They used the clinician's couch to consider matters that had troubled them for years, but which they were only able to deal with now because they linked them to their children's victimization. Patricia Crowley and other mothers, for instance, used their sessions to discuss incest and molestation they had experienced as girls but never talked about.[75] By the time they went to therapy, sexual abuse had become an overarching metaphor for feminine distress—particularly among the clinicians they were referred to. What this meant was that talking about abuse, whether their children's or their own, validated current problems in these mothers' lives. For example, the fact that Crowley's five-year-old daughter, Hannah, had not immediately told her she was molested reminded Crowley of her long-standing dread that her children would cease confiding in her as they matured.[76] In therapy because of Hannah's ritual abuse, Crowley could voice her anxieties, blame them on her daughter's victimization, and define them as normal and healthy instead of neurotic or pathological.

Many parents used their belief in ritual abuse this way. But to make it work, the clinicians they went to had to concur that the children had been molested and blame the family's problems on abuse. If they disagreed, their services were often terminated—which is what Beth Vargo did with her therapist. A Chicagoan whose child was involved in a day-care case that surfaced in 1984, Vargo went to a counselor who concluded that her most serious problems were marital and urged Vargo and her husband to attend joint sessions. They refused—because, Vargo has said, they did not want to leave their children with baby-sitters. She terminated therapy and went on to become president of Believe the Children, a national organization for families involved in ritual-abuse cases.[77]

The Breakdown of Family

Comments by Vargo and other believer mothers illustrate another finding from the *Behind the Playground Walls* study: wives often resented their husbands' unwillingness to talk about the case, their indifference to attending therapy and parents' meetings, and their skepticism about the children's more lurid stories. These behaviors are products of traditional masculine insensitivity to women's feelings, reticence about displaying emotion, and rationality and logic, which are still culturally constructed as masculine ways of thinking. In the highly charged atmosphere of ritual-abuse cases, women sensed that their husbands' reactions were exaggerations of everyday conflicts, and they tended to vent their hostility by withdrawing affection. This is not the kind of thing they could do in ordinary times, for such behavior usually evokes humiliating social disapproval. In the context of a ritual-abuse case, however, women could rebuke their husbands' masculinity without seeming cold or vicious. They could rationalize their anger with the thoroughly acceptable excuse that they were too emotionally depleted to attend to their mates and too busy comforting their children—whom *Behind the Playground Walls* indicates they showered with extraordinary displays of hugging and kissing.[78]

Amid this reordering of affection, conjugal sex suffered. Again, though, no one—least of all their husbands—could criticize the mothers' lack of libido, because it was expressed dramatically and painfully. There were, for example, paralyzing episodes in the marriage bed. One woman reported that in the middle of lovemaking, she often was overwhelmed by the feeling that she was her preschool-age daughter being raped.[79] *Behind the Playground Walls* investigators found that this experience was common to mothers. During sex, they would "flash" on their children being violated and have to stop.[80]

Not surprisingly, many couples eventually separated or divorced. Ritual abuse thus helped women disengage from unsatisfactory marriages without feeling guilty about being bad wives or mothers. After all, the reason they weren't getting along with their husbands was because they cared so much about their children. Being the parent of a ritual-abuse victim was not just a private nightmare. It was also a way to stand with the angels, to bear a civic cross that evoked society's deepest admiration, and become active in a social movement.

The Prestige of the Child Victim

While adults invented themselves as the shell-shocked parents of ritual-abuse victims, children adopted complementary roles. Very few were at all conscious or conniving about this. Most came to truly believe they had been abused, and once they did, they became severely disturbed by anxiety, insecurity, insomnia, nightmares, terror of strangers, depression, rages, recurrent fears about dying, and suicidal impulses.

Tanya Mergili, whose interview with Kee MacFarlane was described in chapter 4, had been acting normally until CII interviewers diagnosed her as a victim and suggested that she enter therapy. She did, and within weeks she was worried about her parents dying. In a few months, Tanya was obsessed with death, funerals, and cemeteries. Then she began playing games in which she was pregnant and Ray Buckey was slaughtering her babies.[81]

Curt Mrazek's experience was similar. Once his father had played Santa Claus at McMartin's; now he was on the board of directors of the Children's Civil Rights Fund, spoke about the case on radio and television, and joined efforts to unearth molestation tunnels under the preschool. Curt, meanwhile, was having frightening dreams about guns, knives, skeletons, and dismembered bodies. He abandoned his bed and started sleeping in a cardboard box.[82]

It was the same everywhere. In Maplewood, Patricia Crowley's daughter had nightmares about Kelly Michaels's ghost coming out of a light socket. Another child whimpered that "Kelly's in my head."[83] Boys and girls throughout the country complained that they did not want to go on living. Some talked of being "the son of the

Devil," and denounced God.[84] When children from the same case met, they acted in strange and unnerving ways. At a Manhattan Beach counseling center with a day-care program for victims, preschoolers circled the room chanting curses and dis-membering dolls while horrified teachers watched and wept.[85]

The adults who observed this behavior were convinced that brutal molesters had defiled the children—otherwise, why would they act so damaged? In reaching this conclusion, though, parents and therapists could never explain the absence of phys-ical trauma or evidence. Nor did they acknowledge simpler, more logical explana-tions based on the well-known psychological concepts of cognitive dissonance, social desirability, and secondary gain.

Cognitive dissonance describes the profound identity crisis a person typically suf-fers when deeply held beliefs are challenged by contradictory but convincing infor-mation—especially when it comes from powerful and respected authorities.[86] Faced with such a dilemma, the individual experiences a feeling of disorientation border-ing on madness, and must either reject the new information or wholeheartedly embrace it to avoid going crazy.

Parents of children in ritual-abuse cases faced this dilemma when experts told them that people like the Buckeys and McMartins, whom they had loved and respected for years, were malevolent perverts who thought nothing of tormenting lit-tle boys and girls. It was the same with the children. That they had liked, even loved, their caretakers is evident from the many investigative records in which they call their teachers "nice," and wonder why they are in jail. In response, the author-ities insist that the accused are "bad" and "sick," and that the children will feel much better if they admit this and disclose the terrible things done to them. The potential for such an experience to unnerve a youngster is suggested by cognitive dissonance theory. It is borne out by the reaction of one child who showed signs of confusion and anxiety even as he was being interviewed.

Nine-year-old Bruce Stoddard began his session at CII insisting that "I don't remember anything" about abuse at the McMartin Preschool, and that it "didn't happen to me."[87] But after he was encouraged to maul a doll named after teacher Ray Buckey, and after entreaties to "picture" the molesters "in your brain," Bruce began generating scenarios of fondling, rape, and pornography making. He seemed shaken at how he was denouncing his teachers: "God! What do you have here?" he exclaimed after making an accusation, and added that he felt as though the inter-viewer was trying to "[t]ake my brain out."[88] Later he produced florid charges that Ray Buckey and his associates had worshiped Satan and slaughtered animals. Bruce also became wracked with fear that the Devil lived in a jar in his house and was trying to control him.[89]

Another influence on children in ritual-abuse panics is pressure for *social desir-*

ability—or, in simpler terms, the tendency to tell people what we think they want to hear instead of what is really on our minds. Although the effects of social desirability are seldom measured, they constantly undermine the accuracy of public opinion polls and survey research. They are especially common when the people quizzed are socially subordinate to the interviewers: when patients are questioned by psychologists, for instance; when prisoners are surveyed by criminologists; or when poor people are buttonholed by glossy television reporters.

Skewed power relations are the issue here, and for little children, who could be more powerful than the people who house, feed, and love them? Social desirability works so strongly on children that they can easily be made to imagine something terrible happened if an authoritative adult insists it did.[90] In such situations, youngsters defer to grownups not merely to please them but to win approval and privileges. This dynamic is called *secondary gain*, and, while it can bring a child intense pleasure, it can also be terrifying and painful.

Secondary gain exercises both of these effects on the children in involved in ritual-abuse cases. Many studies and anecdotes note that as soon as children are identified as victims, they gain unprecedented status and regard. In some cases, they are elevated to community icons, as when Manhattan Beach's American Martyrs Catholic Church, where many McMartin students' families worshiped, began holding special masses for the child victims. McMartin youngsters who were diagnosed as victims were treated to visits and free performances by media celebrities such as Mr. T and the stars of *Punky Brewster*. (At least one child whose family did not believe she was abused used to cry disconsolately because she did not qualify to attend these fetes.) "Victims" were also coveted by area therapists who went out of their way to recruit them for treatment.[91]

Within their families, meanwhile, the children were showered with attention. Five-year-old Sara Barton's parents, for instance, were told by CII interviewers to hug and praise her continuously for telling her abuse "secrets." The Bartons followed the instructions; at the same time, they made it clear to their daughter that their new affection was predicated on her escalating recitations about rape and torture.[92]

Likewise, in Maplewood, Patricia Crowley and her husband stopped going out for dinner alone once a week. Instead, they stayed home to comfort five-year-old Hannah, and Patricia even took over tasks that the child already knew how to accomplish herself: she dressed Hannah, fed her, put on her shoes, and even wiped her after she used the toilet. The Crowleys had four children, but when Hannah wept at night, Patricia left the others and rushed to her side. Relatives took her out for ice cream and bought her new dolls. Her father gave her a special toy and, as did Patricia, spent more time with her than with their other children. So accustomed did Hannah become to these indulgences that when Patricia's brother was seriously injured in an accident, she angrily complained that the distraught relatives were paying attention to him and not her.[93] "Hannah will always need more from me than my other children," Patricia proclaimed.[94]

Siblings also became embroiled in ritual-abuse dramas. With the "victimized" child suddenly receiving every ounce of community and parental attention, the others became intensely jealous. One ten-year-old girl got so upset at being ignored that her grades dropped and she developed insomnia and an ulcer. In the McMartin case, Mandi, the nine-year-old sister of Sara Barton, regained her parents' attention when she told them several weeks after Sara's CII diagnosis that she, too, had been abused at the preschool. Soon Mandi was echoing her little sister's stories of rituals and torture in "devil houses" and mansions,[95] even though she had not attended McMartin for several years.

The Ritual-Abuse Industry

Satanism in day care, devil houses, preschoolers forced to ingest feces—child-protection workers had never before heard of such things, and neither had politicians. In the War on Poverty era of the 1960s, the country had been concerned about improving nursery schools, and willing to spend money on the effort. With McMartin, the national image of public child care had degenerated from kindly images of Head Start and hot lunches to dark visions of persecution conducted by occult kiddie-porn mafias. Such thinking was promulgated during congressional hearings in September 1984 as legislators responded to the California scandals by considering a proposal to fingerprint all applicants for jobs at day-care centers and preschools.

One of the witnesses they heard from was Kee MacFarlane. When she testified, her paranoia was so intense that she seemed an ideological shadow of her former liberal, feminist self.[96] Powerful conspiracies of sexual predators appeared to be running preschools across the country, she said. She also compared the sexual pillage at these facilities to nuclear warfare and called for community disaster planning to combat it. As for running criminal investigations on day-care job applicants, MacFarlane thought it was a "great" concept.[97]

Two weeks after her testimony, Congress authorized a doubling of funds for child-protection programs: $158 million in the next four years.[98] Days later, an additional $25 million was directed to day-care centers to train staff in how to prevent and detect sexual abuse. States could receive the money only if the centers agreed to do costly criminal records checks, such as fingerprint screenings, on all employees.[99]

While many child welfare and women's advocates sensed uneasily that this money reeked of moral panic and conservative politicking, few complained. As ritual-abuse hysteria rumbled through the legislatures, it pulled domestic violence and neglect along with it and exposed politicians to these less dramatic issues. To be sure, interest was relatively perfunctory, but for activists accustomed to being ignored, any attention at all was welcome. And when the federal government added a $63 million program for family violence victims to the new child-protection funding bill,[100] it was clear that the well-heeled victims from schools like McMartin's were making things easier for women and children in less affluent communities.

The budget for the National Center for Child Abuse and Neglect is another example of the ritual-abuse panic's coattail effect on funding. In 1983, the agency had only $1.8 million to spend on all types of abuse research and demonstration projects (of that, only $237,000 went to sex-abuse studies). Following the McMartin scandal the next year, NCCAN's budget more than quadrupled, and included $146,000 to Kee MacFarlane to interview and examine more McMartin children. (In addition, CII received $350,000 in 1985 from California funds, making the institute that state's first publicly funded training center for child-abuse diagnosis and treatment.)[101]

Hundreds of thousands of dollars were also dedicated to campaigns to teach preschoolers how to avoid being sexually abused, and by the mid-1980s, millions of American preschoolers were going through Good Touch/Bad Touch educational programs. Complaints then began surfacing that children who did not understand the lessons were making false accusations.[102] Eventually, an NCCAN-funded study revealed that even after attending the programs, preschoolers could not tell the difference between appropriate and inappropriate touching, and as many as one-fifth thought that normal parent-child activities such as bathing were "bad." The research concluded that the preschool-age prevention instruction was a waste of money and effort.[103]

When NCCAN funded the prevention research in 1985, it had even more money to work with than the year before. This was mainly because in 1984—again, because of McMartin—the government added maltreatment by out-of-home caretakers to its definition of child abuse. As a result, NCCAN found itself with almost $14 million for research and demonstration grants. Battering and neglect project money dropped, however, to only about $5 million. The rest went to sex-abuse projects.[104]

These disbursals established NCCAN as the country's major funding source for child-abuse research, particularly for sexual abuse. Yet the staff who handled grant applications had minimal research experience and little grasp of what constituted quality scientific inquiry.[105] In the new world of child-protection studies, this incompetence did not bode well. It immediately manifested itself in a surge of funding to apologists for ritual-abuse prosecutions.

One grant, for $449,000, was given to a state mental health department employee who planned to study children supposedly abused at a preschool in Niles, Michigan.[106] The case had surfaced after Richard Barkman, whose wife operated the preschool, reported a pupil's mother for neglect. The mother responded by accusing Barkman of molesting her child, and eventually more than one hundred youngsters described him and other adults photographing them naked, abusing them in a church and in tunnels, giving them injections, inserting foreign objects into their genitals, threatening them with sharks, engaging in blood rituals, unearthing corpses, burying the children, and butchering animals. Barkman was convicted and sentenced to seventy-five years in prison despite an utter lack of material evidence.[107] Nevertheless, the grant applicant and NCCAN described the research as "a followup study of children who experienced sexual abuse at a day-care center."[108]

An equally large disbursal went for *Behind the Playground Walls*, the study of McMartin families discussed earlier in this chapter. Like the Michigan investigators, the researchers who put together that book were unabashedly certain of their subjects' victimization, but they could not have been otherwise, given the politicking that went on in Southern California to monopolize and control knowledge about McMartin.

Government Financing of Belief in Ritual Abuse

Plans for research had germinated a year earlier, in early 1984, when child-abuse professionals, and parents involved in the panic began meeting to discuss the need for a canon that would combat skepticism about the accused teachers' guilt if they were not convicted. When the meetings formalized into a group eager to "study" McMartin, the California Community Foundation, the Conrad Hilton Foundation, and United Way helped it prepare grant applications and solicit funds. The purpose of this remarkable teamwork, as one grant formulator put it, was to prevent "thoughtless or ill-qualified researchers from invading" Manhattan Beach.[109] Presumably, these invaders were anyone who questioned the group's unstinting belief that the defendants were guilty.

Efforts to keep such people away succeeded, and ultimately the recipient of the NCCAN grant was UCLA adjunct psychology professor Dr. Jill Waterman. She was also a member of The Book Club, a group of people who were writing a text about sexual abuse of young children that included Kee MacFarlane and other professionals involved with the McMartin prosecution.[110] Although Waterman's connections with UCLA gave her a degree of independence as a researcher, the same cannot be said for the team she assembled. One member was a Richstone Center psychotherapist who was treating several McMartin children. Another worked with the same health department office and hospital as Roland Summit, and she directed a therapy center that was seeing McMartin clients.[111] When they talked about satanic crimes, she and the rest of the investigative team took the stories literally.

Giving McMartin crusaders hundreds of thousands of dollars was not the only way the government financed belief in ritual abuse. It also sponsored conferences that lent respectability to the idea and enabled proponents to trade information about cases, and tips on how to prosecute them successfully. In October 1984, the Justice Department footed the bill for a four-day conference in Washington that brought together eighty-five child-abuse professionals from throughout the country—including McMartin doctors Roland Summit, Bruce Woodling, David Corwin, and an employee of CII. At the gathering, Summit described a new kind of abuse in which "children are forced to eat feces and drink blood and participate in blood sacrifices and in sexual ceremonies with robed figures and people in costume," and he warned his colleagues not to "hop to the assumption that you're dealing with something that can't be true."[112]

Florida Republican Senator Paula Hawkins also appeared, spoke angrily about children in the Country Walk case who were still being evaluated for abuse, and implied that they had gonorrhea. Bruce Woodling advised investigators to contact CII to learn how to do evaluations. A judge from Wisconsin described how he used a frog puppet in court to get children to talk. Their remarks were collected, published by the Justice Department, and distributed to libraries nationwide.[113]

A few months later, in February 1985, the FBI spent several thousand dollars on a meeting at its Quantico, Virginia, headquarters for personnel from district attorneys' offices and child-protection agencies who were dealing with ritual-abuse cases around the country. Other government-sponsored conferences followed. A glimpse at what went on at these gatherings is provided by handouts from the FBI conference.

Much of the material described satanists and their purported customs, and a good deal of it came courtesy of San Francisco cult cop Sandi Gallant. Gallant and other police officers' obsession with endangered children reflected the fact that many were evangelical Christians convinced that Satan was out to conquer the world by turning the younger generation away from God and Jesus. One "proof" of this sinister plan was the Wicca Letters, a document whose origins and content were remarkably like the rabidly anti-Semitic, nineteenth-century *Protocols of the Elders of Zion*. Like the *Protocols*, the Wicca Letters were "discovered" by the police—only this time, it was not a czarist officer but a San Diego sheriff's deputy who made the find. At least he said he did, but he never made the originals public. Instead, he reported in a fundamentalist Christian publication that the Letters were minutes from an international satanist convention held in Mexico, whose participants formulated a master plan to conquer the world by infiltrating day-care centers and corrupting America's preschoolers.[114]

Gallant did not actively promote the Wicca Letters, but at Quantico she distributed checklists of features common to ritual-abuse cases (enclosing children in secret rooms was typical, the list said, as was sticking needles in their feet and cutting up Barbie dolls). The symptoms this torture was supposed to create in children included masturbation, headaches, nightmares, and an unwillingness to take afternoon naps. The satanist perpetrators, Gallant's material added, commonly used five-pointed stars in their rituals, as well as chalices, capes, altars, and sacrificial animals. Babies, too, were butchered, and the handout quoted from *Michelle Remembers* as it advised the Quantico attendees that among the satanists, "[o]nce every 28 years a human is sacrificed to the Devil."[115]

The FBI conference taught its participants questions to ask of children in ritual-abuse cases, and it instructed prosecutors in what was virtually a tenet of the economically cutthroat Reaganite 1980s: that people who lacked high-powered jobs and large salaries were failures, even morally defective. This was the message Gallant's handout conveyed as it informed readers that while satanist men and women generally were intelligent, they were also "working-class" "underachievers" whose interest in the occult reflected their "mediocre lifestyles"—which included the fact that they worked for minimum wage caring for other people's children.[116]

The organizer of this meeting was Kenneth Lanning, a special agent with the FBI's Behavioral Science Unit (BSU). The criminologists who work there study multiple murderers, homicidal rapists, and child molesters; and the BSU has cultivated a brilliant, daredevil image for itself by advising the authors of several popular works, including the writers of the novel and screenplay for *Silence of the Lambs* (Thomas Harris and Ted Tally). When McMartin surfaced in early 1984, Lanning was the BSU's expert on sexual offenders against children. A former FBI field agent, he had already heard other stories about youngsters being ritually abused, and he had fielded dozens of calls from grown women claiming, Michelle Smith–style, to have been molested years ago in satanic cults run by their parents.[117]

By the time Lanning called the Quantico conference, he was already deeply suspicious of the validity of these claims. Nevertheless, as an FBI official, he is a voice for police and prosecutors, and while he has warned that innocent people sometimes are convicted Lanning has also noted that his job is to use guilty verdicts as grist for his Behavioral Science Unit's efforts to understand the motives of sex criminals.[118] In the early years of the ritual-abuse panic, that meant that when a day-care teacher was convicted, it was Lanning's task to explain what had impelled her to commit the abuse. He performed this job with the help of convoluted logical gymnastics. Since he knew that the behaviors attributed to defendants in ritual-abuse cases did not conform to anything previously known about child molesters, and since he doubted that organized satanists were involved, Lanning came up with a new explanation for the crimes. Ritual abusers, he declared, were motivated not by sexual or pedophilic impulses but by violent ones. "What you are dealing with," he said, "is individuals who have emotional, psychological problems, hostilities, angers, pent up emotions, and they are simply taking them out on available targets . . . who in this case are children."[119]

Lanning made these remarks in late 1985, during hearings before the U.S. Attorney General's Commission on Pornography—popularly known as the Meese Commission. Reflecting the Reagan administration's fundamentalist Christian passions, Justice Department head Edwin Meese III appointed the commission to find "new ways to control the problem of pornography"—even though fifteen years earlier, a similar panel formed during Lyndon Johnson's presidency had found no evidence that sexually explicit material causes antisocial behavior. Now, the Meese Commission launched an attack on everything (including vibrators) that divorced sex from marriage or procreation. Its chairmen were rabid antivice prosecutors, and most of the commissioners had come out strongly for laws restricting pornography.[120]

Although these moral conservatives were indifferent or hostile to the women's movement, they sensed that their efforts would be better received if they were couched in the language of social science and victimology. The commission therefore appointed a few token liberals and women, such as Ellen Levine, editor of *Redbook* magazine, into its ranks. It also courted (and got) support and testimony from feminist antipornography activists like Catharine McKinnon and Andrea Dworkin and child sex-abuse researcher Diana Russell. This accomplished, the panelists played down nonviolent pornography and emphasized far rarer sadistic genres. They also ignored or mischaracterized research showing no demonstrable causal relation between pornography and violence, and based their findings on anecdotal testimony from witnesses, especially women, who told horror stories about boyfriends and husbands coercing and degrading them after viewing smut.[121]

Kiddie porn was naturally a potent weapon in the Meese Commission's assault on sex, and several days of hearings in Miami were devoted to the topic. There ritual abuse made its appearance, as parents from the California preschool cases testified that their children were talking about lights and cameras.[122] The parents' concerns were later amplified by commission member Deanne Tilton Durfee. Newly married to Dr. Michael Durfee and longtime head of Los Angeles's Interagency Council on Abuse and Neglect (ICAN), Tilton Durfee was a supporter of the key players in the McMartin panic. In a statement she wrote for the final Meese report, she intimated that day-care centers were involved in a vast kiddie porn industry that needed investigating by a national task force.[123] Tilton Durfee's fellow commissioners agreed, and they echoed Roland Summit in recommending that victims of day-care sex crimes needed to be studied further.[124]

Though the task force never materialized, the call for additional research was answered the next year, when NCCAN disbursed yet more money for a study of sexual abuse at day-care centers. The grant, for $173,000, went to a group of University of New Hampshire sociologists led by David Finkelhor. Finkelhor had done pioneering sociological investigation into the incidence, prevalence, and aftereffects of child sexual abuse. But he had also established himself as a moral conservative on the issue by promoting the idea that the sexual revolution of the 1960s created "confusion" that was "in part responsible for the occurrence of sexual abuse."[125]

He had also co-authored work on sexual abuse with Diana Russell, the sociologist and Women Against Violence and Pornography co-founder, who was embracing the McMartin case as proof that child pornography was rampant and a likely contributor to incest and other sexual abuse.[126] At the same time Russell was formulating this theory, Finkelhor signed on as a researcher for the *Behind the Playground Walls* McMartin and Manhattan Beach study described earlier in this chapter.[127] He later relinquished the job, but as a supportive colleague of the remaining investigators,[128] he was hardly sequestered from the prosecutorial passions they brought to the work.

The Impact of Nursery Crimes

With his own grant for a national study, Finkelhor scoured the country for day-care cases that surfaced between 1983 and 1985. When he and his team finished two years later, their work was published as a book, *Nursery Crimes*, that promptly became a Bible for ritual-abuse believers.[129] It gained this status for two reasons. First, Finkelhor was no housewife or lay activist; he was a highly regarded social science researcher doing government-funded work. Too, *Nursery Crimes* took information on more than three dozen ritual-abuse scandals[130] and collapsed it into data about scores of much more ordinary, credible-sounding cases. Accusations against the mentally ill sons of day-care operators, or against confessed pedophiles who admitted fondling their victims, were indiscriminately combined with charges against middle-aged women for slaughtering animals, dancing in robes, piercing toddlers' genitals with pins, and flying them to molestation sites in aircraft. No matter how outlandish the charges, the study assumed that all were valid, even if the accused was ultimately never arrested, much less convicted.

The great irony of *Nursery Crimes* is that if anyone should have been suspicious of the data, it was Finkelhor, who earlier had joined Diana Russell in observing that women are nowhere near as likely as men to molest children, and that when they do their offenses tend to be much less coercive or violent.[131] Yet here were the ritual-abuse cases, in which 40 percent of the accused were females engaged in wanton, sadistic assaults.

Instead of expressing skepticism about this dramatic contradiction, Finkelhor assumed that the defendants were guilty and set out to elaborate a new criminal type: the female sex fiend. Like FBI agent Lanning at the Meese Commission hearings, the New Hampshire sociologist had precious little material to work with. He found no evidence that the women in his study had psychiatric records, alcohol or drug abuse problems, histories of criminal sexual deviance, or anything else that would signal a propensity to attack children. Indeed, if the accused had anything in common besides making modest livings working in child care, it was that they seemed utterly unremarkable. They certainly were not people criminologists would expect to suddenly start raping and torturing anyone, much less preschoolers. But in order to cast them as ritual abusers, *Nursery Crimes* implied that normality was characteristic of female day-care molesters. Or to put it more simply: absolutely anybody could be a vicious, satanic child torturer—even the nice, sweet lady at the nursery school.

Embedded in this paranoid sociology was barely concealed fear that the sexual revolution of the 1960s (and, by implication, the feminism that went with it) had engendered a New Woman succubus who, as *Nursery Crimes* put it, was so obsessed with "power and control" that dominating men did not satisfy her—she even had to engage in the "mortification" of innocent children.[132] Such thinking updated myths about insatiable female sexuality that lay at the core of the European witch trials. The fact that feminist-oriented researchers such as Finkelhor would bolster it was ominous. Like the witch hunters who burned females in the name of God and the state to protect society, the modern-day researchers were ready to vilify women in order to save children. As they went about this business, they also discredited public child care, even though in their eyes, they were rehabilitating it. As part of *Nursery Crimes'* analysis, Finkelhor and his colleagues compared the number of youngsters sexually abused in day care with those victimized within families, and concluded that preschools were about 60 percent safer than children's own homes.[133] While at first glance this statistic seems staunchly pro–day care, a second look reveals that two-thirds of the victims in *Nursery Crimes* came from ritual-abuse cases. Removing them from the calculations would have tripled the 60 percent figure and revealed how safe public child care really was.

But while day care was a safer place, it certainly was not a more loving one during the height of the ritual-abuse panic. Many child-care workers began fearing that their charges were, as one journalist put it, "walking time bombs" for false accusations. Nursery school teachers no longer patted students on the shoulder to compliment them, but instead told them to pat themselves. At one Southern California day-care center, staff began changing diapers with toddlers standing up rather than lying down, to give the appearance of less intimate contact. The vice president of the biggest public school teachers' union in Los Angeles advised members to withhold

affectionate pats, hugs, and kisses: "Don't touch. Stay away," she warned.[134] Similar policies cropped up across the country. Fear of false accusations was acute
among men who worked in day cares and grade schools, and to protect themselves,
many abandoned the field—during a time when child development experts and
even politicians were calling for more male influence in the lives of youngsters, especially boys. Child development specialists expressed concern that youngsters were
receiving less attention and nurturing touch from both men and women.[135] Ritual-
abuse charges also jacked up the price of group child care, and drove providers out
of the business. This happened because insurance rates skyrocketed as companies
paid millions of dollars to families in McMartin-style cases who filed civil suits,
even when no criminal convictions were forthcoming.[136]

The Industrialization of Belief

The crisis in day care inspired a modicum of early skepticism about ritual
abuse, but much of the doubt was neutralized as promoters organized themselves
into influential professional groups. Many of the most fervent believers were
already members of the International Society for Prevention of Child Abuse and
Neglect (ISPCAN). The organization had been founded in 1977 by Battered Child
Syndrome originator Dr. C. Henry Kempe, and by the mid-1980s it was the world's
largest and most prestigious child-abuse professional association. But ISPCAN dealt
with all kinds of maltreatment, not just sex abuse, and although MacFarlane was on
the article-review committee of ISPCAN's journal, *Child Abuse & Neglect*,[137] she and
other Americans involved in ritual-abuse cases had relatively little influence in the
organization.

By 1985, many of them were talking about forming a new group dedicated exclu-
sively to sexual abuse. The catalyst for this idea was David Corwin, the psychiatrist
who had studied child abuse under Roland Summit and convened the Preschool-
Age Sexually Molested Children's Group in Los Angeles. By 1984, Corwin was
doing therapy with a McMartin child, and during that time he became convinced
that mental health professionals needed a new psychiatric diagnosis for sexually
abused children. This would enable experts to identify young victims, Corwin
thought, and it would bolster youngsters' claims in court when they could not speak
effectively for themselves.[138]

To formulate the symptoms of this new malady, Corwin called a conference,
obtained Justice Department funding for it, and invited some 100 child-protection
professionals to meet in Los Angeles. There they deliberated about whether a child
could accurately be diagnosed as abused if she seemed to know too much about sex
or masturbated excessively; and they seconded Corwin's call for a new organization

to represent their interests.[139] A few months later, many of the attendees met again in New Orleans at a national convention sponsored by the Washington based Children's National Medical Center. There, while parents from ritual-abuse cases founded Believe the Children, two thousand professionals followed suit and launched plans for a new association. It coalesced shortly thereafter, and was christened the American Professional Society on the Abuse of Children (APSAC).[140]

From its inception, APSAC's leadership roster was a veritable directory of ritual-abuse architects. Kee MacFarlane was an at-large director. Roland Summit was on the board. So were David Finkelhor, Ann Burgess, and Bruce Woodling. Second vice president was David Corwin. President was Jon Conte, the Chicago social worker who earlier had called a ritual-abuse conference, whom Believe the Children listed in its directory of helpful resources, and who rejected the possibility that children making the charges were prompted by adults.[141]

Soon APSAC was publishing the quarterly *Journal of Interpersonal Violence*, with Conte as editor. It became the country's leading forum for child sex-abuse research, and its masthead of consultants and board members was packed with ritual-abuse proponents: most notably, Burgess, Finkelhor, and MacFarlane. APSAC also began a quarterly newsletter, *The Advisor*, which published articles by these writers and other ritual-abuse theoreticians.

At the same time that MacFarlane assumed her position as APSAC director, she joined the advisory boards of several influential organizations: The Center for the Prosecution of Child Abuse of the National District Attorneys' Association; two projects of the American Bar Association; and the conference planning committee of the influential National Symposium on Child Victimization. By 1986, MacFarlane had propounded her views about the McMartin case at more than thirty statewide, national, and international conferences that took her from California to Chicago, Montreal, Germany, and Australia. She had also appeared several times on television programs aired nationally by CBS, NBC, and HBO.[142]

Ritual abuse also propelled Roland Summit into the limelight as the media, hungry for stories about sexual abuse, flocked to him for interviews. He was quoted in dozens of magazines and newspapers, among them *Newsweek, Parade, Women's Day* and the *Wall Street Journal*. He was everywhere on the airwaves, from *Good Morning America* and *Nightline* to *Donahue* and *60 Minutes;* and he acted as a consultant for prime-time entertainment programs such as *Cagney and Lacey, Diff'rent Strokes,* and *Mr. Belvedere*. District attorneys from around the country began asking Summit to appear at ritual-abuse trials to tell juries that just because sexually abused children make delayed, garbled statements and even recantations does not mean they were not abused. He acted as policy adviser to the federal Department of Juvenile Justice and Crime Prevention, the National Office of Victim Assistance, the National Institute of Mental Health, and Attorney General Meese's Advisory Board on Missing Children. He gave the keynote speech at the 1986 congress of the International Society for Prevention of Child Abuse and Neglect, held in Australia.[143]

By the mid-1980s, belief in ritual abuse had been institutionalized by professional societies, journals, the mass media, and a federal government that energetically promoted its champions' claims. Advocates used these forums to develop a new logic and language that made the unbelievable sound credible, despite impassioned efforts by defendants and their attorneys to discredit it. The following chapters examine how this new reasoning and rhetoric were constructed, and how they enveloped common sense, defendants, and children in an impenetrable shroud of silence.

SEVEN

Accusations

Autism, which affects about 400,000 people in the United States, is a bizarre and disturbing disorder that seems genetic and neurological, but whose causes are largely unknown. As newborns, children who are destined to acquire this condition act normally, but by the time they are two years old they develop a chilling aloofness to the social world around them. They do not look at other people's faces, nor do they smile. They seem indifferent when their mothers are nearby and equally unconcerned when they are not. When picked up, they do not cling or cuddle, and they turn away from interactive games like peekaboo or pat-a-cake. Instead, as autistic children grow older they become preoccupied with objects and with using their bodies like objects. Some whirl around or walk on tip-toe. Some flap their arms. Others bang their heads repetitively or twitch their lips. Their faces often eventually take on the slack, vaguely ecstatic look of people who are profoundly mentally disabled, and in fact, most autistics are thought to be retarded. No one is certain about this, though, and the children themselves can do little to explain things because many do not speak. Others merely repeat sounds and nonsense phrases over and over, like parrots. Or they utter only a few words.

Dr. Douglas Bicklin is an educator and autism researcher at Syracuse University. In 1990, on a trip to Australia, he chanced upon a new method used there to improve the lives of cerebral palsy patients. Called facilitated communication, or

FC, the technique involved assigning a helper—or facilitator—to steady the palsied person's wrist and guide it to a diagram resembling a typewriter keyboard. With the facilitator's assistance, patients pointed at letters, one at a time, and spelled out a message. Thus they were able to bypass their physical disabilities and communicate with the world.

When Bicklin saw FC in action, he immediately felt it would work with autistics, and when he returned to Syracuse he began training facilitators and pairing them with disabled students. The results were stunning. People who previously had been doomed to lives of silent, menial toil in sheltered workshops were suddenly composing complex messages to their parents and teachers. Six-year-olds were writing perfectly spelled, grammatically precise, and conceptually precocious lines such as "I cry a lot about my disability. . . . It makes me feel bad when I can't do my work by myself." And poetry: "I greatly fear for the ruin of the Earth/Unless humans jointly find a cure."[1] Teenagers like seventeen-year-old New Hampshire student Matt Gherardi, who seemingly had never learned to read, were mainstreaming into regular classes and earning A's in biology and advanced math.

Teachers and parents were ecstatic. No longer were these children retarded. In fact, many seemed highly gifted. Their problems, FC implied, lay not in their minds but in their anarchically coordinated bodies. With a facilitator's help, though, the spastic movements of autism could be slowed down, smoothed out, and rendered on a keyboard into speech.

At Syracuse University, the Facilitated Communication Institute was founded to train more practitioners, and soon hundreds of people from across the country had learned the method and returned home to teach it to others. By 1993, FC was a veritable social movement. Bicklin called it "revolutionary, a means of expression for people who lacked expression . . . a way that you could find out what people were feeling and what they were thinking." The media agreed: FC was "a miracle," Diane Sawyer told her viewers on *Prime Time Live,* "a story about hope."

But hope was soon dashed by children like Matt Gherardi, the New Hampshire boy. Before he met his facilitator, Matt's vocabulary had consisted of about fifty words. Afterward he was doing well in grammar, algebra, and Shakespeare. His teachers were delighted, but Matt's parents were perplexed. They found it strange that he could suddenly be so literate, and even stranger that he refused to facilitate with his mother, with whom he was very close.

One day, while working at school with his facilitator, Matt pointed to his keyboard and spelled out these words: "dad herts me." "What happens?" his facilitator typed back. "his balls next to mine," the boy replied. "make me very horney Thursday. Dad give love to my ass and dad give love to my cock with his mouth. the bastard eats cock in mouth then kneel over and—you know."

When Matt's father arrived home that night, there was a warrant for his arrest and orders not to set foot in his house.

Insisting he was innocent, he and his wife began investigating the latest developments in autism education, and discovered two things. One was that researchers recently had begun stressing that the incidence of sexual abuse among disabled children is very high. The other was that with the help of FC, several other autistic students around the country had accused their parents, teachers, and care workers of molesting them.

Because so many of the accused were denying the charges, authorities started wondering just who was authoring these messages about abuse: the children or their facilitators? In Maine, after a teenage girl accused her entire family of molesting her, the defendants and prosecutor called in researchers to determine the answer. A study was designed in which the girl and her facilitator sat at a table with a panel dividing them, so that although they could hold hands and touch a keyboard together, their visual fields were separated. Each was then shown pictures of simple objects and asked to type what they saw. The results were chilling. When both looked at a key, for instance, the girl typed "key." But when she saw a cup and her facilitator saw a hat, the girl typed "hat." When she saw a dog and her facilitator saw a pair of shoes, she typed "sneakers." The test went on, and for every picture, the girl always typed not what she saw, but what her facilitator saw.

Many similar tests have since been conducted elsewhere, including in New Hampshire with Matt Gherardi and his facilitator.[2] Unfailingly, they have produced identical results, and it is now clear that facilitated communication never gave autistics their own voices. Instead, with their hands functioning like planchettes and the typewriters like Ouija boards, these students served as nothing more than amplifiers for the thoughts of the people who held their wrists. The "facilitators had no idea they were controlling," one researcher has noted. It is a completely unconscious phenomenon, and when the study results were released, many facilitators were devastated. One described the dedication he felt to his autistic students, the overwhelming joy he had experienced at seeing them communicate with FC, and finally, his shock and heartbreak when he learned that the method had never worked at all—that it simply had overlaid his thoughts, and his colleagues' concerns about sexual abuse, onto other people's silence.

The Investigative Interview

Although the children in ritual sex-abuse investigations generally have normal IQ's and communication skills to match, the dynamic between them and the adults who construct the cases is eerily similar to what went on between autistics and their well-meaning but misguided facilitators. In both instances, those who purport to be helping victims speak are actually the ones doing all the talking. The victims, meanwhile, remain virtually mute.

We know this about the ritual cases mainly because of records that were made of investigations done in the 1980s. Before large-scale cases like McMartin unraveled, police and social workers often kept extensive notes and tapes of their work, and they were so caught up in the power of the accusations that they did not realize how vividly these records portrayed children as clay being molded by driven adults.

In McMartin, for instance, in which hundreds of children were recorded on videocamera, the jury refused to convict the accused because the tapes answered the obvious question raised by the charges: How could preschoolers invent such terrible things without having experienced them?

The interviews had been conducted in cheery playrooms at CII, where Director Kee MacFarlane and her associates dressed in brightly colored clothes and plied the children with toys. Their talks never began with open-ended questions such as: "Tell me what it was like at school." Instead, sessions followed a script that began with an interviewer drawing the human body on a piece of paper and labeling its anatomy for the child. The adult would then display naked dolls with breasts, pubic hair, and genitalia, "the kind you can't buy at the store," and tell the child they were "funny" and their breasts were "cupcakes." Now it was time to name them after accused perpetrators Ray and Peggy Buckey and, that having been done, to laugh at and beat them. Then the body parts were named again, culminating with the genitalia. Whenever a child pointed out a sex organ, he or she was warmly praised.

Next, pictures of the McMartin students and teachers were brought out, including Ray Buckey's, which no child reacted to and many did not recognize. Even so, the interviewer routinely remarked that she already knew what had happened and that the child's classmates had been brave enough to talk about being molested, even though the teachers had terrorized them so they would stay silent. These teachers were bad, the interviewer said, but the police were watching and following them, so now it was safe to talk about the "yucky secrets." Such talk was characterized as a game, complete with puppets and a microphone called the "secret machine." Just tell the secrets to the microphone, the interviewer said, and they will go into a box and be gone forever.[3]

The transcripts that survive from these sessions show that many children did not immediately comply. "I haven't seen anyone playing Naked Movie Star," insists Keith, an eight-year-old, during his interview with Kee MacFarlane. In response, MacFarlane scolds: "Are you going to be stupid, or are you going to be smart and help us? You must be dumb." Trying to please her, Keith answers her demand to describe Ray Buckey's ejaculate by noting that it was yellow, smelled like "poo," and tasted like "barf" and "a rotten snail." Minutes later, he has forgotten all these details. Meanwhile, he desperately tries to distinguish his own perceptions from the hearsay swirling through Manhattan Beach and in the interviewing session. Speaking through a puppet, he points out that his knowledge of Ray Buckey touching children's private parts comes not from firsthand experience, but from what his mother and father told him. MacFarlane ignores this, just as she ignores Keith's later statement, after an hour of relentless demands that he recall abuse, that "[s]ome of the stuff I sort of forget, and like then I remember, and I'm not really sure . . . maybe I accidentally said the wrong thing." Keith is diagnosed a victim, and he ends the session trying to throw a Ray Buckey doll out the window.[4]

One of the most astonishing things about Keith's interview and the many others for which records survive is how little talking the children do: from start to finish, it is adults who speak. In page after page of transcripts, there is not one spontaneous disclosure of abuse. One juror remarked after the first McMartin trial that the interviewers' questions were so leading that "we never got the children's story in their own words."[5] Others cited videotapes of the sessions as key evidence in the defense's favor.[6]

The techniques used at CII were exceptional only in their assembly-line scale. In case after ritual-abuse case across the country during the 1980s, cassettes are filled with the voices of adults urging children to recover hidden memories (see chapter 4), leading them, bribing and threatening them, in order to obtain confirmation of preconceived notions about the guilt of the accused. In the following example, a five-year-old boy is interviewed by a police officer and a social worker investigating the case against Kelly Michaels:

ADULT: Did she put the fork in your butt? Yes or no?
CHILD: I don't know, I forgot.
ADULT: . . . Oh, come on, if you just answer that you can go.
CHILD: I hate you.
ADULT: No you don't.
CHILD: Yes I do.
ADULT: You love me I can tell. Is that all she did to you, what did she do to your hiney?
ADULT #2: What did she do to your hiney? Then you can go.
CHILD: I forgot.
ADULT #2: Tell me what Kelly did to your hiney and then you can go. If you tell me what she did to your hiney, we'll let you go.
CHILD: No.
ADULT: Please.

CHILD: Okay, okay, okay.
ADULT: Tell me now . . . what did Kelly do to your hiney?
CHILD: I'll try to remember.
ADULT: What did she put in your hiney?
CHILD: The fork.[7]

The investigators pressed on blindly, unfazed by denials or insults, paying no attention when children asked to stop, and making no effort to sort out inconsistencies, to decipher incomprehensible statements, or to ask children to explain what they meant. In their campaign to obtain disclosures, they flattered preschoolers by telling them they were old enough to help their younger friends; or they challenged them to act maturely by repeating what the bigger kids said.

In the day-care cases, parents typically played an active role in helping the prosecutors assemble evidence. But when the parents themselves were charged and prosecutors had to extract accusations from the children against their own mothers and fathers, they subjected youngsters to the same techniques of persuasion used by both "cults" groups and their adversaries, "deprogrammers." In both instances, the goal is to alter people's belief systems by totally isolating them from their customary social settings, while simultaneously surrounding them with individuals who press another way of thinking. Oppositional figures from the old milieu, such as parents, are pitied rather than hated, and characterized as needing help because they are "lost."[8]

This is what happened to Byron and Billy Kniffen in the Bakersfield case. Kern County officials scooped the brothers up early one morning and took them to the county holding unit for children, where they were isolated from frantic family members. The boys were interviewed all that first day by Carol Darling, the social worker who had just stepped into the Sex Abuse Coordinator position in the DA's office, and social worker Velda Murillo. After talking to Billy and Byron, the women told law-enforcement officers that the boys had admitted participating in several ritualized orgies and being taken to motels and sold to strangers for group sex.

Though no records were kept of these first interviews, portions of sessions conducted five days later were audiotaped. In surviving recordings, Deputy District Attorney Don McGillivray's voice is heard first as he questions six-year-old Billy: "Don't get scared! Don't get scared Billy! Don't get scared on me now!" "I miss my mommy," Billy replies, through tears and sniffles. "I know you do," answers McGillivray. He turns off the tape recorder.

When the tape resumes some time later, Billy is telling a fantastic tale about six naked people cutting up his clothes with scissors and throwing toilet paper at him. After being told what sodomy is, he talks of the six people, three men and three women, putting "stuff" in his "butt" and describes watching a stranger who drove up in a red car to his friend Robert's front yard and "got wax in [Robert's] butt," then drove away. Robert's mom came out, says Billy, and Robert told her what happened as "he was, um, pulling it out of his butt." Such stories seem much less an account of how perverse adults behave with children than a six-year-old's desperate attempts to guess what they do.

Yet Billy continues to deny that his parents abused him. So he is told that his big brother has already admitted it—which is not true, since at that point Byron had not yet been interviewed—and is given exact details of what Byron supposedly said. After hearing this disinformation, Billy agrees that, yes, his parents did do bad things. When he reverses himself and again insists nothing happened, the recording stops.[9]

Now it is Byron's turn. During his entire interview, with some 340 leading questions about sex abuse, his responses consist of little more than "yes," "no," "I don't know," and one-word echoes of the interviewers' questions. The "no's" and "I don't know's" with which Byron begins displease his interviewers. One of them, Sergeant Don Fredenburg, tries another tack. He effectively tells Byron that his parents are in trouble and that if Byron says what the sheriff wants to hear, they will get help and he will be able to see them. The child is never told, though, that if he makes allegations of sex abuse his mother and father will probably be imprisoned.

Finally, Byron gives in to the two interrogators:

McGILLIVRAY: Now Billy told us that men stuck their penis in his butt and that he saw men stick their penis in your butt.
FREDENBURG: (whispering) It's okay.
McGILLIVRAY: Was he telling the truth when he told that?
(No audible response)
FREDENBURG: What's your answer?
McGILLIVRAY: What's your answer?
BYRON: Yes.

The two men then shower praise on Byron, calling him an "absolute good boy" who is "almost a man."[10]

Police reports summarizing these interviews bear little relationship to the tapes. Fredenburg's report of this session with Byron places long, fluent narratives of abuse in the child's mouth, but in fact Byron offered monosyllabic answers to leading questions and changed "no" to "yes" only after being questioned relentlessly. None of this is noted in Fredenburg's report, nor are any of the boy's scores of denials. When the interviewers' words are edited out of the transcript, the reader is left with page after page of virtually unbroken white space.

What happened to Billy and Byron Kniffen was no exception in Bakersfield. In August 1986, an investigation by California's attorney general into the Satanic Church case found that children were removed from their homes as soon as they were named by others; some were kept from their families for years, even though no charges were filed. In their new, alien surroundings, they were interviewed as many as two dozen times apiece by deputy sheriffs, and countless more times by social workers, sex abuse coordinators, and deputy district attorneys.[11] Similar scenarios were played out in Jordan, Minnesota.[12]

In every ritual-abuse case where interview records survive, it is obvious that the children were subjected to pressure and coercion before they disclosed abuse. It seems a wholesale violation of common sense that investigators—and parents— could be so blind to the risks they were taking when they interviewed the children relentlessly; meticulously described sex to them; cajoled and badgered them when they were silent; praised, hugged, and sated them with treats when they gave the "right" answers; berated or threatened them when they offered "wrong" ones. How could the adults involved in these cases have overlooked the almost certain distortions such pressure was bound to produce?

Windows of Disclosure

The answer lies in an article of faith embraced by investigators who developed ritual-abuse cases: that children never lie about sex abuse. Over and over, early investigators and theoreticians made this point.[13] CII's Dr. Heger told the McMartin jury that "children cannot be led to disclose having been sexually abused if it didn't happen"—a claim that echoed Roland Summit's observation that "[i]t has become a maxim among child sexual abuse intervention counselors and investigators that children never fabricate the kinds of explicit sexual manipulations they divulge in complaints or interrogations."[14]

These words appeared in Summit's article "The Child Sexual Abuse Accommodation Syndrome" and were accepted by case investigators as a truism about children's nature rather than about their behavior in the years before sexual abuse became a widely discussed public issue that even youngsters heard and talked about. Believing that children could not mention sex abuse unless they had actually experienced it assured investigators that they could never be too suggestive. It also implied that since children would not disclose abuse to an indifferent, emotionally distant or passive interviewer, it was appropriate to use all sorts of aggressive and intrusive methods to get a discussion going.

In ritual-abuse cases, the less often voiced but no less ardently believed corollary to Summit's theory was that if children in an investigation denied having been sexually abused, they were *always* lying. So said Sergeant Fredenberg in a 1986 newspaper interview; his source for this was "research" by Roland Summit.[15] But Summit has never done any research (his writings, including the "Child Sexual Abuse Accommodation Syndrome," are all, in his words, "impressionistic"), nor had he done therapy with children under the age of seven since 1966, and even then his young patients were not in treatment for sexual abuse.[16] Summit's career has been with public bureaucracies, teaching, speaking at conferences, seeking grants, and testifying in court cases for prosecutors.[17] During one such appearance, in a hearing to overturn a Kern County sex-ring conviction, he dismissed a child's recantation of abuse as most likely false. In explaining why, he delineated a blueprint for creating ritual-abuse allegations that was followed in virtually every case:

[T]he investigator must wait to build a trusting relationship and hope to find some way to pry open the window of disclosure. This usually requires [subjecting the child to] multiple interviews, ingratiation, and separation from suspected perpetrators.

Direct questioning may be unproductive unless coupled with confrontation, presenting the child with a reassurance that the examiner already knows what happened. The investigator provides either a hypothetical based on experience with other cases, or assures the child that another victim has already broken the secret.

. . . [W]hatever leverage is required to pry open the window of disclosure, an opening crack affords only the first hint of a larger picture. Acceptance of each hint without prejudice or punishment by the investigator allows for exploration of the more painful or more dangerous secrets.

Victims typically reveal awareness before participation, a passive role before an active one, genital or oral contact before anal, an individual perpetrator before group exploitation, male before female perpetrators, and nonviolent sexual interactions before ritually sadistic and humiliating experiences.

The child may therefore proceed in sequence from nothing happened, to something happened, to other kids but not to me, to he tried to do it to me but I wouldn't let him, to he did it to me one time, to he did it a lot of times, to he made me do it to him once, to I had to do it a lot, to she was there, to she did it, to they made us eat pooh, to they killed a bird, to I killed a bird.[18]

Some of these prescriptions might be appropriate in cases where charges have already been independently corroborated and adjudicated, and the victim is now in therapy. But they are squarely at odds with forensic guidelines for the investigative interviewing of children that California law officers were supposed to be following by 1983. Those rules emphasized the importance of open-ended questions; a sympathetic but neutral demeanor; avoiding threats, games, bribes, and repeated questioning or interviews; as well as the need to avoid "cross-germination"—telling one child what another has already said (or supposedly said) about sex abuse. They cautioned against putting words in the child's mouth and urged that interviews, particularly the crucial first one, be recorded.[19]

In other parts of the country, similar guidelines were also in effect by the mid-1980s.[20] But it was Summit and his co-thinkers who actually taught front-line child-abuse investigators how to do their work. And in ritual-abuse cases, the latter were usually social workers and therapists whose concern was not so much to investigate the validity or falsehood of the allegations as to assume from the beginning that they were true and to help children heal emotionally by pressing them to reveal the atrocities.

Consider what is recommended to investigator trainees by an acknowledged master of the art of prying open windows of disclosure: Bakersfield's Velda Murillo. She obtained many of the first disclosures of sex abuse in the Kern County ring cases. In early 1984, she and fellow social worker Ann Harris conducted a seminar to demonstrate how to interview children using anatomically detailed dolls. In the videotape of the session, Harris holds up the dolls and urges the audience to become completely at ease with them by keeping them on their desks, taking them home, undressing them, looking at them, and feeling them. Murillo then describes how to create the proper interview environment. One must start in the morning, she advises, when everyone is fresh; and the session should last a full day. Only the investigator and child should be present—this is essential if the latter's skittishness about talking is to be overcome. In fact, solitude is so vital that the room must be locked so that disclosures will not be derailed by someone walking in unannounced.

Murillo and Harris devote much of their presentation to the problem of denials and how to squelch them if they emerge. When a disclosure is finally obtained, Harris cautions that it is still not the whole story. The perpetrator committed additional violations, and so did other culprits. Investigators must therefore learn how to make the child talk about these crimes as well. And if no revelations are forthcoming despite all these efforts, everyone is urged to rise above egotism and to ask another person to question the child.

In this training session, obtaining disclosures emerges as less a forensic science than an art, an act of intuition, a personal gift. One social worker describes the time she extracted an admission from a child even though no one had ever told her the child had been abused: "I've . . . had a child say, 'Well, how did you know?' and I would say, 'Well, honey, I really didn't know . . . nobody told me. All the dynamics were there.'" And Harris boasts about how

I had a four year old and she would just not even pick up the rag dolls. She just told me she didn't want to come in, she didn't want anything to do with me. And so I had that little bitty doll and she had real long hair and her body's about this big. . . . So she got her out and . . . got those little legs apart and simulated oral copulation. And why that doll instead of the big rag dolls, I don't know, but . . . when everything else fails, try something else. You're the grown up. You are creative. You are in control. This is a statement that you are facilitating for the child. They need you to help them. And you can do it![21]

This fervor to help the victims in ritual cases by "trying something else" was so strong that it typically overwhelmed forensic considerations. In McMartin, investigators said they were trying to aid the children in their emotional recovery, even though none had previously disclosed sexual abuse or other harm. In El Paso, a social worker testified that her session with a child in the Michelle Noble–Gayle Dove case was "about as leading as you can get," but that the assistant district attorney directing the investigation ordered her to ignore legal considerations and interview the child "for therapeutic reasons."[22] During such sessions, the adults often adopted a style that combined the humble confession with a Rasputinlike megalomania. In the Kelly Michaels case, social worker Lou Fonolleras interviewed eighty-two children and disclosed to at least one of them that he had been molested as a boy.[23] Later, when New York therapist Eileen Treacy saw these same children, she told them: "God gave me a special blessing. He did. You know how some big people can't talk to kids too good? You know, they don't seem to listen? . . . Well, you know what? God gave me the blessing that I am able to listen and I help kids with this stuff. I go to tell people how the children feel."[24]

That Treacy would tell five-year-olds she had extraordinary abilities is telling, since at trial she testified that her interviewing techniques constituted "an effort to disempower Kelly of these super powers that she allegedly has."[25] This obsession with transcendental power was another reflection of the investigators' preconceived ideas about what happened—ideas derived from sources such as *Michelle Remembers* and from seminars about satanic cults, kiddie porn conspiracies, and ritualistic nursery crimes.

The Word of Children

Treacy's effort to speak for the children reflects investigators' tacit assumption that by themselves, youngsters cannot describe their experience accurately. In the United States, this attitude derives in large part from the colonial witchcraft trials in Salem, Massachusetts.

The trials began in 1692, after three girls ages nine, eleven, and twelve in the household of the Reverend Samuel Parris met with other girls and with a Caribbean slave named Tituba. She showed them charms, spells, and ways of predicting the future—such as how to identify the men they would marry. The Puritan girls became frightened that they had participated in pagan "conjurations." They began to behave strangely, "getting into holes, and creeping under chairs and stools . . . , [with] sundry odd postures and antic gestures, [and] uttering foolish, ridiculous speeches which neither they themselves nor any others could make sense of."[26]

The girls' parents took them to a doctor who was unable to find a physical cause for their ailments. So he diagnosed satanic possession, and at this, ministers and experts in witch finding were called. The questioners were convinced that community residents had cursed the girls. All they lacked were the culprits' names. But when they asked the simple question, "Who torments you?" the girls did not answer. Other inquiries were equally futile. So Parris, Reverend Nicholas Noyes, and several other villagers peppered the girls with the names of Salem residents and then watched how they responded. This interrogation process went on hour after hour, week after week. Finally, after a month of it, the youngest girl named Tituba as a witch, along with two other women who were community outcasts. Eventually, the girls fingered dozens more people, both women and men.[27]

These events, and the subsequent trials, exercise a deep and continuing hold on the national imagination. Some scholars have condemned the children as fraudulent attention-seekers,[28] while others have pitied them as being afflicted with mental diseases.[29] What is overlooked in these discussions is that the girls who started the persecution were in no hurry to assume the role of accusers. They made their charges only after being subjected to relentless interrogations, pressed on them by the most powerful adults in their lives. Because historians generally ignored or downplayed this fact, for generations after Salem the whole cloth of American children's testimony was discredited. Never again, said jurists. They tended to agree with Robert Louis Stevenson that children should not be allowed on the witness stand, since, as Stevenson wrote: "In all the child's world of dim sensations, play is all in all."[30]

Even so, by the late nineteenth century in America, children's testimony had been somewhat rehabilitated, and sexual abuse was not entirely a public secret. "Our criminal annals," a Michigan judge wrote, "are full of cases where little girls under seven years of age are outraged and maltreated by fiends in human form." Without these girls' testimony, the judge warned, justice could not be reached.[31] He wrote in dissent to a reversal of a case, based on the testimony of a five-year-old found by the trial court to be candid and credible, because the child could not define the word *oath*. Eventually Michigan reformed its laws so that children could

testify in any case where they appreciated the importance of telling the truth. Jurisdictions around the country began eliminating arbitrary refusals to hear youngsters
simply because of their age or their inability to make formulaic recitations of an
oath. Instead, judges were allowed to make case-by-case rulings about whether a
child could testify.[32]

The tension between discrediting children's testimony and valorizing it continued
into the early twentieth century. Surviving records from the period offer both prejudice and shrewd insights. On the one hand, children were seen as pure beings, lack-
ing the sexual or other corrupted interests said to taint adults' perceptions and testimony. The influential professor Dr. Hans Gross felt that children could indeed be
easily led, but absent such manipulation, they made keen observers. An "intelligent
boy," he felt, "as a rule is the best witness in the world." On the other hand, Gross
believed that while girls were superb observers of human relationships, their ability to provide good evidence was far inferior to boys'.[33]

The attitude that girls' perceptions were not to be trusted was closely related to
suspicions about women who brought charges of sexual assault and rape. By the
1930s, the legal scholar John Henry Wigmore had set forth the widely accepted
principle that women and girls were predisposed to falsely accusing men of sex
crimes, and that courts should not be fooled by their falsehoods. Particularly in
cases where a girl accused her father of incest, Wigmore recommended that she be
examined by a psychiatrist to determine her credibility.[34] Since prevailing psychiatric opinion had it that stories about incest were typically manifestations of Oedipal fantasies or hysteria, a visit by a girl to a follower of Freud was almost a guarantee that her testimony would be dismissed.

Suggestibility

Even so, early-twentieth-century prosecutors continued to file sexual assault
cases, particularly in instances where the accused was not a family member. Such
cases combined with others, not about sexual abuse, that hinged on the testimony
of children. All of them fueled an interest in children's suggestibility that spread
beyond the medical and legal fields to the newly emerging discipline of psychology.

To assess credibility, European courts have long relied on experts rather than
jurors, so judges on the Continent welcomed the new psychological research. Contemporary American psychologist Steven Ceci and his Canadian colleague Maggie
Bruck have summarized the work of four leading European researchers at the turn
of the century—Alfred Binet, Otto Lipmann, J. Varendock, and Wilhem Stern—and
found that their research included strategies often used today. Binet, for example,
had a board with buttons glued to it, which he would show to children for ten sec-
onds. Then he would ask some of them questions such as, "How was the button

attached to the board?" The correct answer, of course, is that it was glued. But some children were asked, "What was the color of the thread that attached the buttons to the board?" These children often "remembered" threads where there had been none, and they even described the color of thread. Misleading questions, Binet found, generated inaccurate recall.[35]

In several articles published in the *Psychological Bulletin* between 1909 and 1913, G. M. Whipple presented the work of European researchers and concluded that young children are so highly suggestible that they are dangerous witnesses in court.[36] These articles essentially closed the discussion of children's suggestibility in the United States for decades. That is not to say, though, that children never testified, especially older children—even in sex-abuse cases. Appellate records from 1920 to 1975 contain numerous examples of girls taking the stand to describe rapes and assaults. Even so, society considered such crimes exceedingly rare.

In the late 1970s and early 1980s, sex-abuse cases mushroomed, and judges increasingly began allowing younger and younger children to testify. The vast majority of these trials involved incest accusations against a family member, or fondling by nonrelatives such as priests or scout leaders. Compared to these, ritual cases were rare. But no matter what kind of scenario was alleged, the new wave of sex-abuse trials dramatically raised the issue of children's suggestibility for the first time in sixty years. It was not long, then, before a new generation of cognitive psychologists began designing new studies.

They had already supplied courts with research demonstrating that adults' memories are quite prone to suggestion. In court, there is nothing more powerful than a witness on the stand who confidently points a finger and tells the jury, "That's the man!" But the annals of criminal law are replete with examples of eyewitnesses singling out as the perpetrator someone who was locked in the jail of a city a thousand miles away on the night of the crime. Beginning in the 1970s, cognitive psychologist Elizabeth Loftus and her colleagues began exploring the causes of such errors. Their research found that when people witness crimes and then later give inaccurate testimony, often it is because their memories have been distorted by suggestion. It is not easy to get a fleeting glimpse of a stranger and then later identify him or her—particularly, in this culture, when the stranger is of another race. Yet if the police are pressing hard for an answer, it may be very difficult to avoid feeling increasingly sure about the identification. And once a witness enters this state of mind, the police can both deliberately and unwittingly communicate their own belief about who the guilty party is.[37]

Many people are completely unaware of such complications. In fact, several studies have found that the more certain eyewitnesses feel about their identifications, the more likely they are to be wrong. And while a wrong selection at a line-up might feel shaky at first, by trial time it has often hardened into certainty.[38] This problem is now so widely recognized that in many jurisdictions defendants are allowed to call experts such as Loftus to warn the jury about it.[39]

Loftus's suggestibility research is informed by a now generally accepted view of memory as a complex process of production rather than simple reproduction. When a memory is acquired, or encoded, it is subject to distortion from influences that come from both inside and outside a person. Once encoded, bits of information that were acquired through perception do not reside in memory passively. Instead, they, too, are subject to many changes—from events that happen later, or from hearing about other people's experiences.[40] All this is called "post-event information," and often it can significantly alter the way the witness remembers the original incident: how noisy it was, how violent, who was there, and so on.[41]

Finally, the way an event is recalled can be changed again, when it is "retrieved" from memory and talked about. Particularly when witnesses feel pressure to give a detailed account, they may fill in memory gaps with mistaken information. After repeated questioning, these errors may congeal in memory and begin to feel like fact. And once they feel real, without independent corroboration there is no way to tell whether they are or not.[42]

By the early 1980s, these distortions were well documented in adults, but little new research had been done on children. As the courts overflowed with sex-abuse cases, more and more young witnesses were taking the stand. This fueled an interest in researching their cognitive abilities, and soon a new spate of studies suggested that youngsters are also prone to having their memories altered. And it showed something else: contrary to earlier claims, children who are interviewed properly are not so different from their elders when it comes to suggestibility.

The work of cognitive psychologist Gail Goodman is illustrative. In one of her studies, six dozen girls between five and seven years old were given a checkup by a pediatrician. Half got a genital and anal exam and half were examined for scoliosis, which merely involves checking a child's posture. Later, the girls were asked to tell what had happened, to reenact it with anatomically detailed dolls, and to answer questions—some of which were misleading. In open-ended interviews, less than half the girls who had the genital and anal exam reported it; when they used the dolls, even fewer mentioned being touched until they were asked directly. On the other hand, of the children who were not touched, three said they had been, and one added that the doctor had put a stick in her rectum.

To Goodman, these errors reflected confusion and anxiety, and they were easily corrected by asking the girls follow-up questions. After doing so, she optimistically concluded that the chances of obtaining a false report of genital or anal touching are slim, and that normal children are unlikely to fabricate details about sexual acts or to yield easily to adults' misleading suggestions that something sexual happened when it didn't. This is particularly so, she noted, when interviewers are not intimidating and when they ask easy-to-understand questions.[43]

Goodman's studies and others that emphasize young children's resistance to suggestion are characterized by neutral interviewing styles, the absence of motive to make false reports, and limited use of misleading questions. They led former American Psychological Association president Gary Melton to write: "There is now no real question that the law and many developmentalists were wrong in their assumption that children are highly vulnerable to suggestion, at least in regard to salient details."[44]

The handful of studies on which Melton relied, with their models of appropriate interviewing technique,[45] bear little resemblance to what has occurred in ritual-abuse cases, where children are taken from familiar contexts and asked not one or two but hundreds of leading questions during repeated and relentless interviews. Because replicating this scenario with preschoolers in a laboratory would be abusive and unethical, researchers have faced a dilemma as they ponder how to build what they call "ecological validity" into their experiments. How, in other words, can a sex-abuse investigation be imitated without traumatizing the children?

Obviously, it can't. But since the late 1980s, cognitive psychologists Ceci, Bruck, and others have devised several studies that excise sexual themes, yet preserve other important elements of the typical ritual-abuse interview. In doing so, they have demonstrated the ease with which false memories can be created by using simple techniques of persuasion.[46] They have also shown how children can even be led to fabricate stories about having their bodies touched.[47]

Repeating a question over and over, for instance, tells the young child that her first answer must have been wrong because the adult is not satisfied with it. If the question is leading, such as "Grace made everybody kiss her vagina, didn't she?" the child quickly intuits that her "no" should be a "yes." Even repeating a question that is not leading signals the child that she has yet to produce the right response. This can trigger fantasies so rich in detail that therapists and investigators cannot distinguish them from memory of real events.[48] And after such answers are repeated during several interviews, what began as suggestion may be remembered as history.

These effects are heightened when accompanied by adult displays of emotion. If the interviewer seems annoyed or exasperated with the child's reply, she soon learns to change it; if her next attempt is greeted with warm affirmations or caresses, she learns the direction she is expected to move in.

Another powerful form of suggestion is "stereotypical inducement": if the interviewer repeatedly characterizes someone as bad or dangerous, a child may incorporate this view and then struggle to flesh out the image. Ceci and a colleague designed a study to test the effects of stereotypical inducement on preschoolers at a day-care center. As part of the research, an assistant who called himself "Sam Stone" came to the center. Each week, beginning a month before his visit, two groups of children were told that Sam was coming soon. This was all one group heard. The other listened to stories in which Sam was depicted as being very clumsy. For example: "You'll never guess who visited me last night. That's right. Sam Stone! And guess what he did this time? He asked to borrow my Barbie and when he was carrying her down the stairs, he tripped and fell and broke her arm. That Sam Stone is always getting into accidents and breaking things!"

When Sam finally came to the center, he stayed for two uneventful minutes, then left. Later, on four different occasions over a ten-week period, both groups of children were asked what had happened during his visit.

Those who had heard nothing about Sam beforehand were simply asked to describe what happened in as much detail as possible. Then, a month after the last interview, the children spoke with a new interviewer who asked whether Sam had done anything to a teddy bear or a book. He hadn't, of course, and most of the children correctly noted this. Only 10 percent of the youngest ones mistakenly said he had, but when gently challenged, most returned to the true version of events.

On the other hand, children who heard stories about Sam's clumsiness were asked on four different occasions, "Remember that time Sam Stone visited your classroom and spilled chocolate on that white teddy bear? Did he do it on purpose or was it an accident?" and "When Sam Stone ripped that book, was he being silly or was he angry?" By the last session, about three-quarters of these children were claiming that Sam had committed misdeeds. The figure dropped when they were asked whether they had actually seen him hurt a bear or a book. Still, one child in five continued insisting having seen Sam damage playthings, even when challenged by the interviewers.[49] Transcripts of interviews with children in ritual-abuse cases are typically filled with detailed stereotypical inducements of the accused by interviewers.

Young children are also sensitive to the superior status and power of adults, and studies have shown that simply by altering an interviewer's apparent prestige level—by putting him in a police uniform, for instance—children are more likely to change their answer to conform with what they think they are supposed to say. In real-world abuse cases where their parents are being accused, children often understand that the people who interview them will influence who cares for them and where they will live. In day-care scenarios, mothers and fathers join law-enforcement officials in pressuring disclosures. Their authority is often more powerful to the child than any policeman's.

A child's superiors are not the only people capable of inducing false accusations. Since the work of Binet at the turn of the century, studies have shown that children will also change their answers to agree with their friends' experience, even when the response is clearly wrong.[50] A recent study of students whose elementary school was attacked by a sniper found many of the children reporting vivid recollections of seeing their friends shot. But the "witnesses" had been nowhere near the scene of the attack.[51] In ritual-abuse cases, as previously mentioned, interviewers frequently introduce peer pressure into their questioning. Byron and Billy Kniffen, for instance, did not accuse their parents until each was told that the other had already disclosed being sexually abused by them.

Babes in Toyland

Another technique used in virtually every ritual-abuse case was anatomically detailed dolls, with genitalia, breasts, and pubic hair. Advocates of the dolls believe they allow children to reenact the abuse and thereby trigger additional memories and disclosures. They also think the dolls help alleviate shame and shyness. Too, even if a child says nothing while playing with the dolls, sexual abuse is supposedly suggested if she avoids them, seems anxious when they are undressed, or demonstrates "unusual" interest in their genitals.[52]

But what constitutes "unusual" is largely speculation, since data about what normal, nonabused children do with anatomically detailed toys are sketchy and hard to interpret.[53] A study seeking to demonstrate that experienced professionals could accurately assess whether a child had been sexually abused from videotapes of doll play instead showed that not only were these professionals wrong more often than not, but they frequently disagreed with one another about the meaning of what they saw.[54]

What does seem clear is that dolls with breasts and genitals encourage some children to play in ways that many adults would consider sexual. Recent studies suggest that preschoolers will grab a pretend penis simply because it is there to grab, and put a finger into a doll's vagina in much the same spirit as when they explore the hole of any hollow toy. In the context of a criminal investigation, such "disclosures" could prove explosive, particularly considering what other research findings show: that dolls do not help small children talk about embarrassing things.

All this was demonstrated in a recent study by Ceci and Bruck in which forty three-year-olds visited their pediatrician for an annual checkup. Half the children got an examination in which the doctor touched their buttocks and genitals. The other half were not touched. Immediately after the exam, the interviewer pointed to the genitalia or buttocks of an anatomically detailed doll and asked, "Did the doctor touch you here?" Of those children who did not have the exam, half incorrectly said he had, and when given dolls, even more depicted touching. Meanwhile, fewer than half the children who did get the exam mentioned being touched. And when asked to demonstrate with the dolls, their accuracy plummeted—partly because several girls stuck their fingers into the dolls' anuses and vaginas.

The researchers in this study noted other behaviors that ritual-abuse case investigators would consider evidence of sexual abuse. When the children were given a stethoscope and asked to show what the doctor did with it, some demonstrated that he used it on genitals. When shown a spoon and asked if the doctor had used it, several wrongly stated that he had, to give them medicine. Then, when asked, "How might he use this spoon?" one child in five stuck it into the dolls' vagina or anus, and some even hit the genitals.[55]

Ceci and Bruck also videotaped the pediatric exam of a presumably nonabused preschooler who correctly told an interviewer immediately afterward that the doctor had not touched her genitals or buttocks. When shown a regular doll and asked to describe how she had been examined, she again answered appropriately. But three days later, when given an anatomically detailed doll, she put a stick into its vagina and said this happened to her at the doctor's. When pressed, she retracted her story, but when the process was repeated three days later, she again inserted the stick— this time hammering it—and then put a toy earscope into the doll's anus.

When asked whether this really happened, the child said, "Yes, it did." Her father and the experimenter demurred. "Your doctor doesn't do those things to little girls," they said. "You were just fooling. We know he didn't do those things." Nevertheless, the little girl clung tenaciously to a tale that adults would most likely interpret as horrific sexual abuse.[56]

Anatomically detailed dolls are not the only tools that investigators and therapists have used inappropriately during investigations. Children's artwork has also been exploited by child-protection workers unaware that it should never be used to make forensic determinations. One procedure frequently implicated in this malpractice is the Draw-A-Person test, in which the person being examined is asked to make a picture of a human figure. The drawing is then evaluated by the tester to determine the examinee's emotional state. This is done by searching pictures for features that supposedly reflect the artists' feelings. Drawing small figures, for instance, is said to reveal inferiority. Using mainly the left side of the paper shows impulsiveness. Leaving out arms signifies guilt or depression. And, according to literature on one test that was published in the 1950s, "when the sexual characteristics of the figures are confused and inconsistent, sexual problems and maladjustment are indicated."[57]

The problem with the Draw-A-Person test and similar exercises is that, despite their immense popularity among therapists, they are completely useless for reliably diagnosing emotions and should never be employed to assess whether a person has experienced a crime such as sexual abuse. As one expert in psychological testing has noted about the drawing tests, "administration and scoring instructions are vague and inconsistent, norms for interpretation are unclear and nonsystematic, statistical data to support clinical observations are sparse, and objectivity in scoring is minimal."[58]

These facts about the tests' unreliability have been known since the late 1970s.[59] Even so, in 1980 the National Center on Child Abuse and Neglect began promoting the use of Draw-A-Person and similar tests to diagnose sexual abuse in children.[60] Shortly afterward, Ann Burgess—author of the Rape Trauma Syndrome and promoter of the concept of the sex ring—published work encouraging psychiatric workers to examine children's drawings for indications of abuse.[61] Elaborating on this work, Boston pediatric nurse Susan Kelley claimed that "[n]urses can also identify suspected cases of child sexual abuse by recognizing characteristics unique to these children's drawings."[62] The telltale features, according to Kelley, are: shaded genital and chest areas, missing hands or arms, emphasis on the upper body, the mouth rendered too large, and—reflecting outdated, sexist ideas about how people should look—"elaborate jewelry on males, or male and female figures with little or no difference in their sizes, shapes, clothing or details."[63]

In many ritual-abuse investigations and prosecutions, therapists and police have used Draw-A-Person procedures and interpretations as evidence that children were victimized. In the Kelly Michaels case, a preschooler's crayoned picture of himself with a red scribble near the legs—done months before the case even surfaced—was later interpreted by a therapist as his depiction of bloody abuse inflicted by Michaels. Her guilt was also said to be evident in children's self-portraits that lacked hands, a feature cited by clinicians in other cases, too, as evidence that abuse occurred.

Besides using drawings and anatomically detailed dolls to diagnose abuse, child-protection workers have also used play therapy, which is also completely unreliable as a diagnostic tool. A model for this malpractice is supplied by psychotherapist Catherine Gould, in an article about how to find evidence of satanic victimization in young patients. All children, Gould writes, should be checked for behavioral signs of ritual abuse, even if they are asymptomatic. To accomplish this, they should be given playthings such as string, toy airplanes, monsters, police cars, masks, costumes, and weapons; and provided with a tray filled with sand, in which they can play out "themes of burial, caves, tunnels, basements, dirtiness and hiddenness." It is hard to imagine what children could do with these materials except enact scenes that—to adults, at least—include mayhem and violence. And once they construct these dioramas, Gould interprets them as indicative of the death, mutilation, bondage, cannibalism, burial, and magic characteristic of ritual abuse.[64]

Gould's theories are illustrated in a 1989 training videotape for child-protection professionals in which she and other therapists show how to diagnose ritual abuse using toys.[65] Another therapist, Catherine Graham-Costain, supplies a smiling toddler with tiny plastic animal and human figures, as well as with a toy electric food grinder. As the machine hums and buzzes, the little girl pushes its switch with obvious delight and shovels toys into it. "The kitty goes in the grinder with the fishies!" coos Graham-Costain, then she faces the camera and explains that this play is the child's reenactment of how humans and animals were pulverized and cannibalized during a ritual.

Amid criminal investigations, other therapists have reached similar conclusions. In one ritual-abuse trial, a social worker testified that a little boy claimed his daycare teacher had slaughtered rabbits, an elephant, and a giraffe. He made these charges after staging a battle between toy dinosaurs in the social worker's sandbox, prompting her to ask whether his the teacher had "hurt animals."[66] Other similar disclosures occurred after therapists have exposed children to *Don't Make Me Go Back, Mommy: A Child's Book About Satanic Ritual Abuse*, a book with large print and colorful illustrations of preschoolers being spirited to a countryside satanic ritual by their robed and hooded teachers. *Don't Make Me Go Back, Mommy* is available not just in therapists' offices but also in the children's section of many public libraries. For therapists wishing to supplement the book, there is also the *Child Exploitation Series*, a package of similar drawings marketed with instructions to use them, flashcard-style, on suspected abuse victims.[67] Critics of the use of toys, drawings, and dolls to diagnose abuse point out that people who employ them are quite likely to project their own mental processes onto the interviewee. Indeed, as with the autistic students and their facilitators, children's false memories in sex-abuse cases seem to emanate from one basic source: the thoughts and perceptions of the adults who are trying to help them speak. Studies have shown that interviewers given erroneous information about an event will elicit the same incorrect material from children, despite all exhortations to avoid suggestion and leading questions. This phenomenon is called the "expectation effect," and it pervades all kinds of human behavior, from visual perception to scientific research. It is a problem that can never be entirely avoided, but careful interviewers try to be as aware of it as possible so they can control for it.

Yet no such caution is discernible in the records of ritual-abuse case investigations. In fact, in one such case, an ad hoc piece of research exists that successfully bypassed all the ethical caveats about making guinea pigs of children. Dr. Barbara Snow is a Utah psychologist whom Roland Summit has called one of the "vital, scientifically objective new generation" of sex-abuse professionals.[68] In the late 1980s, several cases that Snow investigated evolved into large-scale ritual scenarios in which children described pornography making and abuse by dozens of adults.

Utah police eventually became suspicious of the carbon-copy similarity of Snow's cases, so they decided to do an experiment: They invented allegations and fed them to Snow. The allegations soon appeared in the statements of children she questioned.[69]

We do not know what happened to the children Snow interviewed, but more conventional studies suggest that they may well have integrated her suggestions into their memories, then woven reality and fantasy into a seamless web of recall that they may never successfully untangle. This is often what happens with false memories: they may be embellished with vivid details and with emotions so convincing that most adults would swear the child experienced a real event.

In the Sam Stone experiment, for instance, many children who described Sam damaging toys embroidered a wealth of detail into their made-up stories. One claimed that Sam took a teddy bear into the bathroom, soaked it with hot water, then smeared it with a crayon. Another said there was more than one Sam Stone. Another saw him go to a corner store to buy chocolate ice cream. Videotapes of children telling these stories were shown to some thousand professionals who conduct research, provide therapy for sex-abuse victims, and do investigative interviews. As they watched the tapes, most were sure they knew which children's accounts were accurate and which were not. But when Ceci and his colleague reviewed these professionals' assessments, the majority had guessed wrong. In fact, their ability to distinguish truth from falsehood would have improved if they had simply flipped a coin.[70]

Although much work on children's suggestibility remains inconclusive, experts now generally recognize that even preschoolers can give accurate information if interviewed properly. If they are pressed with insistent, misleading, and directive questions, however, they will likely give false information that can seem convincingly true. Virtually every researcher agrees that the techniques documented in ritual-abuse cases such as Wee Care generate completely unreliable testimony.

In an amicus brief to the New Jersey Supreme Court, several dozen prominent North American cognitive psychologists concluded that the way the children in that case were questioned was so overwhelmingly suggestive that all of their statements about sex abuse must be considered unreliable. The psychologists found it "difficult to believe that adults charged with the care and protection of young children would be allowed to use the vocabulary that they used in these interviews, that they would be allowed to interact with the children in such sexually explicit ways, or that they would be allowed to bully and frighten their child witnesses in such a shocking manner."[71]

Indeed, they concluded, the techniques officials and therapists in ritual-abuse investigations had used to pry open children's "windows of disclosure" constituted another form of child abuse, a psychological one.

EIGHT

Confessions

During the Salem witch trials, dozens of people admitted to being witches, including Tituba, the West Indian slave who was the first to be named by the accusing girls (see chapter 7). None of those who confessed were killed, or even brought to trial. But twenty defendants who steadfastly denied being servants of Satan were killed, by hanging or being slowly crushed with rocks.[1]

Nearly three hundred years later, Kern County officials arrested Gina Miller, a twenty-five-year-old single mother of three who was eight months' pregnant, and charged her with dozens of counts of child pornography making and ritualistic sex abuse. Miller had initially been lumped with six other Pitts case defendants because of a mistaken identification: when she was brought into court, most of the child witnesses did not even recognize her. Because she was considered the least culpable of the defendants, her lawyer began negotiating for a plea bargain.

Just before trial, presecutors offered Miller immunity from all criminal charges, as well as money, custody of her young children, a new name, and a new life in a witness-protection program if she would confess and testify against her co-defendants. Adamantly proclaiming her innocence, Miller refused the deal, and in the spring of 1985, she was tried, convicted, and sentenced to 405 years in prison—several decades more than what the defendants thought to be the ringleaders received.[2]

Besides Miller, the same thing had happened to the McCuans, the Kniffens, the Dills, the Pitts, and other Kern County "ring" defendants who insisted they were not guilty. The fate of all these people was not lost on defendants in unresolved cases. Defendants in the Cox and Wong cases agreed not to fight the charges, in return for dismissal of all but one count and sentences of probation or minimal prison time. In July 1986, six defendants in the Weatherly-LeCaine cases each pleaded no contest to one count each of child abuse in return for dismissal of dozens of other charges.

A plea of no contest means that the accused does not admit guilt, but does agree that there was a factual basis for the charge. As he went through the legal procedures to make his plea, defendant Allen LeCaine explained that "the reason I'm taking this deal is I feel this case is bogus and that I feel that at this time I could not get a fair hearing. I have seen too many people railroaded, and I feel that this has been a witchhunt, and this is probably a good point and a wise point to step out."[3]

LeCaine's sentiments are a modern formulation of the explanation Reformation-era German Jews gave to a sixteenth-century religion scholar, Andreas Osiander, who doubted claims that Jews ritually slaughtered Christian children, yet puzzled over why they often confessed when accused. The reason, Osiander was told, was simple:

> When a Jew is being tortured, it doesn't matter whether he speaks the truth or not because his tormenters would not stop until they have heard what they want to hear. It is enough for us that God will punish our tormenters and that every reasonable man may judge for himself whether such confessions are lies or truths.[4]

Confessions have always been the most expedient way of solving crimes. They eliminate the expense and difficulty of investigation, and they ease the intolerable anxiety that infects a community when a notorious wrongdoing remains unprosecuted. They have been ardently sought after in ritual-abuse cases, where the lack of material evidence and adult witnesses invariably threatens successful prosecution.

Physical Coercion

Many accused witches of the Middle Ages believed that since they were innocent, God would see them through their ordeal. But the thumbscrew, the Spanish boot (which broke the shinbone into pieces), the *gresillon* (which crushed the tips of the fingers and toes in a vice), the *strappado* (a pulley that suddenly jerked the body in midair), the rack, and the witch chair (a seat of spikes heated from below)—these instruments and others reliably extracted statements that the suspects' interrogators wished to hear. Hugh Trevor-Roper notes that none of these was as effective as the *tormentum insomniae,* or sleep deprivation.[5] And in an atmosphere permeated with torture, women confessed to flying off on broomsticks to midnight *sabbats* before any torture was applied.[6]

Inquisitorial procedures that focused entirely on the suspect became the law of every land in Europe except England, where the process of compulsion came to share the odium attached to the ecclesiastical courts that relied on it—the Star Chamber and High Commission. The English elite believed in witches as strongly as their brethren on the Continent did, but charged, tried, and convicted far fewer people.[7] This discrepancy flows from England's comparative reluctance to use torture to obtain confessions and accusations.

Confessions were integral to witch trials, and today they remain the lifeblood of the criminal justice system in the United States. Currently, with more than 90 percent of felony cases in this country disposed of by guilty pleas that in effect are confessions, the administration of punishment would collapse if very many defendants exercised their right to a jury trial. While this fact gives the accused person a modicum of leverage, criminal codes are structured so that prosecutors routinely "overcharge": they indict a suspect with more crimes than they actually think he or she committed, or with counts that investigation has not produced sufficient evidence to pin convincingly onto the defendant. Even so, there is always the chance that a judge or jury will convict, because of solid evidence showing that the accused did something bad, whether or not it meshes nicely with the formal charges. During plea bargaining, this threat puts the state in a superior position as the prosecutor promises to throw out some charges, or even all of them, if the defendant will only confess to others or give evidence against fellow suspects.

But what happens when agreements aren't reached? In the United States in the nineteenth century and well into the twentieth, suspects were often brutally beaten in order to extract confessions. The difference between that era and the sixteenth century, though, was that rather than proudly displaying their instruments of torture, American police concealed their beatings by using more furtive tools such as the rubber hose.

In 1928 Herbert Hoover appointed what came to be known as the Wickersham Commission. Following an extensive investigation, the commission released a review of use of the "Third Degree"[8] by police in every part of the United States. Delivered to Hoover in 1931, the report documented examples of brutality from every part of the country, and of tag-team interrogators persisting hour after hour, depriving suspects of sleep by uninterrupted questioning. The report was a meticulously assembled collection of data demonstrating that police use of extreme physical and mental coercion was pandemic in station houses across the United States.[9]

Shortly after the Wickersham report became public, the U.S. Supreme Court handed down the first reversal of a state conviction obtained via a coerced confession. The Arkansas deputy sheriff who had presided over the beating of the defendants conceded that one had been whipped, but "not too much for a Negro; not as much as I would have done if it were left to me."[10] A series of Supreme Court cases soon followed that reversed convictions based on brutally coerced confessions, even though the statements obtained were quite credible and not contradicted by other evidence. Following this judicial rejection of the Third Degree, police gradually ceased the routine practice of beating suspects during interrogations.

Psychological Coercion I: Police Interrogation Manuals

By the 1950s, the rubber hose had been replaced by police interrogation manuals as the route to a confession. In describing how to question suspects in custody, these texts accepted a ban on physical force, but in its place they offered sophisticated techniques of influence and psychological coercion. According a leading manual of the day, "the interrogator's task is somewhat akin to that of a hunter stalking his game. Each must patiently maneuver himself into a position from which the desired objective may be attained."[11] Such successful maneuvering could be achieved, according to the book, by conducting interrogations in private and extending them for several hours if necessary. The suspect should not be permitted to talk to a lawyer or family member, and should not be taken before a judge until questioning was finished. Also recommended was that no record of the questioning be made, so that any dispute about what really occurred could be resolved only by a swearing contest between the defendant and the police—a contest that the defendant was almost guaranteed to lose. Amid all this, prisoners were not to be told they had the constitutional right to remain silent. Nor should they be routinely informed of the crime they were charged with.

Methods for interrogation included displaying "an air of confidence in the subject's guilt" and sternly refusing to let him "indulge in repeated denials."[12] The use of pretended sympathy was recommended, along with other sentimental appeals to the suspect's emotions. The manual encouraged interrogators to stress that they already knew the prisoner was guilty, even if they did not. Two ways to do this were offered: the bluff, where the interrogator claimed that a co-defendant had already confessed and implicated the prisoner; and the false claim that physical evidence existed when it didn't.

Interrogators were also taught to belittle and blame the crime victim, to minimize the seriousness of the offense, to offer justifications for it, and to suggest that the accuser exaggerated the accusation. Prisoners should be berated for lying, and they should be accused of additional, trumped-up crimes. Another helpful technique was to get very close, physically, and use "nonviolent" contact, such as securing the suspect's knees between the interrogator's legs; holding the chin and staring into the eyes; and clasping fidgeting hands and twitching shoulders in order to "bottle up" expressions of nervousness.[13] These stratagems will produce confessions from the guilty, but they are so discouraging, humiliating, and disorienting that they can also induce admissions of guilt from the innocent. This is particularly so if interrogations go on for several hours, or if a suspect is not familiar with the ways of the police.[14]

Excerpts from these interrogation manuals made up a good portion of the briefing in *Miranda v. Arizona* (1966), and they were cited extensively by the Supreme Court in its decision that before the police question suspects, they must read them the "Miranda warning," informing them of their right to remain silent and to secure a lawyer's assistance.[15] As these principles became common knowledge, police and prosecutors realized that in many investigations, getting enough evidence for a conviction was going to be harder than in pre-Miranda days. As a result, interrogators began developing new ways to produce confessions, methods that are more subtle than the older ones, but no less insidious.

After Miranda: Ritual Abuse and the Jailhouse Snitch

The systematic use of jailhouse informants, or "snitches," has a long history in America. It also has a unique history: in no other criminal justice system in the world is the judge or jury so routinely presented with vicarious confessions supposedly offered by defendants to people they never met before being jailed—and whom they would have every reason to distrust and certainly no reason to confide in about anything. Throughout the United States, snitches have become a regular part of major criminal trials.

In the Kelly Michaels ritual-abuse trial in New Jersey, a jail inmate, Charlene Munn, testified that Michaels had made admissions of guilt. According to Michaels, when she was isolated in the protective-custody wing of the Essex County Jail women's annex in June 1987, Munn was working as a messenger and inmate representative on Michaels's jail wing. At the time, she was charged with first-degree murder; she had shot in the back a thief who had made off with her jacket. Once in jail, Munn was allowed to move about freely and chat with inmates, some of whom would routinely shout that she must be a snitch. Michaels, who had been instructed by her lawyers not to talk with anyone in jail, says she was so lonely that she did not heed their orders. She remembers how Munn would "camp out in front of my cell and ask me all about my case." Instead of maintaining her silence, Michaels responded to Munn: "I told her that I had no idea what was going on, that I was completely innocent, saying what I always said, and she was very sympathetic, asking me what I wanted. She even offered to bring me a Bible."[16]

After Michaels made bail, Munn wrote her a letter vowing "I'll always believe your very innocence, regardless of who may disown you." Yet shortly afterward, Munn told prosecutors that she had heard Michaels talking to herself, saying over and over, "I didn't mean to harm those kids the way I did," and that "her and her old man made love in the car." Munn assumed that the "old man" was Michaels's father, which added fuel to the prosecutors' otherwise baseless contention that Michaels must be an incest victim and therefore predisposed to abusing children. When she testified against Michaels in 1988, Munn had just pled guilty to manslaughter and was awaiting her sentence. The prosecution, she said, had promised her "cooperation."[17]

Jailhouse snitches also made appearances in several of the sex-ring trials in the Bakersfield, California, area.[18] But no jurisdiction in that state—or probably anywhere else, for that matter—ever engineered the production of vicarious "confessions" as systematically and lavishly as did Los Angeles County. The institutionalized snitch system that developed there in the 1980s swelled to gargantuan proportions, with Module 1700 of the Bauchet Los Angeles Jail evolving into an evidence factory that ground out "confessions" in virtually every major criminal case of the era. In this factory, the foremen were sheriff's deputies who classified, reclassified, and transferred inmates in order to increase their production. The line workers were a handful of police detectives, district attorney investigators, and their crew of several dozen snitches. The task of these men, whose numbers were augmented by occasional one-shot "temporaries," was to testify in court—after coaching from the district attorney's office—that the defendant had confessed to the charges.

Snitches learned the appropriate text of these confessions by impersonating law-enforcement officers on the telephone; by reviewing police and coroner's reports; by listening to the detectives who interviewed them; and by gleaning information from friends, relatives, and the media. The defendant might even provide an opening unwittingly, by telling the snitch what the charges against him were. Experienced snitches did not even have to wait for such conversation to happen by chance: if an inmate was housed in another part of the jail, they could schedule court appearances that placed them on the same bus with the accused (a striking number of Los Angeles County "confessions," in fact, were said to have been confided during bus rides).[19]

In the biggest, most notorious cases, several snitches would audition for the role of the concerned informant coming forward to tell the truth for the good of the community. To prepare for these sessions, snitches both cooperated and squabbled with one another, forming a production team in which one snitch acquired information on a case, then relayed it to another, who spread it to others, and finally each would present his own version of the "confession" to the police. Detectives presided over these tryouts, evaluating each snitch's presentation for sincerity and delivery, and correcting it when the details contradicted official knowledge of the case.[20]

The lucky snitch chosen to testify in court would be rewarded with cash, leniency in sentencing, and a reserve of credit for future misconduct that amounted to a license to rape and rob. Informants who were discredited by overexposure ended up in the "undesirable snitch" file in the Los Angeles County district attorney's office, but it was always possible for good workers to change their names and reappear as virgin informants with no criminal past.[21]

The institutionalized snitch system steadily metastasized through the 1980s until one of the most notorious of its workers betrayed it. In late 1988, inmate Leslie White showed the Los Angeles sheriff's office how he could fabricate a detailed confession of someone he had never even met, by adroit use of the jail tier telephone.[22] A few months later, after White repeated the procedure for *60 Minutes* from a hotel room, a scandal flared that led to an exhaustive investigation by the Los Angeles County grand jury.[23]

One of the many steps the grand jury took in investigating the snitch system was to order district attorney's office personnel to explain exactly how they had used snitches in particular cases. Prosecutors generally complied, but Deputy District Attorney Lael Rubin did not; she wrote back to say she was too busy.[24] Indeed, she was preoccupied, for at the time she was trying Ray and Peggy Buckey in the McMartin case. And in the process, she had used a snitch.

The prosecutors of the Buckeys and of the other five McMartin defendants had been stymied in their efforts to obtain a confession and guilty plea from even one defendant in return for testimony against the others. "There was no question that the first one to turn would have been given the moon," notes Glenn Stevens, one of three assistant district attorneys initially assigned to the case. Their hopes centered on Betty Raidor, a sixty-seven-year-old teacher whose involvement in the putative crimes was said to be the most peripheral. Raidor was represented by Arthur Urban, an attorney with a reputation for plea bargaining when he thought it advantageous for his client. When the prosecution made a generous offer, Urban consulted his client, but returned to say, "She just doesn't know anything."[25]

Charges against Raidor and four other women were ultimately dropped. Ray Buckey's attorney, meanwhile, hoped to win an acquittal, and from the beginning he warned Buckey not to discuss the case with anyone. Thus, the only confession the prosecution could hope for would have to be snitch-induced; and indeed, several informants were eagerly waiting in the wings for the job.

On March 23, 1984, Buckey was indicted and booked without bail into the hospital section of the county jail. Three days later, he was moved from a one-man cell to a room for two men, where he was placed with veteran snitch George Homer Freeman. Freeman was a hulking six-footer with the well-buffed muscles of a convict who did little besides lift weights. Within hours, Freeman told the sheriff's deputy who was in charge of placing informants near high-profile defendants that Ray Buckey had talked about his involvement in the "Manhattan Beach preschool child molesting case." Two days later, Freeman met with a sergeant who was the snitch liaison. According to the sergeant's report dated mid-April, Buckey had told Freeman all about child molesting, incest, cult worship, and pornography making.[26] Freeman was released from jail on April 6, after serving less than a year on a robbery charge. Within two months, he was breakfasting with television reporters and telling them that he had posed as a child molester to gain Buckey's confidence, and that he wished to go public now because as a father himself, he was outraged that anyone would do such things to children.[27]

Freeman had a slew of previous felony convictions, including armed robbery, and he had perjured himself in court by relaying phony confessions.[28] Nevertheless, if he testified against Ray Buckey, the prosecution was prepared to give Freeman a new identity, a job, and monthly rent payments. This was not the first time he had prepared false testimony in exchange for his freedom, nor did Freeman think it would be his last. In essence, he was owned by the Los Angeles district attorney's office, since in 1979 he had been charged with rape and murder but never tried.[29] Because murder has no statute of limitations, Freeman knew that he could be tried and convicted if he stopped cooperating with the state snitch enterprise. Thus he was ready to testify on cue against Buckey at the preliminary hearing.

But the prosecution did not place all its McMartin eggs in George Freeman's basket. In June 1986, Buckey was moved to Module 1700 of the Bauchet jail, where several men who later would become Southern California's most notorious snitches buzzed with excitement at his arrival. Within weeks, a blizzard of notes, memos, and taped interviews revealed that seven snitches were charging one another with inappropriate efforts to snitch, or claiming that Buckey had confessed. They talked of child sex trafficking, pornographic filmmaking, and a kiddie prostitution network enjoyed by prominent Los Angeles businessmen. According to one inmate, Israel Issac, Buckey confided that his prosecution would be hindered by clients of the prostitution service, as well as by prominent actors, who, if the child victims fingered them, would take revenge calculated to "tear . . . the fabric of our society in Los Angeles and its neighboring cities." Issac added that Buckey admitted to burning children in order to frighten them into silence.[30] Less florid was inmate Leslie White, who reportedly offered that he heard Buckey say, "What I did, I did."[31]

None of these snitches made the cut. At trial, the chosen one was Freeman. He appeared for the prosecution in late 1987, and at the end of his direct examination, the prosecution revealed that Freeman had admitted to one prior instance of perjury. Then he disappeared, and the judge ordered him arrested. Captured and back in court again, Freeman acknowledged lying at Ray Buckey's preliminary hearing. He admitted that he had committed perjury on countless occasions and that the state often had helped him avoid jail. When Freeman said that he told his lies to help his family, defense lawyer Danny Davis asked him if he meant his mother and sister? "Yes," Freeman answered. "And isn't it true," Davis continued, "that in 1983 you tied up your mother and sister and robbed them and burglarized their home?" Freeman's work in the Buckey case was finished.[32] He stepped down from the witness stand, returned to the streets, and next month was arrested for robbing a woman at gunpoint.[33]

Psychological Coercion II: Mind Control

In the post-Miranda period, confessions produced by snitches are often powerful prosecution tools. But for jurors to take such evidence seriously, they must discount the fact that the sources of these damning statements are often felons, career perjurers, or at best, accused criminals whose word upstanding citizens may find difficult to believe. In the long run, a confession is far more credible when it comes not from a third party but from the suspect's own mouth. Miranda has not changed this. But it has encouraged the development of new forms of manipulation, some of which are extremely coercive, even though at first they might not appear to be.

One of these is investigative hypnosis. In the 1970s, the practice of putting suspects and witnesses into trance became widespread in the United States, until research made it clear that hypnotized subjects would conform their memories about a crime—and ultimately their testimony—to the hypnotists' perceptions, even when those perceptions were inaccurate. It soon became evident that confessions evoked under hypnosis could also be false. Eventually, evidence produced through trance was limited or excluded entirely from courts.[34]

But at the same time that hypnosis was being discredited as a forensic tool, interrogators were developing techniques that did not put a suspect into trance but still challenged the integrity of memory. Known as "guided imagery," "visualization," and "relaxation," these procedures have become familiar to many people who have tried to stop smoking, lose weight, or simply calm down after a stressful day at work. With their soothing injunctions to "close your eyes . . . empty your mind . . . imagine yourself in a beautiful, peaceful place," visualization, relaxation, and guided imagery exercises have lately become staple patter in the offices of psychologists and massage therapists and at countless self-improvement seminars. Such routines feel calming and benign, but many practitioners are not aware that they can cause people to become extremely suggestible, even make them enter trances. In fact, many psychological researchers now believe that individuals who undergo the procedures are as likely to embrace false memories as are people who have been formally hypnotized.[35] Given this possibility, it is noteworthy that—aside from no contest and guilty pleas for minimal prison time or no time at all by people who usually specified that they were doing so under duress—only two of the hundreds of people charged with ritual-abuse crimes have confessed, and their statements were elicited when they apparently were absorbed in guided imagery, visualization, and relaxation states.

One of these cases is that of Paul Ingram, an Olympia, Washington, sheriff's deputy officer whose two daughters suddenly "remembered" that for years, Ingram had been raping them in satanic cult rituals. The daughters developed these memories in 1988 after one of them attended a women's retreat sponsored by the fundamentalist Christian church the Ingram family belonged to. When first arrested and told of his daughters' accusations, Paul Ingram said he had absolutely no memory of committing the crimes. Yet he did not deny them; he told police that his daughters loved him, so if they were saying these things about him, they must be true. Further, as a law-enforcement officer exposed to the latest theories about sexual assault and its effects, Ingram was familiar with the claim that victims might "repress" such crimes from memory, and that perpetrators could, too.

As Ingram sat alone in his jail cell, he became insomniac, confused, and anxious. Meanwhile, interrogators repeatedly suggested to him that he had a devil in him and that he did not remember ritually abusing his daughters because he was afflicted with multiple personalities. Ingram underwent trancelike prayer sessions, as well as relaxation and visualization exercises in which he was instructed to meditate on the crimes and to try to recall the details. Soon he was remembering sadistic sexual assaults and a satanic cult of which he was a member.

Prosecutors then called in Richard Ofshe, a specialist in cult behavior, to help them investigate Ingram's occult group. But when Ofshe examined the record of the interrogations, he began to suspect that Ingram's confessions were false. He tested his theory by ordering Ingram to meditate on a crime, one that Ofshe had invented. When Ingram then "remembered" this particular act, Ofshe was convinced that his other memories—and thus his confession—were delusionary. By the time Ofshe prepared a report with his findings, Ingram had pled guilty to lesser charges of rape. He was convicted and imprisoned.[36]

The other ritual-abuse "confession" was that of Ileana Fuster, the young Honduran woman who was accused of sexual abuse after a three-year-old in the Miami suburb of Country Walk commented to his mother that "Ileana kisses all the babies' bodies." The child's statement may well have been a description of common caretaker behavior toward small children in some Latino cultures (see chapter 6). But the case snowballed when investigators discovered that Ileana's husband, Frank, had pleaded guilty to manslaughter years earlier and had recently been convicted of lewd assault after being charged with fondling the clothed breast of a nine-year-old relative late one night after a party.

Within a few weeks after the investigation against both the Fusters started, dozens of children were accusing the couple of bizarre and violent acts of ritual molestation. Miami-area head prosecutor Janet Reno, who was preparing to campaign in a hotly contested reelection, promised to do "everything humanly possible to see that justice is done" in the Fuster case—that is, obtain the couple's convictions.[37] There were the usual evidentiary problems, however, including the fact that Joseph and Laurie Braga, whom Reno appointed as child interviewers, used patently leading, deceptive, and coercive questioning methods to elicit the Country Walk allegations.

Amid doubts sown by the Bragas' poor techniques, Ileana's confession to the same things the children were charging cinched the prosecution's case. The details she supplied in the depositions in which she admitted her guilt are the foundation on which many descriptions of ritual abuse are constructed,[38] and her confession is cited as rock-hard proof that children's accounts of ritual abuse are reliable, even when obtained during flawed interviews.[39] A closer look at how the confession was obtained, however, shows that this "rock" more closely resembles clay that was shaped and fired by both the prosecution and Ileana's own lawyer, using the newest techniques of persuasion together with methods that facilitated confessions by accused witches centuries ago.[40]

Ileana Fuster was seventeen years old when she was arrested. In August 1984, she was placed in solitary confinement in the Dade County jail. Her cell was small, bare, and lit twenty-four hours a day. She would remain there for six months. In October, the state attorney's office offered to reduce Ileana's sentence drastically if she would turn state's evidence. The offer was formalized in the spring, but Ileana refused.[41]

During all this time, defense investigator Stephen Dinerstein visited both the Fusters in jail. According to him, Ileana was not in good condition. Isolation terrified and depressed her. She told him that she was not being fed regularly or given medical attention when she requested it. She and Frank both complained that their calls to each other were unduly restricted, their mail undelivered, and their communication with their attorneys insufficient. To Dinerstein, she looked anxious and emaciated.[42] Ileana had no appetite, could not rest, and was taking medications to help her sleep.[43]

Still, she would not confess to any wrongdoing, and her intransigence was becoming as tricky for the defense attorneys, Michael Von Zamft and Jeffrey Samek, as it was for the state. Von Zamft in particular was having troubles: the case was so notorious and the Fusters so vilified in the media that he was losing clients and being ostracized in the community simply for defending them. In addition, state senator Roberta Fox, a child-protection advocate closely tied to parents in the Country Walk case, attacked Von Zamft's qualifications to become head of a new, multimillion-dollar state program to provide death row inmates appellate attorneys, citing his connection to the Fusters. It was a job he coveted.[44] Pressures on Von Zamft apparently were becoming unbearable. How could he simultaneously fulfill his job as the Fusters' attorney and relinquish his role as defender of child sex-offender pariahs?

He resolved the dilemma by, in effect, becoming one of Frank Fuster's prosecutors. In April 1985, he and Samek decided a conflict existed in their joint representation of the defendants. Next month, the couple's defense was legally separated. Von Zamft chose Ileana as his client. Samek was left with Frank.[45]

Von Zamft then began crafting his strategy: to admit that Ileana was indeed a perpetrator, but only because she herself was a child victim—of her husband. She would have to testify that even though she and Frank both abused the children, she only did it because Frank forced her. Logically, the way to elicit such testimony from Ileana would be to cast her in the role of a battered wife.

In fact, evidence did emerge that Frank had hit Ileana. Shirley Blando was a chaplain in the women's jail where Ileana was detained during 1984 and 1985. In a deposition given during that time, Blando stated that she often talked with Ileana; the two became so close that Ileana called her "mom Shirley."[46] Sometime after her defense was separated from Frank's, Ileana was confronted with the statements of some Country Walk parents that they had seen her with a black eye. She then admitted to Blando that Frank had hit her.[47]

But she denied that he did this more than once; and according to Blando, the denials were consistent. In fact, Ileana wrote Frank love letters almost every day and regularly told Blando that he was "a loving husband; that he was good, and that there were no problems."[48]

On the other hand, according to Blando, Ileana often confided that

she did not trust her lawyer . . . she was afraid of her lawyer. . . . She would say: "They want me to say something that is not true." . . . She thought that about the District Attorney. She thought that about the lawyers for both of them. She thought that everybody wanted her to say: "I saw my husband do these things," and it was the thing everybody wanted from her.[49]

But Blando said Ileana insisted that she could not "say things that are not true."[50]

In March 1985, to Ileana's great excitement and relief, she was moved to an "open pod," one of six cells from which the inmates could freely move into a day-room, watch television, and visit with each other. A few weeks later, however, close to the time her case was separated from Frank's, she was returned to isolation. According to Blando, it was extremely traumatic for her.[51] Dinerstein said: "She couldn't take that. . . . When I would visit her, the fact that she was in isolation would be half the conversation. She really had it tough."[52]

By summer, she was locked up again by herself and separated from Frank for almost the same length of time that she had been married to him. During this time, she began changing her story about her one-time black eye and claiming that Frank had hit her often. Then she began refusing his mail and stopped calling him. Soon she was claiming that before they were married, Frank "forced" her to have sex—though what she meant by "forced" is unclear, since she said he had not touched her or threatened her to make her submit.[53] She also said that Frank hit and slapped his son. Now, according to Ileana, Frank Fuster was a wife and child batterer. Yet she continued to insist that no sexual abuse of any kind had ever occurred at their baby-sitting service.

In further attempts to elicit information for plea-bargaining negotiations, prominent Miami psychiatrist Charles Mutter was called in by both prosecutors and defense attorney Von Zamft. Mutter, who has evaluated witnesses and defendants in numerous Florida criminal cases, has since said that Ileana's "was a very unusual case." His involvement in it was "the first time in my life I was ever called by both the state and the defense" to evaluate the same person. Mutter conducted at least fourteen sessions with Ileana, but in none of them did she ever admit that she or Frank had sexually abused children.[54]

The psychiatrist considered various methods by which he might prompt Ileana to reveal the truth. He told her that a lie detector test had found deception when she answered that she had neither seen nor been aware of Frank molesting children. Ileana replied that the test might have registered a lie because when asked the question, she thought about a child who once had been scared by a Halloween mask belonging to Frank's son.[55]

Mutter concluded that Ileana did not have any amnesia or memory disturbance. Instead, he thought that if Frank really had molested children, Ileana was denying it—either because she didn't know about it or because she was afraid of her husband. Mutter apparently believed the latter. He felt that Ileana fit the profile of a battering victim rather than a sex offender.[56]

In mid-July, Dinerstein visited Ileana again. At the time of her arrest she had looked well nourished and stylishly groomed, with long, shiny hair and clear skin.

Now she appeared to be suffering from massive weight loss, her hair was matted, her body smelled, she had sores and infections on her skin, and she was clothed in a housedress that looked many sizes too large.[57]

"Over the period of incarceration," Dinerstein wrote years later in an affidavit, Ileana had "changed from a 17-year-old somewhat quiet small little scared girl to a constantly crying shaking tormented person who understands little if anything about the whole process and is now being threatened and promised and is totally now in a state of confusion to the point of not having the slightest idea as to month and date." Dinerstein told Ileana's attorney about his client's condition, but Von Zamft said not to be concerned. He added that Ileana would be receiving intense psychological counseling, and instructed Dinerstein to make no more visits to her.[58]

It was now almost a year after the investigation had begun, and Ileana continued to insist on her and her husband's innocence. "I would tend to believe her," said Blando during a deposition she gave on August 1.[59] Assistant State's Attorney John Hogan asked Blando what the chances were that Ileana "would ever take the stand and say: 'Frank abused the children, and I did not say anything because I was afraid of him.'" "There is nothing to indicate to me that she would do that, . . . " Blando answered, "because her feeling and belief is that she did not see him do those things . . . she will only testify to what she sees as being true."[60]

Another psychologist who had examined Ileana in late July had concluded that her basic functioning was that of "an extremely needy child" who "would have come under the domination of Francisco Fuster while living with him" and "done things that she would normally not done [sic] if he demanded it of her." According to the psychologist, he himself could "get her to respond in any way that I pushed her."[61] Von Zamft told Ileana that the trial date was coming up, and she needed something to say. "I always say that I have nothing to say, that I was innocent," Ileana recalled recently. "He said that I needed to remember something . . . and I kept telling him no. And then he thought I had problems and that I should be seen by a psychologist."[62]

In a competency hearing on August 2, Von Zamft told the court that Ileana was so immature and dependent upon Frank that if she had to stand trial with him, she could not be expected to defend herself. "The only valid defense that counsel perceives in this case requires that this defendant be prepared to give testimony against the co-defendant," he said.[63] He then told the prosecution that by the time his client took the stand, she would be able to testify, since she had psychologists working with her—"to bring back her memory," as he later put it.[64]

Von Zamft was basing his defense on "memory" that wasn't yet "back," on a confession that so far did not exist. A trial was scheduled in less than a month, and if he wanted to avoid it, he would have to produce a guilty plea fast. He did.

In an interview with the authors several years later, Von Zamft reported that after calling in Dr. Mutter to examine Ileana, and after determining that she still was "unable to say anything clearly," he contacted Miami psychologists Michael Rappaport and his partner, Merry Sue Haber, who ran a business called Behavior Changers.[65] Rappaport and Haber visited Ileana in her isolation cell at least thirty-five times and possibly forty. In an interview with the authors in 1991, Rappaport said that while he was working with Ileana, she was also visited by Janet Reno.[66] Reno later denied making visits prior to Ileana's guilty plea;[67] Von Zamft has said that he doesn't know whether she did or not. (It is now impossible to check Reno's claims against old visitor sign-in logs at the Women's Detention Center, because they are discarded every five years.) And Rappaport refuses to elaborate.

But he has not been hesitant in recounting what went on during his and Haber's sessions with Ileana. He describes doing "relaxation" and "visualization" exercises with her, while constantly telling her that there was "a deal being made" and that if she confessed she would be sentenced lightly, but if she pleaded innocent and was convicted, she would get life in prison. "It's a lot like reverse brainwashing," according to Rappaport. "We just spent hours and hours talking to her. . . . It's kind of a manipulation. It was very much like dealing with a child. You make them feel very happy, then segue into the hard things." Ileana's confession, he says, finally "started flowing out and she would say little bits of things and we'd stop." He describes the process as "almost like a hypnotic thing."[68]

According to Ileana, the psychologists said she could not remember the crimes because she was suffering from "blackouts." They were there to help, they said, and they began to visit her every day, even at night and on weekends. Ileana remembers being wakened for these sessions, but being so disoriented that she did not know whether it was daytime or nighttime. Her mother came to see her during this period; Ileana did not recognize her.[69]

Rappaport and Haber read Ileana excerpts of what the children were telling prosecution-appointed interviewers Joseph and Laurie Braga, who were using grossly leading and suggestive questioning techniques on the preschoolers. Over and over, the psychologists told Ileana the horrible things the children were saying. When she still could not remember any of them, they instructed her in how to recall her former home in Country Walk and how to visualize sex crimes there: "before going to bed . . . I was supposed to close my eyes and I was supposed to think of the house. And I was supposed to be standing in front of the door. And that I was afraid to open it, and I was supposed to open the door, and I was supposed to see what was happening. And before I know it I would fall asleep."[70]

It was then that Ileana began having nightmares about the same things Rappaport and Haber were telling her, "about games and stuff happening in the house."

The nightmares, they said, meant that their treatment was starting to work. Ileana's dreams were the way she was starting to remember the crimes.

They also warned her that she would grow into an old woman in jail and remain there until she died if she could not remember. Then they reminded her how it was to be free. Investigators from the district attorney's office twice took Ileana to upscale restaurants, where she dined on expensive Spanish food while they asked whether she missed such pleasures.[71]

At first, said Ileana, she argued with the psychologists when they told her that her nightmares were her system's way of recalling what had happened: Why can't I remember? she asked. Gradually, though, she came to believe that the crimes were so shocking that she had repressed them from consciousness to protect herself.[72]

As the sessions continued, the psychologists told her to think about bad times with Frank, and to tell them about her nightmares. She would close her eyes, trying to picture the house. If she was unable to visualize the subject matter mentioned by Rappaport and Haber, "[T]hey would get mad." They told her she had to dream about the crimes in order to help the children; and that her testimony must exactly match what the youngsters were saying. Eventually, whatever the therapists suggested, "I would dream about it, even if it took two, three days later, it was true, I would dream exactly the same things. And I started to believe it that they really happened." But Ileana still had no conscious memories.[73]

Finally, on August 21, she stated during a polygraph test that she and Frank had molested children. Next day she pleaded guilty to several counts of sexual abuse. But the speech she made in court that day was hardly a definitive admission. "Judge," she said,

> I would like you to know that I am pleading guilty not because I feel guilty, but because I think—I think it's the best interest . . . for my own interest and for the children and for the court and all the people that are working on the case. But I am not pleading guilty because I feel guilty. . . . I am innocent of all those charges. I wouldn't have done anything to harm any children. I have never done anything in my life. . . . I am innocent. I am just doing it—I am pleading guilty to get all of this over. . . . For my own good.[74]

Ileana then gave a series of "confession" depositions that gradually evolved into full-blown descriptions of ritual sex abuse. She developed these statements while sitting between psychologist Rappaport, who often hugged her, and Dade County chief prosecutor Reno, who held her hand.[75] Frequently, when Ileana couldn't answer a question because she did not remember, Rappaport would intervene. In one typical exchange, when asked to describe an incident of abuse, Ileana answered, "I couldn't do it. I don't recall." Rappaport interrupted, insisting that "it's not that you can't recall; it's that you don't want to recall." "Oh," Ileana answered. "They don't understand," Rappaport continued, "I understand you better than they do."[76]

When she said she couldn't remember, Rappaport often would request and receive "breaks" in which he and Ileana would retire for several minutes in private. They would then return to the proceedings and Ileana would supply an answer. For example, once she was asked to describe Frank assaulting her. She could not supply details. Rappaport asked for a recess so she could "put her thoughts together." On returning, Ileana remembered a "tool thing," or "crowbar," that Frank put "around" her vagina.[77]

When she emerged from other breaks with Rappaport, she claimed to have just recovered memories of Frank wanting to be diapered, forcing his son to perform fellatio, kissing a five-year-old boy, and making Ileana kiss the five-year-old's penis. Ileana continually generated new testimony alleging extraordinary events, for example: "He took me from my hands and my feet and he threw me in the shower in our bedroom and he turned the water on. I just remember today."[78] One of her charges against Frank was that he had put snakes inside her and the children's genitals. The testimony was developed as she was asked to elaborate about Frank's abuse. "Well, I remember a snake," she answered. "What about a snake?" asked a lawyer. "Having bad dreams about it," she replied.[79]

Before her trial testimony against Frank, the psychologists again met with her and repeated what her testimony should be, "because they didn't want me to make no mistakes, they said."[80] Frank Fuster was convicted and sentenced to six life terms and 165 years in prison. Prosecution officials agreed that he probably would not have been convicted without Ileana's confession and her testimony against him. As for Ileana, she served 3½ years in a juvenile prison program and was then released and deported to Honduras. Her education has since been financed by Honduras-based associates of a Florida church that befriended her while she was in prison and who have since attempted to keep the U.S. media from contacting her.[81] In 1994, she recanted her confession in a sixty-one-page sworn deposition, and described the yearlong ordeal of isolation and intensive interrogation that produced it. This document became part of legal proceedings seeking to overturn Frank Fuster's conviction. In response, the prosecution argued that Ileana's statement could not be used in court unless she returned to the United States, where she could be tried for perjury. Shortly after the court ruled against the prosecution, the church minister traveled to Honduras and returned with a one-page general retraction of the recantation, apparently drafted by him, that was signed by both him and Ileana.[82] At this writing, investigation and Frank Fuster's appeal continue.

As for Country Walk prosecutor Janet Reno, during Senate hearings to consider her nomination for the Clinton administration's attorney general, numerous supporters cited her concern for children and their welfare. Country Walk was never mentioned. Neither was another ritual-abuse case she prosecuted, one that surfaced in 1989 within a few blocks of the Fusters' old home. Fourteen-year-old Bobby Fijnje ultimately was acquitted, but only after being tried for sadistically assaulting several children at the church his family attended. As with Country Walk, Bobby's case was characterized by a prosecutorial mania to extract a confession. He was a diabetic, and only after he was detained, deprived of food, and made to suffer the first throes of insulin shock did he agree with the police that he had touched a preschooler. As soon as he was released from questioning, he retracted his confession. But as the charges spread to other children and became increasingly bizarre, Reno ordered Bobby separated from his family and jailed in a juvenile facility. The child needed to be isolated, she said, because his parents were probably satanist pornographers and that was why he was afraid to talk about his own abuse.[83]

Years after Reno prosecuted the Country Walk and Fijnje cases, one of her first actions as attorney general was her intervention into the Waco, Texas, confrontation between federal agents and David Koresh's Branch Davidians. After a weeks-long standoff, Reno seized on FBI claims that the Branch Davidian compound needed to be invaded because the group was engaged in systematic and ongoing child sexual abuse during the standoff. The information turned out to be unfounded, but instead of checking it, Reno ordered her agents into the compound with tanks and chemicals. The attack apparently provoked mass suicide among the Branch Davidians; as a result, entire families perished by gunshot and conflagration. Amid the national soul searching and congressional probes that followed, there was only the barest mention of Reno's history of seeming obsession with child sex abuse—an obsession that, in Miami as in Waco, ended with children themselves being severely damaged and even destroyed in the name of protecting them.

In Florida, after all, Reno cast Ileana Fuster as, simultaneously, an adult who committed crimes and a child who by any means necessary must be made to disclose the wrongs done to her. With Ileana, with Bobby Fijnje, and with the preschoolers who said they were mortified by them, we see how the authorities use the same methods to evoke false accusations as they do to win false confessions. Accused and accusers become both victims of the investigative process and victimizers of each other. It is a strange, harlequin role in which the idea of cannibalization comes to mind. Such images fit well with the masks, clowns, magic, and sadism of the ritual-abuse tale. Indeed, the people who construct these cases added their own details—real ones—to the myth.

NINE

The Medical Evidence

A crucial part of ritual-abuse prosecutions in the 1980s involved testimony from doctors who examined young children and then appeared in court to tell juries that new theories and high-technology instruments had detected evidence of molestation. In case after case, physicians bared, stretched, and measured anuses and vaginas, took high-magnification photographs, projected the images onto giant courtroom screens, and testified about the smoking gun: hitherto unobserved physical signs that comprised hard evidence of sexual abuse. With the help of such testimony, young children's sketchy, contradictory stories were clothed with a mantle of objectivity that helped sway uncertain jurors. As a result, hundreds of people in the United States were convicted. Only later would scientific research reveal that the new "signs" of abuse were found as often in nonabused children as in victims.

The Search for Devil's Marks

Using health-care workers to gather evidence of Satan's crimes has a long tradition in America. In the colonies during the era of the Salem trials, one way to identify a witch was to conduct an expert search of her body. Evidence of her guilt consisted of "Devil's marks," which one authority described as "some big or little Teat" on the suspect's body, often in a secret place, where the Devil had left suck marks and other signs, including blue or red spots, wounds that resembled flea bites, or depressions where the flesh looked "sunk in and hollow."[1]

It is no accident that these signs were found on the intimate parts of females. Though the genitals of both sexes are generally covered up in Western culture, those belonging to women connote hiddenness and sin even more than men's. Our language reflects this: as a woman stands disrobed, her pubic area, the only visible part of her genitals, is called the *pudendum*, from the Latin *pudere*, "to be ashamed." The sex organs themselves were seldom closely observed even by physicians or midwives during colonial times. With the intense secrecy ascribed to the area, women's genitals were an understandable focus for experts as they searched for signs of the Devil's machinations.

They found them with regularity. In the first colonial witchcraft trial, of a woman in Charlestown in 1648, John Winthrop noted that an examination of her body uncovered "an apparent teat in her secret parts . . . and another began on the opposite side." A defendant in Connecticut had a strange growth similar "in shape to a dogs eare." And in Salem, accused witch Rebecca Nurse was tainted with "a preternatural excressense of flesh between ye pudendum and Anus" that the searchers noted was very similar to a teat, and "not usual in women."[2]

Rebecca, who was seventy-one years old and had borne eight children, begged for a second opinion, on the grounds that the oldest and wisest of the nine women who searched her the first time "found nothing in or about yoer Honor's poare pettissioner But what might Arise from a Naturall cause."[3] Another examination was ordered. It was done by the same women as before, but this time they were surprised to find that instead of the excrescense noted before, now Rebecca's genitals were blemished by nothing more damning than a spot of "dry skin." The jurors initially refused to convict Rebecca, but finally did so only after the judges ordered them to reconsider. The defendant was hanged.[4]

Three centuries after Salem, Rebecca Nurse is remembered as a martyr to community hysteria. Gynecology has made doctors familiar with how women's genitals actually look: with their occasional excrescenses and other minor anomalies that come from age, childbirth, or simply from having been born that way. Today, Devil's marks are deemed a bizarre historical footnote, and to imagine that a class of criminals—even sex criminals—could be identified by how their genitals look seems ludicrous. But in the early 1980s, another search for Satan's signs began. Now, though, it was not the demonic perpetrators who were scrutinized. Instead, it was the bodies of their innocent, silent child victims.

Dr. McCann's Work

At an early-morning workshop at the San Diego Children's Hospital's annual conference on child maltreatment in 1988, conference director Dr. David Chadwick stood before an international gathering of doctors and health-care workers and introduced a very special speaker. "For the last five or six years," Chadwick told his audience, "everyone has been saying, 'Why doesn't someone look at normals?'" He was referring to children's genitals, and he answered his question by presenting Dr. John McCann.[5]

McCann is a prematurely gray-haired, avuncular-looking pediatrics professor at the University of California's San Francisco School of Medicine who also works at a large Fresno hospital. When he took the podium in San Diego, he had just spent four years photographing the anuses and vaginas of hundreds of young children who presumably were not sex-abuse victims, then cataloging the results. Now he was here to talk about his findings.

He began his presentation by describing how he and his colleagues had designed the study. To gather a nonabused group of subjects, the Fresno hospital had advertised that local children could get free physicals for school or summer camp by participating in some research. No mention was made of sex abuse, but when families showed up at the hospital, the parents were told the exam would include a careful check for it. At that point several withdrew, but ultimately some three hundred boys and girls remained.

McCann described how they lay in frog-leg and knee-chest positions to reveal their genitals, how they were photographed, and what the exams revealed. On the young subjects' anuses, for instance, his team had found redness (particularly on babies still in diapers), dark spots (especially on Asians and Hispanics), and little tags of tissue near the opening. And the researchers were surprised when they noticed something else: after the children had spent a few minutes in their awkward examination positions, the anuses of almost half began opening and closing, or "winking," as McCann called it.

Then there were the girls' hymens. The hymen is a thin membrane that covers the vagina, and in a child who is not sexually experienced, it almost always has a small opening. But for several years, doctors who worked in child protection had been wondering exactly what size opening was normal. And if it was bigger, did that mean sexual abuse had taken place? Now McCann had some answers. Hymenal orifice size, he found, depends on several variables. They include how old a girl is, how relaxed she is during the exam, and whether she lies on her back or her stomach. Based on these factors, a hymen can change size even during the same exam. He also pointed out that not every girl has a gossamer-thin, circular hymen. His subjects had a variety of shapes, and some even had rolled edges, bumps, bands, and tags of tissue.

At first all this variation shocked the researchers. As he and his colleague looked at hundreds of photographs of ordinary children, McCann told his audience, "We kept saying, 'Oh my God, that's bizarre, that can't be. . . . It took us three years," he quipped dryly, "before we found a 'normal.'"[6]

No one laughed. And as McCann continued his presentation, he half-expected the audience to gasp, as he had earlier, "Oh my God!" That would have been a natural response from people who for the past five years had been telling police, prosecutors, and juries that children had been chronically molested—based on signs McCann was now saying were perfectly ordinary.[7]

During the 1986 El Paso trial of Michelle Noble, for instance, a doctor had testified that three-year-old Patti had been "ruptured" from sexual penetration. The evidence? Her hymen had a "shredded" edge. Yet now McCann was reporting that just such a frayed-looking edge showed up on some of his girls who presumably had never been abused. And he noted that during the research exams, almost half his nonabused children's anuses "winked." This was the same sign that led to guilty verdicts against several adults in Bakersfield after juries heard a prominent doctor's testimony that the such winks were a result of molestation.

Searching for Evidence

How many other physicians in other cities had sent defendants to prison based on signs that McCann was now saying meant nothing? Was the child sex-abuse medical evidence of the 1980s only wild inference and pseudoscience? If so, where had it come from?

Certainly not from malfeasance. Like the interviewing techniques their social worker and therapist colleagues were using, these physicians' hymenal micromeasures, anal winks, and classification of tiny skin tags constituted a brand new field of knowledge that rushed to fill a vacuum. By the late 1970s, mandatory reporting laws and a sharpened cultural and legal focus on sex abuse meant that doctors were treating more and more victims for injuries, venereal diseases, and pregnancy. Physicians were also gathering evidence for use in criminal prosecutions, but for most of them, forensic work was novel and puzzling. Until then, they had seldom looked closely at children's genitals, and when they did, it was usually to check for the signs of acute rape: fresh tears, bruises, and bleeding, or ripped, sodomized anuses. Because the assaults that produced this kind of trauma generally involved struggle, the child's body often bore additional injuries. On the lips or in the mouth there might be broken blood vessels from being gagged, on the throat choke marks, on the ankles rope burns, on the thighs scratches or bite marks. In the most extreme cases, the victim might be dead from battering or strangulation, leaving the physician with horrifying yet unequivocal evidence: a corpse.

Incest cases, however, concern long-term molestation by family or friends—abuse that usually escalates gradually, progressing from touching or kissing to genital or anal contact, without forceful penetration. In 1983, Roland Summit's Child Sex Abuse Accommodation Syndrome canonized what by then was already widely known among child-protection workers: that children who suffer this kind of crime are often reluctant to talk about it, and by the time they do, months or years may have passed since the last assault. By then, the semen, bruising, and blood are long gone.

Until quite recently, if any evidence at all remained, it was typically met with institutionalized disbelief. A 1950 textbook on communicable diseases assured readers that little girls could contract gonorrhea from towels and toilet seats, or by merely sleeping in the same bed with an infected adult.[8] A popular obstetrics and gynecology book from the same period taught physicians that if they found gonorrhea-infected pus on a child's genitals, this did not necessarily indicate sexual assault. Instead, they should suspect malevolent mothers, since the pus "may have been put there, with blood and scratches, for purposes of deception."[9] Yet another book offered a more scientific-sounding, and prurient, rationale: "Little girls are remarkably susceptible to gonorrheal vulvovaginitis. The external genitalia at this age are soft and succulent and devoid of hair. . . . Although it is believed that transmission of the infection is always by direct contact, many cases occur despite every precaution."[10]

By the 1980s, as part of the new climate of concern about sexual abuse, epidemiological research had debunked the toilet-seat theory of girls and gonorrhea. It had also put emergency room doctors and pediatricians in the unprecedented position of being asked to identify legal evidence based on microorganisms and anatomy that most knew little about. For these doctors, bleeding and tearing were clear and convincing evidence of trauma. But in incest cases they seldom found anything like this, and in ritual-abuse scenarios there was even less to see. The truth in these cases was elusive. No one wanted to buttress a false accusation, but no one wanted to overlook an actual assault either. Among investigators and prosecutors, there was a yearning to find a foolproof way of resolving competing versions of reality—something akin to the Battered Child Syndrome.

The Battered Child Syndrome focused on the hard evidence of physical abuse—multiple fractured bones at different stages of healing, for example—evidence that, until radiology became widely available, had lain deep within the body, invisible and undetectable. But with the advent of X rays and knowledgeable physicians to interpret them, the secret of domestic physical abuse was revealed and the child could be protected. All it took was technology, combined with sensitive and specially trained medical personnel.

But even health workers accustomed to identifying fractures had seldom examined the genitals of children, and they certainly had not studied them in medical school. Thus, the only model they had to refer to was the typical visitor to the gynecologist's office: the grown woman. This was a problem, because by cultural definition, a woman's private parts are supposed to mirror her sexual experience. Consider, for example, the adult hymen. Often it looks wider on one side than the other, or it may have narrow, irregular or ragged edges. Its tissues are frequently thickened and folded, with the labia richly pigmented and darker than the surrounding skin. Some of these features appear to be effects of sex play and coitus. Others, though, have nothing to do with sexual intercourse, stemming instead from hygienic practices or from mild infections.

A thick hymen may also result from the fact that when a girl matures, increased production of hormones such as estrogen enlarge her genital tissues as they swell her breasts.[11] Color is related at least partly to overall complexion and ethnicity: darker people tend to have darker genitals. And the hymen can be shaped several ways and still be quite normal. It can resemble a doughnut or a horseshoe. It may have one opening, two, three, or in rare cases none at all. It can be thin and smooth, thick, notched, folded, or frilly.[12]

Anatomical theory explains this difference: the less useful a feature is biologically, the more it varies from individual to individual. The hymen apparently follows this rule. It serves no discernible function; instead, it seems to form from the fusing of the embryo's two halves during gestation, constituting a sort of afterthought at the midline, exactly like the raphe—the wiggly line that bisects every man's scrotal sack.[13] The hymen does have one use, but it is cultural rather than biological. Named for the Greek god of marriage, it has long served to mark virginity, but it actually does not even do that job very well. Contrary to popular belief, it does not burst during first intercourse, much less disappear. In fact, many a woman who has been sexually active for years retains all or part of it, particularly when her hymen was relatively flexible to begin with or when sex partners have entered her gently. Nevertheless, in medical folklore, the "deflowered" adult hymen, with its unsightly bumps, spots, and thickenings, is contrasted to the romanticized virginal tissue, which is supposed to be undamaged and thus perfect: gossamer-thin, crisp-edged, with a sharp, circular opening.

The idea of the perfect virginal hymen persisted even among a group of Southern California doctors who began meeting in the early 1980s to compare notes on what constituted physical evidence of sexual abuse. At these gatherings, led by San

Diego Children's Hospital's Dr. David Chadwick, the doctors brought medical histories of their child patients, along with color photographs and slides of their genitals. The group then compared the accusations with the pictures and tried to correlate children's stories with their body signs. Chadwick remembers spirited arguments about whether a girl's oddly shaped hymen was normal or whether it indicated molestation. Discussions sometimes would go on for hours, until someone finally called for a wrap-up. At that point, an election would be held, with doctors raising their hands to vote for "normal," "abnormal" or "don't know."[14]

But the use of consensus to define what constitutes forensic medical evidence is unscientific; essentially it is no more advanced than the practice followed by physicians of the Middle Ages in deciding the best place on the body to apply leeches. Science requires not democratic consensus but controlled studies. Such research conducted to determine normal genital anatomy in children would include two things. First, several doctors. Second, two groups of children: one in which every member is known to have suffered abuse, and the other made up of girls and boys no one suspects of having been molested. Without knowing who was in which group, each doctor would check each child's genitals and document anything that looked abnormal. Their findings would then be tabulated, and the resulting statistics would indicate which signs correlated strongly with abused children, versus which showed up frequently in both the nonabused and abused groups. In court, expert witnesses would review these percentages. They would then leave it to judges and juries to decide whether the likelihood of abuse was high enough to warrant a conviction.

Without such studies, it is impossible to say with scientific confidence that any physical sign is the result of a sexual act—particularly when the features observed are so-called traumas so tiny that they are invisible without a microscope. In the early 1980s, though, when it came to researching sexual molestation, normative descriptions and controlled studies were more easily proposed than accomplished. This was true partly because it was hard to obtain funding and staff, and even harder to gather a large group of nonabused children whose parents would let doctor after doctor examine their genitals. Consequently, as abuse cases flooded courtrooms and doctors' offices, physicians had to make do with subjective observations, anecdotes, and votes such as those taken at the San Diego meetings.

Their only other resources were articles just starting to appear in medical journals. The authors of some of these called their work studies, but in fact they were much more reflective of a prosecutorial than a research mentality. This was predictable, given that the first doctors to examine regularly children for sexual assault were not academics and researchers. They were front-line child-protection people who worked with law-enforcement authorities and got their funding from them.

Sodomy, Virginity, and the Magnifying Machine

One such physician was Bruce Woodling. He was a young family practitioner who had finished medical school at the University of Southern California in 1972, then did a residency in obstetrics and gynecology. During his tenure in this specialty, Woodling demonstrated great interest in minutely studying, with chemical assays and microscopic examinations, abnormalities in the placenta—the organ the pregnant female body develops to nourish the fetus. When he was not doing this research, Woodling was diagnosing and treating many women and children who had been sexually assaulted. Later, he moved to a family practice residency at the county hospital in Ventura, just north of Los Angeles.

He had not been there long when he was approached by the district attorney, who could not find doctors willing to examine rape victims—much less children—because they did not want to be bothered with going to court to testify at trials. Woodling took on the work, and soon he was doing all the county's sexual-assault and child-molestation exams. He would do them on call, sometimes in the middle of the night, and his fees were very low. He believed in the moral significance of his work. By 1975, he was directing a program funded by the district attorney's office to teach area doctors how to diagnose child molestation.

Within a few years Woodling was considered an expert in sexual-abuse forensics, not just locally but statewide. The Southern California doctors began bringing him to San Diego to advise their consensus sessions, and Woodling in turn busied himself with resolving his profession's dilemma: how to find signs of sexual violation when the abuse was chronic and insidious rather than acute and violent. In theory, this was an admirable preoccupation. In practice, though, Woodling's alliance with prosecutors rather than scientists propelled him back to a school of thought that was riddled as much with patriarchal hostilities toward homosexuals and women as it was graced with concern for children.[15]

Woodling inherited this attitude from nineteenth-century forensic medicine, most notably the work of French doctor Ambroise Auguste Tardieu. In his critique of Freud's abandonment of the seduction theory, *The Assault on Truth*, Jeffrey Masson—a former psychoanalyst and currently the fiancé of feminist antipornography activist Catharine MacKinnon—lauds Tardieu as the first physician to describe the "full range of abuses that adults, most often parents, inflict on young and helpless children."[16]

In his book, the *Étude médico-légale sur les attentats aux moures* (*The Medico-Legal Study of Assaults Against Decency*), first published in 1858, Tardieu focused on the prevalence of sexual assaults against children, mostly young girls.[17] Tardieu's interest in these cases was part of a larger political agenda that sought to describe—

and, in so doing, to proscribe—all transgressions of sexual convention. He was one of the premier nineteenth-century taxonomists of deviance. Additionally, Tardieu and his followers were deeply suspicious of any behavior in men that seemed feminine, such as homosexuality. According to Arno Karlen, a modern historian of homosexuality, Tardieu spent much effort trying to determine "whether the disgusting breed of pederasts could be physically identified for courts."[18] In searching for evidence to facilitate such identifications, he had certain precedents to draw on— the belief many of his contemporaries held, for instance, that the appearance of the rectum was changed by frequent acts of sodomy.

In Tardieu's *Medico-Legal Study*, he discussed "more than two hundred cases of sodomy" that he had examined "for purposes of legal proof."[19] He suggested that the sodomist's rectum lacked certain skin folds found in normal men, but this was not necessarily due to sexual acts—in homosexuals, the absence of folds could also be congenital. There were other signs: the passive homosexual's rectum was "funnel shaped," and the penis of the active pederast "slender, undeveloped . . . with a small glans, tapering from root to tip like a dog's."[20] The *Medico-Legal Study* became so popular among medical practitioners that by 1878 it had been reprinted six times, and the signs of sodomy were passed down to generations of physicians.

Another belief also survived the nineteenth century—that when a patient is prepared for a rectal examination, if his anus spontaneously opens, this means he is accustomed to being sodomized. By the 1970s, this "sign" of homosexuality had been discredited, but belief in its reliability persisted, even among physicians sympathetic to gay men. One of these doctors was a San Francisco–area proctologist whom Karlen described as "a guru" to the staff of *Ramparts*, a popular, nationally circulated leftist magazine published in the Bay Area. When Karlen asked the doctor about Tardieuian signs such as the funnel-shaped anus, the physician shrugged them off. He did believe, though, that in homosexual men "the rectal canal will dilate if the anus is touched . . . the whole lower canal opens up immediately."[21]

During medical school, Bruce Woodling had heard these same anecdotes about the dilated rectum as a sign of sodomy in gay males.[22] Now, in Ventura County almost a decade later, he decided to check for its presence in another population: young boys and girls. During exams, he began separating their buttocks and touching a spot near the rectum with a cotton swab. If the anus opened, Woodling took this to be proof of sodomy. He dubbed his procedure the "anal wink test," and in 1981, in the prestigious medical journal *Pediatric Clinics of North America*, he published an article recommending that it be used to check for sexual abuse in children. His co-author was not a doctor but an assistant from the district attorney's office.[23]

The same year Woodling's recommendations were published, the *American Journal of Forensic Medicine and Pathology* published an article by Wilmes Teixeira, the chief medical examiner in São Paulo, Brazil, instructing colleagues how to do virginity checks on girls and women.[24] In Brazil, such determinations were legally important, since a rapist could be prosecuted only if his victim was sexually inexperienced, and a groom could annul a marriage if he found out that his bride had lovers before him.[25] In his article, Teixeira reported that he had checked the genitals of hundreds of females with a specialized new instrument, the colposcope. Originally developed to diagnose cervical cancer, the colposcope is a kind of binoculars that magnifies up to thirty times and attaches to a film or video camera. If an accused wife denied indiscretions before her marriage, he attempted to distinguish the fresh irritations inflicted by her husband's penis from other infinitesimal woundings that might have been wrought by a former boyfriend. In working for the state, the São Paulo medical examiner's office also gathered evidence for rape and child-molestation investigations. Now, without consulting any colleagues, Teixeira combined these with his virginity cases, wrote up his observations, and concluded that the colposcope helped clarify his findings.[26]

Teixeira's work was no more scientific than Tardieu's nineteenth-century musings about French perverts. But in 1983, when Woodling read it for the first time, he was so impressed that he acquired a colposcope and began using it to examine children. Immediately, he saw things on their genitals that he had never seen before: tiny abrasions, minuscule blood vessels, and little bands of tissue running inside and outside vaginas. There were fine lines, almost invisible bumps, and subtle light and dark spots on the genital and rectal area. Woodling honored these features with medical terminology. The abrasions, for instance, he labeled *microtraumas*— wounds too small to see with the naked eye. The vaginal bands he called *synechiae*, a technical term for scar tissue.[27] Thus, through linguistic sleight of hand, these features became medically valid signs that a child had been hurt.

Woodling also read the findings of Hendrika Cantwell, published in 1983 in the journal *Child Abuse and Neglect*. A pediatrician in Denver, Cantwell had done a study purporting to show that the normal girl's hymenal opening measures no more than four millimeters, and that anything more suggested she was molested. Like the Brazilian work, Cantwell's was flawed. For one thing, her subjects were all homeless or had histories of abuse and neglect, and thus were hardly "normal." Further, the diameter of any orifice depends on the size of one's entire body.[28] Yet Cantwell's study neglected to list how old the girls were. Even so, many doctors accepted her claim that for every child, a hymenal opening larger than four millimeters signaled abuse. Others, like Woodling, thought the orifice could be somewhat bigger and still be normal, but they still assigned arbitrary measurements to gauge abuse.[29]

Woodling first applied his newfound expertise to ritual abuse during the investigation of the initial Bakersfield sex-ring case. This was the scandal that surfaced in

1982, when Alvin and Debbie McCuan and their friends Scott and Brenda Kniffen were accused of child abuse (see chapter 3).

In a recent affidavit, one of the children in the case, Tricia McCuan, remembers Woodling "telling me I had been molested," but when she denied it, he retorted: "This examination will tell who's right and who's wrong." He then told Tricia what he was about to do. By now, his standard exam involved rubbing the anus with swabs, inserting glass test tubes into the rectum, and taking photographs of the genitalia. Eight-year-old Tricia became distraught and wanted no part of it. But though she was embarrassed, frightened, and tearful, and begged not to be examined, Woodling insisted. When he finished, he told Tricia that he now had proof she had been molested, and so had her cousins and the Kniffen boys. Years later, Tricia remembers this encounter as "the worst thing that ever happened to me." Woodling, she says, violated her against her will.[30]

Woodling's testimony about his findings on the child witnesses played a major role in convicting their parents. He testified that Darla McCuan's hymen measured between five and ten millimeters, larger than the supposedly normal four. He also said her hymen had two synechiae and another scar visible only under the intense magnification of the colposcope. As for Darla's sister, Bobbie, her vagina gaped open and her hymen had "lost its shape." It was marred by several synechiae and a cut, and the opening measured fifteen millimeters. Bobbie's vagina also harbored an organism that was considered sexually transmitted, and her ano-rectal area showed "fissuring and thickening." As if all this were not enough, both girls had anally winked the doctor. The Kniffen brothers had, too, and according to Woodling, that by itself proved molestation.[31]

In response, the McCuans' attorney called Dr. David Paul, a British coroner who had for several years been warning his colleagues about the unreliability of the old Tardieuian signs. Paul debunked Woodling's new one as well. The anal wink, he said, was not evidence of penetration. Rather, it was a normal reaction to having an erogenous zone stimulated. Paul's testimony dramatically underscored how much one doctor's perceptions can differ radically from another's. When he looked at photographs of the McCuan girls' hymens, he did not see scars, as Woodling had. To Paul, Bobbie's hymen was not rounded, nor did her vagina gape, and her anal area was normal.[32]

Darla showed no evidence of any abnormality.[33] But Paul did agree with Woodling that Bobbie had some abnormalities on her hymen, suggesting that she had been fondled.[34] That opinion echoed early findings in the case, before it blew up into a ritual-abuse scandal. It had begun when Bobbie purportedly said that her step-grandfather had molested her. This was in 1980, before most doctors had ever heard of Woodling and his new evidence. Even so, a physician who examined Bobbie back then also noticed that her hymen was not intact. And Bobbie's mother, Debbie McCuan, admitted that when she was a teenager the same man had molested her. Paul's agreement with Woodling, therefore, and his concurrence with medical findings from years before, buttressed intimations of incest in the McCuan family and seriously weakened Alvin's and Debbie's protestations of innocence.

No such problems plagued Scott and Brenda Kniffen. Recall that they had not even been charged until after Scott agreed to testify about his friend Alvin McCuan's good character. The Kniffens were by all indications a happy family with no history of abuse, and the state was never able to find evidence to impeach their unwavering denials of guilt. For them, much more than for their co-defendants, the case boiled down to nothing more than a swearing match between them and their children.

But Woodling tipped the balance against the parents. He told the jury that when he stroked Byron Kniffen's anus, it gaped so wide that it could have accepted a fully erect penis. Billy revealed a similar opening, and Woodling testified that he had never seen this response in a nonabused subject. He simply had no explanation for it other than sodomy—even when a child had no history of abuse and there was no other evidence.[35] The wink test was infallible, Woodling said, and in this case it was damning.

The trial judge was impressed, calling Woodling's testimony "very persuasive."[36] The jury agreed. They voted guilty on 289 felony counts, and the defendants received a total of 1,000 years in prison, then the longest single-case sentence in California history. (Debbie McCuan got 252 years, the most ever given a woman.)

Woodling later went on to discredit witnesses for the defense in the Pitts trial (see chapter 5). But this time, instead of debunking adults, he impeached children. The case had started when a five-year-old boy was caught playing doctor with a girl at school. In typical Kern County fashion, that child and several others ended up accusing their relatives of orchestrating rapes, orgies, and pornography production. There was another group of Pitts children, though: two sisters who lived in the house where all these evil machinations were said to have regularly occurred. Yet the girls consistently denied that anything bad happened at their house. That meant that the case would materialize as yet another swearing match, this time between two teams of children.[37]

Just before the trial was set to start, in early 1985, the district attorney's office insisted that the sisters visit Woodling. As in Tricia McCuan's case, prosecutors told the doctor the details of the case before he saw the girls, and again, Woodling found marks on their bodies to buttress the charges: large hymenal orifices, scars, light-colored tissue near the vagina, skin tags on the anus. Again, Woodling diagnosed rape and sodomy in both children. At trial, he repeated his findings while the jury stared at his exhibits: jumbo photographs of the sisters' vaginas and rectums being pulled open by his fingers.[38]

Lawyers for the defendants had asked several doctors to counter Woodling at trial, but all declined. Some were unsure of their own opinions about hymenal size and microtrauma. Others privately condemned Woodling's theories as unscientific, but feared that by testifying for the defense, they would be seen by their colleagues and community as pro–sex abuse. Woodling's testimony thus prevailed over that of the two girls, and the Pitts and their co-defendants were convicted. For this work, the doctor was not nearly so charitable as he had been during his early days doing rape exams in Ventura County. Now he billed the State of California nearly $3,000 a day. He was paid in full.[39]

With the McMartin Preschool scandal, Woodling's theories gained national and international attention. McMartin had surfaced after Judy Johnson told Los Angeles–area authorities in the summer of 1983 that her two-year-old son said he was sodomized sodomized by teacher Ray Buckey. Like Mary Ann Barbour, the grandmother who started the satanic sex-ring case in Kern County, Johnson was later diagnosed as psychotic and paranoid. When she took her son to doctors, though, they were unaware of her mental problems and noted redness and possible fissures around her little boy's anus. The police were notified and the case snowballed.

In late 1983, the Los Angeles County district attorney's office began sending hundreds of McMartin students to a local diagnostic and treatment clinic, Children's Institute International (CII). There, some 200 were examined by pediatrician Astrid Heger, a former classmate of Bruce Woodling's at the University of Southern California's medical school. After graduating in 1972, Heger had spent several years working in pediatrics, but she almost never saw patients complaining of sexual assault. She was concerned about the issue, though, and kept in touch with Woodling, particularly since she was impressed with his reputation for doing rape exams. After she was recruited by CII in 1982, Heger contacted Woodling and asked him to teach her his methods with children.[40]

When the first McMartin students were brought to her, she had never used a colposcope and had done only about a dozen exams on chronically abused children.[41] Many of these had been done with Woodling supervising, and during Heger's first exam on a McMartin child, he was there with her, too. Thereafter, he returned intermittently and checked some children by himself. During the first year after she began seeing McMartin children, Heger had no one to compare her findings with but Woodling, since his office and CII were the only places in California—probably in the entire country—that were using colposcopes to check for abuse. On the basis of these exams, Heger concluded that four-fifths of the students had been sexually assaulted.[42]

Often she reached this conclusion after noting scars, bands, neovascularization, rolled hymenal edges, and large openings. But Heger also diagnosed abuse in children whom MacFarlane and her colleagues, based on interviews, had already decided were abused, but who showed no evidence, not even Woodling's signs. Heger found some boys to be normal, for instance, but she wrote in her reports that their negative findings were "consistent with history of sexual abuse."[43] In this she was following Woodling's warning that even if physicians found no signs, they should "never make a diagnosis 'No evidence of sexual abuse' . . . because if you make that conclusion, the case will never go forward."[44] This principle was a rephrasing of Tardieu, who advised his students that when investigating "assaults against morals," "[i]n cases where the examination is inconclusive, the physician should not be satisfied with pointing out negative signs when it is possible that the act took place without leaving traces; to be completely truthful it is necessary to indicate at least the possibility of the act [having taken place] even in the absence of positive signs."[45]

Doctors as Detectives, Medicine as Politics

The updated version of these old instructions infuriated advocates for defendants; they angrily noted that when doctors made findings like Heger's, all skepticism about the allegations ceased. Some protested that calling negative medical findings "consistent with history of abuse" bowdlerized the very concept of a medical history. The traditional meaning of the term implies that people visit doctors because they are sick or injured, and will do whatever is needed to get well. Under such circumstances, it was only logical to assume that patients tell doctors the truth about how they became wounded or ill. If the physician sees an abdominal scar, for instance, and the patient says it came from an appendectomy, no doctor will suspect that this is a lie and that the scar really came from some other operation. But children examined for sexual abuse are very seldom sick, much less physically injured. In such circumstances, a "history" is not part of an effort to get well. Instead, it is an element of a criminal investigation. Defendants and their lawyers could not understand why physicians refused to grasp this fact, or what that refusal implied for a sex-abuse case.

But neither did they understand that the California doctors were operating from their own logic. More than a century has passed since Tardieu advised his colleagues of the terrible frequency of child sexual abuse. Since then, consciousness of the problem had waned for generations. Now it was suddenly reviving, and American physicians like Heger and Woodling were passionately conscious of their power either to stifle this new awareness or to nurture it. But in many cases the doctors were only dimly aware of how the allegations presented to them had been produced in the first place. In the ritual-abuse cases, it was not children who first offered the abuse "histories"—it was adults speaking for them. But, like other professionals working closely with prosecutors, many doctors did not seem to understand this. As Heger put it, the role of the physician in a child-abuse exam was above all Hippocratic—"First, do no harm"—and she understood this mandate to mean that the physician must always and unfailingly advocate for the young patient against the abuser. This attitude sometimes induced doctors like Heger actually to encourage charges that they should have been merely reporting.[46]

For example, Heger believed that the women defendants accused in the McMartin case were innocent, and she once confided to one of the defendants that she was praying for her and that "angels are surrounding you, taking care of you."[47] On the other hand, Heger was convinced that Ray Buckey was guilty, and she manipulated at least one child's "history" to conform to her opinion. In one CII videotaped interview, Heger examines a girl who repeatedly denies being abused. Heger tells the child: "I don't want to hear any more 'no's. No, no! Detective Dog and we are going to figure this out. Every little boy and girl in the whole school got touched like that . . . and some of them were hurt. And some were afraid to tell. . . . And they were afraid to tell because they thought . . . Ray might come and hurt their parents or hurt them. . . . I think there's something to tell me about touching."[48]

It did not occur to Heger that her style might be coercive. Indeed, she was convinced that it was therapeutic and caring. In a 1986 CII videotape titled *Response: Child Sexual Abuse—A Medical View,* she reminds her fellow doctors that they seldom will find sexual abuse unless they are willing to entertain the possibility that it has occurred. Roland Summit also appears in the videotape to warn viewers that unless they can commit themselves 100 percent to their child patients' welfare, they should not be doing sexual-abuse exams at all. Amid these admonitions, the tape presents school-aged actors playing molestation victims while horror movie–style music plays in the background. Heger displays enlarged photographs of "normal" genitals. She instructs viewers that a young girl's hymen is smooth-edged and thin, and the illustration she displays has the precise circularity of a wedding band. Then she shows examples of "abuse": bumpy hymens, vulvas with white lines, and an anus surrounded by dark-colored skin.[49] The tape was sent free to journalists covering the McMartin case and marketed, for $195 a copy, to medical schools and sexual-abuse diagnostic facilities.[50]

The video was not the only way professionals learned Woodling's signs. At training sessions, he indoctrinated hundreds of doctors, many of whom worked in hospitals and clinics with contracts to examine alleged sexual-assault victims for police and district attorneys' offices. He also became increasingly influential in policy circles. By 1985, he was chairman of California's State Medical Protocol Committee, empowered to revise the sexual-abuse reporting form required in all of the state's emergency rooms. He was also on the child- and sexual-abuse task forces of the California Medical Association, the American Medical Association (AMA), the U.S. attorney general, and the surgeon general.[51]

Heger's career, too, took off dramatically. Before she examined the McMartin children, she had never testified as a child sex-abuse expert; afterward, she was deluged by requests to testify in court for prosecutors and to make media appearances. She also began traveling throughout California, the United States, and Canada to address sex-abuse congresses, give professional trainings, deliver lectures, and participate in committee reviews. In 1985, she became director of the Child Sexual Abuse Clinic at the Los Angeles County–University of Southern California Medical Center.[52]

Germ Theory

At around the same time, both Heger and Woodling were invited to meetings to help draw up AMA guidelines for diagnosing child abuse, published in 1985 in the *Journal of the American Medical Association.* Among the physical signs in the published guidelines: lax anal tone, a hymenal opening bigger than four millimeters, candidiasis (a fungal infection that causes everything from vaginal irritation to diaper rash), recurrent urinary tract infections, and vaginal discharge.[53]

These last two conditions can result from microorganisms such as the bacterium that causes gonorrhea, which studies show is virtually always sexually transmitted. Most agents that infect the genital area can migrate there in nonsexual ways as well, though, and it is often impossible to tell the difference with any legal certainty. Recent research has shown, for example, that the irksome growths popularly known as venereal warts are usually spread sexually. Yet in some infected children studied, no such contact is documented. The same ambiguity applies to *Gardnerella vaginalis,* an organism that generally infects sexually active women but which is also found in young girls with no history of abuse.[54]

Diagnosing molestation solely on the basis of discharges and infections is thus by no means foolproof. But some doctors remembered their profession's earlier use of scientific pretense to ignore sexual abuse—its cavalier dismissal, for example, of gonorrhea in little girls. Now, their determination to redress history outpaced their concern for empirical caution. One such doctor was pediatrician Carol Berkowitz, who worked at the same University of California medical center as Roland Summit, and who examined some of the McMartin children.[55] By the mid-1980s, Berkowitz was encouraging parents and doctors to suspect sexual abuse in every female child with itchy genitals. Conventional wisdom had it that this problem usually arose from poor toileting habits, but Berkowitz vehemently disagreed. "Why should wiping the wrong way cause vaginitis?" she asked a news reporter rhetorically.[56] Later, at a conference of her colleagues, she elaborated: "For years we've said, 'Little girls don't wipe good; that's how come they all have urinary tract infections.' I think that's another one of the great lies, along with 'The check's in the mail' and 'I'll respect you in morning.' "[57]

Indignation such as Berkowitz's blinded doctors to another problem: their new passion to diagnose abuse sometimes outstripped the new techniques and technologies they were using. Many methods were still plagued by glitches. It soon became clear, for instance, that laboratory tests deemed useful for diagnosing a host of newly discovered venereal infections were not always sensitive enough to distinguish these pernicious organisms from innocuous ones.

The case of four-year-old Sandy Johnson is one example. In 1986, when Sandy's mother took her to a San Bernardino County, California, pediatrician to treat a vaginal discharge, the doctor diagnosed possible sexual abuse and notified Child Protective Services. Over and over, the little girl denied being molested. But lab cultures of her discharge indicated that her vagina harbored *Gardnerella vaginalis,* which the pediatrician recently had learned was always spread sexually. Sandy was forcibly removed from her home and examined by a Child Protective Services–affiliated doctor, who observed that her hymen's opening was larger than normal and had cuts on it. Later, other doctors found no abnormalities, and when a second lab cultured Sandy's discharge, it found not *Gardnerella vaginalis* but another bacteria that usually lives in the upper respiratory tract and which can infect the vagina if a child wipes her nose and then her genitals. Sandy was finally returned to her family after spending eleven terrifying days in foster care.[58]

The Country Walk ritual-abuse case contained similarly faulty lab work. The Miami doctors who examined the children in late 1984 were on opposite sides of the country from Woodling and his colleagues, so they were still ignorant about hymenal notches and anal winks. Predictably, they found no anatomical evidence of molestation. But when the children had their throats cultured for gonorrhea, one test came back positive: it belonged to defendant Frank Fuster's six-year-old son, Jaime. To the prosecution, Jaime's test was the smoking gun, the hard proof that sexual abuse had occurred at the Fusters' baby-sitting service. Jaime denied it, however, and this pushed investigators to grill him further. In one session, state-appointed therapists Joe and Laurie Braga questioned the little boy relentlessly for seven hours. "I know you are not telling me the truth because you said no one put their penis in your mouth," Joe Braga scolded. "I don't remember," Jaime answered. The interviewers pressed on: "Do you think it was your father?" Braga insisted, and when the child said he didn't know, Laurie Braga suggested that "Maybe it was your dad?" "Did you ask him to stop?" Joe added. Again Jaime repeated that he remembered nothing about being abused. "Maybe you can remember after lunch," Joe ordered. "That's what I want you to think about."[59]

Indeed, after lunch Jaime did say that his father had molested him. But as soon as he was removed from the questioning room he reversed himself, and today he insists that neither he nor any other children were ever abused at Country Walk.[60] Nevertheless, during a trial in late 1985, Jaime's positive lab findings were used to convict Frank Fuster. Three years later—long after the throat culture had been discarded—researchers at the federal Centers for Disease Control revealed that they had tested hundreds of children's samples sent in by laboratories throughout the country. In more than a third of the samples that indicated gonorrhea, the CDC said, the actual organism turned out to be something else. What had happened was that the test used on these children (and on Jaime Fuster) could not distinguish bacteria that cause gonorrhea from other harmless ones that normally live in children's throats.[61]

So Frank Fuster's son probably never had a sexually transmitted disease. Yet believers in ritual abuse still cite the gonorrhea findings in Country Walk as proof that such crimes happen. They also commonly refer to long-discredited medical evidence and in other cases hold it out as proof that allegations have substance. During the investigation of Kelly Michaels, two years after the purported molestations were said to have occurred, children were taken to New Jersey's sex-abuse diagnostic and treatment program in Newark. A pediatrician there examined one girl and observed that her hymenal opening was "not entirely symmetrical," since "on [the] child's right at 9 o'clock position there is more of a dip, a notch, than on her left." The doctor recognized that her finding could be normal, but she thought that, alternatively, it might be "an area of healed trauma."[62]

During the next few years, research on nonabused girls would show that this pediatrician's first guess was as likely as her second, if not more so. Nonetheless, the prosecution's reply to Kelly Michaels's appeal of her guilty verdict, filed in 1991, continued to note, as supposed proof of Michaels's guilt, that the little girl had hymenal notches.[63] And a popular book that vilifies Michaels carries things a step further by suggesting that the child's notches mean her teacher lacerated her hymen with a knife.[64]

The Power of the Body

Why do believers cling so tenaciously to physical evidence that science has disgraced? Primarily because no matter how meaningless notches and winks and hymenal sizes may be, they still constitute something tangible and scientific-sounding. Like black eyes, broken bones, gunshot wounds, and bruises, they are physical, measureable, and apparently easy to understand. They are evidence of the traditional kind—the kind that children's halting disclosures, parents' retrospective descriptions of bed-wetting, and therapists' talk of syndromes can never be.

Related to this reassuring physical evidence is the urge to help the body speak by elevating its involuntary behaviors and unconscious signs to the level of social critique. For instance, the hysterical nineteenth-century woman with her paralyzed limbs has been given a voice by psychoanalytically oriented feminists who interpret such postures as a protest against the social constraints of being female. If this type of symbolism feels profound and compelling, it seems even more so when extended to children, who—to a greater extent than women—are supposed to be seen but not heard. To lend speech to the silent youngsters in sex-abuse cases, their advocates have been tempted to look to their bodies for a language of victimization. The effort produced at least one ironic result: the neopoliticization of the anal wink. The process had already begun when Woodling assigned the feature to California children, but it gained force as other doctors shipped the wink back to its native England. In 1986, the British medical journal *The Lancet* introduced doctors to Woodling's test so they could check children for what the journal still called *buggery*—that old word that in England has for so long been associated with male homosexuality.[65]

The test was immediately adopted by doctors at a public hospital in Middlesborough, an impoverished working-class town in Cleveland County, England. When children were brought in to be examined for abuse, neglect, or sometimes simply for earaches, physicians there found many anal winks, and they also discovered what they described as genital redness, enlarged or damaged hymenal openings, and scars. Within six months, more than one hundred Cleveland County children were diagnosed as abuse victims. Many were removed from their homes. The abuse diagnoses were widely accepted, especially since some parents had good reason to believe their children had been molested (and, indeed, subsequent investigation produced confessions from several male perpetrators). But charges were believed even by mothers and fathers who could not fathom how the abuse might have happened or who the offender might be. Soon many parents grew suspicious, as did police and forensic examiners, especially after children separated from their accused molesters persisted with anal winks and even developed new ones. The situation escalated into a national scandal, as the British government investigated the child-protection system. After extensive hearings, doctors were advised to use caution in drawing conclusions about winks until rigorous research had been done on their "natural history and significance."[66]

But the issue would not die. A woman social worker and a psychologist who helped doctors diagnose and remove Cleveland children from their homes justified their actions by calling themselves warriors in a political struggle to liberate children. They were joined by Beatrix Campbell, a journalist and feminist who is one of Britain's most vocal supporters of the existence of epidemic ritual child abuse.[67] Following the Cleveland scandal, Campbell called the anal wink a "coded message" about how children's bodies open to avoid the pain of rape. The wink, in other words, was the physical manifestation of Roland Summit's Accommodation Syndrome. Further, Campbell asserted that the wink made a radical point about gender: it proved that many so-called heterosexual men were sodomizing their sons, which meant that being straight was not so different from being gay in that regard.[68]

But even as Campbell was throwing down this gauntlet, scientific research was emerging that would dash her theories. In 1987, doctors at a children's hospital in Boston published results of their study comparing abused girls with a group seen for simple vaginal and urinary tract infections, as well as with another group who had no history of either infection or abuse. No matter what group they were in, many of these girls' hymens measured larger than four millimeters.[69] In addition, some of the "normal" girls had bands, bumps, and tears. As for those with vaginal and urinary tract problems, their bottoms looked even more like the abused girls'. After McCann's work was published two years later, the myth of the normal four-millimeter hymen was finally laid to rest, along with synechiae, six o'clock tags, and neovascularization. Woodling's anal wink was also summarily retired, and he has not since been seen in court—though at this writing, several people convicted with his testimony, including Scott and Brenda Kniffen, are still incarcerated in California prisons.

As for Astrid Heger, she managed to emerge from Woodling's shadow and from McMartin with her professional reputation almost unscathed. As a member of several child-protection and pediatrics journal peer-review committees in the late 1980s, she was aware of the normative studies on children's genitals long before they were published, so she had ample time to reverse herself before her older work was discredited. Even before the first McMartin trial started, in 1987, she was already testifying in criminal cases for the defense, where she would tell juries that the four-millimeter measure for hymens was forensically meaningless. She later went on to participate in more research on nonabused children and eventually co-authored an authoritative study of hundreds of young girls, which again found the usual lines, bumps, and tags on many of them.[70]

Nevertheless, at the McMartin trial, Heger continued to insist that the findings she had first made on the children were correct. During the first days of the case, for instance, she had identified a scar on one boy's anus. Now, three years later, she again, called it a scar—but another physician witness identified it as only shadows caused by hairs.[71] Her seeming desperation to save face led to absurdities: once she looked at a slide and saw massive trauma, yet in an earlier report she had indicated nothing out of the ordinary.[72] At no time in court did she do the logical thing: simply admit that the findings she made in McMartin were based on theories she now knew were wrong.

Nor did public corrections come from the many other prominent physicians who took such theories into court. Their failure to concretely acknowledge their mistakes has allowed lesser lights to continue taking the stand during trials and presenting misdiagnoses as fact. That such errors persist is evident from the discussion we heard during a 1994 San Diego Children's Hospital conference workshop, "Anogenital Anatomy: A Developmental Approach to the Evaluation of the Sexually Abused Child." The presenter was John McCann, who had debuted his groundbreaking research at the same gathering six years earlier. This time, he brought up the topic of objects commonly found in youngsters' vaginas. "How many of you," McCann asked the doctors in attendance, "have seen children—little girls—who have put something in their vaginas?" Several raised their hands, and one physician talked about how, in court, he always said that a little girl would never willingly insert an object into her own vagina because "its hurts too much." Other audience members disagreed. Several told of removing crayons and other toys from children who were apparently playing doctor, and McCann mentioned extracting a flashlight battery and screw from a child he felt was not abused but who had simply inserted the objects herself. He then projected slides of a four-year-old girl's genitals, and asked for a poll of how many audience members saw signs of sexual abuse. Several raised their hands. Then McCann commented that in his opinion, it was impossible to diagnosis abuse with any confidence.

There was much chuckling during the vote taking and good-natured ribbing at the participants' disagreements with one another about the meaning of the hymens portrayed in the slides. Amid the camaraderie, there was no discussion of what to do about a defendant who might have been convicted because a doctor wrongly thought little girls never put crayons up themselves; or of what might have happened to the four-year-old's parents if the physician who checked her genitals had been a seminar audience member and not McCann.

Neither was there talk of the problem faced in many U.S. communities: that, although researchers have challenged a raft of child-abuse pseudoscience during the past few years, their corrections have trickled slowly to the hinterlands, and in many communities, doctors have yet to learn them. The problem is illustrated by what happened in San Diego, where even though workshop attendees left with updated information, no one else was destined to have it. That is because McCann had ordered that, unlike the conference's other seminars, his not be taped for distribution. Recording it would have made an issue of the scientific uncertainty regarding crayons and batteries and four-year-old hymens. And it would have revealed the chilling results of not discussing that uncertainty, both in the past and currently.

TEN

Extraordinary Laws

I n Washington, D.C., in October 1984, at a national symposium on child
molestation, dozens of lawyers, judges, therapists, police, and government officials from around the country listened intently as Steve Chaney, an attorney
with the district attorney's office in Fort Worth, Texas, began to speak. Chaney
was there to tell the members of the audience that for years, they had been pos-
ing the wrong issues in the courthouse. "We're not asking the question, 'Was the
child abused?'" he noted. "We're asking . . . , 'Can the child perform for us in the
courtroom?'"[1]

"Children don't do that well," Chaney continued,[2] and he went on to describe how
he had solved the performance problem in Texas by reforming the law so that videotaped testimony could substitute for youngsters' live appearance in court. When he
proposed the change in the early 1980s, Chaney assumed it would take at least two
years of lobbying state legislators to get it passed. He was amazed when it flew
through both the Texas House and Senate, with hardly a vote of opposition.

Now, as symposium attendees like Roland Summit listened, Chaney encouraged
child-protection activists in other states to follow the Texas example, and he praised
the superior truth-telling capabilities of children by comparing them to grownups.

As a prosecutor for thirteen years, Chaney said, he was constantly faced with adult witnesses who lied:

> And they were all under oath. I'd rather have a child recite something that I have some believability in, because unless they have actually experienced [sexual abuse], these experiences are beyond their realm of understanding. I trust a child telling about these things more than I do an adult who takes his hand and raises it and swears to tell the truth so help me, God, and then commits perjury from Fort Worth to Washington.[3]

Chaney's search for justice for sexually violated youngsters followed on the heels of feminist attempts to do the same for women in rape cases, and his efforts were in many ways equally laudable. Recognizing that children's testimony could be reliable was a welcome change from the long-standing and reflexive courtroom attitude that boys and girls were not to believed—particularly in cases involving charges of incest and molestation. What Chaney and most other child-protection professionals did not understand during the 1980s, though, was that unlike women, children are not the equals of men. They are not grownups, and under the sway of adults who hold power over them, twelve-year-olds, nine-year-olds, and certainly four-year-olds are subject to strong pressures to comply with their caretakers' wishes, including when they give testimony. Even when they are not thus influenced, very young children often lack the cognitive or verbal skills necessary to give accurate accounts of events and the self-confidence needed to face a courtroom. As Chaney pointed out, they may become too frightened to convey information. And as he neglected to mention, many lack a mature understanding of the extent to which the fact-finding process is damaged if they tell an untruth.

If those attributes sound insulting, it is only because women have been traditionally described in the same ways: irrational, without moral conscience, incapable of conducting themselves appropriately in the civic realm. But women are grownups, capable of achieving equality with men. Is it wise or even possible to propel children into a realm that, like driving, drinking, working, or sex, demands adult capabilities? To put it more concretely: Is it right to make witnesses of preschoolers?

That question is often asked from the defendant's perspective, but seldom from children's—or women's. Much feminist history centers on attempts to differentiate women from children, to raise women to adult male status. The recent move by courts to acknowledge females as competent witnesses in sexual-assault cases reflects these efforts. But the parallel attempt to do the same for children raises difficult questions. One is whether justice is truly served by bending the rules of evidence to accommodate witnesses who simply are not adultlike. Do such changes seriously weaken the judicial process? If they do, does that mean that the problem of child sexual abuse is not addressable through the courts? And if so, how should sexual abuse be realistically dealt with in our society?

The legal history that follows does not answer these perplexing questions. It does, however, demonstrate the tragic consequences of ignoring them.

Rape

In the Anglo-American legal tradition, females and minors have long been treated as equals, both when they were denied rights and when they gained them. Nineteenth-century efforts to free women from their position as their husbands' chattel, for instance, led to similar challenges to fathers' absolute right to beat or even kill their children and to the first state efforts to regulate family life. It is therefore not surprising that the transformation of legal procedure affecting children in sex-abuse cases began with changes in the law regarding rape.

By 1970, shifting sexual mores had made it more socially acceptable for American women to say yes to sexual activity, but as far as the legal system was concerned, they still did not have the right to say no. The centuries-old accretions of statutes designed to protect men charged with rape remained staunchly in place, and in several states, judges still gave juries formal warnings that charges of sexual assault by women were "easily made, and, once made, difficult to defend, even if the person accused is innocent."[4] The law also required a woman bringing a rape charge to prove that she had physically resisted the assault, since, according to influential law review articles in the 1950s and 1960s, psychiatry had demonstrated that women felt so ambivalent about sex that when they said no, this could actually be an invitation to more "masterly pursuit."[5]

In addition to these long-standing impediments to obtaining a rape conviction, the popularity of psychiatry as explanation for human behavior—particularly female behavior—led courts in the 1960s to order psychiatric examinations for women who brought sexual assault charges, in order to assess their "credibility."[6] This policy was endorsed by the American Bar Association, by prestigious commentators on the law of evidence, as well as by prominent psychiatrists Karl Menninger and William White.[7]

As the feminist movement coalesced in the early 1970s, activists vowed to redress these indignities. They established rape crisis centers and targeted rape laws for reform by working to eliminate attitudes and statutes that denigrated women. Throughout the country, crisis-center staffers came to know police officers and prosecutors, as well as lobbyists in statehouses. Coalitions of feminists, police, district attorneys, and politicians testified before legislative committees in California, Washington, and many other states about the damage done to women by archaic rape laws. Constitutional rights organizations such as the American Civil Liberties Union (ACLU) were also enlisted to help.

The results were dramatic. By 1980, California had abolished the instruction to juries about the ease with which rape charges are made, and the requirement that a woman must physically resist had also been eliminated. Statutes also banned the term "unchaste character" and prohibited jury instructions about inferring consent from the fact that a woman was sexually active outside of marriage. The mandatory psychiatric examination was rescinded, spousal rape was criminalized, and a new "rape shield" law restricted inquiry into a woman's sexual history.[8] Similar laws passed throughout the country.[9]

The coalition that cleansed the law of its former hostility toward women charging rape pressed on to gain additional "affirmative action" for them in criminal trials. In response, in the late 1970s, courts began allowing a "rape expert" to bolster a woman's credibility by explaining to the jury the behavioral symptoms of the "Rape Trauma Syndrome" (RTS).

The term was coined in 1974 by Boston nurse Ann Burgess (who later developed the concept of the "sex ring") and sociologist Lynda Holmstrom in their study of women and girls treated in a hospital emergency room after making sexual-assault reports.[10] RTS, according to Burgess and Holmstrom, encompassed the range of reactions women experience after forcible or attempted forcible rape. Most women in the study were assumed to be victims of coerced sex,[11] and the researchers did not investigate whether their claims were true. Instead, Burgess and Holmstrom tried to identify RTS symptoms in order to validate the women's reports and speed their psychological healing.[12]

Within a therapeutic context, this practice makes good sense. But soon, Burgess and other self-proclaimed "RTS experts" were going into court at prosecutors' behest and using the syndrome to prove a forensic matter: that a rape had indeed occurred. This practice credited RTS with scientific pretensions it did not deserve. Women's reactions to rape are varied, ranging from profound distress to perfect composure;[13] because such reactions can follow any traumatic event, they do not in themselves prove sexual assault.

American courts have traditionally been hostile to the idea of experts telling juries whether or not a particular witness should be believed. Nevertheless, when the rape laws were reformed, courts moved from favoring attacks on women's credibility to bolstering it with expert testimony.[14] The use of testimony about RTS to prove that a rape had occurred was criticized in the mid-1980s and modified. Nowadays, testimony about the syndrome is used to explain to juries that a woman's delayed report to the police, her calm demeanor, or her failure to resist are normal responses to sexual assault and do not in themselves indicate a false accusation.[15]

Changing Laws for Children

The legal shift from stigmatizing women witnesses in rape trials to rehabilitating them with expert testimony coincided with efforts to change laws affecting children in sex-abuse cases, efforts that were initiated by the same activists who had worked to change the rape laws. "Women who organized and staffed the rape crisis centers have been among the first to recognize the scope of the problem of child sexual abuse, to develop innovative services for abused children, and to fight for legal reforms." So wrote Judith Herman in 1981 in *Father-Daughter Incest*. Herman envisioned providing a support person to shepherd children through the criminal justice system, beginning when a complaint was filed and continuing through the trial. She favored softening the harsh environment of courtrooms and getting rid of competency rules and corroboration requirements that kept very young children from the stand and devalued their testimony. Herman also promoted the concept of minimizing contact between the child and the accused adult by using videotaped testimony or by separating defendant and child altogether. She wanted children to take the stand in special, cheerfully appointed rooms where the only other people present were the judge, prosecutor, support person, and defense attorney. As for the public, they could watch from the courtroom via closed-circuit TV along with the jury and the defendant, who would communicate with his lawyer via an intercom.[16]

The legal community, mental health experts, and the popular press echoed Herman's concerns. Impassioned authors wrote that the entire criminal justice process in child sexual-abuse cases was a grueling waste of time, and the Constitution little more than a refuge for molesters. Proponents of this view denounced trials themselves as a form of abuse, and believed that to submit already victimized children to these ordeals was to assault the youngsters even further. A *Houston Chronicle* series on child abuse and the courts wrote about victims who dream not only about people sticking things into them but "about being raped at the courthouse."[17] Children's truth-telling abilities were easily tainted by their immaturity, this argument asserted, and by their fear of defendants and other adults in the courtroom. Further, children were so vulnerable that they might even be permanently damaged by having to testify. So they should be kept out of court and allowed to present their statements on videotape or closed-circuit television, or through "hearsay"—statements made to another person even before the trial.[18] Finally, these advocates wanted experts to interpret children's words, gestures, and even silences, and to tell jurors why they should disregard youngsters' denials of abuse.[19]

The Sixth Amendment Under Fire

The sticking point for these efforts was the Sixth Amendment of the U.S. Constitution, which includes a defendant's right "to be confronted with the witnesses against him." Neither history nor psychology convincingly shows that face-to-face confrontation is an effective method of forcing the truth,[20] but the requirement that an accuser must face the accused is deeply rooted in Western culture and the Anglo-American legal system.[21]

Yet during the 1980s, the confrontation clause came to be viewed with great impatience by reformers who counterposed the rights of child accusers to those of adult defendants. In arguing for reforms to the Sixth Amendment, they repeated their claims that children were vulnerable in court. But they also developed the diametrically opposed argument that youngsters were invulnerable.

This latter piece of logic was based on a growing tendency to dignify the word of children, a trend that tracked the process by which women's testimony had gained credibility in rape cases during the 1970s. During the 1980s, the requirement that children undergo psychiatric examinations to test their credibility was increasingly abandoned,[22] for instance, and there was a growing tendency to credit children with the rational and moral abilities required of witnesses during criminal trials: the capacity to observe, to remember what one has experienced, to be able to communicate one's perceptions, to know the difference between truth and falsehood, and to appreciate the obligation never to lie in court.[23]

While it has been more than two hundred years since Anglo-American law fixed an arbitrary age below which children are deemed incompetent,[24] during most of the twentieth century, U.S. judges conformed to an aside in a late-nineteenth-century Supreme Court opinion that said "no one would think of calling as a witness an infant only two or three years old."[25] In the 1980s, however, the unthinkable became fact as preschoolers were allowed to take the stand. In 1984, a two-year-old testified in Washington. Since then, three-year-olds have appeared in several molestation cases.[26]

New research showing that children could be reliable witnesses if questioned properly (see chapter 7) encouraged eager child-protection advocates and prosecutors to romanticize youngsters as being free of the "taint of interest" that biases grownups. As one prosecutor wrote, "children do not make good liars."[27] This view of children as naturally possessed of acute observational abilities and sterling truthfulness endowed them with exceptional moral power and cast them as perfect witnesses. On the other hand, the same reformers who lionized children's senses and sensibilities argued that they were so weak and vulnerable to adult pressures that they should be excused from cross-examination and from face-to-face confrontation with defendants. Reformers also sought to lessen the prosecutor's burden of proof in child sex-abuse cases by permitting convictions based on children's testimony about events the youngsters were unable to fix at a particular time.[28]

The practical consequences of the legal changes that flowed from these contradictory visions of children can be seen in the 1984 trial of Bronx day-care teacher's aide Jesus Torres, for sexually assaulting several preschoolers. Denying the charges, Torres showed that the boys who testified against him were not even in his class. He produced nine witnesses to corroborate his testimony that during his six-month tenure at the center, he had little or no contact with these children and was never alone with them. Torres could not, however, account for every single moment of his time at the day-care center, and the prosecution's indictment did not specify when the crimes had been committed. A pediatrician in the Torres prosecution justified the children's failure to say when the abuse occurred by testifying that preschoolers hardly understand abstractions like time,[29] and Torres's alibi was rendered useless. He was convicted and sent to prison.[30]

The evidence against Torres and defendants in similar cases was based on directly opposing ideas about children's abilities, but this contradiction was lost on reformers bent on making drastic changes in the law. In the 1980s, a deluge of writings and testimony by social workers, psychologists, professors, newspaper reporters, judges, and law students urged the passage of reforms. The political forces behind them included not only prosecutors and feminist organizations but also "victim's rights" groups such as SLAM, Believe the Children, and other organizations of believers in ritual abuse, the American Bar Association, the American Academy of Child Psychiatrists, the American Psychological Association, the American Professional Society on the Abuse of Children, the federal government–funded National Center for the Prosecution of Child Abuse of the National District Attorney's Association—in short, every group recognized as concerned with crime and children.

It might be expected that organizations dedicated to safeguarding the Constitution would have rushed to dispute moves to tamper with the Sixth Amendment. But civil liberties groups were largely silent on the matter. In their writings and public relations efforts to change the criminal law, reformers seized the rhetorical high ground and always referred to child witnesses as "victims."[31] That done, criticizing their reform efforts would make civil liberties groups look "soft" on molesters and hostile to children. Given the other battles that rights organizations were fighting in the 1980s—over deteriorating abortion rights and attacks on artistic expression, for example—defending accused child molesters was seen as a political liability,

Groups like the ACLU, the National Lawyer's Guild, and the Center for Constitutional Rights remained silent, even as many child sexual-abuse cases grew bizarre and scores of people were put on trial under unprecedented circumstances.

Legal opposition to the plethora of proposed reforms was left to the accused themselves, or their friends and relatives. Without opposing voices raised by people speaking from positions of power or principle, there was nothing to block the proposed changes, and they sailed through legislatures nationwide. By the mid-1980s, the right of an accused to face-to-face confrontation with a complaining witness had been decimated for defendants in child sex-abuse cases. Most states permitted videotaped testimony from the children, half authorized one-way closed-circuit television testimony, and eight allowed a two-way system in which the child witness is permitted to see the courtroom and defendant on a video monitor and the jury and judge can view the child during the testimony.[32] New exceptions to the hearsay rule were also created, and old ones were expanded.[33]

Removing Children from the Courtroom: High Tech and Hearsay

In 1984, the publicity from McMartin and from a sex-abuse scandal involving several day-care centers in the Bronx led the New York legislature to pass a law allowing children to testify via closed-circuit television, away from the defendant and the "scary and intimidating surroundings of a courtroom." According to Bronx DA Mario Merola, in the prosecution of Puerto Rican Association for Community Affairs (PRACA) day-care center teacher's aide Albert Algarin, a five-year-old who had "done fine" during pretrial sessions with assistant DAs Nancy Borko and Charlie Brofman later became dumbstruck on the witness stand. So Merola decided to use the TV regardless of the consequences on appeal.[34] Several children then became the first witnesses in New York to testify outside the courtroom, in a room separate from the defendant.[35]

Child witnesses against day-care operator Sandra Craig also appeared on closed-circuit television, away from the judge, jury, and Craig. The relevant Maryland law allowed this kind of testimony when children would otherwise suffer such emotional distress that they could not reasonably communicate in the courtroom.

Another way of avoiding face-to-face confrontation between defendant and child is to let adults—parents, investigators, and therapists—give hearsay testimony about what the child said to them out of court about sexual abuse. One justification for this reform came from the new rape laws, which assumed that although a woman might not immediately go to the authorities after being victimized, she might well tell a friend or relative who could appear in court to bolster her claim of having been raped. Now, the same logic was applied to children's victimization, and the result was that in ritual-abuse cases, parents came to court to tell juries what their sons and daughters had supposedly revealed to them about molestation and torture.

The 1986 trial of Texan Michelle Noble on ritual-abuse charges is an example of how the new hearsay laws were applied against defendants. Noble and another teacher, Gayle Dove, were matronly employees of a day-care center in El Paso who were charged with multiple counts of aggravated sexual assault and indecency with a child. It was alleged that the two women, under the pretext of taking their charges to a nearby park on sunny days, had instead walked them to Noble's home, where they fondled the children's genitals and had the children touch theirs; stuck pencils and syringes up the anuses and penises of little boys; helped an unknown man rape a three-year-old girl; photographed the children defecating; terrified them into silence by sawing open stuffed animals; and did much of this while wearing monster masks.

At the first trial, Noble never saw any of her accusers. Instead, the prosecution showed videotapes of social workers interviewing the preschoolers. Then parents took the stand and reported disclosures that their children had made in piecemeal fashion over several months, until just before the trial began. The mothers and fathers talked of breast sucking, the licking of vaginas, pencils being stuck up rectums, stuffed animals being sawed open to evoke terror, and threats that the children's loved ones would be killed if they told of the abuse. Jurors almost recoiled from the graphic material and from the parents' overwhelming emotions as they recounted it. One mother began sobbing and wailing as soon as she started testifying. Other hearsay witnesses, including fathers, wept every time they said "peepee" and "boobies." The jury found Noble guilty on eighteen counts. She was sentenced to life in prison plus 311 years.[36]

Besides parents, therapists and physicians have also been allowed to present secondhand testimony about children's disclosures of abuse. The logic of this "medical exception" to the principle of disallowing hearsay is the venerable and reasonable assumption that since sick people want to get well and avoid death, patients tell their doctors the truth about how they got ill. But the idea that infirmity engenders honesty has lately been stretched to include children's statements about sexual abuse made to doctors and psychotherapists—even though the youngsters are not "sick" in the traditional sense of the word, and even though they may have little or no understanding of the consequences of what they are saying.

In a ritual-abuse trial of child-care workers Martha Felix and Francisco Ontiveros, for instance, in Carson City, Nevada, psychotherapist Patricia Bay was allowed to tell the jury about abuse allegations made by a child in response to Bay's leading questions during some of the ninety-eight therapy sessions she conducted with the girl. Ontiveros and Felix were convicted by a jury and sentenced to maximum terms.[37] In another case, against a woman named Laura Wright, police took one of Wright's daughters to the doctor because the child's two-year-old sister, shortly after returning to the custody of Wright's estranged husband for a six-month stay, had reportedly said that both girls had been abused by their mother and her boyfriend, whom the girls called Daddy.

The two-year-old was not physically injured or ill during her sexual-abuse medical evaluation. Nevertheless, at Laura Wright's trial, the physician who did the exam was allowed to testify about his "patient's" response to questions he asked while he took her medical "history": "Do you play with daddy?" "Does daddy play with you?" "Does daddy touch you with his pee-pee?" and "Do you touch his pee-pee?"

When asked how the little girl answered the first two questions, the doctor testified that she had said nothing more than "we play a lot" and then went on calmly to describe several benign play activities with her mother's boyfriend. But after the physician persisted and asked, "Does daddy touch you with his pee-pee?" he said that the child "did admit to that," and though she said nothing in response to "Do you touch his pee-pee?" she later volunteered that the boyfriend "does do this with me, but he does it a lot more with my sister." The doctor had made no record of his interview, and he had discarded a picture he worked with to help the child understand what he meant by "daddy's pee-pee." Nevertheless, Laura Wright was convicted.[38]

Experts in Court

Allowing children to be removed from the courtroom was not the only way that legal reforms paved the way for successful ritual-abuse prosecutions. As with the Rape Trauma Syndrome in trials involving women complainants, new laws also allowed experts to appear before juries and tell why they thought children were telling the truth. In the Country Walk trial in Miami, for instance, four psychologists, one for each child who testified, told Frank Fuster's jury that the children had made incriminating statements about him during therapy. Then, the psychologists changed abruptly from hearsay witnesses to experts on child behavior as they assured the jury that they believed the charges against Fuster were true.

Psychologist Ira Poliakoff led off as he told the jury about his sessions with two-year-old Scott M. According to Poliakoff, in their third meeting, Scott revealed that Fuster and his wife had hurt him. When Poliakoff pressed Scott for details, the child became distraught, crawled on the floor, and rocked—which to Poliakoff meant that Scott was telling the truth.[39] Poliakoff had also read a "neurolinguistics" study about how one can differentiate between a person who is telling the truth and one who is lying by looking at his or her eyes. And he believed he could determine when a child was lying by paying attention to voice and facial expression. If children are hesitant to speak or seem upset, the therapist said, this means they are telling the truth. He further concluded that Scott's statements about Frank Fuster molesting him were valid, since "[a] child Scotty's age would have difficulty presenting something as true if it were not."[40] Other psychologists gave similar testimony.[41]

The appearance of experts like Poliakoff in ritual-abuse trials is not without precedent. Since the Progressive era in the United States, juvenile courts have given children who break the law special treatment, with the aim of rehabilitating them. In these courts, testimony by mental health experts has long been a mainstay;[42] by mid-century, psychiatrists were routinely supplying arbitrary opinions that justified years of incarceration in reformatories. It was not until 1967 that the U.S. Supreme Court applied the rudiments of due process to decisions affecting children's liberty.[43]

That decision, though, did nothing to stem the rising tide of mental health experts in children's courts, even as the larger areas of criminal and civil law remained apprehensive about them. This uneasiness has a long tradition. In the eleventh and twelfth centuries, an important method of resolving disputes was "trial by compurgation," in which each side would present *compurgators*—people who swore that the litigant was a believable person[44]—and the party who assembled the most compurgators won the case. This system of seeing who could muster the most imposing array of supporters eventually fell out of favor, and was replaced with testimony from witnesses describing what they had observed with their five senses. The task of determining who was telling the truth was assigned to jurors, on the assumption that a range of ordinary people who are litigants' peers but not connected to them through financial or blood ties have the best chance of discerning the truth.

In response, litigants have long sought to influence the jury with experts whose opinions are cloaked in impenetrable and thereby impressive jargon. Jurors have been overwhelmed by the confident assertions of obscurantist professionals whom they are in no position to evaluate critically, and who have later been shown to be entirely wrong. Knowledge from well-established experts is extremely useful, however. Fingerprints are a valid and reliable way of identifying someone, for example, because many different experts will typically reach identical conclusions about who left them. But how can a court determine which assertions of truth are speculation and which are scientifically reliable?

For seventy years, the answer was found in *Frye v. United States*, the 1923 case that held that evidence based on lie detectors could not be used in a criminal trial. The judges who heard *Frye* noted that "the courts will go a long way in admitting expert testimony deduced from a well-recognized scientific principle or discovery." Nevertheless, they continued, "the thing from which the deduction is made must be sufficiently established to have gained general acceptance in the particular field in which it belongs."[45] In simpler terms, an expert's claims about what is scientific are admissible only when other experts in the field agree.

This test—that a claim be accepted by the relevant scientific community—became the rule in most federal and state courts. It has been applied to dozens of new forensic techniques, including the Rape Trauma Syndrome, the profile of a rapist, the use of hypnotically induced testimony, psychological testimony on eyewitness identifications, and the use of anatomically correct dolls.[46] But, like the traditional refusal to allow experts to preempt the jury by telling it which party to believe, the long-standing requirement that scientific evidence meet minimal standards before experts may present it to the jury has often been ignored in ritual-abuse prosecutions.

The *Frye* test for determining whether or not to admit expert testimony has often been criticized for overrating consensus, which by itself cannot establish a claim as scientific.[47] A consensus existed for centuries, for instance, that using leeches to suck blood from sick people was a valid medical treatment.

The child-protection professionals whose stories fill this book have been quite aware of the courts' reliance on Frye's notion of the scientific community, and they have devoted much effort to stitching together a polity of their own who can present a legally acceptable consensus about the symptoms of sexual abuse and how to diagnose it.

California psychiatrist David Corwin, who did therapy with a child in the McMartin case, mounted an effort in 1985 to have his Sexually Abused Child's Disorder (SACD) named as a category in the American Psychiatric Association's *Diagnostic and Statistical Manual*. One of Corwin's main goals was to allow experts to give testimony that a child had been abused. SACD would resemble the use of Battered Child Syndrome in legal proceedings.[48]

Ultimately, the APA rejected the proposed new category, but Corwin was more successful in his other goal: to define the "relevant scientific community" from whom courts would permit expert assessments of child sexual abuse.[49] He did this by organizing the American Professional Society on the Abuse of Children, whose leadership is packed with child-abuse moral crusaders, including the country's most active proponents of the belief that ritual abuse is real and widespread.

The *Frye* test has also been steadily criticized in recent years for being so easily manipulatable by determined professionals. In 1993, the U.S. Supreme Court finally jettisoned the test in federal trials.[50]

At the state level, however, *Frye* is alive and well. As we have seen in the Country Walk prosecution, for instance, therapists were allowed to tell the jury the children had been abused. This was permitted because even though experts are not supposed to testify about witnesses' credibility, many states allow them to use their "experience and familiarity with the literature" to formulate an opinion that sexual abuse took place.[51] But research shows that no one can reliably make these kinds of determinations. No agreement exists about the behavioral characteristics of an abused child, or whether such characteristics even exist.[52] Even though there are a few behaviors that many child-protection professionals agree suggest abuse, none has been incontrovertibly verified as such.[53] Experts who examine children often cannot agree among themselves about which ones were abused. In fact, there is some indication that when asked to tell whether or not a child is telling the truth about such claims, the experts are less accurate than a coin flip.[54]

Experts' Theories

When No Means Yes: Doubting the Children

In the 1950s and 1960s, psychiatrists and lawyers said women could not be believed when making rape charges, because they did not know whether they wanted to have sex or not: if they said no, they probably really meant yes. These days, children are subject to the same psychologizing, except now, instead of emanating from the defense, these mind-reading efforts come from the district attorney's office. Once again, the precedents are the Rape Trauma Syndrome and the experts who used to instruct juries that women were really victims even if they did not report an assault for days or weeks.

Likewise, in a child sexual-abuse case, if months went by and a youngster had not disclosed the alleged abuse, a defendant would be sure to use that fact to attack the validity of the charges. Because this happened often, prosecutors in the 1980s began using experts to explain children's seemingly normal behavior after abuse or to justify improbable elements in their stories. The most common themes these professionals touched on concerned the observation that children involved in cross-generational sex often make hesitant disclosures over a long period or deny having had the experience. Such behaviors are features of Roland Summit's Child Sexual Abuse Accommodation Syndrome, or CSAAS (see chapter 1).[55]

Currently, prosecution experts routinely caution jurors not to believe children's initial denials or recantations of their earlier charges. The most eloquent admonishment comes from the CSAAS, whose use of the word *syndrome* give it a scientific ring, just as Battered Child Syndrome has. But in fact, CSAAS has no scientific basis. The 1983 article by Dr. Roland Summit that defined it was, in the author's words, "entirely impressionistic"; Indeed, Summit had conducted no research on sex-abuse victims, nor had he done significant amount of therapy with children. He employed one sensible observation—that incest victims may be pressured by their families into hiding or denying their abuse—to defeat another sensible observation—that in the absence of external pressure, children who repeatedly say they were never abused probably weren't.

Ritual-abuse prosecutions have relied heavily on testimony from experts that particular children fit Accommodation Syndrome–like patterns and therefore should be believed, even when their statements are inconsistent. Summit himself has used his work this way. In late 1984, the state of Florida paid him $75 an hour to view videotapes of Jason, a five-year-old accuser in the Country Walk prosecution of Frank Fuster. Jason had been videotaped during interviews by child-development "experts" Joseph and Laurie Braga, using leading and suggestive questioning techniques. After viewing Jason's tapes, Summit was paid an additional $1,000 per day to opine to the jury that the child's statements about being abused by Fuster were "reliable."[56]

After telling the jury that Justin's responses to the Bragas' questioning had been "spontaneous" and "candid," Summit explained why the little boy had nevertheless denied knowing about abuse at the Fusters' when the police first questioned him. Jason, Summit said, had to open the "window of disclosure" that is usually closed by fear and shame about abuse. Having thus certified Jason as a victim, Summit played on jurors' emotions by assuring them that "[w]e need to find a way to pry open that window" because "the child will first try and claw it back closed and protect against divulging a secret."[57] The clear implication was that the only way to help Jason was to believe the abuse charges. Fuster was convicted.

That was in 1985, and since then, courts have gradually restricted mention of CSAAS to rebuttal testimony, to "clarify juror misconceptions"[58] after a child's credibility is challenged.[59] Professionals generally understand now that "syndrome" testimony cannot be used to diagnose sex abuse.[60] But CSAAS language still confuses more than it enlightens.

Doll Play

Some courts have found that the use of anatomically detailed dolls to diagnose sex abuse is a novel scientific technique that cannot be presented in court until it has met the *Frye* test of general scientific acceptance.[61] This finding guarantees that testimony stemming from dolls will be excluded, since there is no consensus about whether the way children play with toys that have genitals, breasts, and pubic hair says anything about their prior exposure to sex.

One study examined whether professionals who used the dolls regularly would agree with one another about their significance. Participants were shown videotapes of children playing with dolls, then asked to identify which boys and girls had been abused. Only one expert of more than a dozen got most of the answers right.[62] Even so, many courts admit doll play into evidence by claiming that it is not a scientific technique, but rather a language used by children too young or frightened to speak in words.[63] While the image is inspiring, it promptly breaks down when one realizes that the experts do not agree among themselves about this "language's" grammar, syntax, or vocabulary.

Deciphering the Body

Throughout the 1980s, physicians told jurors that "microtraumas" discerned by powerful magnifying devices indicated sex abuse (see chapter 9). Recall that in the midst of the McMartin investigation, Dr. Astrid Heger traveled to a San Bernardino sex-abuse trial and told the jury there that nonabused young girls' hymens are perfectly round, thin-membraned, and no bigger than four millimeters in diameter. Therefore, Heger said, a child's intact hymen that looked lumpy or streaked in a colposcopic photograph and which measured seven millimeters must have been damaged by chronic penetration with a penislike object. The defendant's protestation that Heger had no scientific basis for her statements was rejected in *People v. Mendibles*,[64] the leading case on the admissibility of testimony on the physical signs of sex abuse.

The court called Heger an expert because she had written one article and was preparing another. It added that she had examined hundreds of McMartin children, and that she knew the "growing body" of literature on the emerging specialty of diagnosing physical evidence of sex abuse. There was no need, the court said, to ascertain whether Heger's use of the colposcope to find sex abuse was a novel scientific technique, since examining children's genitals microscopically was "no different than the analysis of any other wound or injury."[65] But even though research has since shown that Heger's theories were wrong, *Mendibles* continues to be cited as authority for allowing expert testimony that microtraumas are lingering traces of sex abuse.[66]

From Theory to Practice: The Kelly Michaels Case

The cumulative effect of the changes in courtroom procedure described in this chapter can be seen in the trial of Kelly Michaels, which started in 1987 and ended almost a year later. None of the children who testified against Michaels ever confronted her in the courtroom. Instead, they gave evidence in chambers in the presence of the trial judge, prosecutors, and defense attorneys. Michaels, meanwhile, had to stay in the courtroom with the spectators and jury, who watched on closed-circuit television as the judge complimented the children, held them on his lap and knee, and whispered in their ears. They whispered back to him.

The children's direct testimony, however, was a fraction of the prosecution's case. Thirty-two parents, relatives, and friends of the young accusers appeared, along with eleven investigators and psychological experts. These adults testified about what the children had told them and interpreted their behavior for the jury, including their play with dolls and other toys. At the prosecution's behest, parents had spent months keeping diaries about their children's behavior. At trial, they read entries from these journals to the jury.

Psychologist Eileen Treacy also testified for the prosecution, about stages in young children's cognitive development. Later in the trial, she returned and spent several days describing what she called the "child sex-abuse syndrome," which included typical behavioral indicators of sex abuse. Treacy then meticulously reviewed the children's investigative interviews, their trial testimony, and their parents' reports of troubling behavior. In her opinion, Treacy said, almost all the children were behaving as though they had been abused by Michaels. Defense lawyers countered with their own experts, but they were not allowed to see the children. Michaels was convicted of 115 counts and sentenced to forty-seven years in prison.

The fact that Michaels spent the first two years of her prison sentence futilely searching for help with her appeal illustrates civil libertarians' continuing reluctance to challenge ritual sex-abuse convictions, even as the 1980s turned into the 1990s. After her conviction, Michaels seemed an excellent candidate for a case to test the new child sex-abuse evidentiary laws, especially after a 1988 article in *The Village Voice* raised serious doubts about her guilt, and a sympathetic follow-up piece in *Harper's* two years later publicized her plight nationally.[67] Desperate to find an attorney willing to contest the findings of her multimillion-dollar trial and its thousands of pages of transcripts, Michaels and her parents had written to every public-interest law firm they could think of. They received no response.[68] Finally, Morton Stavis, a retired attorney who was a founder of the National Lawyer's Guild and of the Center for Constitutional Rights (CCR), agreed to take the case. Because of its gargantuan complexity, he solicited support from the CCR, which has since its inception been one of the staunchest defenders of the civil rights of unpopular individuals and groups. Stavis made his case to CCR's board, but members refused to join him. They felt that defending a convicted child molester would be too politically controversial.

In cases besides Michaels, some of the most egregious guilty verdicts brought about by the new child sex-abuse laws were reversed during the late 1980s and early 1990s, and a handful of statutes were struck down. In the main, though, the reforms have been accepted by the courts. Even the U.S. Supreme Court has validated them in fits and starts. Challenges to laws overriding face-to-face confrontation, for instance, reached the high Court in 1988, in *Coy v. Iowa*. The court held that an Iowa statute allowing alleged child victims of sex abuse to testify from behind a screen violated the Sixth Amendment.[69] The vote was close, though, and when the court considered a conviction for ritual abuse two years later, it changed its mind.

In that case, Maryland day-care operator Sandra Craig was tried and found guilty of assaulting children in scenarios that included killing rabbits and twirling possums. Craig's convictions were reversed by the Maryland Court of Appeals because her right to face-to-face confrontation had been denied.[70] But in 1990, the Supreme Court told the Maryland court to reconsider because, the judges said, protecting young victims from the trauma of giving testimony in sex-abuse cases outweighed Craig's right to face her accusers in court.[71]

Although the Supreme Court has recently demonstrated great sophistication in its understanding of what constitutes quality empirical investigation, in this case it succumbed to junk science. The Court relied in part on the "growing body of academic literature documenting the psychological trauma suffered by child abuse victims who must testify in court" as presented to it by a brief by the American Psychological Association (APA) and a study of the "emotional effects of criminal court testimony suffered by child abuse victims" headed by child witness and memory researcher Gail Goodman. It further cited the APA brief as support for its conclusion that face-to-face testimony might taint criminal trials by causing significant emotional distress in child witnesses.[72]

In its amicus brief, the APA claimed that recent psychological research made its arguments much stronger than those contained in its brief of three years earlier.[73] The much-vaunted new findings, however, were actually sparse and equivocal. One study noted that drawn-out criminal proceedings hurt children, but that the important variable in how they reacted was the delay, not the confrontation. Another study, of forty-six children involved in criminal cases, found that only 10 percent indicated they were afraid of the accused, and that of those who testified in court, fewer than 10 percent seemed upset on the stand. While these children's negative experiences are regrettable, the study provides no information on whether adult witnesses would have reacted any differently. It did not talk about the youngsters' emotional recovery, either; but a third study, headed by Goodman, found that children upset at testifying before a defendant nevertheless showed no long-term emotional effects.[74] Thus, the studies the Supreme Court relied on to justify removing children from court laid a decidedly uncertain foundation for the judges' decision.[75]

What is inarguable, however, is that face-to-face confrontation is so much a part of our legal culture that when a defendant is isolated from a child witness, the clear message to the jury, aside from the content of the testimony, is that the defendant is a threat to the child—a menace so great that centuries-old customs have to be broken to protect the young witness from harm. This drastic restructuring destroys the presumption of innocence and propels the defendant toward conviction.

Meanwhile, children's behavior during ritual-abuse trials suggests that what is really avoided by keeping them from the accused is not their own trauma but the prosecutors'. In the Kelly Michaels case, a defense lawyer asked one little girl whether she would like to see Kelly; she smiled and said she would.[76] Similar reactions have been noted in other cases.

Beyond the Law

Throughout the 1980s, legal arguments about what is wrong with child sex-abuse prosecutions focused on events in court, ignoring how cases were put together in the first place. As one commentator on pretrial investigative methods has pointed out:

> The courtroom is a splendid place where defense attorneys bellow and strut and prosecuting attorneys are hemmed in at many turns. But what happens before an accused reaches the safety and enjoys the security of this veritable mansion? Ah, there's the rub. Typically, he must first pass through a much less pretentious edifice, a police station with bare back rooms and locked doors.[77]

Children, too, are interrogated behind closed doors in police stations, as well as in their own homes and at the therapist's office, often for months. As in all other criminal cases, the charges in child sex-abuse proceedings are made or broken by the witness interviews.

Because the way witnesses and suspects are questioned is so important, criminal law has always been concerned with what happens during an investigation. Nevertheless, when it came to children's interviews, the frequency, circumstances, and techniques used were rarely discussed by appellate courts and legislatures through the 1980s. Although the issue was a live one during trials, appellate courts did not tackle it until 1989, when the Idaho Supreme Court, in Laura Wright's case, ordered that henceforth, all interviews of child witnesses in that state would be videotaped. The court also forbade blatantly leading questions, such as those the doctor apparently asked, and warned against questioning a child with a preconceived idea of what had happened.[78]

The U.S. Supreme Court reviewed the Idaho decision. The high court has never been comfortable with the idea that law-enforcement investigators should have to follow specific procedures (the one grand exception is the *Miranda* warnings that are familiar to every fan of police thrillers, as well as to anyone questioned as a suspect in a criminal investigation). Because of judicial reticence to intrude on police practice, confessions in the United States do not have to be recorded. Nor is there any rule in America that child witnesses must be video- or audiotaped when they are interviewed. The Supreme Court rejected the Idaho court's order that investigators record their interrogations. At the same time, the court agreed that Laura Wright's convictions should be reversed, since her daughters had been interviewed in a suggestive manner. Generalizing to other situations, the justices concluded that children's hearsay statements about abuse may not be trustworthy if there is evidence of prior interrogation, prompting, or manipulation by adults.[79]

In another state ruling, in 1993, New Jersey judges finally ruled on Kelly Michaels's appeal, which had been filed a year earlier by Stavis. The appellate division held that if interviews of child witnesses were too leading and suggestive, children might not be allowed to give testimony at all.[80] That decision was unanimously affirmed by the New Jersey Supreme Court in 1994.[81] The *Michaels* decisions relied on long-established precedent that forbids testimony from witnesses who have been hypnotized or otherwise had their sensibilities tainted before giving evidence. The New Jersey ruling brings children under the same umbrella that protects adults from bullying or other overly directive police tactics.

The result may not be what the judges intended, however. When investigators and prosecutors have preserved records of their faulty interviewing methods on film and tape, juries and appellate courts—such as those involved in the McMartin and Michaels cases—have cleared defendants of guilt. Meanwhile, in cases where records have been "lost" or never kept at all, the accused have often been convicted and their guilty verdicts upheld. This dichotomy suggests that in future investigations, no recordings will be made and no detailed logs kept. It is just this kind of silence that is now being recommended by the nation's leading prosecutors of child sex-abuse cases.

PART IV
Taming the Demon

ELEVEN

Silences Broken, Silences Made

Although not a description of ritual abuse, Roland Summit's famous 1983 article, "The Child Sexual Abuse Accommodation Syndrome," has been a guiding light for investigators in cases where satanic assaults are alleged. Despite its dry, scholarly style, the article tells a heartrending story—one that, like the tragedy described in *Uncle Tom's Cabin*, cries out for listeners.

Summit writes about a prepubescent daughter who is sexually molested by her father. "This is our secret," he says to her. "Don't tell anybody. Nobody will believe you." The abuse goes on as he wakes her at night to probe her with his hands, mouth, and penis. She submits quietly to these terrors, too confused and ashamed to cry out, resist, or escape.[1]

Because she loves her abuser, the daughter eventually comes to believe that *she* has provoked the sex, and she tries to make amends by being a good girl. Her father shows her how, and his main requirement is that she comply with his continuing demands. ("It's a good thing I can count on you to love me, otherwise, I'd have to turn to your little sister. I'd have to hang out in bars and look for other women," he tells her. Or, even more threateningly, "If your mother ever found out it would kill her. If you ever tell they could send me to jail and put all you kids in an orphanage.") In a perverse reversal of the adult and child roles, the daughter is made responsible for preserving her family.[2]

Finally, the secret can no longer be contained. The girl reaches adolescence and tells a teacher or some other authority—haltingly, partially, but she tells. The reaction is cataclysmic. The abuser vehemently denies the accusations, and calls her a liar. Her mother does not believe her, or she decompensates into hysteria and rage. All the children are placed in custody. The father is threatened with disgrace and imprisonment. The girl is blamed for causing the whole mess, and everyone treats her like a freak. She is sent to a juvenile home or foster care while her father remains in the home.[3]

Finally, she "admits" that she made up the story. "I was awful mad at my dad for punishing me," she says. "He hit me and said I could never see my boyfriend again. I've been really bad for years and nothing seems to keep me from getting into trouble. Dad had plenty of reason to be mad at me. But I got real mad and just had to find some way of getting out of that place. So I made up this story about him fooling around with me and everything. I didn't mean to get everyone in so much trouble."[4]

The daughter's lie, cautioned Summit, "carries more credibility than the most explicit claims of incestuous entrapment. It confirms adult expectations that children cannot be trusted. It restores the precarious equilibrium of the family. Children learn not to complain. Adults learn not to listen. The authorities learn not to believe."[5]

Summit's chilling tale galvanized child-abuse specialists and the culture at large, for who would not want to help such a child tell her secret? The possibility of providing her with words and a voice to obtain justice has proved irresistible to case investigators. Even more tempting is the prospect of illuminating darker crimes—including the evils of ritual abuse.

Persuasive Rhetoric

Since the 1980s, then, ritual abuse believers have used the image of the child in need of a voice and the metaphor of the terrible secret to arouse popular support for their claims and to stifle skepticism. Families of Crimes of Silence is the name of a Southern California parents' group, organized in the wake of the McMartin case, that has lobbied to increase prison time for people convicted of ritual abuse. VOICES (Victims of Incest Can Emerge Survivors) includes purported ritual-abuse victims in its membership. Journalists, too, have relied on this rhetoric. Jan Hollingsworth's *Unspeakable Acts* is about Miami's Country Walk case, while John Crewdson's *By Silence Betrayed* includes credulous accounts of similar accusations.[6] Believers in ritual child abuse compare society's unwillingness to acknowledge the phenomenon with the refusal before the end of World War II to recognize the mass murder of Jews in Europe. In confronting skeptics, the San Diego County Ritual Abuse Task Force has declared: "It is useful to draw correlations to other atrocities which were not originally believed, such as the Holocaust, to illustrate that such things can happen in a civilized, advanced society."[7] Believers also have accused skeptics of suffering from collective denial and shared negative hallucinations, of encouraging child abuse, and of being child molesters themselves, or even satanists.

The opposite of callous indifference, according to the same believers, is "breaking the silence," and the job of child protectionists is to accomplish this task by helping victims express what is hidden.[8] "Come on, Ronnie," pleaded Deputy Sheriff Jack Rutledge to a reluctant, confused eight-year-old boy in a Kern County, California, sex-ring investigation; "go ahead and let it out!"[9] In McMartin, Sara Barton's father encouraged her to recall abuse at the preschool, and when she told about eating feces covered with chocolate sauce, he showered her with praise for revealing her "secrets" and thereby strengthening their family.[10] Children like Sara who disclosed abuse were commended in direct proportion to the gravity of their charges, since it was thought that the more appalling the crimes, the greater the courage needed to break the silence about them.

Behind this injunction to speak out is the premise that liberation from the dead weight of one's past can be achieved by unearthing painful material, then publicly disclosing it. This idea flows not just from psychoanalysis and psychotherapy but also from the politics of the 1960s, when women and minorities proclaimed the need to remember and rewrite their own histories, including the chronicles of their oppression. In another sense, though, breaking the silence meant something different in the 1980s from what it meant in the 1960s, because for many people, what was repressed in the 1960s was not suffering but desire. Overcoming inhibitions meant overcoming the strictures of a puritanical society, and if one was too "hung up" to express one's deepest feelings, it meant that one was estranged from one's body and erotic needs.[11]

Feminists have been particularly taken with the idea of breaking the silence. During early days of the 1960s-era counterculture, public discussion about sexuality was male-dominated and equated liberation with the traditional male fantasy of having sex with as many partners as possible. The demand that women make themselves freely available to men troubled feminists, and they began formulating definitions of sexual liberation that took women's perspectives into account. In consciousness-raising sessions, for instance, women who discussed how they achieved orgasm were amazed when others reported that their clitorises were more sensitive than their vaginas. This was a subversive disclosure, since according to common knowledge, mature, well-adjusted women were supposed to enjoy penile penetration more than any other kind of stimulation.[12] This reinterpretation of female sexuality was an example of how women broke the silence about their desires regarding sex.

Feminists then set out to do the same with the injuries sex caused, and one of their first projects was to change the laws that made it difficult to convict men of rape. Remembering their girlhoods, many of these same women turned sexual abuse into a public issue, and the idea of a youngster breaking silence about molestation resonated strongly with them. By the 1980s, disclosing ritual abuse was the most dramatic way of all to break the silence, one that Gloria Steinem likened to the revelations of the early feminist consciousness-raising groups.[13]

But there are problems with Steinem's comparison, for when women equate their experiences of sexual violation with children's ritual abuse stories, they ignore the fact that the youngsters' purported narratives do not really come from them. This becomes obvious when one looks at what happened to the earlier practice of recording those voices on tape.

Suppressing Children's Accounts

When ritual-abuse cases first surfaced, it was thought vital to preserve children's original disclosures. In May 1984, Kee MacFarlane told Congress: "What we capture on videotape on the first interview is an incredible kind of spontaneity, this eye-opening reality that comes from children's first descriptions of abuse."[14] Recordings of accusations played a major part in prosecuting child-abuse cases in the 1970s. For a father to watch a videotape of his daughter describing his abuse often led the man to "fall apart and admit" (see chapter 1), and if he still insisted on his innocence, the tape could be played in court in some states, and used as compelling evidence that often led to a conviction. Because of this, the McMartin children's interviews were taped.[15]

But instead of revealing heartfelt narratives by children, the recordings starred the interviewers themselves, and showed them working strenuously to lead children from denials to "yes" answers. The same tapes were instrumental in producing jury verdicts favorable to Peggy Buckey and her son, Ray. Similar recordings led the New Jersey courts to reverse Kelly Michaels's convictions.

Case investigators quickly realized that in ritual-abuse cases, preserving the interviews would create problems for the prosecution. In Bakersfield, where dozens of people were convicted of large-scale sex abuse, recordings were rarely made after 1982. The Kern County district attorney commented in 1985 that his deputies did not like taping, because of its value to the defense.[16] Likewise, in 1984, prosecutors in a Memphis day-care ritual-abuse case found that even though preschoolers were naming more and more people as abusers, they volunteered almost nothing about what these supposed offenders had done to them. The authorities ultimately made no recordings because they knew that "these tapes would be a part of the discovery proceedings."[17] They also destroyed tapes already made.[18]

The same year, in the Bronx, the district attorney and FBI officials investigating the Puerto Rican Association for Community Affairs (PRACA) day-care center declined to record interviews, nor did they take notes. Even without these records, there are several indications that the children were badgered into making accusations. The first one to be interviewed underwent five days of questioning.[19] In court, it was revealed that many others made accusations only after assistant DA's like Nancy Borko gave them toys, "real good candy," and "horsey rides."[20] In his 1988 autobiography *Big City D.A.*, Bronx district attorney Mario Merola wrote: "I've been accused of giving them candy. I plead guilty. I stroke them, I kiss them. . . ."[21] (Years later, investigation into accusations against imprisoned former PRACA day-care worker Albert Ramos revealed that the Bronx district attorney's office went beyond simply failing to preserve evidence. Ramos had been convicted in 1985 of raping a five-year-old at his workplace. Nine years later, his guilty verdicts were set aside because the prosecution never gave his lawyers several exculpatory documents it possessed, including one showing that Ramos's young accuser had earlier made an unfounded sex-abuse accusation against a five-year-old boy.)[22]

Investigators became so diligent in their efforts to avoid giving exculpatory information to defense attorneys that they apparently have even hidden or deliberately destroyed material. In Kern County's Pitts case, prosecutors said they never preserved their sessions with the children, even though one youngster testified that he saw a tape recorder running during his interview. Recantations and statements by the children that would undermine their credibility were also kept from the defense. During the Pitts's trial, for instance, prosecutor Andrew Gindes sequestered the three accusing boys in a juvenile home where they were in constant contact with several other children who were making satanic ritual-abuse allegations.

Before going to the home, the boys had never mentioned ritual abuse. But shortly after their arrival, a social worker told Gindes that one of them, eight-year-old Timothy Martin, had described seeing the defendants stab animals, behead them, and throw them into fires before molesting the children. At the time Gindes said nothing about these allegations, which would have discredited the boy as one of his key witnesses. "I was saying that stuff," Timothy would disclose five years later, "because everyone else was. I thought that's what you were supposed to do there, so I just listened and then made something up."[23]

In cases where recordings were made, preserved, and given to the defense, juries often handed down not-guilty verdicts. Where there were no tapes, defendants were typically convicted. As attendees learned at the FBI's 1985 ritual-abuse conference (see chapter 6), abandoning their tape recorders and notepads "worked" for prosecutors.[24]

Child-protection authorities institutionalized their phobia about interview records in 1987, when the National Center for the Prosecution of Child Abuse (NCPCA) published a voluminous manual instructing district attorneys on how to handle child abuse cases. Titled *Investigation and Prosecution of Child Abuse*, many of its writers and editors were people who had fomented ritual-abuse cases: Bronx Assistant District Attorney Nancy Borko, for example, and Kee MacFarlane.

Investigation and Prosecution of Child Abuse contains reams of advice on how to gather pro-prosecution expert witnesses; how to discredit those who testify for the defense; how to pick juries sure to vote guilty; and—perhaps most important— on not videotaping interviews with children, since doing so may help the defense.[25] The text was published by the National District Attorneys Association, and was federally funded by the Justice Department and the National Center on Child Abuse and Neglect. By late 1990, it had sold more than 8,500 copies, and was considered the standard text for prosecutors, police, and social workers involved in child protection.

The movement from disclosing how a case was put together to concealing the process is demonstrated in a series of ritual-abuse prosecutions in Chicago. The case against Rogers Park Day Care janitor Deloartic Parks, which was tried in 1984, unraveled largely because children were repeatedly interviewed by workers from three separate agencies, each of whom made written reports. Documentation of the many interviews showed how implausible the accusations were. Children reported twenty-seven incidents of teachers urinating or defecating on them in class, for instance, yet none of the many other adults at the school had ever noticed. Such reports were credited with destroying the case, which ended with Parks's acquittal.[26]

But Chicago's next ritual-abuse case was handled differently. The defendant was day-care operator Sandra Fabiano, who was charged in 1987, just after Cook County formed its new Task Force on Mass Molestation of Children. The task force systematically tried to keep Fabiano's attorneys and the public from finding out how they built the case. Assistant State Attorney Diane Romza ordered investigators not to record interviews, and only one of the three task force members present during each session took notes. Prosecutors then impounded the records, which meant they were sealed to the public, including the media.

However, Chicago's press and television stations would not tolerate suppression of the material. They obtained and published leaked documents, such as reports of medical examinations that showed no credible evidence of abuse and interviews with children about events that could not have happened. Fabiano was tried amid a public clamor to drop the charges, and she was promptly acquitted.[27]

Elsewhere, efforts to conceal records have been more successful. In some cases, investigators have destroyed notes. In others, diaries and other written records of therapists, social workers, and foster parents have been sealed. Sex abuse coordinators in district attorneys' offices, and even prosecutors themselves, have asked children investigative questions under the guise of merely preparing them to testify, thus developing state's evidence while maintaining immunity from having to record their conversations.

Further, the media's custom of omitting accusing children's names from the news has meant that their parents have also remained anonymous, and this has kept the public from learning about the power and politics behind many ritual-abuse cases. In San Diego, for instance, the grandparents of two children who accused church day-care volunteer Dale Akiki of rape and animal killing were Jack Goodall, CEO of the parent company of the fast-food chain Jack-in-the-Box, and Goodall's wife, Mary. At the time, Mary Goodall was a substantial contributor to a sexual-abuse foundation of which assistant district attorney Mary Avery was a member. Mary Goodall also sat on the San Diego Ritual Abuse Task Force.

Sally Penso, the deputy district attorney originally in charge of Akiki's case, initially did not indict him because she felt there was insufficient evidence to prosecute. When the Goodalls heard this, they met privately with San Diego's district attorney and urged him to reconsider. A week later, the case was reassigned to Avery, who prosecuted Akiki on forty-three counts of child abuse.[28] The Goodalls, meanwhile—and Avery's connections with them—were kept out of the press until the trial began almost three years later.[29]

The Akiki case was constructed using the most advanced methods of obfuscation. Not only were few records kept of the interviews, and the Goodalls' role kept silent, but Avery asked the court to ban the term "ritual abuse" from being used by the defense—even though one therapist for children in the case testified that Avery had directed her to attend a conference on the topic.[30]

In other cases, damning information was concealed, even from juries and the defense. In McMartin, Judy Johnson's mental problems were obvious enough for prosecutors to joke about, even as they used her delusionary statements to question children (see chapter 4). Johnson's mental health records, however, were allegedly kept from the defense for years, at the direction of assistant district attorney Lael Rubin.[31] And trial judge William Pounders later refused to allow evidence of Johnson's problems to reach the jury.

Perhaps the most striking example of the way exculpatory evidence was concealed occurred during the New Jersey prosecution of Kelly Michaels. Shortly after Michaels was charged with abuse in 1985, employees at a commercial photo-developing laboratory in New Jersey impounded a roll of film sent for processing from a nearby drugstore. According to the laboratory manager, every picture on the roll depicted young, naked girls in "spread shots" so well posed and explicit that he could not imagine they were innocent accidents. He called authorities, and was soon visited by investigators from the Essex County prosecutor's office. So convinced were they that the pictures were deliberate pornography that they scrutinized them for images of semen on the children. They also looked at the customer bag that the roll had been sent in. On it was written Schocken, the name of a couple with a little girl in the Wee Care case.[32]

The case was never publicized, and two years later, an attorney for the Wee Care children (who was also the father of a child in the case) appeared at a closed hearing in the trial judge's chambers and asked that the photographs and negatives be destroyed. By then, the state had decided not to indict the parents whose names were on the bag; prosecutors now claimed that the pictures were the innocent products of children horsing around with a camera. The judge denied the request to destroy the photographs, but he also forbade anyone at the hearing, including Michaels's attorneys, from ever mentioning anything about them.[33]

A few months later, Marla Schocken was called to the witness stand by the state. There she claimed that Michaels once confided to her that she was going to a doctor because she was bleeding from the rectum. This was a devastating assertion, since it backed up children's stories about Michaels inserting sharp objects up their anuses and having them do the same to her. Michaels vehemently denied ever having a bleeding rectum or any such conversation with Schocken, but many trial watchers said that the woman's testimony was the most damning evidence of the trial. After Schocken gave it, Michaels's attorneys were gagged from cross-examining her about her involvement in a child-pornography case—which would have discredited her and suggested the obvious, that Schocken's testimony was part of a deal to escape her own criminal indictment.

Emerging Doubts

Suppression of exculpatory evidence propelled many cases to guilty verdicts. Others, however, quickly fell apart. Prosecutors in Jordan, Minnesota, dropped all charges against twenty-one defendants in late 1984—only a year after the first allegations surfaced—because the accusations had ballooned so wildly that many of them, such as accounts of anonymous mulatto children being slaughtered, were utterly improbable. In early 1985, the state attorney general's office issued a report placing the blame for an investigation gone awry on relentless, unending interviewing of children.[34]

Some cases never made it to indictment. In 1990, Montgomery County, Maryland, police detective Richard Cage described a day-care investigation that began after a three-year-old complained of pain on his buttocks and blamed a person he called David. After repeated questioning by his anxious parents, the child said "David" was a "midget doctor." Cage detailed how leading interrogations and cross-germination spread allegations from parent to parent and child to child, and how therapists and investigators unwittingly encouraged the process. Soon, preschoolers were accusing their female teachers of sadomasochistic acts, satanic rites, and animal killing. Police eventually determined that all the stories were false and that the first child had been trying to tell his parents that his best friend, four-year-old David from day care, hit him while they were playing.[35] Confronted with similar charges at the Breezy Point Day School, in suburban Philadelphia, prosecutors and police investigated for five months. In a lengthy report, District Attorney Alan Rubenstein concluded that the allegations had no basis in fact, and that they had been fueled by parents' hysteria and panic.[36] (Unswayed, two parents vowed to continue their civil lawsuits against the school.)[37]

Other cases went to conviction, then unraveled on appeal. In Bakersfield's Pitts case—the country's most successful prosecution—Catherine Hogan, the leading child witness, told her stepmother in early 1987 that her testimony had not been true and that she had only given it because the authorities kept "talking at me and talking at me" and threatened to remove her from her home if she did not describe abuse.

At a meeting with a defense attorney where she repeated her recantation, Catherine mentioned that on the eve of trial, just after she had said she was molested, she was taken to the hospital for a medical evaluation. That was news to the lawyer. Earlier, he had fought to have the child witnesses seen by doctors, but the district attorney had argued that forcing genital exams on the youngsters would "invade their privacy." During the trial, the prosecutor told the jury that the absence of medical exams with negative sex-abuse findings was further evidence of the defendants' guilt. Now, Catherine's medical exam, done at the district attorney's request, was revealed, and it showed absolutely no evidence of sexual abuse. [38]

Catherine's recantation and the new medical evidence led to legal proceedings to reverse the case. In 1990, an appellate court threw out all convictions in the Pitts case, citing as its reason egregious prosecutorial misconduct throughout the trial.[39] When the district attorney's office attempted to retry the defendants, their six child witnesses had all recanted their testimony, and were describing how they had been badgered and duped into becoming witnesses for the prosecution.

At about the same time that the Bakersfield case fell apart, El Paso, Texas, day-care teachers Michelle Noble and Gayle Dove had their guilty verdicts thrown out by higher courts. Noble was soon thereafter retried and quickly acquitted by a jury who told the press that the district attorney's office should be investigated for having indicted her in the first place. The dramatic turnabout reflected a calmer attitude in the community and the local media, and a feeling—expressed even by the judge—that perhaps the teachers had been "done wrong" during the earlier trial.

Four years after Noble's acquittal, the FBI's Kenneth Lanning published a monograph for child-protection authorities in which he reported that, after hundreds of investigations by law-enforcement authorities into cases of alleged satanic cult abuse, no corroborative evidence was found.[40] Following this authoritative pronouncement, other convictions were overturned: those of Kelly Michaels in New Jersey, Martha Felix and Francisco Ontiveros in Nevada, and Franklin Beauchamp and Alberto Ramos in the Bronx. Defendants finally walked out of prison, bitter at having lost years of their lives. Others still languish in penal institutions around the country. At this writing, to name a few: Francisco Fuster remains in prison in Florida; a middle-aged Texas couple, the Kellners, are locked up in Texas; Gerald Amirault is jailed in Massachusetts, former day-care operators Frances and Daniel Keller are serving decades in Texas; and Bakersfield defendants Scott and Brenda Kniffen and Alvin and Debbie McCuan, and many others from Kern County, continue to serve sentences that in some cases add up to centuries. This despite the fact that in 1994, another federal government study that was five years in the making concluded that rumors of organized satanic child abuse were unfounded and that there was no evidence of any such incursions into public child care.[41]

While panic was subsiding in the United States, American ritual-abuse believers were exporting their claims into the rest of the English-speaking world. In Canada, the first charges had been made early, in Hamilton, Ontario, in 1985, against the parents of two young children and the mother's boyfriend. Years later, in 1992, the town of Martensville, just north of Saskatoon, erupted with more charges, from thirty children against nine adults, including a group of day-care-center operators and several police officers. With its rumors of rampant devil worship and clouds of suspicion hanging over the local authorities, the "Martensville nightmare," as the case was known in the press, burgeoned into a classic, communitywide moral panic. The convictions were ultimately overturned in 1995, on grounds that the children had been questioned improperly.[42]

A rash of cases also surfaced in Great Britain, beginning in 1988, after San Francisco "cult cop" Sandi Gallant—a major spokeswoman for the day-care panic in America—was interviewed in an English newspaper. During the same period, after therapists such as Pamela Klein visited that country to talk to colleagues about ritual abuse, cases flared up in Orkney, Rochdale, suburban London, and Nottingham.[43]

The British romance with ritual abuse, though torrid, was brief. As early as 1989, an investigation of the Nottingham charges concluded that they were unfounded, and a report leaked to the press revealed that children's talk of animals, witches, and blood was probably triggered by toys and "therapeutic aids" used by social workers, including witches' costumes, plastic syringes, and rubber snakes.[44] By late 1990, the British media had turned skeptical,[45] and the government commissioned an anthropologist to investigate the cases. Her report, released in 1994, concluded that most of the charges were brought against extremely indigent families, many of whom were being supervised by social workers from welfare agencies. These social workers had taken satanic-abuse seminars led by U.S. "experts." The Americans then acted as consultants in many of the cases that resulted.[46] Meanwhile, in New Zealand, a day-care case surfaced in Christchurch shortly after U.S. ritual-abuse consultants made presentations in 1991; it was followed by a wave of similar charges throughout the country.[47]

Northern Europe and Scandinavia have also experienced ritual abuse cases: in Holland, one scandal included claims that 1,600 babies had been murdered; an investigation found nothing to support the charges. In Norway, a day-care case that surfaced in 1992 led to arrests of seven adults accused by twenty-one children. Charges were dropped against six defendants in 1993, and the seventh was subsequently tried and acquitted, amid a national discussion about the poor investigative techniques and questionable theories that had built the case.[48]

The Crime of Doubt

If many ritual-abuse cases were so easily discredited, even as early as the late 1980s, where were the doubters in this country whose public protests might have dampened the panic? They existed, but glaringly absent from their ranks were the prominent civil libertarians and political progressives who usually denounce police overzealousness and witch hunting. So taken were these people with the feminist and pro-child pretensions of ritual-abuse claims makers that they failed to question the hysteria, even as dozens of defendants were marched off to prison desperately insisting on their innocence. A vacuum thus existed where skeptics should have been, and it was at first filled with critics whom believers found easy to ignore or attack.

Curiously, the early doubters occupied diametrically opposing points on the cultural spectrum. One was fundamentalist Christian writer Mary Pride, whose book, *The Child Abuse Industry*, is highly critical of government intervention into family life and parental authority. Pride's work demonstrates that even when they believe in the dangers of satanism, many moral conservatives find the government more dangerous than the devil. Another book, *The Politics of Child Abuse*, was authored by longtime iconoclasts Paul and Shirley Eberle.[49] In the 1960s, the Eberles worked for the freewheeling Los Angeles *Free Press,* and by the early 1970s they were editing another antiestablishment publication that attacked civil-liberties violations such as police misconduct. As was common with alternative newspapers during this period, the Eberles financed their enterprise by publishing ads from the sex industry. As staunch free-speech advocates, they later started a newspaper that solicited and published readers' sexual fantasies, including occasional drawings and verbal depictions of pedophilia[50] (for this, they have been vociferously condemned as kiddie pornographers by ritual-abuse believers).

Christian Mary Pride and the counterculture Eberles could not have come from more opposite backgrounds. Yet their books both attack the excesses of state intrusions into private life, without addressing the question of how to define children's rights as separate from their parents'. Indeed, the most outspoken ritual-abuse skeptics have tended to promote the conservative view that parental authority is inviolable. The same is true of the first organization of skeptics, Victims of Child Abuse Laws, or VOCAL, established in late 1984 by Bob and Lois Bentz, and several other Jordan, Minnesota, residents who had been accused of ritual abuse and then been acquitted or had their charges dropped. Since then, VOCAL has lobbied in state legislatures around the country for laws to limit state intervention into families. Its resources are used mostly by defense attorneys and by people accused of sexual abuse, and members generally drop out as soon as their cases are resolved. The organization operates on a shoestring budget, and has never achieved a significant national presence as a think tank or policy maker.

The few mental health experts who were pioneer ritual-abuse skeptics also tended to be conservative on sex and family issues. One is Ralph Underwager, a former Lutheran minister and currently a psychologist in Minnesota. Since testifying for the defense in Jordan, Minnesota, in 1984, Underwager has taken the stand in many other trials, usually as an expert on the issue of children's suggestibility and the effect of improper interviewing on their testimony. Underwager and his wife, Hollida Wakefield, publish the journal *Issues in Child Abuse Accusations,* which prints articles skeptical of ritual-abuse cases, as well as other problematic sex abuse prosecutions. The couple has written several books about false accusations and consider themselves scientists when it comes to the subject.[51] They frequently stray from empiricism, though, and when they do, their moral conservatism is glaring.

They share with child protectionists the political theory that cross-generational sex can never be a positive experience for the younger party (at least not in the United States, Underwager notes), even though the scientific data indicate otherwise. In odder flights from empiricism to morality, Underwager has suggested that pedophiles consider their sexual proclivities "part of God's will,"[52] and that false sex-abuse allegations are at least partly due to women who "may be jealous that males are able to love each other."[53] Further, in their most recent book, *Return of the Furies*, the couple claims that the main problem with the child-protection system is its hostility to the family. The book praises patriarchy as the basis of Western civilization, and warns that society is under attack by "radical feminists."[54]

A more sophisticated moral conservative skeptic is Richard Gardner, a professor of clinical psychiatry at Columbia University. Gardner has generated a massive amount of work, most of it self-published, attacking both ritual-abuse charges and the child-protection system. He has also invented his own malady, the Parental Alienation Syndrome, to describe a psychiatric "disorder" that arises during custody disputes, when one parent—almost always the mother—feels compelled to "alienate" the children from the other parent by pressuring them to see the latter as despicable and even inducing them to make false abuse allegations.[55] This "disorder" has not been empirically researched, let alone recognized by the American Psychiatric Association. Even so, just as accusers have used Roland Summit's Child Sexual Abuse Accommodation Syndrome in court, experts testifying in behalf of the accused have cited Gardner's syndrome to have abuse charges thrown out and the syndrome-afflicted parent's visitation rights restricted. Most of those certified as ill by Gardner's syndrome are ex-wives rather than husbands, but Gardner seems unconcerned that he has developed yet another female malady in a field notorious for pathologizing women. This is perhaps predictable, since he also believes that male promiscuity, female monogamy, and other behaviors that differ between the sexes are genetic.[56]

Perhaps the only pioneer skeptic to avoid the conservative political fray and stick to questions of scientific validity is Berkeley child psychiatrist Lee Coleman, who has testified as a defense expert in child sex-abuse cases throughout the country since the early 1980s. Contending that mental health clinicians' knowledge of behavior is strictly impressionistic, Coleman believes that they should not be allowed to give expert testimony in court about matters that juries are equally good, if not better, at judging—such as whether a child "appears" abused. He also believes that commonly used interviewing techniques produce unreliable statements from children. Further, although not a pediatrician, a gynecologist, or an anatomist, Coleman was one of the first physicians who appeared in court to point out that prosecution "medical evidence" was grossly unscientific.

Regardless of their politics about larger issues of child protection and family intervention, subsequent research on suggestive interviewing and children's genital anatomy has proved Underwager, Gardner, and Coleman correct about the issues they testified to in ritual-abuse cases during the 1980s. Their opinions were readily available then to muckraking journalists, but even in the media, it was hard to find a reporter willing to look critically at ritual-abuse claims. An exception, by 1990, was *The Nation* and *Los Angeles Times* columnist Alexander Cockburn, who questioned the McMartin prosecutions. But his work proved the earlier rule. In an article critical of Kelly Michaels's conviction, published in *Harper's* magazine the same year, writer Dorothy Rabinowitz recounted her experience in New Jersey covering the investigation and trial: "Youngish journalists who prided themselves on their skepticism—types who automatically sniffed with suspicion at any and every pronouncement by a governmental official—were outraged by the merest suggestion that the state's charges against Kelly Michaels lacked credibility."[57]

The few press skeptics who did exist in the 1980s often fared poorly, even as apologists for ritual abuse were lionized. Rabinowitz's article was accepted by *Harper's* months after she wrote it, on assignment, for *Vanity Fair*—the editors there killed it. They felt that Rabinowitz's conclusion, that Michaels was innocent, was too controversial to print.[58] On the West Coast, two years after the Los Angeles district attorney's office dropped charges against five McMartin defendants and called the charges against them "incredibly weak," Bob Williams, an editor and award-winning reporter for the *Los Angeles Times*, investigated the case for several months, concluded that the Buckeys were also innocent, and wrote several sympathetic stories about them. The *Times* reporter who covered McMartin on a day-to-day basis, however, was Lois Timnick. In a series of memos Williams wrote to his superiors, he dissected Timnick's coverage, argued that she was seriously biased for the prosecution, and asked to be assigned more stories about the case. He was rebuffed, eventually disciplined for criticizing Timnick and interviewing Ray Buckey, and chastised for demonstrating "strong bias" toward the McMartin defendants. In frustration, Williams resigned.[59]

Hostility toward skeptics undoubtedly had to do with media intimations—in venues ranging from *Geraldo* to the *New York Times*—that regardless of exculpatory evidence or acquittals, children really had been abused at the McMartin Preschool. A veritable genre of ritual-abuse believer books also spurred popular belief in other defendants' guilt, particularly because some were produced by major publishers and touted as authored by journalists—even though they were little more than screeds for the prosecution.

Lisa Manshel's *Nap Time*, for instance, was released by a major publisher, William Morrow, and praised by child-protection professionals as an objective account of the Kelly Michaels case.[60] Manshel was hardly a disinterested observer, however. Her parents were close friends with a New Jersey social worker who had been involved in the prosecution from its beginning, and who later promoted Manshel's book on nationwide talk shows. Manshel is also related to the former head of New Jersey's Department of Youth and Family Services, the agency that gathered most of the prosecution's evidence against Michaels.[61] Jan Hollingsworth's book, *Unspeakable Acts,* favorably reviewed in 1986 by the *New York Times,* has likewise been praised as an objective journalistic account of the Country Walk case, even though Hollingsworth was actively involved in developing the case. She called in the first complaint against the defendants on behalf of a friend, and shortly thereafter quit her job at a Miami television station, became a paid consultant to the husband-and-wife team who interviewed the Country Walk children,[62] and joined parents in lobbying the Florida legislature to allow closed-circuit testimony of children. Hollingsworth acknowledged none of these activities in her book.

While writers with doubts about defendants' guilt were ignored or refused assignments, skeptical mental health professionals fared worse. Throughout the 1980s, psychologists and physicians who publicly opposed ritual-abuse prosecutions were subjected to harassment and attacks. In 1987, Ralph Underwager sent a questionnaire to thirty-three such experts "who had testified that not every accusation is fact and that there are significant problems with the way such accusations are handled."[63] Of the seventeen who responded, all but one reported a variety of repercussions. Dossiers with slander and ad hominem attacks on them were circulated among prosecutors. There were efforts by child-protection authorities to blacklist them, cut off their referrals, stop their research funding, and cancel their classes and workshops. Complaints were made against them to regulatory bodies. Some were threatened with physical violence. One had his office picketed.[64]

One organization that systematically targeted skeptical experts was the National District Attorneys Association (NDAA), which established its National Center for Prosecution of Child Abuse (NCPCA) in 1985. During its first year, the NCPCA received some $646,000 from the Justice Department and $109,000 from National Center for Child Abuse and Neglect.[65] By 1988, the Justice Department had provided almost $2 million, and by 1991, almost double that.[66] The NCPCA has used this money to develop model statutes concerning hearsay exceptions, videotaped testimony, closed-circuit television testimony, and the competency question.[67] It also teaches prosecutors and allied child-protection workers how to investigate and convict offenders. Many of the organization's most supportive prosecutors have handled ritual-abuse cases, and the NCPCA has bolstered belief in their validity with a vengeance.

One way it has done this is through its *Investigation and Prosecution of Child Abuse* manual,[68] which includes boilerplate motions to close the courtroom, restrict media access, seal records, and block disclosure of child witness records to defendants. The text includes sound bites designed to counter defense arguments, such as: "Children don't lie to get into trouble, they lie to get out of it."[69] The NCPCA also provides prosecutors with lists of expert witnesses. To discredit those who habitually testify for the defense, it distributes transcripts of their testimony and explains how to debunk their theories and research.

One of its thickest files is on Underwager. In late 1990, the organization advertised summaries of seven cases in which he was disqualified as an expert; it also offered information about his odd remarks about pedophilia.[70] Samples of Paul and Shirley Eberle's sex newspapers from the 1970s could be obtained in order to discredit anyone who mentioned their book during a trial. Critiques were also available of many other experts with far more prestigious credentials and nary a hint of iconoclasm, who, the NCPCA derisively noted, "regularly testify on behalf of accused molesters."[71]

Remembrance of Ritual Abuse Past

By the time NCPCA published this advertisement, the McMartin case was over. But shortly afterward, another kind of ritual-abuse criminal case surfaced nationally. The new variety involved accusations made not by children but by adults receiving psychotherapy who, as a result of pressure and suggestion by their therapists and from self-help books, were remembering family-based childhood ritual abuse they supposedly had completely forgotten for years. Such claims had been circulating since the early 1980s, as evidenced by the best-selling book *Michelle Remembers* (see chapter 2). But by the end of the decade, a veritable recovered-memory industry had developed among therapists and psychiatric hospitals, and a significant percentage of the purported victims were suing their relatives for damages.[72] These actions promptly generated skepticism, mainly because instead of discrediting public child care and blue-collar parents, they constituted an attack on the solid, middle-class family.

The flagship case in the new controversy involved criminal charges against Paul Ingram, whose confession is described in chapter 8. Ingram's accuser was his daughter, Ericka, who was twenty-one years old when she brought her charges after suddenly "remembering" one day that her father had raped her for years when she was a child as part of a satanic ritual.

Ericka's accusations against Ingram, a police officer and Republican party official in Olympia, Washington, first came to light when she went on a retreat for women members of the charismatic Christian church that the Ingram family attended. During a highly emotional gathering, a faith healer looked at Ericka, who was already distraught, and told her, "You have been abused as a child, sexually abused." The healer then said she had received a message from God that the abuse was "by your father, and it's been happening for years."[73] Ingram's other daughter later said that she, too, had been raped by him. These accusations reached the sheriff's office, and the deputies, whom Ingram knew well, embarked on a long process of interrogation—which included sleep deprivation and hypnosislike procedures—that eventually had him describing murderous satanic rituals and molestations in the company of several male friends.

After massive efforts to corroborate Ingram's stories produced nothing, authorities called on University of California at Berkeley sociologist and cult behavior specialist Richard Ofshe for help (see chapter 8). Another of Ofshe's specialties, one that the Washington authorities were unaware of, was how police use psychological techniques of persuasion to gain false confessions. Reviewing the case, Ofshe concluded that Ingram had not really experienced the events he was remembering. He set out to publicize Ingram's confession and subsequent conviction as a miscarriage of justice,[74] and shortly thereafter joined the board of the newly formed False Memory Syndrome Foundation (FMSF).

The FMSF is currently the main organized resistance to the notion that recovered, or repressed, memories of sexual abuse are inherently reliable. One issue the group addresses is the phenomenon—increasingly common since the mid-1980s—of grown women (and a few men) entering therapy and suddenly remembering having been abused, as children, during satanic rituals. Parents of many such patients have been sued. Others have been subjected to criminal investigations, and even prosecuted and convicted.[75]

These new and increasingly widespread charges of evil in heretofore respectable families have met a dramatically different response than children's earlier accusations of sexual mayhem at preschool or in blue-collar enclaves. Adults who recover sexual-abuse memories usually do so during psychotherapy. The fact that they can afford such treatment, and that they seek it out, means that most come from prosperous, well-educated families. This in turn means that most of their parents also have money, education, and social prestige—unlike the accused in the children's ritual-abuse cases.

FMSF parents thus have fought the charges against them with far greater success than their predecessors. Illustrative of the difference is the background of VOCAL's leaders versus those of the FMSF. VOCAL founder Bob Bentz was employed in the paint department of a Ford automobile factory in St. Paul, and his wife worked night shift at a print shop.[76] FMSF founder Pamela Freyd, on the other hand, is an education researcher at the University of Pennsylvania; her husband, Peter, is a mathematics professor there, and has taught throughout the world.[77]

Peter Freyd was accused by his daughter Jennifer, a psychology professor at the University of Oregon, of molesting her for years when she was young. She did not remember any of this until she entered therapy. Peter has vehemently denied the abuse, and, as if to lay claim to their professional status, the Freyds' organization has coined the False Memory Syndrome to label women who make accusations like Jennifer's.[78] Founded in 1991, the FMSF board is studded with prestigious psychologists and psychiatrists (including some whom the Freyds previously knew personally), and it has grown with phenomenal speed.[79] In 1992, *Update,* the newsletter of the National Center for the Prosecution of Child Abuse, expressed alarm at the foundation's expansion and influence, and next year, FMSF held its first convention, which featured some of the country's most prominent cognitive psychologists discussing their research into memory.[80]

What many have found suggests that adults may permanently or intermittently fail to recall sexual-abuse incidents they suffered as children.[81] But the researchers also note that people forget all kinds of experiences, whether traumatic or not, and that suggestive questioning by authorities such as therapists can generate false memories that seem very real, even down to the strong emotions that accompany them (see chapters 2 and 7).[82]

Unlike mental health skeptics of the early 1980s who questioned ritual abuse prosecutions, many FMSF advisory board members are prestigious academics who studiously avoid making pronouncements about issues beyond their specialties. One will not hear a disquisition on the decline of Western civilization from renowned memory scholar Elizabeth Loftus, nor a word about feminism from her colleague, Emory University researcher Ulric Neisser.

On the other hand, the FMSF shares many of the same highly charged political assumptions as the child protectionists who fomented satanic-abuse panic. Both sides, for instance, proclaim that sexual abuse is inevitably the most devastating thing that can happen to a child. The FMSF makes this argument in order to posit its corollary, that being falsely accused of sexual abuse is the worst thing that can happen to its members. While this kind of hyperbolic rhetoric may be good organizing strategy, it puts the group in the same camp as ritual-abuse believers, who ignore research that suggests that, in general, neglect and physical abuse, which are far more common than sexual abuse, are also more destructive to children's development.[83]

Further, many FMSF luminaries are editorial board members of *Cultic Studies Journal,* a publication of the American Family Foundation.[84] As its name implies, the AFF is a conservative group that distrusts nonmainstream religions, uses the nonscientific term cult to characterize them, blames them for breaking up traditional families, and believes in organized satanic groups of the kind that the child protectionists imagine are abusing children in day care. In fact, AFF's "satanism information packet," which it distributes to the public, contains a McMartinesque "ritual abuse behavioral checklist" for children.[85] It also recommends *Ms.* magazine's "chilling personal account of generational Satanic ritual abuse by a survivor"—a pseudonymously written article that lists the AFF as a resource to help such victims.[86]

FMSF's attraction for the AFF centers on the fact that the former group's members are obsessed with the idea that, like the preschoolers at day-care centers, their adult children are being brainwashed by "therapy cults." FMSF board member psychiatrist John Hochman condemns these "cults" as controlled by malign antifamily activists who teach hapless patients that the private home is less a haven in a heartless world than a nest of sexual predators.[87] Sounding like the most diehard child exploitation cop or Meese Commission member, Hochman also blames the 1960s counterculture for current social ills, including the "moral chaos" that has engendered "cults."[88] Once the science gets sorted out in the ritual-abuse dispute, it appears that politically, the crusaders and naysayers have much in common—even as angry recovered-memory advocates like Gloria Steinem denounce the FMSF as a front group for perpetrators, one that protests false accusations as a straw man to deflect attention from real sexual violence against women and children.[89]

These bitter denunciations from both camps reflect two things. One is that, unlike the earlier arguments about ritual abuse, in the current debate adversaries are equally matched, and the public is paying much closer attention than it did before to the pros and cons of the argument over child-abuse treatment and intervention issues. Too, the FMSF debate, by legitimizing skepticism about ritual abuse, is inspiring a second look at the early children's cases. Many of them, after all, were predicated on the same highly questionable assumptions that the FMSF challenges: that victims—in this case, actual children rather than grown ones—dissociate or repress experiences of sexual abuse even when the abuse happens incessantly, over weeks or even years. Indeed, amnesia has been cited repeatedly by ritual-abuse believers to explain why it takes children many months of therapy to "remember" their victimization, and why many acted perfectly normally until then. Such reasoning, which is usually introduced by experts who have given the children diagnoses of post-traumatic stress disorder, has contributed to guilty verdicts against several defendants.

Banishing Satan

Amid the new climate of doubt fueled by the FMSF, however, even some child protectionists have broken ranks with their colleagues and publicly questioned the use of traumatic forgetting theory in ritual-abuse cases. In the 1993 trial of San Diego day-care volunteer Dale Akiki, for instance, which ended with Akiki's acquittal, childhood trauma researcher Dr. Anthony Urquiza, a board member of the American Professional Society on the Abuse of Children (APSAC), testified for the defense. Urquiza questioned therapists, including Dr. Lenore Terr, who suggested that Akiki's alleged victims couldn't remember their victimization because they were suffering from post-traumatic stress disorder.

Following his testimony, many of Urquiza's colleagues criticized him for assisting the defense of an accused child molester.[90] But for the child-protection profession, the handwriting was on the wall: there was no longer a united front among APSAC luminaries about ritual abuse. The breech widened as government-funded researchers completed a study of ritual-abuse reports made across the country. Even before it was released in late 1994, the study's conclusion, that claims of widespread, devil-worshiping conspiracy were unfounded,[91] was already common knowledge among leading child protectionists.

Meanwhile, clinicians who treated adult ritual-abuse "survivors" were having their own problems. The False Memory Syndrome Foundation's spectacular success in the media prompted leading dissociationists—many of whom were helping craft the American Psychiatric Association's revised 1994 diagnostic manual—to press for removal of Multiple Personality Disorder from the prestigious text and replace it with the more neutral Dissociative Identity Disorder.[92]

That change made, dissociation theorists also dropped Multiple Personality from the title of their professional organization, formerly the International Society for the Study of Multiple Personality and Dissociation. In the new, shorter-named International Society for the Study of Dissociation (ISSD), president Colin Ross stopped warning about a CIA plot to turn middle-class youngsters into Manchurian candidate spies and assassins by torturing them with drugs, flotation tanks, electric shock, and the deliberate creation of multiple personalities who could be summoned with special letter and number codes.[93] By late 1994, he was publicly denying that he believed all patients' satanic-abuse stories to be true, and calling for dialogue between his organization and the FMSF.[94]

New Demons

The move to save dissociation by sacrificing multiple personality disorder and satanic ritual abuse was an effort not only to defend many psychiatrists' reputations but also to preserve the very essence of what sexual abuse had come to mean for the child-protection profession. Victimologists still insisted that, by definition, the younger parties to cross-generational sex are inevitably psychologically devastated and in dire need of therapy. And the larger culture still required that women's complaints about inequality and sexual violence be communicated through the innocent, mortified voice of the child. Thus, even as the devil-worshiping sex cultist departed the culture, a more secular, reasonable-sounding demon was needed.

Law-enforcement specialists had already provided a template for the new villain in the late 1980s, by suggesting that ritual-abuse cases be renamed "multivictim-multiperpetrator" phenomena, or as the FBI's Kenneth Lanning later suggested, "multidimensional sex rings." Just who would populate these new institutions was unclear, though, until Satan's replacement was finally found in the early 1990s: a composite of Charles Manson, Ted Bundy, Jeffrey Dahmer, and other sadistic murderers, real or imagined, who terrorize the modern imagination.

The substitution of sadist for Satan was first proposed by ISSD luminary and APSAC board member Jean Goodwin. A psychiatrist, Goodwin had worked with incest victims in the late 1970s,[95] and by the mid-1980s she was doing therapy with multiple-personality-disorder patients and promoting belief in their stories of satanic ritual abuse. By 1990 she was writing about the similarity between modern-day descriptions of ritual abuse and pre-Inquisition accounts of what Satan worshipers did at their sabbats.

The texts she drew upon constitute what contemporary historians and folklorists suggest are Christian subversion-myth literature instead of historical fact. Nevertheless, child-protection journals and dissociation conferences featured Goodwin's material, as well as her discussions of how to perform exorcisms on patients complaining of ritual-abuse histories.[96]

Still, Goodwin knew that believers in satanic ritual abuse faced a serious credibility problem. To counteract it, she proposed that *ritual abuse* be replaced with the term *sadistic abuse*.[97] The change, she wrote, would reinforce adults' and children's claims for various reasons. For one, while talking about satanic ritual abuse posited behavior that criminologists and the public had never before heard of, the term *sadist* recurred to real historical precedents: Caligula, the Spanish inquisitors, Jack the Ripper, John Gacey.

Adding scientific cache to her new terminology, Goodwin referred to criminological studies of serial killers. Citing one such study, she noted that sadistic criminals typically torture, bind, gag, rape, and murder their victims, often using electric shock, burning, amputation, cutting, and assaults with weapons and animals. These behaviors, she wrote, are "precisely the characteristics found in accounts of ritual abuse."[98] When described by a child or a psychiatric patient, she added, they "might seem fantastic and unbelievable,"[99] but they should not be dismissed, because sadists and serial killers are very real.

Goodwin's reasoning ignored several obvious facts. First, serial killers usually murder their victims within minutes or hours—they do not allow them to leave the scene of the crime day after day, then return for more torture, as described in ritual-abuse scenarios. Second, unlike the gangs of perpetrators in ritual-abuse stories, criminal sadists are generally loners. Occasionally they recruit a partner, and sociopathic authoritarians such as Charles Manson sometimes direct several people to do their criminal bidding. In these groups, however, maintaining secrecy is virtually impossible, and the police soon obtain evidence and confessions. The same is never true in ritual-abuse cases.

Finally, and most significant, all the criminal sexual sadists thus far identified and studied have been men,[100] leading authorities to conclude that raping, torturing, and mutilating victims for erotic pleasure is masculine activity. Yet in the ritual-abuse cases, the accused are often women. To try to explain them by calling them "sadistic" creates a new criminal type: the female sex murderer. She is far more terrifying than her satanist predecessor, since, instead of being a church invention, she is a contemporary therapeutic and feminist construct who writes her young victims' names not in grimoires but in day-care rollbooks.

Goodwin began publicizing her new *sadism* term in 1991, and soon *ritual abuse* and *satanism* had largely dropped out of child protectionists' vocabulary. By 1994, their major conferences had replaced workshops about ritual abuse with presentations on sadistic sexual maltreatment. Holdouts who still insisted on talking about transgenerational cults and national satanic sex rings found themselves increasingly marginalized, and their claims grew more and more bizarre. Members of the Los Angeles County Commission for Women's ritual-abuse task force called a press conference and announced that satanists were trying to poison them by pumping pesticides into their homes and through the ventilation system at the county building where they held meetings (health officials investigated and found no pesticides).[101]

Roland Summit, meanwhile, began publicizing claims by several McMartin parents that they had found molestation tunnels under the preschool site. Efforts to find the tunnels had begun in 1985, but yielded nothing of interest except evidence that the parents were implanting bogus evidence.[102] On the eve of Ray Buckey's second trial, in 1990, a group of mothers and fathers started a new dig by hiring an archaeologist and retaining as coordinator the cult cop Ted Gunderson, who had discredited himself a year earlier by making unfounded claims about mass satanic killings on the television show *Geraldo*.[103] After digging was completed, the team issued a report claiming they had found tunnels under the preschool, and Summit summarized the findings in an issue of *The Journal of Psychohistory* devoted to credulous articles about ritual-abuse claims.[104]

He and other tunnel publicizers have refused to distribute the archaeological report on the dig, however, which includes a section, written by a geologist, strongly questioning whether they are really tunnels.[105] Further, Summit has said nothing publicly regarding the McMartin parents' seeming implantation of bogus evidence during the 1985 dig, nor about the related fact that they again had access to the site in 1990 and apparently helped with the digging.[106] Nevertheless, production of the report was supported financially by Gloria Steinem,[107] the dig was reported on favorably in mainstream publications such as *Lear's*,[108] and the McMartin tunnels entered the intransigent lore of ritual-abuse conspiracy theory. That theory is now disseminated at crackpot therapy conferences and in publications put out by everyone from mental health professionals to ultra-right-wingers. Further, it can be found on computer bulletin boards devoted to Kennedy assassination obsessions; UFOlogy; and claims that the FBI is covering up a nationwide child-kidnaping and murder ring in which the White House is implicated; or that the CIA is coercing middle-class children into sex-abuse and Manchurian Candidate brainwashing schemes, employing trained dolphins as rapists under the direction of a shadowy Hasidic physician named Greenbaum.

At the same time that ritual-abuse conspiracy theory has grown flagrantly bizarre and anti-Semitic during the past few years, the major child-protection professional journals have published new research that clearly contradicts the jerry-rigged medical, criminological, and interviewing theories used to construct earlier ritual-abuse cases. Some of this material has been funded by the federal government's National Center on Child Abuse and Neglect (the same agency that financed many of the older studies promoting ritual abuse), and the new work mitigates against unjust prosecutions and convictions in the future.

But instead of squarely owning up to its history of sordid involvement in fomenting ritual-abuse panic, the child-protection profession remains officially silent on the issue. This is so primarily because many of its leading figures were so involved in bolstering ritual-abuse theory and prosecutions that to correct themselves would damage their reputations and, worse, threaten their own self-image. To realize how much power these leaders wield, and how much they stand to lose by admitting their mistakes, one has only to look at the board of the country's most influential child protection professional association, the American Society on the Abuse of Children (APSAC).

Board members in 1995 included President Linda Meyer Williams, co-author of *Nursery Crimes*, the government-funded study whose statistics are widely used to advance the claim that women are sadistic sex offenders. Also on the board was APSAC newsletter editor Susan Kelley, who did highly suggestive interviews of children in a Boston-area ritual-abuse case during the early 1980s that led to convictions for sixty-one-year-old day-care operator Violet Amirault, her daughter, and her son (he remains imprisoned at this writing). Kelley has since made her career by publishing research predicated on the assumption that the abuse happened, and she continues to defend her interviewing techniques in the Amirault case.[109]

On APSAC's executive committee in 1995 were Katherine Coulborn Faller, who helped investigate a day-care ritual abuse in Michigan in 1984 in which a defendant was convicted, and who is now on the advisory board of Believe the Children;

and Harry Elias, Kee MacFarlane's husband and formerly on the San Diego County Task Force on Ritual Abuse, a group of child-protection professionals who encouraged ritual-abuse investigations and prosecutions in the early 1990s.

In addition, APSAC's at-large and advisory board included David Corwin, a therapist involved in the McMartin case, and Ann Burgess, promoter of the use of children's drawings to diagnose sexual abuse, developer of the idea of the sex ring, participant (with Susan Kelley) in developing the case that imprisoned the Amirault family, and currently a researcher into the traumatic aftereffects of ritual abuse.[110] Also on the advisory board were North Carolina psychologist Mark Everson, whose testimony in 1992 about traumatic dissociation helped convict Little Rascals daycare operator Robert Kelly to life in prison in a massive ritual-abuse case; David Finkelhor, the lead researcher for *Nursery Crimes*; and Roland Summit, the McMartin tunnel publicist, who is also an advisory board member of Believe the Children, the country's major supporter of ritual-abuse claims. Summit is still frequently quoted by the media as an authority on child sexual abuse. And Kee MacFarlane— who is still a social worker—teaches in the psychiatry department at the University of Southern California, and continues to work at Children's Institute International, the center where the prosecutorial foundation of McMartin was laid. Far from being discredited by that case, the Institute has prospered: under MacFarlane's tutelage it recently received a subcontract from $1.2 million of federal money awarded to the Giarretto Institute by the state of California to train a new generation of child-protection workers in investigative interview techniques.[111]

Some of these individuals, as well as others involved in ritual-abuse cases, also sit on the editorial boards of prestigious child-abuse publications such as *The Journal of Interpersonal Violence* and *Child Abuse and Neglect*. Many continue actively to promote belief in ritual abuse under its new rubric, sadism, and still others advocate dissociation and repression theories of traumatic amnesia. Their typical response to criticism is twofold. Some pay lip service to the idea that their profession's past mistakes are at least partly to blame for the opprobrium directed against them. Yet they have never made any effort to publicly review those mistakes in particular cases—to reexamine the transcripts of Kee MacFarlane's child interviews in the McMartin cases, for instance—or to take concrete steps to overturn convictions based on such errors. Instead, they dismiss public concern about false charges as a political backlash against feminism and efforts to ensure children's welfare.[112]

At their conferences, symposia, and colloquia, such talk still evokes thunderous applause. Embedded in the noisy ovations, though, is a deep quiet that belies all the well-intentioned efforts of MacFarlane, Summit, and their colleagues to lend a voice to youngsters. The children of ritual-abuse cases are still silent, and so are the adults who remain imprisoned, some for more than a decade now.

TWELVE

Toward Real Child Protection

When we started work on this book in the early 1990s, expressing skepticism about ritual abuse had ceased being the practically indictable stance it was when the panic first erupted ten years earlier. Yet belief in the charges was still so strong that we wondered whether we could make much of a dent in it. Now, as we finish writing, the tide has turned dramatically. At least weekly, we get calls from people working on print and television stories about sex-abuse allegations that appear to be false. The older reporters always passionately recount how, while everyone else at their newspaper or TV station ten years ago thought Kelly Michaels or the McMartin teachers were guilty, they saw the whole thing as a witch hunt (even though they filed no stories to that effect and did not argue the point with their colleagues).

We also hear from younger members of the media, but they often sound less impassioned than bored. For them, skeptical treatments of sex-abuse charges are becoming so commonplace that they seem like just another story. Little remains to be done, except to spice them up with mention of the final unraveling of ritual-abuse conspiracy theory—which includes the fact that the McMartin tunnel-dig coordinator Ted Gunderson has appeared with paramilitarist leaders and asserted that a demonic element within the U.S. government, and not Timothy McVeigh, bombed Oklahoma City's federal building.

The patently paranoid and ultra-right-wing tenor of ritual-abuse culture, and child protection's obvious involvement with it, have closed the book on satanic-abuse claims for most people, Even conservative legislators, whose politics a decade ago helped push the panic, are now exploiting the new skepticism to promote their Contract with America. Immediately after the 1994 congressional election upheaval, House Republicans moved to scrap Walter Mondale's Child Abuse Prevention and Treatment Act (CAPTA), the bill passed in the early 1970s whose history introduces this book. They propose that federal child-protection money be shunted into state-by-state welfare block grants. With an irony characteristic of his party, the bill's sponsor, California congressman Randy "Duke" Cunningham, claimed the changes would help poor children—even as his proposals took their place in legislation designed to cut school lunches and food stamps, deny youngsters medical care if they are not U.S. citizens, and consign many to orphanages.

As part of the anti-CAPTA campaign, Cunningham arranged hearings that showcased witnesses narrating first-person horror stories about false accusations and ritual-abuse charges. Their painful recitations were intended not to encourage rational discussion of child protection but to disengage Washington from the entire issue. In response, longtime critics of false accusations—"the backlash," their adversaries call them—recommended that CAPTA be saved, if only to preserve a federal agency through which reforms in sexual abuse reporting, investigation, and litigation could be enforced nationwide, with an eye to diminishing unfounded charges and cleansing the field of its worst irrationalities. To these ends, the reformers recommended better training for child-protection workers, abolition of total immunity for malicious false reporting and incompetent investigations, and mandatory taping of all child interviews.

When the bill reached the Senate, CAPTA was resurrected. It lacked the changes needed to significantly ameliorate the false accusations problem, however, and the block-grant proposal for funding still seemed destined for enactment. Money for child welfare and child-protection services thus is likely to diminish during the next few years. Couple that decrease with intensified anxiety in this country over declining living standards, and it seems clear that expressions of those anxieties—including false sex-abuse charges—are not going to disappear on their own.

Instead, they will endure, sans black robes and ritually murdered infants, but with more secular-sounding scenarios like incest and sex rings. (Even now, in Wenatchee, Washington, a mega-ring case against more than two dozen men and women—all of them poor and uneducated—is winding its way through the courts, with virtually no evidence and no audio- or videotaped recordings of interviews with the accusing children.)

Complaints about unjustified accusations will increase, along with grassroots anger over them that has been smoldering for several years now, its sparks fanning out through other fervors of social ire and frustration. The patriot movement, for example, has its CIA and ritual-abuse conspiracy theories. But it also has members who believe that Janet Reno's ritual-abuse prosecutions in Miami were part of a deliberate federal effort that included her order to attack Waco's Branch Davidians. Further, the theory goes, Reno is a feminist, and feminism is behind the persecution of innocent people in the current wave of false sex-abuse charges.

It is difficult to explain to justifiably indignant and frightened people that feminist theory and practice are not monolithic, and that many women's advocates abhor that part of the movement that demonizes masculinity, forges alliances with the antifeminist right, and communicates such a profound fear and loathing of sexuality that—as the ritual-abuse cases demonstrate—it is even willing to cast women as demons.

These currents are most strongly expressed among antipornography and victimology feminists. But lately it has become clear to many that proponents of these ideas are engaged not so much with a political movement as with a moral crusade engaged in dangerous flirtation with antiabortionists, homophobes, racists, and proponents of the principle that a woman's place is in the home. It is also obvious that the antipornographers and victimologists are feminism's main contributors to the ritual-abuse panic. Catharine MacKinnon, for instance, has publicly proclaimed her belief in the existence of widespread ritual sex abuse. So have Gloria Steinem and countless psychotherapists, social workers, doctors, lawyers, and writers who call themselves feminists.

Indeed, during the past decade, belief in ritual abuse has become so esconced in this wing of feminism that the arrest, trial by ordeal, and lifelong incarceration of accused women have occasioned hardly a blink from its proponents. They have remained silent as convicted mothers and teachers are sent to prison. Or some have admitted that a handful of defendants are probably innocent, but dismissed their fate as the inevitable casualties of a war in which the claims of truly abused youngsters cannot be threatened by talk of even one false accusation. In the name of feminism, then, these women end up playing their bleak, age-old role: sacrificing themselves for the children, whether they want to or not.

This irony is the result of a feminist movement battered by demoralization during the years when ritual-abuse panic simmered in the popular culture and on the right. Things had not always been so bad for women, particularly when feminism was revived during the 1960s' height of the black civil rights struggles and New Left antiwar organizing. Animated by these forces, and by a dramatic democratizing of sexual mores, feminists urged women to take up traditionally masculine pursuits and to question the arbitrariness of everything deemed womanly, including chastity and maternity.

The great difficulty with these politics, of course, was that they were deeply unsettling, and not just to men. Challenging tradition frightened women, too, because it asked them to rethink themselves as individuals during a time when there were few models aside from masculine ones. It was also a time when feminism was increasingly vilified as a threat to morality, family, and the national welfare.

It was amid this attack and deepening sense of beleaguerment that feminists took up the issue of domestic violence and incest, characterizing both as the result of male domination over women and girls in patriarchal families. This bold, structural analysis was soon silenced by the push to frame child abuse as a neurosis that could be cured with therapy. Viewing the problem this way extended a long American tradition of blaming child neglect and maltreatment on the moral failings of parents, and of using child-welfare interventions as an excuse to discipline and break up families who failed to meet native-born, white, middle-class standards. Thus, by the time modern feminists starting making an issue of sex abuse, it was practically a foregone conclusion that institutional responses would obscure the fact that sexual assault rates are much higher among poor women and children than more affluent ones, and that the national policy that would arise to deal with incest would ignore its roots in the patriarchal family.

Still, feminists' concern with sexual abuse has persisted—and understandably, since on the surface it seems to be a simple and highly profitable political issue. Unlike battering and neglect, in which many offenders are mothers, sex offenders traditionally have been cast as males. Further, sexual abuse is about the violation of little children, not grown women, and this eliminates the problem of establishing the victims' "innocence." Proving one's virtuousness and chastity has always been a prerequisite for women trying to make claims on patriarchal institutions. But children are deemed blameless, and this gives organizing against sexual abuse tremendous potential to advance other feminist concerns—about rape, wife beating, and sexual harassment, for instance—that society has been known to dismiss with the taunt "she asked for it."

Crusades against child sexual abuse can also serve as a symbolic focus for women's frustration and anger over disparities between the much-touted promise of gender equality versus the bleak reality of continuing power imbalances at work and at home; and of increasing reports of sexual violence and harassment.

But if victimology exercises any political clout, that is only because it echoes the obdurate social requirement that in order for their claims to be respectable, the women making them must cast themselves as the asexual, devastated casualties of male lust. Much contemporary therapy accepts this demand and promotes it. Once women's personal histories are structured this way, it is tempting to flesh them out with grotesque, gothic detail. These tales can also serve the useful function of expressing forbidden fantasies.

Expressions of desire are sanctioned in our culture, even hyped, as long as they are confined to stylized representations of adult heterosexuality. Meanwhile, there is growing animus toward portrayal or even discussion of the panoply of minority and outlawed impulses, from homosexuality to fetishism, bestiality, sadomasochism, and the ultimate evil: attraction between adults and children.

As we have seen with homosexuality's decertification as a psychopathology during the past generation, ideas about deviancy and normality are subject to change—although pedophilia will likely always be condemned. It is tempting to censor art and literature that portrays perversions, as well as popular discussion about them, because the ensuing silence creates an illusion of safety and social purity. But forcing fantasies underground does not eliminate the impulses behind them. Instead, they return to haunt us as projections, paranoia, and "true crime" stories that aren't true, but which can lead to very real campaigns against the scapegoats forced to stand in for our hidden desires.

Forbidden fantasy also erupts in mental health and even forensic contexts, particularly when clinicians and investigators demand sexual material and abuse "memories" from their patients and interviewees. In interpreting the resulting stories literally, therapists and their allies in child protection and criminal justice have tapped into women's rage. They have also won public sympathy and nominal funding for many feminist-inspired efforts, from battered women's shelters to programs to discourage child beating.

But indulging the patriarchal insistence on sexual purity has proved a Faustian bargain that has emotionally damaged children, demonized their adult caretakers, and terrorized society with a bogeywoman: the female sexual psychopath who lurks everywhere, even in nursery schools. With her genesis, the public world—always considered a threat to nice women and innocent children—becomes all the more frightening as its "victims" are encouraged to abandon work and public child care and to retreat to the seclusion of the clinic and home.

By insisting that sex abuse has nothing to do with poverty, and by fetishizing toddlers and prepubescents as its primary victims, women's and children's advocates contribute to this society's hostility toward the poor and, particularly these days, toward adolescent girls—those under eighteen who are least frequently described as children but most commonly involved in sexual relations with adults.

Indeed, the vast majority of unwed mothers younger than eighteen are indigent, and a substantial minority of their babies' fathers are men who are at least six years their senior—which in most states legally defines the mothers as child sex-abuse victims.[1] Yet teenage mothers usually call these men their boyfriends. And although their attempts to find fulfillment with older partners may in the long run fail, few would call themselves victims of sexual abuse. The lack of better words to describe their problematic experience with older men, and the young women's own refusal to adopt victim identities, make them easy scapegoats for conservatives anxious to cast them not as innocent children but as sluts—and to justify cuts in welfare spending for them and their offspring.

Attempting to shanghai these attacks, some feminists and political progressives lately have been pushing the idea of young, unmarried mothers as child sexual-abuse victims. No one has yet specified how the "offenders" should be punished (conservatives will no doubt favor shotgun marriages for starters). But given the near universality of law-and-order perspectives when it comes to child sexual abusers, we can imagine a scenario in which venues like *Ms.* magazine and *The Nation* were to propose hard time for unmarried men in their twenties who make babies with girlfriends in their teens.

If this happens, the sociology—and racism—of the policy will quickly become obvious. Because although hardly anyone talks about it, the census category of young women most likely to parent children with older men are Latinas (white teenagers take second place, and African Americans come in third). These cross-cultural differences suggest that it is not male depravity that fuels the age discrepancy. Rather, it is the long-standing patriarchal arrangement, still stronger in Latino immigrant cultures than others, that bestows greater earning potential on men and makes them sought-after mates for young women who continue to see motherhood as their sole purpose in life.

It is not just the poor who can be hurt by inflamed, moralistic language about cross-generational sex. Children of all classes have been touched sexually by adults, yet a significant minority show no ill effects, and a few report positive outcomes. In such cases, the contact often was confined to kissing and fondling. When data about these children's experiences get folded into statistics about the aftermath of acts like forcible penetration, rape victims' trauma gets washed out in the averages. The destructiveness of physically brutal assault may thus be trivialized by victimology's tendency to conflate nonviolent cross-generational sex with rape. The two problems are both serious; but calling them the same thing leads to confusion and ultimately to a crying-wolf effect that threatens to steal attention from both.

This is what is happening now. Having reached a flashpoint in public consciousness, False Memory Syndrome and other questionable sex-abuse allegations currently are a hotter topic than actual offenses. Clearly, there is plenty of grist for the new mill. We have learned of innumerable people who apparently have been falsely convicted of fondling their kin, their students, or the neighborhood children, and the accusations convince us that ritual-abuse and sex-ring prosecutions are only the tip of a national iceberg. The flaws in the more dramatic cases—the leading interviews, coerced confessions, bogus medical evidence, and denial of courtroom confrontation—also characterize thousands of more pedestrian-sounding accusations. At the same time, we believe that real child sexual abuse, particularly incest, remains grossly underreported. This means that most of it is never dealt with, least of all by the criminal justice system.

Ignoring actual abuse is unacceptable. Yet how can the police and courts be the right response, when sex, whether egalitarian or exploitive, legal or illegal, is almost always a private, physically nonviolent event between two people? And if there are no wounds or witnesses, how can we adjudicate the competing claims of accused and accusers in criminal courts without guaranteeing widespread miscarriages of justice—and not just against defendants? As weak as the presumption of innocence has become in sexual-abuse and assault cases, it still operates in many of them. An undetermined percentage of perpetrators do go free, and this is something we must accept if we hope to preserve justice for the falsely accused.

But the presumption of innocence will always stick in the social craw if we continue to depend on law and order as our main response to sexual abuse. To restore the order and authority of the courts, we need to look beyond them. We also need to stop fetishizing child-protection authorities as the solution to sexual abuses, for even if they mend their investigative ways, the most careful workers will frequently encounter a dearth of evidence and child victims who are too immature or compromised by family ties to testify convincingly.

The only real answer to these dilemmas is to cease thinking obsessively about what to do after sexual abuse has occurred, and take real steps to prevent it in the first place. Here we are not talking about current good-touch/bad-touch programs, which are little more than laundry lists of taboo body parts and warnings about accepting candy bars from sex killers. Such presentations are one-shot affairs that do very little to help children define their psychological and sexual integrity or be able to react effectively when it is being threatened or denied. These abilities do not come from occasional didactic sessions. Children develop them by being given the chance to live in egalitarian families, to study in schools that value their intellectual, moral, and creative capabilities, and to live in a society where they are encouraged to engage in meaningful decision making, with peers and with adults.

Prevention lessons do not address these needs. Neither do they help make nurturers of fathers, encourage economic parity between parents, or otherwise change family relations so that if abuse happens or is about to, a mother—or children them-selves—can muster the economic and emotional independence to stop the mis-treatment, or leave home if need be. In the long run, nothing short of these changes will make much of a dent in the frequency of incest, the most common type of sex-ual abuse.

Current "child-abuse industry" measures will have little effect, either, on out-of-family molestation. Younger children who are imposed upon sexually by child-care personnel and other older people are often incapable of distinguishing threatening situations from benign ones, and they shouldn't have to. They deserve a level of attention from their adult caretakers sufficient to protect them from all kinds of dan-gers, of which molestation is only one. Parents, teachers, and others who work with children need enough time, energy, and resources to provide that care. But poverty, overwork, and understaffed facilities with substandard floor plans encourage neglect and all sorts of injuries.

Older children drawn into sexual contact with adults are also victims of everyday social neglect and abuse far more often than they are of stranger abduction and vio-lence. Often they have been taught not to question adult demands. They may be very curious about their developing sexuality but—and this is particularly true for children with homosexual impulses—have a dearth of information about it and lit-tle opportunity to explore it with peers. In addition, older children whose parents and other caretakers cannot attend to them emotionally or materially may be so needy that they end up trading sex for adult affection and care.

Sex between children and adults, then, is but another symptom of this society's most profound political-economic inequities, inequities that foster authoritarianism and neglect by fathers against dependents, adults against children, and rich against poor. The best of progressivism and feminism has always outspokenly condemned these conditions, described them unflinchingly, and refused to exempt sacred cows from investigation. Yet ironically, the demonization of child sexual abuse as soci-ety's ultimate evil has rendered it so holy as to be virtually immune to reasoned analysis. Unexamined, it is now an altar for our unresolved conflicts about sex and gender—a part of the culture that curses women, children, and the legal system.

It is time to topple this noxious shrine, beginning with immediate steps that can inspire widespread commitment to more thoroughgoing policies to improve women's and children's lives. The child-protection system should be addressed first, by enrolling all its personnel in a national training program that teaches them scien-tific and forensically valid ways to do their work. At the same time, the virtually total immunity that abuse investigators and prosecutors enjoy should be abolished. Replacing it with the limited immunity that covers other law-enforcement authori-ties would mitigate against sloppy or venal behavior. Malpractice would also be avoided by mandating audiotaping of all interviews with accusers and suspects in child sexual-abuse investigations. In addition, a federal commission should be formed to review every sex-abuse conviction of the 1980s and 1990s that was based on erroneous and malicious evidence-gathering methods or on community hysteria.

For all their rigid intolerance, even the Puritans of Salem quickly repented their behavior after the witch hunts of 1692. "We walked in clouds and could not see our way," apologized the Reverend John Hale five years after his testimony against an accused Salem woman helped put her to death.[2] The same year that Hale penned his regrets, Salem declared a day of public contrition, and in 1709 the families of those who were executed received reparations. These displays of repentance helped heal the community at the same time that they preserved it.

In Salem, it was an an act of moral strength, political self-interest, and social progress to say "we were wrong." Three centuries later, it is up to all who sanctioned our modern-day sex-abuse witch hunt to help redress this terrible mistake. It is not only the justice system that is at stake. Restoring the presumption of innocence to those who never should have lost it can be a rallying point to rethink what it means to truly protect children and a gesture of willingness to deal constructively with our anxieties about working women, public child care, single motherhood, and other momentous alterations in gender and family relations. Demanding that the government redress its errors would be a step in holding it truly accountable for empowering women and children against unwanted sex and for advancing their well-being in general. The involvement of women's activists in this effort would also help cleanse feminism's sullied reputation among people who have suffered from false charges.

Child protectionists and feminists who refuse to help make these amends will ultimately be remembered as the deluded commanders of a crusade whose enemies were phantoms, but whose casualties were all too real. The past decade's war against ritual abuse and other imagined sexual offenses has devastated people, including the women and children it was supposed to help. To repair the damage and prevent more of it, we need to exorcise our demons by dealing thoughtfully and publicly with what they stand for. Only then can we hope to break the silence that still belongs to Satan.

Notes

Introduction

1. Gail S. Goodman et al., *Characteristics and Sources of Allegations of Ritualistic Child Abuse* (Washington, D.C.: National Center on Child Abuse and Neglect, 1994).

2. Doris Sanford, *Don't Make Me Go Back, Mommy: A Child's Book About Satanic Ritual Abuse* (Portland, Oreg.: Multnomah Press, 1990).

3. "True Believers," A. S. Ross, "Blame It on the Devil," *Redbook*, June 1994, p. 88.

4. According to an unpublished survey conducted in Southern California in the early 1990s, 45 percent of a sample of fifty-three area therapists agreed with the statement "Satanic ritual abuse involves a national conspiracy or network of multi-generational perpetrators where babies, children, and adults are sexually assaulted, physically mutilated, or killed." See Martha Rogers and L. Brodie, "Front Line Providers in Investigation of Child Abuse: Personal Background, Experience, Knowledge Base and Attitudes of Social Workers Regarding Child Sexual Abuse Survivors and Recovered Memories," paper presented at the conference of the False Memory Syndrome Foundation, Valley Forge, Pa., April 1993 (available from Martha Rogers, 17662 Irvine Blvd., Tustin, CA 92680).

5. The American Bar Association Center on Children and the Law reported in 1993 that in a nationwide survey of prosecutors, 26 percent reported having handled at least one case involving elements of ritual abuse. See American Bar Association Center on Children and the Law, *The Prosecution of Child Sexual and Physical Abuse Cases, Final Report* (Washington, D.C.: American Bar Association, 1993), pp. 29–31.

6. Kelly's and Wilson's convictions were overturned on appeal in 1994. At this writing, new charges have been brought against Kelly.

7. Gloria Steinem, "Making the Invisible Visible," audiocassete of a presentation to the 11th International Conference on Dissociative States, Chicago, 1994 (avail-

able as tape no. 1b-973-94 from Audio Transcripts, Alexandria, Va.; E. Gary Stickel, *Archaeological Investigation of the McMartin Preschool Site, Manhattan Beach, CA*, 1993 (unpublished manuscript, in author's possession); Howard Witt, "Amid Oklahoma Mysteries, Conspiracy Ideas Win Hearing," *Chicago Tribune*, 9 May 1995.

Chapter 1. The Best of Intentions

1. All information about the Arizona Children's Home and working conditions there is taken from telephone interviews conducted during August 1994 with people employed at the Home in 1970 and 1971, the same time MacFarlane was. Those interviewed were Marge McFerron, formerly a social worker at the Arizona Children's Home, and the following former child-care technicians: Dee Ann Barber, currently the Home's assistant executive director; Sandy Staples, now a social worker in Tucson; Gregg Scott, a teacher in the Nogales, Arizona, public school system; Bill Graham, currently a Tucson social worker; and Mary Graham, Bill's wife and a special education teacher in the same city.

2. MacFarlane's last name then was Hall. She would divorce a few years later and take her maiden name again. Mary Meinig, "Profile: Kee MacFarlane, M.S.W," *Violence Update* 3, no. 1 (September 1992); Kee MacFarlane, Curriculum Vitae, (Children's Institute International, Los Angeles, CA, 1987, photocopy in author's possession). Kee MacFarlane did not respond to our request for an interview.

3. Meinig, "Profile"; MacFarlane, Curriculum Vitae; U.S. House Committee on Science and Technology, Research into Violent Behavior: Domestic Violence, 95th Cong., 2nd sess., 14–16 February 1978, p. 69.

4. MacFarlane, Curriculum Vitae.

5. U.S. House Committee on Education and Labor, Fair Labor Standards Amendments of 1973: Hearings on H.R. 4757 and H.R. 2831, 93rd Cong., 1st sess., 13–15 March 1973 and 10 April 1973, p. 242.

6. Robert E. Litan and Robert Z. Lawrence, eds., *American Living Standards: Threats and Challenges* (Washington, D.C.: Brookings Institution, 1988), p. 4; Kevin Phillips, *The Politics of the Rich and Poor* (New York: Random House, 1990), p. 18 and appendix C.

7. Barbara J. Nelson, *Making an Issue of Child Abuse: Political Setting for Social Problems* (Chicago: University of Chicago Press, 1984), p. 189.

8. Nelson, *Making an Issue of Child Abuse*, p. 102.

9. Ibid., pp. 106–8.

10. Child Abuse Prevention Act, S. 1191, Hearings Before the Subcommittee on Children and Youth of the Committee on Labor and Public Welfare, U.S. Senate, 93rd Cong., 1st sess., 26, 27, 31 March and 24 April 1973, pp. 49–59.

11. MacFarlane, Curriculum Vitae.

12. Ibid.

13. MacFarlane, Curriculum Vitae.

14. Kee MacFarlane and Leonard Lieber, *Parents Anonymous: The Growth of an Idea* (Washington, D.C.: NCCAN, June 1978).

15. Patte Wheat and Leonard L. Lieber, *Hope for the Children: A Personal History of Parents Anonymous* (Minneapolis: Winston Press, 1979), pp. 76–77.

16. For data and discussion about the linkage between poverty and child abuse, see

Leroy H. Pelton, "Child Abuse and Neglect: The Myth of Classlessness," in *The Social Context of Child Abuse and Neglect*, ed. Leroy H. Pelton (New York: Human Sciences Press, 1981); National Center on Child Abuse and Neglect, *Study Findings: National Study of the Incidence and Severity of Child Abuse and Neglect* (Washington, D.C.: U.S. Department of Health and Huamn Services, 1981); National Center on Child Abuse and Neglect, *Study Findings: Study of National Incidence and Prevalence of Child Abuse and Neglect* (Washington, D.C.: Department of Health and Human Services, 1988); Murray A. Straus, Richard J. Gelles, and Suzanne K. Steinmetz, *Behind Closed Doors: Violence in the American Family* (Garden City, N.Y.: Anchor Press/Doubleday, 1980).

17. Judith Lewis Herman, *Father-Daughter Incest* (Cambridge, Mass.: Harvard University Press, 1981).

18. Kee MacFarlane and Josephine Bulkley, "Treating Child Sexual Abuse: An Overview of Current Program Models," in *Social Work and Child Sexual Abuse*, ed. J. Conte and D. Shore (New York: Haworth Press, 1982), p. 73.

19. Judith Stacey, *Brave New Families: Stories of Domestic Upheaval in Late Twentieth Century America* (New York: Basic Books, 1990).

20. Lucy Berliner, "Deciding If a Child Is Abused," and Francis Sink, "Studies of True and False Allegations: A Critical Review," in *Sexual Abuse Allegations in Custody and Visitation Cases*, ed. E. Nicholson (Washington, D.C.: American Bar Association, 1988), pp. 60, 44.

21. Henry Giarretto, "Integrated Treatment of Child Sexual Abuse: Treatment and Training Manual" (Palo Alto, Calif.: Science and Behavior Books, 1982), pp. 6–7, 67; U.S. House Committee on Education and Labor, Sexual Exploitation of Children, 95th Cong., 1st sess., 27, 28, 31 May 1977 and 10 June 1977, pp. 129–30, 133–35.

22. National Center for Child Abuse and Neglect, *Child Sexual Abuse: Incest, Assault, and Sexual Exploitation* (Washington, D.C.: Government Printing Office, 1981), p. 5.

23. Giarretto, "Integrated Treatment," p. 67.

24. Ibid., p. 10.

25. Herman, *Father-Daughter Incest*, p. 206.

26. Shulamith Firestone, *The Dialectic of Sex: The Case for Feminist Revolution* (New York: Morrow, 1970); Florence Rush, "The Sexual Abuse of Children: A Feminist Point of View," in *Rape: The First Sourcebook for Women*, ed. N. Connell and C. Wilson (New York: New American Library, 1974).

27. Herman, *Father-Daughter Incest*.

28. Roland Summit and JoAnn Kryso, "Sexual Abuse of Children: A Clinical Spectrum," *American Journal of Orthopsychiatry* 48, no. 2 (April 1978); Mary Springer, "Most Incest Cases Are Not Reported; Area Has Its Share," *Torrance* (California) *Daily Breeze*, 5 July 1977, pp. A1, A3; Roland Summit, Curriculum Vitae, Department of Psychiatry, Harbor-UCLA Medical Center, Torrance, CA, 1982 (photocopy in author's possession).

29. Wheat and Lieber, *Hope for the Children*, pp. 71, 166; deposition of Roland Summit, M.D., in Chancery Court for Davidson County, Tennessee, *Richard G. Gotwald v. Susan C. Gotwald*, no. 86-463-111, 28 April 1986 (photocopy in author's possession).

30. Deposition of Roland Summit.

31. Springer, "Most Incest Cases Are Not Reported," p. A1.

32. Summit and Kryso, "Sexual Abuse of Children," p. 243.

33. Ibid., pp. 242–43.

34. Springer, "Most Incest Cases Are Not Reported," p. A1.

35. Summit and Kryso, "Sexual Abuse of Children," p. 243.

36. Ibid., p. 243.

37. Springer, "Most Incest Cases Are Not Reported," p. A1.

38. Wheat and Lieber, *Hope for the Children*, pp. 169–70.

39. Giarretto, "Integrated Treatment," p. 10.

40. H. Giarretto and A. Einfeld-Giarretto, "Integrated Treatment: The Self-Help Factor," in *The Incest Perpetrator*, ed. Anne L. Horton et al. (Newbury Park, Calif.: Sage, 1990), p. 224.

41. Giarretto, Giarretto, and Sgroi, "Coordinated Community Treatment of Incest," p. 236.

42. Sexual Exploitation of Children Hearings Before the Subcommittee on Select Education and Labor, House of Representatives, 95th Cong. 1st sess., p. 150.

43. Giarretto, "Integrated Treatment," p. 231.

44. Herman, *Father-Daughter Incest*, p. 160.

45. Ibid., p. 161.

46. House Committee, Sexual Exploitation of Children, pp. 137–38.

47. Ibid., p. 127.

48. Ibid.

49. Giarretto, "Integrated Treatment," pp. 120–21.

50. MacFarlane and Bulkley, "Treating Child Sexual Abuse," p. 85.

51. Mona Simpson, "Incest: Society's Last and Strongest Sexual Taboo," *California* (San Francisco) *Living Magazine,* 4 October 1981, p. 38.

52. Giarretto, "Integrated Treatment," p. 113.

53. Ibid., p. 117.

54. Ibid., p. 114.

55. Herman, *Father-Daughter Incest*, pp. 130–31, 171.

56. Berliner as cited in ibid., p. 171.

57. Diane Hamlin, "Harbor View's Sexual Assault Center: Two Years Later," *Response to Violence in the Family* 3 (March 1980): 3, as cited in Herman, *Father-Daughter Incest*, p. 171; and Giarretto, "Integrated Treatment," p. 295.

58. Kee MacFarlane, "Program Considerations in the Treatment of Incest Offenders," in *Sexual Aggression: Current Perspectives on Treatment*, ed. J. Greer and I. Stuart (New York: Van Nostrand Reinhold 1982).

59. National Center for Child Abuse and Neglect, *Child Sexual Abuse*, p. 10.

60. California Legislature, Assembly Bill No. 2288, Regular Session 1975 (Sacramento, 6 May 1975).

61. Deposition of Rowland [*sic*] C. Summit, M.D., *State of Florida vs. Bob Fijnje, In the Circuit Court of the 11th Judicial Circuit in and for Dade County, Florida,* Dade County Florida. Case No. 89-43952, Vol. 2, 8 January 1991, pp. 6–7

62. Deposition of Roland Summit, M.D., *In the Chancery Court for Davidson County, Tennessee*, pp. 15–19.

63. Roland Summit, foreword to Kee MacFarlane et al., *Sexual Abuse of Young Children: Evaluation and Treatment* (New York: Guilford Press, 1986).

64. Roland C. Summit, "Abuse of the Child Sexual Abuse Accommodation Syndrome," *Journal of Child Sexual Abuse* 1, no. 4 (1992): 153–63.

65. Roland Summit "The Child Abuse Accommodation Syndrome," *Child Abuse & Neglect* 7 (1983): 191.

66. Ibid., p. 183

67. George E. Fryer et al., "The Child Protective Service Worker: A Profile of Needs, Attitudes, and Utilization of Professional Resources," *Child Abuse & Neglect* 12 (1988): 481–90.

68. Summit, foreword to *Sexual Abuse of Young Children*.

69. MacFarlane, Curriculum Vitae.

70. Clearinghouse on Child Abuse and Neglect Information, *National Center on Child Abuse and Neglect: Compendium of Discretionary Grants, Fiscal Years 1975–1991* (Washington, D.C.: NCCAN, April 1992), p. 89.

71. MacFarlane, "Program Considerations"; MacFarlane and Bulkley, "Treating Child Sexual Abuse," pp. 69–91.

72. Giarretto, "Integrated Treatment," p. 59.

73. Gene G. Able et al., "Multiple Paraphiliac Diagnoses Among Sex Offenders," *Bulletin of the American Academy of Psychiatry and the Law* 16 (1988): 153–68.

74. San Diego County Grand Jury, *Child Sexual Abuse, Assault, and Molest Issues, Report No. 8, A Report by the 1991 San Diego County Grand Jury*, 29 June 1992.

Chapter 2. Demonology

1. "Those Treats May Be Tricks," *New York Times*, 28 October 1970, p. 56, as cited in Joel Best and Gerald T. Horiuchi, "The Razor Blade in the Apple: The Social Construction of Urban Legends," *Social Problems* 32, no. 5 (June 1985): 488.

2. Best and Horiuchi, "The Razor Blade in the Apple," pp. 488–99.

3. Ibid.

4. Jan Harold Brunvand, *The Choking Doberman and Other "New" Urban Legends* (New York: Norton, 1984).

5. Jan Harold Brunvand, *The Vanishing Hitchhiker: American Urban Legends and Their Meanings* (New York: Norton, 1981), p. 3.

6. Lauri Honko, "Memorates and the Study of Folk Beliefs," *Journal of Folklore Research* 1 (1964): 5–19; D. Hufford, *The Terror That Comes in the Night* (Philadelphia: University of Pennsylvania Press, 1982); Bill Ellis, "The Satanic Ritual Abuse Claim as Contemporary Legend: Second Thoughts," paper presented at the 12th International Conference on Perspectives on Contemporary Legend, Paris, France, July 1994.

7. Bill Ellis, "Introduction," *Western Folklore*, special issue: "Contemporary Legends in Emergence," 49, no. 1 (January 1990): 1–7.

8. James S. Gordon, "The UFO Experience," *Atlantic Monthly*, August 1991, pp. 82–92.

9. Ellis, "Introduction," pp. 1–10.

10. Veronique Compion-Vincent, "The Baby Parts Story: A New Latin American Legend," *Western Folklore* 49, no. 1 (1990): 9–25; Norman Cohn, *Europe's Inner Demons* (New York: Basic Books, 1975), p. xi.

11. Cohn, *Europe's Inner Demons*, pp. 3–4.

12. Bill Ellis, "De Legendis Urbis: Modern Legends in Ancient Rome," *Journal of American Folklore* 96 (1983): 200–208; H. R. Trevor-Roper, *The European Witch-Craze* (New York: Harper Torchbooks, 1969), p. 127 *n.* 1; Gavin Langmuir, "Thomas of Monmouth: Detector of Ritual Murder," in *The Blood Libel Legend: A*

Case Study in Anti-Semitic Folklore, ed. Alan Dundes (Madison: University of Wisconsin Press, 1991), pp. 7–9.

13. Abraham G. Duker, "Twentieth-Century Blood Libels in the United States," in Dundes, *The Blood Libel Legend,* pp. 233–60.

14. Edgar Morin, *Rumour in Orleans* (New York: Random House, 1971).

15. Compion-Vincent, "The Baby Parts Story"; "American Woman Beaten by Mob," *Los Angeles Times,* 31 March 1994, p. 7A.

16. Jeffrey S. Victor, *Satanic Panic: The Creation of a Contemporary Legend* (Chicago: Open Court, 1993), pp. 80–81.

17. Steve Robrahn, "Satanic Rumors Terrify Thousands," Associated Press, 12 September 1988.

18. J. Phillips Stevens Jr., "The Demonology of Satanism: An Anthropological View," in *The Satanism Scare,* ed. James T. Richardson, Joel Best, and David G. Bromley (New York: Aldine de Gruyter, 1991), pp. 22–24.

19. Jeffrey Burton Russell, "The Historical Satan," in Stevens, *The Satanism Scare,* pp. 41–48.

20. Trevor-Roper, *The European Witch-Craze;* Joseph Klaits, *Servants of Satan: The Age of Witch Hunts* (Bloomington: University of Indiana Press, 1985), pp. 17–19; Richard Kieckhefer, *European Witch Trials: Their Foundation in Popular and Learned Culture* (Berkeley: University of California Press, 1976); Russell Hope Robbins, *Encyclopedia of Witchcraft and Demonology* (New York: Crown, 1959), pp. 167–69, 174, 279.

21. Murray B. Levin, *Political Hysteria in America: The Democratic Capacity for Repression* (New York: Basic Books, 1971), pp. 141–75; Jay W. Baird, *The Mythical World of Nazi War Propaganda, 1939–1945,* (Minneapolis: University of Minnesota Press, 1974); David Welch, *Propaganda and the German Cinema, 1933–1945* (Oxford: Clarendon Press, 1983); Z. A. B. Zeaman, *Nazi Propaganda* (London: Oxford University Press, 1973).

22. Some of the better known of these are Larry Cohen, *It's Alive* (Warner-Larco, 1974); Richard Donner, *The Omen* (TCF 1976); Peter Sasdy, *The Devil within Her*—(originally titled *I Don't Want to Be Born*) (Rank-Unicapital, 1976); and Peter Medak, *The Changeling* (Chessman Polk Productions, 1979).

23. U.S. Department of Labor, Bureau of Labor Statistics, as cited in Children's Defense Fund, *The State of America's Children, Yearbook 1994* (Washington, D.C.: Children's Defense Fund, 1994), p. 32.

24. Catherine S. Newman, *Falling from Grace: The Experience of Downward Mobility of the American Middle Class* (New York: Free Press, 1988), p. 38.

25. Juliet B. Schor, *The Overworked American: The Unexpected Decline of Leisure* (New York: Basic Books, 1993); Arlie Hochschild with Anne Machung, *Second Shift: Working Parents and the Revolution at Home* (New York: Viking, 1989).

26. Clyde Nunn, "The Rising Credibility of the Devil in America," in *Heterodoxy: Mystical Experience, Religious Dissent and the Occult,* ed. R. Wood (River Forest, Ill.: Listening Press, 1975); George Gallup Jr. and Frank Newport, "Belief in Paranormal Phenomena Among Adult Americans," *Skeptical Inquirer* (Winter 1991): 137–46.

27. James T. Richardson, Joel Best, and David G. Bromley, "Satanism as a Social Problem," in *The Satanism Scare,* p. 6.

28. David G. Bromley and Anson D. Shupe Jr., eds., *New Christian Politics* (Macon,

Ga.: Mercer University Press, 1984); Sara Diamond, *Spiritual Warfare: The Politics of the Christian Right* (Boston: South End Press, 1989).

29. David G. Bromley and Anson D. Shupe Jr., "The Trevnoc Cult," *Sociological Analysis* 40, no. 4 (1979): 361–66.

30. David G. Bromley and Anson D. Shupe Jr., *Strange Gods: The Great American Cult Scare* (Boston: Beacon Press, 1981), p. 3.

31. Richardson, Best, and Bromley, "Satanism as a Social Problem," pp. 7–13.

32. David G. Bromley and Anson D. Shupe Jr., *The New Vigilantes* (Beverly Hills, Calif.: Sage, 1980).

33. David G. Bromley and James T. Richardson, eds., *The Brainwashing/Deprogramming Controversy* (New York: Edwin Mellen, 1983).

34. Victor, *Satanic Panic*, p. 9.

35. Robert D. Hicks, *In Pursuit of Satan: The Police and the Occult* (Buffalo, N.Y.: Prometheus Books, 1991), p. 119.

36. Richardson, Best, Bromley, "Satanism as a Social Problem," p. 7; Russell, "The Historical Satan," pp. 47–48.

37. Gordon Melton, "Satanism and the Church of Satan," in *Encyclopedic Handbook of Cults in America*, ed. Gordon Melton (New York: Garland Publishing, 1986).

38. "'Satan Cult' Death, Drugs, Jolt Peaceful Vineland N.J.," *New York Times*, 6 July 1971, p. 29, cited in Victor, *Satanic Panic*, p. 10.

39. Victor, *Satanic Panic*, pp. 136–40.

40. Ibid., pp. 137–88; Bill Ellis, "Legend-Trips and Satanism: Adolescents' Ostensive Traditions as 'Cult' Activity," Richardson, Best, and Bromley, in *The Satanism Scare*, pp. 279–87.

41. Ellis, "Legend-Trips and Satanism," pp. 279–95.

42. Ibid.; Victor, *Satanic Panic*, p. 23.

43. Bill Ellis, "Cattle Mutilation: Contemporary Legends and Contemporary Mythologies," *Contemporary Legend* 1 (1991): 39–80; Jacques Vallee, *Messengers of Deception* (Berkeley, Calif.: And/Or Press, 1979), pp. 178–83.

44. Brunvand, *The Choking Doberman*, p. 172.

45. Victor, *Satanic Panic*, pp. 13–14.

46. Lucy Komisar, "The Mysterious Mistress of Odyssey House," *New York Magazine*, 19 November 1979, pp. 43–50.

47. Myra MacPherson, "Children: The Limits of Porn," *Washington Post*, 30 January 1977, p. C1.

48. U.S. House Committee on the Judiciary, Sexual Exploitation of Children: Hearings Before the Subcommittee on Crime, 95th Cong., 1st sess., 23 and 25 May, 10 June, and 29 September 1977, pp. 42-48.

49. Ibid., pp. 57–73; Lloyd Martin, personal interview with author, May 17, 1994.

50. House Committee, Sexual Exploitation of Children, pp. 61, 42, 49.

51. Ibid., pp. 48, 62, 43.

52. After her 1977 congressional testimony, Judianne Densen-Gerber arbitrarily doubled her "sexually exploited children" estimate from 1.2 million to 2.4 million. The new figure was then cited by the national media. See Joel Best, "Dark Figures and Child Victims: Statistical Claims About Missing Children," in *Images of Issues: Typifying Contemporary Social Problems*, ed. Joel Best (New York: Aldine de Gruyter, 1989), pp. 21–37.

53. Irene Diamond, "Pornography and Repression: A Reconsideration," *Signs* 5, no. 4 (Summer 1980): 688.

54. Pat Califia, *Public Sex: The Culture of Radical Sex* (Pittsburgh: Cleis, 1994), pp. 12, 116, 121 *n.* 8.

55. Wendy Kaminer, "Feminism's Identity Crisis," *Atlantic Monthly,* October 1993, pp. 51–68.

56. Susan Brownmiller, *Against Our Will* (New York: Simon & Schuster, 1975), p. 16.

57. Robin Morgan, *Going Too Far* (New York: Random House, 1978), p. 93.

58. Andrea Dworkin, "Why So-Called Radical Men Love and Need Pornography," in *Take Back the Night,* ed. Laura Lederer (New York: Morrow, 1980), p. 152.

59. Andrea Dworkin, "Sexual Economics: The Terrible Truth," reprinted in *Letters from a War Zone: Writings 1976–1989* (New York: Dutton, 1989), p. 119.

60. Catharine A. MacKinnon, "Feminism, Marxism, Method, and the State: An Agenda for Theory," *Signs* 7, no. 3 (1982): 541, 533.

61. *Adult Video News Buyer's Guide 1991,* cited in Marcia Pally, *Sense and Censorship: The Vanity of Bonfires* (New York: Americans for Constitutional Freedom: Freedom to Read Foundation, 1991), p. 167. See also Marjorie Heins, *Sex, Six, and Blasphemy: A Guide to America's Censorship Wars* (New York: New Press, 1993), p. 35; Nadine Strossen, *Defending Pornography: Free Speech, Sin, and the Fight for Women's Rights* (New York: Scribner, 1995), p. 144; John R. Wilke, "Porn Broker: A Publicly Held Firm Turns X-Rated Videos into a Hot Business," *Wall Street Journal,* 11 July 1994.

62. Daniel Linz, Steven Penrod and Edward Donnerstein, "The Attorney General's Commission on Pornography: The Gap Between 'Findings' and 'Facts,'" *American Bar Foundation Research Journal* (1987): 713.

63. David McCabe, "Not-So-Strange-Bedfellows," *In These Times,* 7 March 1994, pp. 22–23.

64. Ellen Goodman, "Sexploiting Kids—An Abuse of Power," as cited in U.S. House Committee on Education and Labor, Sexual Exploitation of Children: Hearings Before the Subcommittee on Select Education, 95th Cong., 1st sess., 27, 28, and 31 May and 10 June 1977, pp. 348–49.

65. Illinois Legislative Investigating Commission, Report to the General Assembly, 1980, p. viii, cited in Lawrence A. Stanley, "The Child Porn Myth," *Cardozo Law Journal* 7, no. 2 (1989): 313–15.

66. Senate Committee on Governmental Affairs, Child Pornography and Pedophilia, 99th Cong., 2nd sess., 9 October 1986, Senate Report 99–537, pp. 4, 43, 16–17.

67. Ibid., pp. 19–26.

68. Ron Kermani, "'Kid Porn': A Billion-Dollar Scandal," *Albany Times Union,* 25 April 1982; Rita Rooney, "Innocence for Sale," *Ladies' Home Journal,* April 1983, pp. 79–132.

69. For a comprehensive summary of this phenomenon, see Paul Okami, "Sociopolitical Biases in the Contemporary Scientific Literature on Adult Human Sexual Behavior with Children and Adolescents," in *Pedophilia: Biosocial Dimensions,* ed. J. R. Feierman (New York: Springer Verlag, 1990).

70. Diana E. H. Russell, "The Incidence and Prevalence of Intrafamilial and Extrafamilial Sexual Abuse of Female Children," *Child Abuse and Neglect* 7 (1983): 133–46.

71. Gail E. Wyatt, "The Sexual Abuse of Afro-American and White American Women in Childhood," *Child Abuse and Neglect* 10 (1985): 231–40.

72. Jeffrey J. Haugaard and Robert E. Emery, "Methodological Issues in Child Sexual Abuse Research," *Child Abuse and Neglect* 13 (1989): 89–100.

73. Ibid.; Russell, "Incidence and Prevalence."

74. David Finkelhor, *Sexually Victimized Children* (New York: Free Press, 1979); Judith L. Herman and L. Hirschman, "Father-Daughter Incest: A Feminist Theoretical Perspective," *Signs* 2 (1977): 735–56; K. A. Kendall-Tackett, Linda M. Williams, and David Finkelhor, "Impact of Sexual Abuse on Children: A Review and Synthesis of Recent Empirical Studies," *Psychological Bulletin* 113 (1993): 164–80; Edward O. Laumann et al., *The Social Organization of Sexuality: Sexual Practices in the United States* (Chicago: University of Chicago Press, 1994).

75. Paul Okami, "Self-reports of 'Positive' Childhood and Adolescent Sexual Contacts with Older Persons: An Exploratory Study," *Archives of Sexual Behavior* 20, no. 5 (October 1991): 437–57; Allie Kilpatrick, "Some Correlates of Women's Childhood Sexual Experiences: A Retrospective Study," *Journal of Sex Research* 22 (1986): 221–242 and 20, no. 5 (October 1991): 437–57; Diana E. H. Russell, *The Secret Trauma: Incest in the Lives of Girls and Women* (New York: Basic Books, 1986).

76. "Child's Garden of Perversity," *Time,* 4 April 1977, pp. 55–56; House Committee, Sexual Exploitation of Children, pp. 57, 60.

77. D. Kelly Weisberg, *Children of the Night: A Study of Adolescent Prostitution* (Lexington, Mass.: Lexington Books, 1985); Eli Coleman, "The Development of Male Prostitution Activity Among Gay and Bisexual Adolescents," in *Gay and Lesbian Youth,* ed. Gilbert Herdt (New York: Haworth Press, 1989), pp. 131–49; Debra Boyer, "Male Prostitution and Homosexual Identity," in Herdt, *Gay and Lesbian Youth,* pp. 151–84; Frank Rose, "Men and Boys Together," *Village Voice,* 27 February 1978.

78. B. Drummond Ayres Jr., "Miami Debate over Rights of Homosexuals Directs Wide Attention to a National Issue," *New York Times,* 10 May 1977, p. 18.

79. Nicholas A. Groth and Ann Wolbert Burgess, "Motivational Intent in the Sexual Assault of Children," *Criminal Justice and Behavior* 4, no. 3 (September 1977): 253–64.

80. Ann W. Burgess, Nicholas A. Groth, and Marueen P. McClausland, "Child Sex Initiation Rings," *American Journal of Orthopsychiatry* 51, no. 1 (January 1981): 129–33.

81. Mitzel, "NAMBLA Pickets Confab on 'Child Victimization,'" (Boston) *Gay Community News,* 28 March 1981.

82. Joel Best, *Threatened Children: Rhetoric and Concern About Child-Victims* (Chicago: University of Chicago Press, 1990), pp. 46–47.

83. David Gelman, "Stolen Children," *Newsweek,* 19 March 1984, pp. 78, 85.

84. David Finkelhor, Gerald Hotaling, and Andrea Sedlak, *Missing, Abducted, Runaway, and Throwaway Children in America: First Report* (Washington, D.C.: U.S. Department of Justice, Office of Juvenile Justice and Delinquency Prevention, 1990).

85. Michelle Smith and Lawrence Pazder, *Michelle Remembers* (New York: Congdon and Lattes, 1980).

86. October 28 and 31, 1993, author interviews with Eva Bradshaw, next-door neighbor of the Proby family (Michelle's maiden name) in 1955; October 29, 1993, author visit to St. Margaret's School, and review of Cardinal yearbooks for St. Margaret's during the 1950s and 1960s; October 31, 1993, author interview with Dorothy Lee, former teacher and yearbook editor during 1950s; October–November 1993, interviews with Diane Lockyear and her daughter Gillian (classmate of Michelle's throughout grade school); Paul Grescoe, "Things That Go Bump in Victoria," *Maclean's,* 27 October 1980, p. 30.

87. Smith and Pazder, *Michelle Remembers,* pp. 62–70, 152. To check these authors' claim about a fatal traffic accident involving Smith, the authors had an independent researcher, Teresa Gray, review all issues of the (Victoria) *Daily Colonist* from December 1954 to January 1955. Gray, who did not know the purpose of the search, was instructed to copy all news about vehicle accidents in the Victoria area. Results of her work are in authors' possession.

88. Elizabeth Loftus and Katherine Ketcham, *The Myth of Repressed Memory: False Memories and Allegations of Sexual Abuse* (New York: St. Martin's Press, 1994); Richard Ofshe and Ethan Watters, *Making Monsters: False Memories, Psychotherapy, and Sexual Hysteria* (New York: Scribner's, 1994).

89. Joseph Breuer and Sigmund Freud, *Studies in Hysteria,* trans. A. A. Brill (Boston: Beacon, 1964); Sherrill Mulhern, "Satanism and Psychotherapy: A Rumor in Search of an Inquisition," in Richardson, Best, and Bromley, *The Satanism Scare,* pp. 145–72.

90. Sigmund Freud, as cited in Jeffrey M. Masson, *The Assault on Truth: Freud's Suppression of the Seduction Theory* (New York: Farrar, Straus & Giroux, 1984), p. 91.

91. Sigmund Freud, *Standard Edition of the Complete Psychological Works of Sigmund Freud,* vol. 3, trans. James Strachey (London: Hogarth Press, 1953–74), p. 153.

92. Janice Haaken, "Sexual Abuse, Recovered Memory, and Therapeutic Practice: A Feminist-Psychoanalytic Perspective," *Social Text* 40 (Fall 1994): 115–45.

93. Mulhern, "Satanism and Psychotherapy," pp. 145–72.

94. Ibid., pp. 147–51.

95. Ilene J. Philipson, *On the Shoulders of Women: The Feminization of Psychotherapy* (New York: Guilford, 1993).

96. Haaken, "Sexual Abuse, Recovered Memory, and Therapeutic Practice."

97. Masson, *The Assault on Truth;* Judith L. Herman, *Trauma and Recovery* (New York: Basic Books, 1992).

98. American Psychiatric Association, *Diagnostic and Statistical Manual of Mental Disorder,* 3rd ed. (DSM-III) (Washington, D.C.: American Psychiatric Association, 1987).

99. Bennett G. Braun, "Forward," *Psychiatric Clinics of North America,* 7 (1984): 1–2.

100. Frank W. Putnam, *Diagnosis and Treatment of Multiple Personality Disorder* (New York: Guilford Press, 1989).

101. Corbett Thigpen and Hervey Cleckley, *The Three Faces of Eve* (New York: McGraw-Hill, 1957).

102. Corbett H. Thigpen and Hervey M. Cleckley, "On the Incidence of Multiple Personality Disorder," *International Journal of Clinical and Experimental Hypnosis* 32 (1984): 63–66.

103. C. Sileo, "Multiple Personalities: The Experts Are Split," *Insight,* 25 October 1993,

pp. 18–22; John Taylor, "The Lost Daughter," *Esquire,* March 1994, pp. 76–87.

104. Mulhern, "Satanism and Psychotherapy," pp. 152–53.

105. Bill Ellis, "Kurt E. Koch and the 'Civitas Diaboli': Germanic Folk Healing as Satanic Ritual Abuse of Children," *Western Folklore* 54 (1995): 77–94.

106. Smith and Pazder, *Michelle Remembers,* pp. 168, 188, 194; November 1 and 2, 1993, author interviews with Lawrence Pazder's ex-wife, Marilyn Steele.

107. Grantia Litwin, "Survivors Emerge Heartier and Wiser" *Times-Colonist* (Victoria, Canada), 5 June 1992, p. 8B.

Chapter 3. Beginnings: Mary Ann Barbour

1. Joan Didion, *Slouching Towards Bethlehem* (New York: Simon & Schuster, 1979), p. 182.

2. *In Re Scott and Brenda Kniffen,* Kern County (Calif.) Superior Court No. HC 5092 A&B, Petition, Exh. 8 (1/15/80 Kern County Sheriff's Office [hereafter KCSO] report of Deputy J. Williams); Kern View Community Mental Health Center and Hospital, discharge summary re: Mary Ann Barbour, 21 January 1980, p. 1 (photocopy in author's possession).

3. *Kniffen,* Petition, Exh. 9 (1/15/80 KCSO report of Deputy D. Morgan).

4. Kern Medical Center mental health emergency report re: Mary Ann Barbour, written by Kristin Stockton, 15 January 1980 (photocopy in author's possession).

5. Kern Medical Center progress record re: Mary Ann Barbour, entry dated 16 January 1980 (photocopy in author's possession).

6. Ibid.

7. *Kniffen,* Petition, Exh. 5 (1/14/80 Child Protective Services report of Velda Murillo, p. 2).

8. *In the Matters of Roberta McCuan and Darla McCuan, Minors,* Kern County (Calif.) Superior Court Nos. 52811 and 52812, reporter's transcript, 7 December 1981, p. 46.

9. *Kniffen,* Petition, Exh. 6 (1/8/80 report of Dr. Flynn), Exh. 5, p. 1.

10. Ibid., Exh. 70 (3/22/84: "Interviewing Child Victims of Sex Abuse," transcript of training tape).

11. *Kniffen,* Exh. 5, p. 2.

12. Ibid.

13. Discharge summary re: Mary Ann Barbour, p. 1.

14. *Kniffen,* Exh. 5, p. 2.

15. Discharge summary, p. 2.

16. *Kniffen,* Exh. 14 (9/13/82 Palko preliminary hearing transcripts [PT], pp. 35–38); Exh. 15 (1/29/80 Palko memorandum); Exh. 16 (2/5/80 letter of Charles E. Vollet).

17. *McCuan,* reporter's transcripts, 7 December 1981, pp. 48–49.

18. Curriculum vitae of Jill Martin, in author's possession; Jill Martin, personal interview with author, August 1994.

19. Curriculum vitae of Jill Martin.

20. Keith Love, "Child Sex Unit Chief Reassigned," *Los Angeles Times,* 12 March 1982, sec. 2, p. 1; idem, "Officer Finds Fame—and Misfortune," *Los Angeles Times,* 28 April 1982, A1+ (morning final ed.); curriculum vitae of Detective Lloyd Martin, in author's possession.

21. Josephine Bulkley, ed., "Innovations in the Prosecutions of Child Sexual Abuse

Cases," a report of the American Bar Association National Legal Center for Child Advocacy and Protection, Section X: Inter-Court, Inter-Office, and Inter-Disciplinary Coordination (November 1981), p. 1.

22. *People v. Scott Kniffen, Brenda Kniffen, Alvin McCuan and Deborah McCuan*, Kern County (Calif.) Superior Court No. 24208, reporter's transcripts, 2 February 1984, pp. 8,357–61; 1 March 1984, pp. 8,791, 8,798–99, 8801.

23. *Kniffen*, part of Exh. 18 (10/22/81 KCSO report of Deputy Shaneyfelt).

24. Ibid. part of Exh. 18 (10/21/81 KCSO report of Deputy Shaneyfelt).

25. Ibid., Exh. 19 (11/2/81 report of Supervisor Warren Irvine).

26. *McCuan*, reporter's transcript, 7 January 1982, pp. 113ff.

27. Ibid., reporter's transcript, 7 December 1981, pp. 28–38.

28. *Kniffen*, Exh. 12 (1/27/82 case report of social worker Carla Fogle); Exh. 23 (casenotes of social worker Dana Marciewitz, pp. 1–2).

29. Ibid., Exh. 22 (Shalimar records re: Darla and Roberta McCuan (pseud.)); Exh. 24 (notes of therapist Barbara Raifel); Exh. 21 (testimony of John Carillo, 9/7/82 Palko PT); Exh. 23, pp. 7, 13–14.

30. Ibid., Exh. 32 (9/13/82 Palko PT, p. 68; 9/14/82 Palko PT, pp. 13, 19–21); Exh. 23, p. 15.

31. Ibid., Exh. 28 (3/31/82 entry of 4/6/82 KCSO Shaneyfelt report, pp. 2–3); Exh. 23, p. 16; Exh. 24, p. 11.

32. Ibid., Exh. 23, pp. 17–18.

33. Ibid., Exh. 23, p. 19; Exh. 32.

34. Ibid., Exh. 29 (8/9/82 Kniffen PT, pp. 72, 76); Exh. 23, p. 20; Exh. 28, pp. 3–11.

35. Ibid., Exh. 31 (4/5/82 District Attorney office memo).

36. Ibid., Exh. 23, pp. 20–21.

37. Billy Kniffen, personal interview with author, August 1993.

38. Ibid., Exh. 23, p. 22.

39. Scott Kniffen, personal interview with author, summer 1994; Scott Kniffen, letter to author, 19 January 1995.

40. Brenda Kniffen, letter to author, 21 January 1995, Scott Kniffen, interview by KCSO Sgt. Don Fredenburg, 8 April 1982 (transcript in author's possession).

41. *Kniffen*, Exh. 47 (4/26/82 notice of motion to withdraw stipulation and declaration of Medelyian Grady); Exh. 48 (5/5/82 Walker PT, pp. 15–16).

42. Ibid., Exh. 26 (preliminary hearing transcript in *People v. Phelps*, Kern County (Calif.) Superior Court No. 24673, 11/16/82 PT 44).

43. Ibid., Exh. 27 (10/27/82 Walker PT, p. 181); Exh. 33 (8/30/82 Palko PT, pp. 100–104).

44. Ibid., Exh. 44 (4/19/82 KCSO report of Inv. Johnson); Exh. 45 (4/16/82 transfer of custody from Medelyian Grady to Shalimar); Exh. 46 (Shalimar visitation records for April 1982); Exh. 38 (declaration of Don Mcillivray).

45. *Kniffen and McCuan*, preliminary hearing transcripts re: testimony of Byron and Billy Kniffen.

46. *Kniffen*, Exh. 86 (court file, *People v. Corene Oliver*, West Kern County (Calif.) Municipal Court No. 34104).

47. *McCuan* (pseud.) *and Kniffen*, preliminary hearing transcripts re: testimony of Darla and Roberta McCuan.

48. Memo of Medelyian Grady, October 1982 (photocopy in author's possession). Grady notified the defense of this incident the following October.

49. *Kniffen*, Exh. 36 (8/31/82 Palko PT, p. 61).

50. Ibid., Exh. 85 (declaration of Georgia Herald, pp. 2–3).

51. Ibid., Exh. 35 (8/9/82 Kniffen PT, pp. 85–86, 94–97, 101–103, 112–117; 9/13/82 Palko PT, pp. 59–60, 68–69, 71; 9/14/82 Palko PT, pp. 9, 28–31).

52. See California Court of Appeal No. 5 Crim. F004423, Slip Opinion, p. 153.

53. Ibid., part of Exh. 63 (testimony of Brad Darling, in *In Re Hubbard,*). Kern County (Calif.) Superior Court No. HC5-5.2378.

54. *Kniffen*, Exh. 62 (4/14/86 Fredenburg interview).

55. *McCuan and Kniffen*, reporter's transcript, vol. 23, p. 5,917.

56. Ibid., re: children's testimony, passim.

57. Ibid., reporter's transcript, pp. 9,331–32.

58. Ibid., pp. 641–52, 657.

59. "Stolen Innocence: Molestation of Children Becoming a Common Crime," (Bakersfield) *Californian,* 27 January 1985, p. A1.

60. *Kniffen*, Exh. 67 (2/6/84 Carol Darling employee performance report).

61. "Victims' Plea: Without You, We're Nothing," *Kiddie Cop Watch* 1 (March 1984): 2 (in author's possession).

62. *Kniffen*, Exh. 93 (chart of Mary Ann Barbour's behavioral parallels in 1980 and 1982); Exh. 88 (10/21/84 declaration of Kenneth I. Schwartz re: defense based on the mental condition of Mary Ann Barbour, p. 2).

63. *Kniffen*, Exh. 89 (12/17/84 notice for motion of discovery of the psychiatric records of Mary Ann Barbour); Exh. 90 (12/17/84 minute order of Judge William F. Stone); Exh. 91 (1/2/85 ruling on defendants Palko and Walker's motion for discovery); Exh. 95 (2/4/85 in camera declaration of Kenneth Schwartz); Exh. 96 (3/18/85 minute order re: discovery of Mary Ann Barbour's medical records); Exh. 97 (3/22/85 minute order to dismiss case).

Chapter 4. Judy Johnson and the McMartin Preschool

1. Sar Levitan, R. Belous, and F. Gallo, *What's Happening to American Families?* rev. ed. (Baltimore: Johns Hopkins University Press, 1988), p. 102.

2. Judith Stacey, *Brave New Families: Stories of Domestic Upheaval in Late Twentieth Century America* (New York: Basic Books, 1990), p. 15.

3. Peggy McMartin Buckey, personal interview with author, May 1994.

4. Shawn Hubler, "Driven to Her Death," *Los Angeles Herald Examiner,* 8 March 1987, pp. A1, A10, A11.

5. Ibid.

6. Peggy McMartin Buckey, personal interview with author, May 1994.

7. Mary A. Fischer, "A Case of Dominoes?" *Los Angeles Magazine* 34 (October 1989): 126–35.

8. Ibid.

9. Roland C. Summit, "The Dark Tunnels of McMartin," *Journal of Psychohistory* 21, no. 4 (Spring 1994): note 4; Los Angeles County District Attorney's Office, notes, June 1984 (photocopy in author's possession).

10. Dr. Robert tenBensel, professor of public health and pediatrics, chairman of Child Abuse and Neglect Consultative Committee of the University of Minnesota, Hospital and Clinics, Minneapolis, telephone interview with author, 14 September 1988; W. D. Erickson, N. H. Walbek, and R. K. Seely, "Behavior Patterns of Child Molesters," *Archives of Sexual Behavior 17*, no. 1: 77–86.

11. Medical report for M. Johnson, 12 August 1984 (in author's possession).

12. Manhattan Beach Police Department, report June–August 1983 (DR. NO. 83-04288), 11 September 1983 (photocopy in author's possession).

13. Paul Barron, defense memorandum, 11 November 1986 (photocopy in author's possession).

14. "Medical Report—Suspected Child Abuse," 17 August 1983, UCLA Medical Center (photocopy in author's possession).

15. Babette Spitler, telephone interview with author, November 1994.

16. Mary A. Fischer, "Ray Buckey: An Exclusive Interview," *Los Angeles Magazine*, April 1990, pp. 91–100; interviews of Ray Buckey's neighbors by Manhattan Beach Police Department, reports from 19–20 November 1983 (photocopies in author's possession); Manhattan Beach Police Department, official channels with Department of Motor Vehicles of California and El Segundo Police Department, Records Division, n.d. (photocopy in author's possession).

17. Interviews of Ray Buckey's neighbors by Manhattan Beach Police Department.

18. Paul and Shirley Eberle, *The Abuse of Innocence: The McMartin Preschool Trial* (Buffalo, N.Y.: Prometheus Books, 1993), pp. 270, 277.

19. Manhattan Beach Police Department, report June–August 1983.

20. Ibid.

21. Manhattan Beach Police Department, letter to parents of former and current McMartin Preschool children, 8 September 1983 (photocopy in author's possession).

22. *People v. Raymond Buckey* et al., Los Angeles Sup. Ct. No. A750900 trial transcript, vol. 212 (28 March 1988): 30676–803. See also handwritten diary of R.O., 9 and 12 September 1983 (photocopy in author's possession).

23. Joan Barton (pseud.), letter to Manhattan Beach Police, 10 September 1983 (photocopy in author's possession).

24. Ibid.

25. Manhattan Beach Police Department, report June–August 1983.

26. Manhattan Beach Police Department, report nos. 83-04288, 83-04929, 83-094390, 83-04931, 83-04932, 83-04932/5202, 83-04933, 83-05088, 83-05201, 83-05202, 83-05207, 83-05340, 83-05464, 83-05560, 83-05589, 83-05590, 83-06218, and report for D.B. (no number), 27 September 1983 (photocopies in author's possession).

27. Manhattan Beach Police Department, report nos. 83-04932, 83-05201, 83-5202, and 83-05340 (photocopies in author's possession).

28. Manhattan Beach Police Department report nos. 83-04288, 83-04929, 83-094390, 83-04931, 83-04932, 83-04932/5202, 83-04933, 83-05088, 83-05201, 83-05202, 83-05207, 83-05340, 83-05464, 83-05560, 83-05589, 83-05590, 83-06218, and report for D.B. (no number), 27 September 1983 (photocopies in author's possession).

29. *People v. Buckey,* preliminary hearing transcript, vol. 168: 9–45, vol. 169: 7–30, vol. 170: 12–51, vol. 171: 10–80, vol. 172: 4–64, and trial transcript, vol. 232:

33,218 and 33,272, as cited in defense memorandum, 4 April 1989 (photocopy in author's possession).

30. See, for example, Children's Institute International interview with C.S. by Sandy Krebs and Stan Katz, n.d., p. 33 (photocopy in author's possession).

31. *People v. Buckey,* trial transcript, vol. 232: 33,220, as cited in defense memorandum, 4 April 1989 (photocopy in author's possession).

32. Ann Hagedorn, "Grinding Slowly: Longest Criminal Trial in American History May Be Shy on Justice," *Wall Street Journal,* 12 January 1990, A1.

33. Kevin Cody, "Passing the Buckey Case: McMartin Preschool Ten Years Later," (Hermosa Beach, Calif.) *Easy Reader,* 17 March 1994, p. 28.

34. U.S. Department of Health and Human Services, *Study Findings: Study of National Incidence and Prevalence of Child Abuse and Neglect,* (Washington, D.C.: U.S. Government Printing Office, 1988), 5.12, 5.23; David Finkelhor and Larry Baron, "High-Risk Children," *Sourcebook on Child Sexual Abuse* (Newbury Park, Calif.: Sage, 1986), pp. 64–66.

35. Michael Durfee, "Child Abuse in Los Angeles County," audiotape of speech from Second Conference of the International Society for the Study of Multiple Personality and Dissociation, Chicago, 1985 available from Audio Transcripts, Ltd, Alexandria, Va.); Michael Durfee, M.D., personal interview with author, 9 June 1995.

36. Roland Summit, foreword to Kee MacFarlane et al. *Sexual Abuse of Young Children: Evaluation and Treatment* (New York: Guilford Press, 1986), pp. xiii–xiv; Michael Durfee, M.D., personal interview with author, 9 June 1995.

37. Mary B. Meinig, "Profile: Roland Summit," *Violence Update* 1, no. 9 (May 1991): 6.

38. MacFarlane et al., *Sexual Abuse of Young Children;* Jane McCord, "A Tale of Two Communities," in *Behind the Playground Walls: Sexual Abuse in Preschools,* ed. Jill Waterman et al. (New York: Guilford Press, 1993), pp. 4–5.

39. *People v. Buckey,* trial transcript, vol. 7 (4 June 1984): 27, vol. 9 (6 June 1984): 37.

40. Ibid., vol. 7 (4 June 1984): 68.

41. Shawn Connerly [*sic*], Resume, Children's Protective Service, Santa Ana, Calif., n.d. (photocopy in author's possession).

42. Sandra Gail Krebs, Curriculum Vitae, Children's Institute International, Los Angeles, n.d. (photocopy in author's possession).

43. *People v. Buckey,* trial transcript, vol. 7 (4 June 1984): 24.

44. See, for example, "Transcription of the Audio Portion of a Videotaped Interview of K.D. by Kathrine [*sic*] MacFarlane," 24 January 1984, pp. 12, 24 (photocopy in author's possession).

45. Jean Matusinka, letter to Kee MacFarlane, 17 October 1983 (photocopy in author's possession).

46. Debbie Nathan, "False Evidence: How Bad Science Fueled the Hysteria over Child Abuse," *LA Weekly,* 7–13 April 1989, pp. 15–16, 18–19; Jean Matusinka, letter to Dr. Astrid Heger, 17 October 1983 (photocopy in author's possession); Jean Matusinka, letter to Dr. Bruce Wooding, 17 October 1983 (photocopy in author's possession).

47. Jean Matusinka, letter to Kee MacFarlane, 17 October 1983 (photocopy in author's possession); Fischer, "A Case of Dominoes?"

48. *People v. Buckey*, trial transcript, vol. 212 (28 March 1988): 30,673–814.

49. Transcript of the audio portion of a videotaped interview of T. M. by Mary Wilson, 20 September 1983 (photocopy in author's possession).

50. Ibid.

51. Dialogue from MacFarlane's session with Tanya Mergili is taken from "Transcription of the Audio Portion of a Videotaped Interview of T.M. by Kee MacFarlane," *People v. Buckey*, 7 December 1983, description of facial expression and movements are from a defense version of the same interview (both in author's possession).

52. *People v. Buckey*, trial transcript, vol. 86 (7 August 1984): 65.

53. Ibid., vol. 232: 33273, as cited in defense memorandum, 4 April 1989 (photocopy in author's possession).

54. Ibid., vol. 232: 33226–230; preliminary hearing testimony, vol. 171: 59, 63–64, 80, as cited in defense memorandum, 4 April 1989 (photocopy in author's possession).

55. *People v. Buckey*, trial transcript, vol. 232: 33274–75, as cited in defense memorandum, 4 April 1989 (photocopy in author's possession).

56. Bruce A. Woodling, examining physician, "Medical-Legal Examination," 7 January 1984 (photocopy in author's possession); *People v. Buckey*, trial transcript, vol. 232: 33274–75, vol. 233: 33313–14, 33384–86, as cited in defense memorandum, 4 April 1989 (photocopy in author's possession).

57. Cynthia Gorney, "The Community of Fear: In Manhattan Beach, Calif., Families Caught in a Whirlpool of Disclosures and Doubts," *Washington Post*, 18 May 1988, p. D-1.

58. Transcript of the audio portion of a videotaped interview of K. W. by Kee MacFarlane, *People v. Buckey*, 1 February 1984, pp.19–20 (photocopy in author's possession).

59. Transcription of the audio portion of a videotaped interview of A.B. by Shawn Conerly, *People v. Buckey*, trial transcript, 5 March 1984, pp. 31–33.

60. Michael Durfee, M.D., personal interview with author, 9 June 1995.

61. McMartin Defense preliminary transcript summary, Witness D.M., vol. 40, 7 October 1984, p. 2 (photocopy in author's possession).

62. Transcription of the audio portion of a videotaped interview of A.B. by Shawn Conerly, *People v. Buckey*, 5 March 1984, pp. 31–33.

63. Transcription of the audio portion of a videotaped interview of K.D. by Kathleen McFarlane, *People v. Buckey*, 24 January 1984.

64. Ibid.

65. *People v. Buckey*, trial transcript, vol. 233: 33362, 33426, as cited in defense memorandum, 4 April 1989 (photocopy in author's possession).

66. Children's Institute International, statement for J.M., April 1984 (photocopy in author's possession).

67. Manhattan Beach Police Department supplemental report on Matthew Johnson (pseud.), DR no. 8304288 (photocopy in author's possession).

68. Eberle and Eberle, *The Abuse of Innocence*, p. 147.

69. Manhattan Beach Police Department supplemental report on Matthew Johnson (pseud.), DR No. 8304288 (photocopy in author's posessession).

70. Manhattan Beach Police Department "Ongoing Investigation," no. 6016, 83-04288 (photocopy in author's possession); *People v. Buckey*, case no. A-750900, supplemental memorandum of points (filed 21 November 1986): 20.

71. Manhattan Beach Police Department supplemental report on Matthew Johnson

(pseud.), DR no. 8304288 (photocopy in author's possession).

72. Manhattan Beach Police Department, supplemental report for A.G., no. 83-04931, 6 January 1984 (photocopy in author's possession).

73. Handwritten notes of Judy Johnson (photocopy in author's possession); *People v. Buckey*, case no. A-750900, supplemental memorandum of points (filed 21 November 1986): 3–5, 12–15.

74. Boston University Conference on Child Exploitation and Pornography, 1981 (photocopy in author's possession); Roland Summit, "Supplement to Curriculum Vitae: Activities Related to Child Abuse" (May 1982) (photocopy in author's possession).

75. Joan Barton (pseud.), letter to Detective Hoag, Manhattan Beach Police Department, 10 September 1983 (photocopy in author's possession).

76. Interview of "S. B.," dated 12 November 1983 [*sic*—actually took place 12 December], Defense version (photocopy in author's possession).

77. All quotes here about Sara are from the diary of Joan Barton, discovery material in *People v. Buckey* (photocopy in author's possession).

78. Joan Barton (pseud.), diary (photocopy in author's possession).

79. *People v. Buckey*, case no. A-750900, supplemental memorandum of points (filed 21 November 1986): 19–20, 23.

80. Nancy Spiller, "Questions of Press Ethics Surface in McMartin Case," (Los Angeles) *Herald Examiner*, 16 July 1985, pp. B1, B7; Robert Reinhold, "McMartin Case: Swept Away in Panic on Child Molestation," *New York Times*, 24 January 1990, pp. A1, A12; Fischer, "A Case of Dominoes?" pp. 133–34.

81. *People v. Buckey*, case no. A-750900, statement in support of defense request for discovery of enforcement information pertaining to history of sexual deviancy and bizarre behavior of former television newscaster Wayne Satz (submitted under seal, 6 September 1988) (photocopy in author's possession).

82. Reinhold, "McMartin Case: Swept Away in Panic," p. A12; "The Next Step in Protecting the McMartin Tapes," (Advertisement) (Los Angeles) *Herald Examiner*, 29 May 1984.

83. David Shaw, "Where Was Skepticism in Media?" *Los Angeles Times*, 19 January 1990, pp. A1, A20–A21.

84. Ibid.

85. Ibid.

86. Mary A. Fischer, "Media Flip-Flop: Why, Four Years Later, the Press Is Taking a Strikingly Different Approach to the McMartin-Preschool Scandal," *Los Angeles Magazine*, December 1988, p. 86; Shaw, "Where Was Skepticism in Media?" p. A20.

87. Shawn Hubler, "At Last, Shadow Has Been Lifted from Manhattan Beach," *Los Angeles Times*, 19 January 1990, p. A18; Eberle and Eberle, *The Abuse of Innocence*, p. 127; Fischer, "A Case of Dominoes?"; Mark Sauer and Jim Okerblom, "A Decade of Accusations: McMartin Case Triggered Charges of Abuse at Scores of Other Preschools," *San Diego Union-Tribune*, 29 August 1993, p. D1.

88. Peggy McMartin Buckey, personal interview with author, May 1994.

89. Untitled police report by Bill Gleason, pp. 00913–18, 19 November 1984 (photocopy in author's possession).

90. Los Angeles County sheriff's department, supplemental report (File #685-00059-2241-120), 21 May 1985 (photocopy in author's possession).

91. Paul Feldman and Pat Manisco, "Columnist Seized in Child Molesting Case," *Los Angeles Times*, 24 August 1984, pt. II, p. 2.

92. Los Angeles County sheriff's department, supplemental report (File #685-00059-2241-120), 21 May 1985 (photocopy in author's possession).

93. Hubler, "At Last, Shadow Has Been Lifted."

94. Los Angeles district attorney's investigator's report no. 002513-002518, 19 November 1984 (photocopy in author's possession).

95. Los Angeles County district attorney's office, notes, 24 October 1984 (photocopy in author's possession).

96. Untitled police report by Bill Gleason 19 November 1984, pp. 00913–18 (photocopy in author's possession).

97. Bob Currie, ENOUGH! Conference on Child Victims of Violent Crimes, San Francisco, Calif., 8 November 1987 (audiotape in author's possession).

98. Glenn Stevens (former Los Angeles County assistant district attorney who left the office in 1985 when he no longer believed the McMartin defendants were guilty), personal interview with author, May 1994.

99. Los Angeles County sheriff's department, supplemental report (File #685-00059-2241-120), 3 April 1985 (photocopy in author's possession).

100. Manhattan Beach Police Department, "Signs of the Occult" (photocopy of checklist in author's possession).

101. Glenn Stevens, telephone interview with author, 28 February 1990.

102. Roland Summit, speaker on tape #GS-1, "Ritual Child Abuse: Disclosures in the 80's, Backlash in the 90's," Believe the Children Second Annual Conference, 1994 (available from Repeat Performance, Hobart, Ind.).

103. U.S. House Committee on Ways and Means and U.S. House Committee on Children, Youth, and Families, Child Abuse and Day Care, 98th Cong., 2nd sess., 17 September 1984, p. 80; A. S. Ross and Ivan Sharpe, "Cases from the Bay Area and the West," in "Ritualistic Child Abuse? A Presumption of Guilt," *San Francisco Examiner*, 29 September 1986.

104. U.S. House Committee on Ways and Means and U.S. House Committee on Children, Youth, and Families, Child Abuse and Day Care, p. 52.

105. Nadine Brozan, "Witness Says She Fears 'Child Predator' Network," *New York Times*, 18 September 1984, p. A21.

106. Roland Summit, as cited in National Symposium on Child Molestation (Washington D.C.: United States Department of Justice, 1984) and National Symposium on Child Molestation (Washington, D.C.: U.S. Department of Justice, 1985), p. 242.

107. "Out of the Mouths of Babes," The 5th Estate (Canadian Broadcasting Corporation), 5 January 1993.

108. Manhattan Beach Police Department, reports, 1, 5, 27–28 June 1990 and 3 July 1990, (photocopies in author's possession); *People v. Buckey,* offer of proof re Jane Hoag, case no. A-750900 (12 July 1989).

109. *People v. Buckey,* supplemental memorandum of points, case no. A-750900 (21 November 1986): 10, 17.

110. Manhattan Beach Police Department, report no. 85-01713, 6 April 1985 (photocopy in author's possession).

111. Hubler, "Driven to Her Death."

112. Hagedorn, "Longest Criminal Trial in American History."

Chapter 5. Chaos in Kern County

1. Lieutenant Brad Darling, "Ritualistic Child Abuse," lecture at the Santa Clara County Conference on Child Abuse, April 1986); tapes and transcript included as exhibits in *In re Donna Sue Hubbard*, California Court of Appeal, Fifth District, No. F021117.

2. *People v. Pitts, et al.*, Kern County, California, Sup. Ct. Nos. 27641, 27774, and 28244, reporter's transcript: 4011–4013, 4015, 4196, 4941, 4943–44, 4959, 5116, 8482.

3. Ibid., pp. 2234–37, 7648, 7661–62, 7687, 7725–26, 7895–96, 8482–83, 8718, 8723; declarations of Jimmy, Timothy, and Bobby Martin (pseuds.), *In re Hubbard*, Petition, Exh. C, D, and E.

4. Ibid., pp. 2467, 2506, 4337, 6064, 6432, 8554, 8573–75, 8577–78, 9678–82, 10679–80, 10682–85.

5. *In Re Pitts, et al.*, Kern County, California, Sup. Ct. Nos. 3676, 3703, et seq., Exh. 27 (Kern County Sheriff's Department Supplemental Report of Deputy Bob R. Fields, 30 May 1984, pp. 1–5).

6. *People v. Pitts,* reporter's transcript: 3351–3352, 4507–4707, 4726, 7730, 8130–53, 8264–66, 8294, 8298, 8315–16, 8318–20, 8733, 8854; *In Re Scott and Brenda Kniffen,* Kern County, California, Sup. Ct. No. HC 5092 A&B Court of Appeal No. F022747), Petition, Exh. 74A (Kern County Sheriff's Office [KCSO] Reports re: Amber Bloom, Wanda Bunch, and Catherine Hogan (pseuds.) denying sexual abuse, pp. 1–3).

7. *People v. Pitts,* reporter's transcript: 2153–54, 2178, 2262–67, 2485, 6049–59, 8577, 11053–11064.

8. Ibid., pp. 2143, 2148, 2161–70, 2180, 2222, 2481–82, 4047, 4051, 4065, 6212–13, 6387–88, 6446, 6448, 6455, 8492–93, 8497, 8501–3, 8506, 8557, 8561, 8563, 9135–44, 10748–56, 11001–5, 11053–64.

9. *Kniffen,* Exh. 74B (KCSO and D.A. reports re: Amber Bloom, Wanda Bunch, and Catherine Hogan (pseuds.) disclosing sexual abuse).

10. The prosecution expert testified that the lights would have felt hot from a distance of six feet and caused second-degree burns from three feet away; the children denied ever feeling especially warm during the orgies. See appellant's opening brief filed on behalf of Rick Pitts, *People v. Pitts,* California Court of Appeal, Fifth District No. F006225, pp. 24–25.

11. *People v. Pitts,* reporter's transcript: 1929–33, 2016, 2122, 2240–41, 2253, 2370–71, 2392–2421, 2428–34, 2447–53, 3927, 3955, 3967–70, 3981, 4183, 4217, 4247, 6236, 6323, 11125–27.

12. Ibid., p. 2511.

13. *In Re Pitts,* 9/18/84 memorandum of Deputy District Attorney Andrew Gindes to Carol Darling and Jack Rutledge, attached to the declaration of Michael Snedeker in support of motion to reopen evidence and for sanctions.

14. Ibid., p. 1.

15. *In Re Pitts,* petitioner's opening brief, sec. V, record citations contained therein; see also reporter's transcript of testimony of Catherine Hogan and Bill Hogan. (pseuds.)

16. *People v. Pitts,* reporter's transcript: 1558–61, 1756.

17. Linda Pitts, personal interview with author, July 1988.

18. *People v. Pitts,* reporter's transcript: 5279, 5373–53.

19. Ibid., pp. 2111–12, 2548, 6475, 7734, 8869, 8981–85, 9392, 10861-A, 10932.
20. Ibid., pp. 1189, 1967, 2009, 2217, 2703, 3304, 4191, 4199–4200, 4203, 4326–27; *Kniffen*, Exh. 56 (4/3/81 Declaration of Amber Bloom).
21. *People v. Pitts*, Reporter's Transcript: 12502–3, 12648–52.
22. Convictions of Grace Dill, Wayne Dill, Coleen Bennett, Gina Miller, Wayne Forsythe, Marcella Pitts, and Rickey Pitts were later overturned on appeal. Charges against Clovette and Clifford Pitts were dropped.
23. UPI, 4 September 1985, dateline Bakersfield, California, regional news section, for distribution in California (available on Nexis).
24. Steve E. Swenson and Michael Trihey, "Sex Abuse Statistics Contrast," *Bakersfield Californian*, 3 February 1985, p. A1.
25. Michael Trihey, "Reports Tip of the Iceberg," *Bakersfield Californian*, from "Part I: Stolen Innocence" (series), 27 January 1985, p. A1.
26. Steve E. Swenson, "Officers Certain Child Pornography Is Made in Kern," *Bakersfield Californian*, 28 January 1985, p. A4.
27. Steve E. Swenson, "Investigators Learn as They Go," *Bakersfield Californian*, 28 January 1985, p. A3.
28. William K. Stoller, Bakersfield Task Force, SAS, Department of Justice, State of California, Kern County Child Abuse Investigation, case number 85-0181-01A, 5/8/86 interview of Velda Murillo, p. 3 (photocopy in author's possession).
29. Darling, "Ritualistic Child Abuse."
30. John Van de Kamp, *Report of the Attorney General on the Kern County Child Abuse Investigation* (State of California, September 1986), p. 39.
31. Ibid., p. 63; Stoller, Bakersfield Task Force, 4/22/86 interview with Deputy District Attorneys Stephen Tauzer and T. Daniel Sparks, p. 8.
32. *Kniffen*, Exh. 105 (4/22/85 KCSO report of Deputy C. Ericsson, p. 2).
33. Van de Kamp, *Report of the Attorney General*, pp. vii, 9.
34. Jim Boren and Paul Avery, "Kern Sex Cult Case Widens," (Fresno) *Bee*, 18 July 1985, valley edition, p. A14.
35. Van de Kamp, *Report of the Attorney General*, pp. vii–viii.
36. Stoller, Bakersfield Task Force, 1/1/86 interview with Cori Taylor Hollingsead, pp. 7–8, 12/17/85 interview with Bill Rutledge, p. 8, "Summary of Involvement—Kern County District Attorney's Office," pp. 42–43; Van de Kamp, *Report of the Attorney General*, pp. 40, 65; Steve E. Swenson, "Child's Molestation Testimony Draws Denial," *Bakersfield Californian*, 10 October 1985, home edition, p. A1.
37. Stoller, Bakersfield Task Force, interview of Tauzer and Sparks, pp. 2–3.
38. Van de Kamp, *Report of the Attorney General*, pp. viii, 32.
39. Eric Malnic, "Bakersfield Torn by Horror Stories of Child Molesting," *Los Angeles Times*, 4 August 1985, p. 3; Jim Boren and Eric Malnic, "Babies Thought Slain by Satanic Cult May Not Be Dead After All," (Fresno) *Bee*, 9 July 1985, final edition, p. A1.
40. Jim Boren and Paul Avery, "Sex Abuse Witness Hypnotized," (Fresno) *Bee*, 25 July 1985, pp. A1, A3.
41. Steve E. Swenson, "Deputy First Told Boy in Satanism Case of 'Babies Dying,'" *Bakersfield Californian*, 11 October 1985, final edition, p. A1.
42. Stoller, Bakersfield Task Force, "Summary of Involvement—Kern County Sheriff's

Department," p. 22; Kathy Freeman and Michael Trihey, "Letter Campaign Gives Jagels a Devil of a Time on Cults," *Bakersfield Californian,* 20 July 1985, final edition, pp. A1, A7.

43. Boren and Avery, "Kern Sex Cult Case Widens," pp. A1, A14.

44. Nokes's grandson was one of the children who eventually named Kern County officials as Satanic Church members. See Stoller, Bakersfield Task Force, interview with Cori Taylor Hollingsead, pp. 7–8, interview with Bill Rutledge, p. 8, "Summary of Involvement—Kern County District Attorney's Office," pp. 42–43; Van de Kamp, *Report of the Attorney General,* pp. 40, 65; Swenson, "Child's Molestation Testimony Draws Denial," p. A1; Malnic, "Bakersfield Torn," p. 3.

45. Roy Nokes, personal interview with author, July 1988.

46. Kathy Freeman, "Grand Jury Seeks Child Rights Probe," *Bakersfield Californian,* 23 July 1985, final edition, pp. A1, A6; Eric Malnic, "State Looks into Alleged Ritualistic Murder Cases," *Los Angeles Times,* 13 August 1985, p. 3; Michael Trihey and Kathy Freeman, "2nd Grand Jury Seeks State Aid in Abuse Cases," *Bakersfield Californian,* 2 August 1985, p. A4; Kathy Freeman and Steve E. Swenson, "2 Agencies to Review Kern Case," *Bakersfield Californian,* 7 August 1985, pp. A1, A2; Michael Trihey, "Full Molestation Probe Vowed: Eight State Agents to Quiz All Case Principals," *Bakersfield Californian,* 19 September 1985, home edition, pp. A1, A2; Jim Boren and Paul Avery, "State Plans Satanic Cult Probe Review," (Fresno) *Bee,* 7 August 1985, valley edition, p. A1.

47. Michael Trihey, "Yard to Be Searched for Bodies," *Bakersfield Californian,* 24 August 1985, pp. A1, A2.

48. Thom Akeman, "Suspects' Yards Will Be Dug Up in Probe of Cult," (Fresno) *Bee,* 24 August 1985, p. B1.

49. Amy Pyle, "Digging for Bodies of Slain Babies Abandoned," (Fresno) *Bee,* 30 August 1985.

50. Stoller, Bakersfield Task Force, "Summary of Involvement—Kern County District Attorney's Office," p. 79.

51. Darling, "Ritualistic Child Abuse."

Chapter 6. A Plague and Its Healers

1. Kathy Sawyer, "Backlash Feared on Child Sex Cases: False Accusations, Mishandled Evidence Could Put Issue Back in Closet," *Washington Post,* 23 March 1985, final ed., p. A13.

2. A Nexis news search for "McMartin" in the year 1984 yielded 328 stories.

3. Martyn Kendrick, *Anatomy of a Nightmare: The Failure of Society in Dealing with Child Sexual Abuse* (Toronto: Macmillan of Canada, 1988), pp. 42–55.

4. Debbie Nathan, "What McMartin Started: The Ritual Sex Abuse Hoax," *Village Voice,* 12 June 1990, p. 37; Mary Ann Williams, "Witch Hunt," *Chicago Lawyer* 11 (October 1988): 24; Illinois Department of Children and Family Services, *Summary of JCC Investigation—Psychiatric Opinion* (Springfield, Ill., February 1985) (photocopy in author's possession).

5. Tom Charlier and Shirley Downing, "Patterns Emerge Across Nation," from "Justice Abused: A 1980's Witch-Hunt" (series), (Memphis) *Commercial-Appeal,* January 1988.

6. Ballard was convicted in 1987 on one count of abuse, but the verdict was over-turned in 1993 and the charge subsequently dropped. See Seth Mydans (New York Times News Service),"Grand Jury Rips Sex Abuse Prosecution, Says Parents, Therapists, Influenced Kids," (Memphis) *Commercial Appeal,* 3 June 1994 p. A1

7. Tom Charlier and Shirley Downing, "Ballard Case: Detours Along Road to Truth," from "Justice Abused."

8. Charlier and Downing, "Patterns Emerge Across Nation."

9. Debbie Nathan, "Reno Reconsidered (Country Walk)," (Miami) *New Times,* 3–9 March 1993. (Sandra Craig's convictions were overturned and charges subsequently dropped.)

10. Lynne A. Daley, "Opening Arguments Are Heard as Baran Trial Gets Underway," (Pittsfield, Mass.) *Berkshire Eagle,* 24 January 1985, p. 11; idem, "Baran Found guilty by Jury of all Charges," *Berkshire Eagle,* 31 January 1985, p. 1; idem, "Baran Receives Life Term; Parole Possible in 15 Years," *Berkshire Eagle,* 1 February 1985.

11. Charlier and Downing, "Patterns Emerge Across Nation."

12. Lisa Manshel, *Nap Time* (New York: Morrow, 1990); Debbie Nathan, "Victimizer or Victim?" *Village Voice,* 2 August 1988, pp. 31–39; *Michaels v. State,* 625 A.2d 489 (N.J., 1993); *State v. Michaels,* 642 A.2d 1372 (N.J., 1994).

13. Tom Charlier and Shirley Downing, "Allegations of Odd Rites Compelled Closer Look," from "Justice Abused."

14. See Kendrick, *Anatomy of a Nightmare,* pp. 36–41; A. S. Ross, "Satanism or Mass Hysteria?: Experts Split on Reason for Rise in Abuse Cases," from "Ritualistic Child Abuse?: A Presumption of Guilt" (series), *San Francisco Examiner,* 28 September 1986.

15. Nathan, "Reno Reconsidered," p. 12.

16. E. N. Padilla, "An Agrarian Reform Sugar Community in Puerto Rico" (Ph.D. diss., Columbia University, 1951); Ramon Fernandez-Marina, "Brief Communications," *Psychiatry* 24 (1961): 79–82.

17. Charlier and Downing, "Patterns Emerge Across Nation."

18. Tom Charlier and Shirley Downing, "Facts, Fantasies Caught in Tangled Web," from "Justice Abused."

19. *People V. Pitts, et al.,* Kern County Sup. Ct. Nos. 27642, 27774, and 28479, reporter's transcript: 4943–44.

20. Emily Yoffee, Diana Marzalek, and Casey Selix, "Girls Who Go Too Far: Affection-Starved Teenagers Are Giving New Meaning to the Term Boy Crazy," *Newsweek,* 22 July 1991, pp. 58–59; Eliana Gil, "Children Who Molest: Responding to the Sexualized, Acting Out Child" (lecture outline, Gil and Associates Child Abuse Treatment and Training Programs, 1989); Hendrika Cantwell, "Child Sex Abuse: Very Young Perpetrators," *Child Abuse and Neglect* 12 (1988): 579–82; Toni C. Johnson, "Child Perpetrators—Children Who Molest Other Children: Preliminary Findings," *Child Abuse and Neglect* 12 (1988): 219–29.

21. Paul Okami, "Child Perpetrators of Sexual Abuse: The Emergence of a Problematic Deviant Category," *Journal of Sex Research* 29, no. 1 (1992): 109–30.

22. John Money and Anke A. Ehrhardt, *Man and Woman, Boy and Girl* (Baltimore: Johns Hopkins University Press, 1972), pp. 21–22, 140–42, 183, 201.

23. William N. Friedrich et al., "Normative Sexual Behavior in Children," *Pediatrics* 88 (September 1991): 456–64.

24. Paul Okami, " 'Slippage' in Research on Child Sexual Abuse: Science as Social Advocacy," in *Handbook of Forensic Sexology: Biomedical and Criminological Perspectives,* ed. James J. Krivacska and John Money (Amherst, N.Y.: Prometheus Books, 1994), p. 565.

25. Sharon Lamb and Mary Coakley, " 'Normal' Childhood Sexual Play and Games: Differentiating Play from Abuse," *Child Abuse and Neglect* 17 (1993): 515–26.

26. Gil, "Children Who Molest"; Johnson, "Child Perpetrators"; Cantwell, "Child Sex Abuse"; Diana E. H. Russell, *The Secret Trauma: Incest in the Lives of Girls and Women* (New York: Basic Books, 1986), pp. 48–49.

27. David Finkelhor and Linda Williams, in *Nursery Crimes: Sexual Abuse in Day Care* (Newbury Park, Calif.: Sage, 1988), write that the highest percentage (63 percent) of parent reports came in multivictim, multiperpetrator cases.

28. Nancy Thoennes and Patricia Tjader, "The Extent, Nature and Validity of Sexual Abuse Allegations in Custody/Visitation Disputes," *Child Abuse and Neglect* 14 (1990): 151–63.

29. Jan Hollingsworth, *Unspeakable Acts* (New York: Congdon and Weed, 1986), p. 40.

30. Madeleine Blais, "Haunted Houses" (Miami) *Herald,* 22 March 1987, *Tropic,* Sunday magazine, pp. 10ff.

31. Debbie Nathan, "The Making of a Modern Witch Trial," *Women and Other Aliens* (El Paso, Tex.: Cinco Puntos, 1991), pp. 122–47.

32. Nathan, "Victimizer or Victim?" p. 35.

33. Shirley Downing, "Tales of Cult Abuse Spiral: Officials Seek Foundation," from "Justice Abused."

34. Children's Institute International (intake form), "Information for Parents or Caretakers," for (child) D. D., by parents J. D. and C. D., n.d. (photocopy in author's possession); Los Angeles County district attorney's office, investigator's notes, no. 007187.

35. Nathan, "Victimizer or Victim?" p. 35.

36. Patricia Crowley, *Not My Child: A Mother Confronts Her Child's Sexual Abuse* (New York: Doubleday, 1990), pp. 110, 234.

37. Nathan, "Victimizer or Victim?" p. 37.

38. Crowley, *Not My Child,* pp. 108, 111, 173.

39. Downing, "Tales of Cult Abuse Spiral," p. A10.

40. Carl Raschke, *Painted Black* (New York: Harper & Row, 1990), p. 76; Shawn Carlson and Gerald Larue, *Satanism in America* (El Cerrito, Calif.: Gaia Press, 1989), p. 137. In the latter publication, Gallant disavowed "police educational materials" she issued before 1986.

41. Robert D. Hicks, *In Pursuit of Satan: The Police and the Occult* (Buffalo, N.Y.: Prometheus Books, 1991).

42. A. S. Ross, "Child-Abuse Cults: How Real?" from "Ritualistic Child Abuse?" 29 September 1986, p. A7.

43. Tom Charlier and Shirley Downing, "Underworld Tales of Terror Echoed through the Land," from "Justice Abused."

44. Department of Children and Family Services, *Summary of JCC Investigation,* psychiatric opinion (cover memo from Bill Ryan to Sexual Exploitation Conference participants, dated 26 February 1985), p. 2; Nathan, "The Making of a Modern Witch Trial," p. 128; Harry L. Kuhlmeyer, letter to Manhattan Beach, California,

chief of police, 8 September 1983 (photocopy in author's possession); Nathan, "Victimizer or Victim?" p. 34.

45. Charlier and Downing, "Ballard Case."

46. See Charlier and Downing, "Justice Abused"; Ross and Sharpe, "Ritualistic Child Abuse?"; Catherine Gould, Ph.D., "Symptoms Characterizing Satanic Ritual Abuse Not Usually Seen in Sexual Abuse Cases: Preschool Age Children (23 May 1986)," in *Satanism: An Information Packet,* published by American Family Foundation (photocopy in author's possession); San Diego Commission on Children and Youth, Ritual Abuse Task Force, *Ritual Abuse: Treatment, Intervention and Safety Guidelines* (San Diego, Calif., September 1991), pp. 18–20.

47. Frances Ilg, Louise Bates Ames, and Sydney M. Baker, *Child Behavior* (New York: Harper & Row, 1981), pp. 155–70.

48. Mary Murray, "What Your Child Fears Most," *Reader's Digest,* January 1994, pp. 109–12.

49. Stephen Kinzer, "For the Dutch, It's O.K. to Despise the Germans," *New York Times,* 8 February 1995, national edition, p. A9.

50. Benjamin Rossen, "Oude Pekela" (Ph.D. diss., University of Amsterdam, 1989); Hicks, *In Pursuit of Satan,* pp. 341–43; Martha Rogers, "The Oude Pekela Incident: A Case Study of Alleged SRA from the Netherlands," *Journal of Psychology and Theology* 20, no. 3 (1992): 257–59; Karel Pyck, "The Backlash in Europe, Real Anxiety or Mass Hysteria in the Netherlands?: A Preliminary Study of the Oude Pekela Crisis," in *The Backlash: Child Protection Under Fire,* ed. John E. B. Myers (Thousand Oaks, Calif.: Sage Publications, 1994), pp. 70–85.

51. Ernest Dunbar, "Sex in School: The Birds, the Bees, and the Birchers," *Look,* 9 September 1969, pp. 15ff., cited by Rosan Jordan de Caro, "Sex Education and the Horrible Example Stories," *Folklore Forum* 3 (1970): 124–27.

52. Manshel, *Nap Time,* pp. 219–20.

53. Bill Ellis, "The Peanut Butter/Ritual Child Abuse Link," *FOAFTale News* (International Society for Contemporary Legend Research), 35 (October 1994); Alan E. Mays, "The Peanut Butter and Dog Surprise," *FOAFTale News* 35 (October 1994).

54. Nathan, "Victimizer or Victim?" pp. 36–39; Lynne A. Daley, "Boys, Parents, Therapists, Police Testify in Bernard Baran, Jr. Case," (Pittsfield, Mass.) *Berkshire Eagle,* 26 January 1985.

55. Finkelhor and Williams, *Nursery Crimes,* p. 132.

56. Paul Eberle and Shirley Eberle, *The Abuse of Innocence: The McMartin Preschool Trial* (Buffalo, N.Y.: Prometheus, 1993), pp. 41–43.

57. Alan C. Kerckhoff and Kurt W. Back, *The June Bug: A Study of Hysterical Contagion* (New York: Appleton-Century-Crofts, 1968).

58. Roseanne M. Philen et al., "Mass Sociogenic Illness by Proxy: Parentally Reported Epidemic in an Elementary School," *The Lancet,* 9 December 1989, pp. 1372–76.

59. M. Mrazek and J. Mrazek (pseuds.), note to "Miss Virginia," 25 September 1983, as cited in defense notes (photocopy in author's possession).

60. *People v. Ray Buckey* et al., Los Angeles Sup. No. A750900, trial transcript, vol. 113 (10 August 1987): 16951–53, and preliminary hearing transcript, vol. 543 (5 December 1985): 10–11.

61. Ibid., preliminary hearing transcript, vol. 543 (5 December 1985): 13, 22–24, vol. 545 (6 December 1985): 50–54.

62. Ibid., trial transcript, vol. 113 (10 August 1987): 16956.

63. Ibid., preliminary hearing transcript, vol. 543 (5 December 1985): 34–35, 63.

64. Transcription of the audio portion of a videotaped interview of C. M. by Kathrine Mac Farlane [*sic*]," *People v. Buckey,* 24 January 1984 (in author's possession).

65. *People v. Buckey,* preliminary hearing transcript, vol. 544 (5 December 1985): 26, 32–40, 102–3, 114.

66. Cynthia Gorney, "The Community of Fear: In Manhattan Beach, Calif., Families Caught in a Whirlpool of Disclosures and Doubts," *Washington Post,* 18 May 1988, p. D-1; memo to (Raymond Buckey's defense attorney) Donald N. Kelly from Robert W. Sabel, 10 February 1984, subject Mrs. J. F.

67. Brett, Doug, Kim, and Rob Wilson, telephone interviews with author, May 1994.

68. Luz Garcia (pseud.), telephone interview with author, March 1987. Some of this material was first published in Nathan, "The Making of a Modern Witch Trial."

69. Susan Kelley, "Parental Stress Response to Sexual Abuse and Ritualistic Abuse of Children in Day-Care Centers," *Nursing Research* 29, no. 1 (January–February 1990): 25–29.

70. Jill Waterman et al., *Behind the Playground Walls: Sexual Abuse in Preschools* (New York: Guilford Press, 1993). By the time this study was completed, in late 1990, the authors were compelled to acknowledge that defendants in the McMartin and related cases in Manhattan Beach had been acquitted or had had charges against them dropped; and that there was widespread skepticism about the allegations. Even so, the study lumps children and parents in its Manhattan Beach sample to those from a verified sexual-abuse case in another state and lauds both for their "continuing struggle to heal and to help others who share their pain." The researchers also write that they believe ritual abuse exists, and they frequently refer to the Manhattan Beach children as "victims."

71. Kelley, "Parental Stress Response," pp. 25–29; Patricia Crowley, *Not My Child: A Mother Confronts Her Child's Sexual Abuse* (New York: Doubleday, 1990); Manshel, *Nap Time;* Kathleen Coulbourn Faller, *Understanding Child Sexual Maltreatment* (Newbury Park, Calif.: Sage Publications, 1990); Lisa Baker as cited from "Panel Discussions" and Beth Vargo, "From Heartbreak Through Healing," Believe the Children, 1st Annual National Conference, 2–4 April 1993, Arlington Heights, Ill. (audiocassettes available from Repeat Performance, Hobart, Ind.); Kenneth Lanning, supervisory special agent, Behavioral Science Unit, Federal Bureau of Investigation Academy, telephone interview with author, 4 April 1994.

72. Baker, "Panel Discussions."

73. Crowley, *Not My Child,* p. 75.

74. Jane McCord, "Parental Reactions and Coping Patterns," in *Behind the Playground Walls,* p. 212.

75. Crowley, *Not My Child,* pp. 204–7; Beth Vargo as cited from "Secondary Victims," Believe the Children, 2nd Annual National Conference, 10–12 June 1994, Arlington Heights, Ill. (audiocassettes available from Repeat Performance, Hobart, Ind.).

76. Crowley, *Not My Child,* p. 44.

77. Vargo, "Secondary Victims."

78. Jill Waterman, "Impact on Family Relationships," in *Behind the Playground Walls,* pp. 177–89.

79. Baker, "Panel Discussions."

80. Waterman, "Impact on Family Relationships," p. 185; Panel of Parents, Spouses, and Professionals, "Secondary Victims," Believe the Children, 2nd Annual National Conference.

81. Report by Detective A. Bell to Los Angeles district attorney's office, 15 July 1985 (photocopy in author's possession).

82. *People v. Buckey,* preliminary hearing transcript, vol. 451 (12 September 1985): 54–55, 81, vol. 544 (5 December 1985): 42–47, 85–86, 92–93.

83. Crowley, *Not My Child,* pp. 134, 159.

84. Faye Fiore, "In Search of Satan: Children Unfold Horrors of Ritualism," *Torrance* (California) *Daily Breeze,* 31 March 1985, p. A1.

85. Gorney, "The Community of Fear."

86. Leon Festinger, *A Theory of Cognitive Dissonance* (Stanford, Calif.: Stanford University Press, 1957).

87. *People v. Buckey,* transcription of the audio portion of a videotaped interview of B. S. by Sandra Krebs, 22 February 1984, pp. 20, 25, 27 (photocopy in author's possession).

88. Ibid., p. 57.

89. Fiore, "In Search of Satan."

90. *California v. Dale Anthony Akiki,* no. CR 129395 (16 September 1993): 14549.

91. Jeff Snyder, "McMartin Child Witness, Mr. T Talk," (Los Angeles) *Daily News,* 24 January 1985, p. 1+; interview with C. M. (mother of former McMartin student B. M.) by Investigator Ferrante, 25 February 1987, 5 P.M., (photocopy in author's possession); Michael Durfee, M.D., personal interview with author, 9 June 1995.

92. Joan Barton (pseud.), diary (photocopy in author's possession).

93. Crowley, *Not My Child,* pp. 71, 101–2, 107, 135.

94. Ibid., p. 241.

95. "Panel Discussion," Believe the Children, 1st Annual National Conference; Joan Barton (pseud.), diary (photocopy in author's possession).

96. U.S. House Committee on Ways and Means and U.S. House Select Committee on Children, Youth, and Families, Child Abuse and Day Care, 98th Cong., 2nd sess., 17 September 1984.

97. Ibid., pp. 46–48.

98. "Symposium Studies Child Molestation," *New York Times,* 4 October 1984, p. C-3; see also P.L. 98-457, in *U.S. Code Congressional and Administrative News,* 98th Cong. 2nd sess. (1984), vol. 1 (St. Paul, Minn.: West Publishing Co.), 98 Stat. 1749–64.

99. Glenn Collins, "U.S. Day-Care Guidelines Rekindle Controversy," *New York Times,* 4 February 1985, p. A16; see also P.L. 98-473, Title IV, Sec. 401, in *U.S. Code Congressional and Administrative News,* 98th Congress, 2nd Sess. (1984), Vol. 2 (St. Paul: West Publishing Co.), 98 Stat. 2195–96.

100. "Symposium Studies Child Molestation," *New York Times;* P.L. 98-457, in *U.S. Code Congressional and Administrative News,* 98 Stat. 1749–64.

101. Clearinghouse on Child Abuse and Neglect Information, *National Center on Child Abuse and Neglect Compendium of Discretionary Grants: Fiscal Years 1975–1991* (Washington, D.C.: U.S. Department of Health and Human Services, National Center on Child Abuse and Neglect, April 1992); "Child Abuse Center Gets State Grant," *Los Angeles Times,* 22 February 1985, sec. 2, p. 3.

102. Jill Duerr Berrick and Neil Gilbert, *With the Best of Intentions: The Child Sexual Abuse Prevention Movement* (New York: Guilford Press, 1991).

103. Howard Levine, "UC Study Urges Dismantling Child Sex-Abuse Program," *San Francisco Examiner*, 24 February 1988, p. B-1; N. Dickon Repucci and Jeffrey J. Haugaard, "Prevention of Child Sexual Abuse: Myth or Reality," *American Psychologist* 44, no. 10 (1989): 1266–75.

104. Clearinghouse on Child Abuse and Neglect Information, NCCAN Compendium of Discretionary Grants.

105. Gary B. Melton and Mary Fran Flood, "Research Policy and Child Maltreatment: Developing the Scientific Foundation for Effective Protection of Children," *Child Abuse and Neglect* 18, suppl. 1 (1994): 1–28.

106. Clearinghouse on Child Abuse and Neglect Information, NCCAN Compendium of Discretionary Grants; Debrah Bybee and Carol T. Mowbray, "An Analysis of Allegations of Sexual Abuse in a Multi-Victim Day-Care Center Case," *Child Abuse and Neglect* 17 (1993): 767–83.

107. Charlier and Downing, "Justice Abused," pp. A-3, A-8; Frank Jones, "Richard Survived False Accusations of Sex Abuse," *Toronto Star*, 24 January 1991, p. F-1. Barkman's convictions were overturned in 1990. Facing a retrial, he then pleaded guilty to a lesser assault charge and was sentenced to five years of probation.

108. Clearinghouse on Child Abuse and Neglect Information, NCCAN Compendium of Discretionary Grants, p. 245.

109. Lois Timnick, "UCLA to Study Development of Victims of Alleged Abuse," *Los Angeles Times*, 20 October 1985, metro sec., p. 1.

110. Kee MacFarlane et al., *Sexual Abuse of Young Children: Evaluation and Treatment* (New York: Guilford Press, 1986).

111. Children's Institute International, "Resource List of Therapists" and "Therapists Currently Treating McMartin Children," n.d. (photocopies in author's possession).

112. Roland Summit, as cited in National Symposium on Child Molestation (Washington, D.C.: U.S. Department of Justice, 1984) and National Symposium on Child Molestation (Washington, D.C.: U.S. Department of Justice, 1985), p. 242.

113. Ibid., pp. 6–12, 72, 125.

114. Arthur Lyons, *Satan Wants You: The Cult of Devil Worship in America* (New York: Mysterious Press, 1988), p. 149; Shawn Carlson and Gerald Larue, *Satanism in America* (El Cerrito, Calif.: Gaia Press, 1989), p. 102.

115. Handouts and notes from the Federal Bureau of Investigation, Day Care and Satanic Cult: Sexual Exploitation of Children Seminar, 18–21 February 1985, Quantico, Va., supplied to author by Glenn E. Stevens, former Los Angeles assistant district attorney, who attended the seminar.

116. Ibid.

117. Kenneth Lanning, telephone interview with author, February 1989.

118. Kenneth Lanning, telephone interview with author, February 1989.

119. Transcript of Proceedings, U.S. Department of Justice, the Attorney General's Commission on Pornography, public hearing, Miami, Fl., 20–22 November 1985, as cited in Lawrence A. Stanley, "The Child Porn Myth," *Cardozo Arts and Entertainment Law Journal* 7 (1989): 295–358 (quotation on p. 301).

120. Carol S. Vance, "Porn in the U.S.A.: The Meese Commission on the Road," *The Nation*, 2–9 August 1986, pp. 76–82.

121. Ibid.; Attorney General's Commission on Pornography, *Attorney General's Com-*

mission on Pornography: Final Report (Washington, D.C.: U.S. Department of Justice, 1986), vols. 1 and 2.

122. Attorney General's Commission on Pornography, *Final Report,* vol. 1, p. 803.

123. Ibid., 182–83.

124. Ibid., pp. 449, 688–89, 731.

125. Clearinghouse on Child Abuse and Neglect Information, NCCAN Compendium of Discretionary Grants; David Finkelhor, "What's Wrong with Sex Between Adults and Children? Ethics and the Problem of Sexual Abuse," in *American Journal of Orthopsychiatry* 49 (1979): 697.

126. Russell, *The Secret Trauma,* pp. 81–82; D. Finkelhor and D. Russell, "Women as Perpetrators: Review of the Evidence," in *Child Sexual Abuse: New Theory and Research,* ed. D. Finkelhor (New York: Free Press, 1984); D. Russell and D. Finkelhor, "The Gender Gap Among Perpetrators of Child Sexual Abuse," in *Sexual Exploitation: Rape, Child Sexual Abuse, and Workplace Harassment,* ed. Diana Russell (Newbury Park, Calif.: Sage Publications, 1984).

127. Timnick, "UCLA to Study Development of Victims of Alleged Abuse."

128. Waterman et al., *Behind the Playground Walls,* p. ix.

129. David Finkelhor, Linda Meyer Williams, with Nanci Burns, *Nursery Crimes: Sexual Abuse in Day Care* (Newbury Park, Calif.: Sage Publications, 1988).

130. The study does not specify how many cases involved ritual abuse allegations, but it includes thirty-six that included more than one perpetrator. Of these, all involved women and were characterized by extreme forms of sadism and threats. In addition, we know of a few ritual-style cases, such as the Wee Care scandal with defendant Kelly Michaels, in which the lone defendant was female, and some where he was male. We thus estimate that Finkelhor and his assistants found about forty ritual cases, or about 15 percent of the total in their sample.

131. Finkelhor and Russell, "Women as Perpetrators," Russell and Finkelhor, "The Gender Gap Among Perpetrators."

132. Finkelhor, Meyer Williams, and Burns, *Nursery Crimes,* p. 47.

133. Ibid., pp. 21–25.

134. B. Baker, "Child Abuse Fears Chill Relationships," *Los Angeles Times,* 19 May 1985.

135. M. Gardner, "Men Who Tend Children: Abuse Cases May Drive Them from Child-Care Field," *Christian Science Monitor,* 24 June 1985; D. Richardson, "Day Care: Men Need Not Apply," *Mother Jones,* 10 July 1985, p. 60; B. Baker, "Child Abuse Fears Chill Relationships," *Los Angeles Times,* 19 May 1985.

136. *New York Times,* "Day-Care Insurance Costs Rise," 30 May 1985, p. C7; Lois Timnick and Carol McGraw, "Initial Hysteria Provoked Positive Changes in Day Care," *Los Angeles Times,* 19 January 1990, p. A18.

137. Kee MacFarlane, Curriculum Vitae, Children's Institute International, Los Angeles, 1987 (photocopy in author's possession).

138. Children's Institute International, "Therapists Currently Treating McMartin Children," n.d. (photocopy in author's possession); David L. Corwin, "Early Diagnosis of Child Sexual Abuse: Diminishing the Lasting Effects," in *Lasting Effects of Child Sexual Abuse,* ed. Gail Wyatt and Gloria Powell (Newbury Park, Calif.: Sage Publications, 1988).

139. MacFarlane, Curriculum Vitae, *Florida v. Bob Fijnje,* "Deposition of Rowland [sic] C. Summit, M.D.," vol. 2 (8 January 1991); Corwin, "Early Diagnosis of Child Sexual Abuse."

140. For Believe the Children's founding, see Waterman et al., *Behind the Playground Walls*, p. 8. For APSAC, see Corwin, "Early Diagnosis of Child Sexual Abuse," pp. 263–64.

141. Debra Cassens Moss, "Are the Children Lying?" *American Bar Association Journal* (May 1987): 59–62.

142. MacFarlane, Curriculum Vitae.

143. *Florida v. Bob Fijnje,* "Deposition of Rowland [*sic*] C. Summit, M.D."; declaration of Roland Summit, M.D., attached to Return, Exhibit A, p. 2 (*in re: Donna Sue Hubbard*, Kern County, Calif., Sup. Ct. No. 5.5-2378); Roland C. Summit, M.D., Curriculum Vitae, 11 December 1989, p. 2 (photocopy in author's possession).

Chapter 7. Accusations

1. All quotes about FC are from "Prisoners of Silence," Frontline PBS-TV, aired 19 October 1993.

2. Jamie Talan, "Words Say: Child Abuse," (New York) *Newsday,* 12 January 1993, pp. 63–64; "Prisoners of Silence."

3. Paul Eberle and Shirley Eberle, *The Abuse of Innocence: The McMartin Preschool Trial* (Buffalo, N.Y.: Prometheus Books, 1993), pp. 242–51. See also, "Transcripts of the Audio Portion of a Videotaped Interview" of fourteen children in *People v. Buckey* (in author's possession).

4. Transcript of the Audio Portion of a Videotaped Interview of K. D. by Kathrine Mac Farlane [*sic*], 24 January 1984 (photocopy in author's possession).

5. Tracy Wilkinson and James Rainey, "Tapes of Children Decided the Case for Most Jurors," (Los Angeles) *Times,* 19 January 1990, South Bay edition, p. A22.

6. Kevin Cody, "Judge Pounders"; idem, "Defendant Raymond Buckey, Juror Mark Basset"; Donald W. Pine, "The Jurors," all in (Hermosa Beach, Calif.) *Easy Reader: A Special Supplement,* 25 January 1990, pp. 3, 16, 9.

7. Child 8C (4 yrs., 9 months), interview by Richard Mastrangelo and Lou Fonolleras, 27 June 1985, *State v. Michaels,* 642 A.2d 1372 (N.J. 1994), appendix.

8. Stanley Clawar and Brynne Rivlin, *Children Held Hostage: Dealing with Programmed and Brainwashed Children* (Chicago: American Bar Association, Family Law Section, 1991), pp. 2–3; Lowell Streiker, *Mindbending* (New York: Doubleday, 1984).

9. *In Re Scott and Brenda Kniffen,* Kern County, Calif., Sup. Ct. No. HC 5092 A&B, Petition, Exhibit 80 (transcript of 4/13/82 interview of Billy Kniffen by Deputy District Attorney Don McGillivray and Sargent Don Fredenberg, pp. 1–46).

10. Ibid., Exh. 79 (transcript of 4/13/82 interview of Byron Kniffen by Deputy District Attorney Don McGillivray and Sargent Don Fredenberg, pp. 1–52).

11. Ibid., Exh. 76 (Declaration of Lynette McCuan, p. 9); John Van De Kamp, *Report of the Attorney General on the Kern County Child Abuse Investigation* (State of California, September 1986), pp. 8–11, 36–37, 40, 71; Kern County grand jury Report of August 1985 (photocopy in author's possession).

12. Hubert H. Humphrey III, *Report of the Attorney General's Office on the Scott County Investigations* (State of Minnesota Attorney General's Office, February 1985).

13. David Raskin and John Yuille, "Problems in Evaluating Interviews of Children in Sexual Abuse Cases," in *Perspectives on Children's Testimony,* ed. Stephen J. Ceci, Michael P. Toglia, David F. Ross (New York: Springer-Verlag 1989), pp.

184–85; Jon Conte and Lucy Berliner, "Sexual Abuse of Children: Implications for Practice," *Social Casework: Journal of Contemporary Social Work* 62 (1981): 601.

14. Eberle, *The Abuse of Innocence,* p. 143; Roland Summit, "The Child Sexual Abuse Accommodation Syndrome," *Child Abuse and Neglect* 7 (1983): 190–91.

15. Michael Trihey, "Tapes Document Boys' Denials, Accusations," *Bakersfield Californian,* 14 April 1986, p. A4.

16. Deposition of Roland C. Summit, M.D., *State of Florida v. Bob Finjnje,* in the Circuit Court of the 11th Judicial Circuit in and for Dade County, Florida, RT vol. 2: 10–13, 39–40.

17. *In Re Donna Sue Hubbard,* Kern County, Calif., Sup. Ct. No. 5.5-2738, Return, Exhibit A (12/11/89 curriculum vitae of Roland Summit, attached to the declaration of Roland Summit).

18. *In Re Pitts, et al.,* Kern County, Calif., Sup. Ct. Nos. 3676, 3703, et seq., reporter's transcript, p. 134.

19. See 1983 California Peace Officers' Standard and Training (P.O.S.T.) Guidelines for the interviewing of children who were suspected victims of sex abuse, and Van de Kamp, *Report of the Attorney General,* pp. 23–29.

20. Investigation and Prosecution of Child Abuse, The National Center for the Prosecution of Child Abuse, chap. 2; New Jersey Governor's Task Force on Child Abuse and Neglect, *Child Abuse and Neglect: A Professional's Guide to Identification, Reporting, Investigation, and Treatment* (1988), p. 31—both quoted in *New Jersey v. Margaret Kelly Michaels,* 642 A.2d 1372, 1378 (N.J., 1994).

21. *Kniffen,* Exh. 70 (transcript of 3/22/84 "Interviewing Child Victims of Sexual Abuse" training tape, pp. 1–42).

22. Gary Scharrer, "Social Worker in Molestation Trial Defends Method of Interviewing Boy," (El Paso, Tex.) *Times,* 7 March 1986, p. 1B. Noble's and Dove's convictions were later overturned on appeal. Noble was retried in 1988 and acquitted; the charges against Dove were subsequently dropped.

23. Debbie Nathan, "Victimizer or Victim: Was Kelly Michaels Unjustly Convicted?" *Village Voice,* 2 August 1988, p. 32.

24. *State v. Margaret Kelly Michaels,* Sup. Ct. of New Jersey, appellate division, docket no. A199-88T4, brief and appendix in support of renewal application for bail pending further proceedings in the appeal herein, p. A175.

25. Amicus Brief presented by Committee of Concerned Social Scientists, prepared by Maggie Bruck and Stephen J. Ceci, *State v. Michaels,* 642 A.2d 1372 (N.J., 1994), p. 12.

26. Paul Boyer and Stephen Nissenbaum, *Salem Possessed: The Social Origins of Witchcraft* (Cambridge, Mass.: Harvard University Press, 1974), p. 25; Robert Calef, *More Wonders of the Invisible World* (orig. pub. London, 1700), in *Narratives of the Witchcraft Cases, 1648–1706,* ed. George Lincoln Burr (1914; reprint, New York: Barnes and Noble, 1968), p. 342.

27. Boyer and Nissenbaum, *Salem Possessed,* pp. 2–3, 23; Marion L. Starkey, *The Devil in Massachusetts: A Modern Inquiry into the Salem Witch Trials* (New York: Anchor Books, 1949), pp. 42–48.

28. Charles W. Upham, *Salem Witchcraft,* 2 vols. (Boston: Wiggins and Lunt, 1867), pp. 6–11, 454–69, 510–11.

29. Starkey, *The Devil in Massachusetts,* pp. 45–47; Ernest Caulfield, "Pediatric Aspects of the Salem Witchcraft Tragedy," *American Journal of Diseases of Children* 65 (May 1943): 788–802.

30. Robert L. Stevenson, "Child's Play," in *Virginibus Puerisque* (1881), quoted in John Wigmore, *Evidence in Trials at Common Law,* vol. 2 (Boston: Little, Brown, 1970), p. 719.

31. *Hughes v. G.G.H. & M. Railway,* 65 Mich. 10, 18 (Michigan, 1887).

32. See, for example, *Wheeler v. United States,* 159 U.S. 523 (1895), in which a five-year-old was deemed competent to testify in a murder trial.

33. Dr. Hans Gross, "Criminal Investigation," cited by Charles Moore in *A Treatise on Facts,* vol. 2 (Northpoint, N.Y: Edward Thompson, 1908), p. 1,056. See also John Wigmore, *Principles of Judicial Proof,* 2d ed. (Boston: Little, Brown, 1931), pp. 287–90.

34. Wigmore, *Evidence,* vol. 3A, pp. 736–44.

35. Stephen J. Ceci and Maggie Bruck, "Suggestibility of the Child Witness: A Historical Review and Synthesis," *Psychological Bulletin* 113 (1993): 405–7.

36. Ibid., p. 405.

37. Elizabeth F. Loftus and Grant M. Davies, "Distortions in the Memory of Children," *Journal of Social Issues* 40 (1984): 51–67; Elizabeth F. Loftus and Hunter G. Hoffman, "Misinformation and Memory: The Creation of New Memories," *Journal of Experimental Psychology: General* 118 (1989): 100–104; Sheri Lynn Johnson, "Cross-Racial Identification Errors in Criminal Cases," *Cornell Law Review* 69 (1984): 934, 938–39; *U.S. v. Wade,* 388 U.S. 264 (1967); *People v. McDonald,* 37 Cal. 3d 351 (1984); Gregory Sarno, Annotation, Admissibility, at Criminal Proceedings, of Expert Testimony on Reliability of Eyewitness Testimony, 46 A.L.R. 4th 1017 (Rochester, N.Y.: Lawyers Cooperative 1986).

38. Gary L. Wells and Donna M. Murray, "Eyewitness Confidence," in *Eyewitness Testimony: Psychological Perspectives,* ed. Gary L. Wells and Elizabeth F. Loftus (New York: Cambridge University Press, 1984), pp. 159–62; Kenneth A. Deffenbacher, "Eyewitness Accuracy and Confidence: Can We Infer Anything About Their Relationship?" *Law and Human Behavior* 4 (1980): 243.

39. "Annotation," 46 A.L.R. 4th 1011.

40. Elizabeth F. Loftus, *Eyewitness Testimony* (Cambridge, Mass.: Harvard University Press, 1979), pp. 86–87.

41. Ibid., pp. 56, 60, 70–72.

42. Ibid., p. 78; Daniel Goleman, "Studies Reveal Suggestibility of Very Young Witnesses," *New York Times,* 11 June 1993, nat'l. ed., pp. A1, A9.

43. Gail S. Goodman and Alison Clarke-Stewart, "Suggestibility in Children's Testimony: Implications for Sex Abuse Investigations," in *The Suggestibility of Children's Recollections: Implications for Eyewitness Testimony,* ed. John Doris (Washington, D.C.: American Psychological Association, 1991), pp. 98–99, 103.

44. See commentary by Melton in Gail S. Goodman et al., *Testifying in Criminal Court: Emotional Effects on Child Sexual Assault Victims,* Monograph of the Society for Research in Child Development (Chicago: University of Chicago Press, 1993), p. 154.

45. Goodman and Clarke-Stewart, "Suggestibility in Children's Testimony," pp. 92–105; Barbara V. Marin et al., "The Potential of Children as Eyewitnesses," *Law*

and Human Behavior 3 (1979): 295–305; Edward M. Duncan, Paul Whitney, and Sean Kunen, "Integration of Visual and Verbal Information in Children's Memories," *Child Development* 53 (1982): 1215–23; Rhona Flin et al., "Children's Memories Following a Five-Month Delay," *British Journal of Psychology* 83 (1992): 323–36; Leslie Rudy and Gail S. Goodman, "Effects of Participation on Children's Reports: Implications for Children's Testimony," *Developmental Psychology* 27 (1991): 527–38; Karen J. Saywitz et al., "Children's Memories of a Physical Examination Involving Genital Touch: Implications for Reports of Child Sexual Abuse," *Journal of Consulting and Clinical Psychology* 59 (1991): 682–91.

46. Alison Clarke-Stewart, William Thompson, and Stephen J. Lepore, "Manipulating Children's Interpretations Through Interrogation," paper presented at the biennial meeting of the Society for Research on Child Development, Kansas City, Mo., May 1989. For a description of the study, see Goodman and Clarke-Stewart, "Suggestibility in Children's Testimony," pp. 92–105; F. Pettit, M. Fegan, and P. Howie, "Interviewer Effects on Children's Testimony," paper presented at the International Congress on Child Abuse and Neglect, Hamburg, Germany, September 1990; Michelle D. Leichtman and Stephen J. Ceci, "The Effects of Stereotypes and Suggestions on Preschoolers' Reports," *Developmental Psychology* (in press); Jennifer Ackil and Maria Zaragoza, "Developmental Differences in Eyewitness Suggestibility and Memory for Source," *Journal of Experimental Child Psychology* (in press); Stephen J. Ceci and Maggie Bruck, *Jeopardy in the Courtroom: A Scientific Analysis of Children's Testimony* (Washington, D.C.; American Psychological Association, 1995); Elizabeth F. Loftus, *The Myth of Repressed Memory* (New York: St. Martin's Press, 1994).

47. Stephen J. Ceci, Michelle Leichtman, and Tara White, "Interviewing Preschoolers: Remembrance of Things Planted," in *The Child Witness in Context: Cognitive, Social, and Legal Perspectives,* ed. Douglas P. Peters (Holland: Kluwer, in press); Gail S. Goodman et al., "Children's Testimony Nearly Four Years After an Event," paper presented at the annual meeting of the Eastern Psychological Association, Boston, 1989; Ann E. Tobey and Gail S. Goodman, "Children's Eyewitness Memory: Effects of Participation and Forensic Context," *Child Abuse and Neglect* 16 (1992): 779–96; Stephen J. Lepore and Barbara Sesco, "Distorting Children's Reports and Interpretations of Events Through Suggestion," *Applied Psychology* 79 (1994): 108–20; Stephen J. Ceci and Maggie Bruck, "Children's Recollections: Translating Research into Policy," *SRCD Social Policy Reports* (1993); Maggie Bruck et al., "I Hardly Cried When I Got My Shot!: Influencing Children's Reports About a Visit to Their Pediatrician," *Child Development* 66 (1995): 193–208; Maggie Bruck et al., "Anatomically Detailed Dolls Do Not Facilitate Preschoolers' Reports of a Pediatric Examination Involving Genital Touching," *Journal of Experimental Psychology: Applied* 1 (1995): 95–109.

48. Stephen J. Ceci et al., "Repeatedly Thinking About Non-Events," *Consciousness and Cognition* 3 (1994): 388–407.

49. Leichtman and Ceci, "Effects of Stereotypes and Suggestions."

50. Alfred Binet, *La Suggestibilité* (Paris: Schleicher Frères, 1900); Pettit, Fegan, and Howie, "Interviewer Effects on Children's Testimony."

51. Robert S. Pynoos and Kathi Nader, "Children's Memory and Proximity to Vio-

lence," *Journal of the American Academy of Child and Adolescent Psychology* (1989), discussed in *Kniffen,* declaration of Elizabeth F. Loftus, Exh. 50.

52. Amicus Brief of Concerned Social Scientists, p. 22; Mary Ann Mason, "A Judicial Dilemma: Expert Witness Testimony in Child Sex Abuse Cases," *Journal of Psychiatry and Law* 19 (1991): 185–219.

53. Amicus Brief of Concerned Social Scientists, pp. 22–28.

54. Paul Realmoto and Sybil Wescoe, "Agreement Among Professionals About a Child's Sexual Abuse Status: Interviews with Sexually Anatomically Correct Dolls as Indicators of Abuse," *Child Abuse and Neglect* 16 (1992): 719–25.

55. Ceci and Bruck, "Children's Recollections: Translating Research into Policy."

56. Ibid.; Stephen J. Ceci, "Cognitive and Social Factors in Children's Testimony," in *APA Master Lectures: Psychology and the Law,* ed. Bruce Sales and Gary Vandenbos (Washington, D.C.: American Psychological Association, 1994), pp. 14–54.

57. Gary Groth-Marnat, *Handbook of Psychological Assessment* (New York: Van Nostrand Reinhold, 1984), p. 135.

58. Ibid., p. 119.

59. Anne Anastasi, *Psychological Testing,* 6th ed. (New York: Macmillan, 1988), p. 611.

60. Clara Jo Stember, "Art Therapy: A New Use in the Diagnosis and Treatment of Sexually Abused Children," in *Sexual Abuse of Children: Selected Readings* (DHHS Publication No. 78-30161), ed. Barbara M. Jones, Linda L. Jenstrom, and Kee MacFarlane (Washington, DC: U.S. Government Printing Office, 1980), pp. 59–63.

61. Ann W. Burgess, Maureen P. McCausland, and Wendy A. Wolbert, "Children's Drawings as Indicators of Sexual Trauma," *Perspectives in Psychiatric Care* 19, no. 2 (1981): 50–58.

62. Susan J. Kelley "Drawings: Critical Communications for Sexually Abused Children," *Pediatric Nursing* 11 (November–December 1985): 421

63. Ibid., p. 424.

64. Catherine Gould, "Diagnosis and Treatment of Ritually Abused Children," in *Out of Darkness: Exploring Satanism and Ritual Abuse,* ed. David K. Sakheim and Susan E. Devine (New York: Lexington Books, 1992), pp. 207–48.

65. "Identification of the Ritually Abused Child," videotape (Ukiah, Calif.: Cavalcade Productions, 1989).

66. Jim Okerblom, "Therapist at Akiki Trial Believes Boy," *San Diego Union-Tribune,* 22 June 1993, p. B-2.

67. Doris Sanford, *Don't Make Me Go Back, Mommy: A Child's Book About Satanic Ritual Abuse* (Portland, Oreg.: Multnomah Press, 1990); *Projective Storytelling Cards, Child Exploitation Series* (Redding, Calif.: Northwest Psychological Publishers, n.d).

68. *Hubbard,* Exh. A (25 August 1992, declaration of Roland Summit, p. 36).

69. *State v. Hadfield,* 788 P.2d 506, 508 (Utah, 1990); Paul Rolly, "Court Orders Hearing in Hadfield Case," *Salt Lake Tribune,* 24 February 1990, p. B-1.

70. Leichtman and Ceci, "The Effects of Stereotypes and Suggestions"; Ceci et al., "Repeatedly Thinking About Non-Events"; Goleman, "Studies Reveal Suggestibility," p. A-9.

71. Amicus Brief of Concerned Social Scientists, pp. 49–50.

Chapter 8. Confessions

1. *The Salem Witchcraft Papers,* comp. Paul Boyer and Stephen Nissenbaum, vol. 1 (New York: Da Capo Press, 1977), pp. 9–10; Kathleen Richardson, *The Salem Witchcraft Trials* (Salem, Mass.: Essex Institute, 1983), pp. 6–8; Paul Boyer and Stephen Nissenbaum, *Salem Possessed: The Social Origins of Witchcraft* (Cambridge, Mass.: Harvard University Press, 1974), pp. 214–16; Carol F. Carlsen, *The Devil in the Shape of a Woman: Witchcraft in Colonial New England* (New York: Norton, 1987), pp. 40–41.

2. *People v. Pitts, et al.,* Kern County Sup. Ct. Nos. 27641, 27774, and 28244, clerk's transcript, pp. 1736, 1741, 3393–97; Gina Miller, personal interview with author, February 1994.

3. *People v. Melvin Weatherly et. al.,* Kern County, Calif., Sup. Ct. nos. 30622A and B., transcript of proceedings on 18 July 1986.

4. Cited in R. Po-chia Hsia, *The Myth of Ritual Murder: Jews and Magic in Reformation Germany* (New Haven, Conn.: Yale University Press, 1988), pp. 139–40.

5. H. R. Trevor-Roper, *The European Witch-Craze of the Sixteenth and Seventeenth Centuries and Other Essays* (New York: Harper Torchbooks, 1969), pp. 120–21.

6. Carlo Ginzburg, introduction to *Ecstasies: Deciphering the Witches' Sabbath,* trans. Raymond Rosenthal (New York: Penguin, 1992).

7. Joseph Klaits, *Servants of Satan: The Age of the Witch Hunts* (Bloomington: Indiana University Press, 1985), p. 135.

8. Zechariah Chafee Jr., Walter H. Pollack, and Carl S. Stern, *Wickersham Commission Reports: The Third Degree Report to the National Commission on Law Observance and Enforcement* (Montclair, N.J.: Patterson Smith, 1968), p. 20. In 1910, the president of the International Association of Chiefs of Police, Major Sylvester Webb, defined the Third Degree as simply the process of questioning after arrest. The term originated in Europe, however, and meant the most severe degree of torture (Klaits, *Servants of Satan,* p. 132).

9. Chafee, Pollack, and Stern, *Wickersham Commission Reports,* pp. 13–263.

10. *Brown v. Mississippi,* 297 U.S. 278 (1936).

11. Fred Edward Inbau and John E. Reid, *Lie Detection and Criminal Interrogation,* 3d ed. (Baltimore: Williams and Wilkins, 1953), p. 185, as cited in Yale Kamisar, Wayne R. LaFave, and Jerold H. Israel, eds., *Modern Criminal Proceedings* (St. Paul, Minn.: West, 1974), fn. 56, p. 503.

12. Fred Edward Inbau and John E. Reid, *Criminal Interrogation and Confessions* (Baltimore: Williams and Wilkins, 1962), as cited in Kamisar, LaFave, and Israel, *Modern Criminal Proceeding,* p. 520.

13. Ibid., p. 521.

14. Edwin D. Driver, "Confessions and the Social Psychology of Coercion," *Harvard Law Review* 82 (1968): 51; Gisli H. Gudjonsson and James A. C. McKeith, "False Confession: Psychological Effects of Interrogation; A Discussion Paper," in *Reconstruction of the Past: The Role of Psychologists in Criminal Trials,* ed. Anne Trankell (Holland: Kluwer, 1982), passim.

15. *Miranda v. Arizona,* 384 U.S. 436 (1966).

16. Margaret Kelly Michaels, personal interview with author, summer 1994.

17. Debbie Nathan, "Victimizer or Victim?: Was Kelly Michaels Unjustly Convicted?" *Village Voice*, 2 August 1988, p. 37.

18. *People v. Pitts, et al.*, 223 Cal. App. 3d 606 (1989); *People v. Duncan*, 204 Cal. App. 3d 613 (1988).

19. Los Angeles County Grand Jury, *Investigation of the Involvement of Jail House Informants in the Criminal Justice System in Los Angeles County* (Los Angeles: Los Angeles County Grand Jury, 1989–90), p. 46.

20. Ibid., pp. 18, 30.

21. Ibid., pp. 13–15; Stachowski memorandum to the William Archibald File re: interview of William Archibald at Soledad Prison to glean information re: Leslie White and Howard Stewart, 23 December 1986 (photocopy in author's possession).

22. Los Angeles County Grand Jury, *Investigation of Jail House Informants*, p. 69.

23. Ibid., pp. 72–73.

24. Gigi Gordon, the Los Angeles attorney whose work sparked the grand jury's investigation. Personal interview with author, summer 1994.

25. Glenn Stevens, personal interview with authors, April 1994.

26. County of Los Angeles sheriff's department memorandum from Sergeant Dvorak to Detective Gunther re: confidential information from an informant, 19 April 1984 (photocopy in author's possession).

27. District Attorney's memorandum to file re: meeting with Pam Moore and Julie Tsitsui, 29 June 1984 (photocopy in author's possession).

28. Michael D. Harris, "Prosecutor Says Witness Admitted to Perjury," *Los Angeles Times*, 1 October 1987; "Key Prosecution Witness Missing," *Los Angeles Times*, 8 October 1987; Paul and Shirley Eberle, *The Abuse of Innocence* (Buffalo, N.Y.: Prometheus Books, 1993), pp. 102–3.

29. Eberle, *The Abuse of Innocence*, pp. 95–100.

30. Memorandum to file from Lael Rubins re: Israel Issac, attachments (Issac's handwritten notes), 10 July 1984 (photocopy in author's possession).

31. Prosecutorial investigative notes, 6 September 1986, 5:36 P.M. entry, discovery, p. 008095 (photocopy in author's possession).

32. Eberle, *The Abuse of Innocence*, pp. 95–104.

33. Lois Timnick, "Trial Judge May Not Achieve Goal as McMartin Case Enters Fifth Year," *Los Angeles Times*, 28 December 1987, metro sec., p. 1.

34. Bernard Diamond, "Inherent Problems in the Use of Pretrial Hypnosis on a Prospective Witness," *California Law Review* 68 (1980): 313–49; *People v. Shirley*, 31 Cal. 3d 18 (1982); *Rock v. Arkansas*, 483 U.S. 44, 97 L. Ed. 2d 37 (1987); *Crane v. Kentucky*, 476 U.S. 683 (1986); *United States v. Roark*, 753 F. 2d. 991 (11th Cir., 1985); *State v. Sawyer*, 561 So. 2d 278 (Fla., 1990); *Reilly v. State*, 355 A. 2d 324 (Conn., 1988).

35. C. Perry and H. Nogrady, "Use of Hypnosis by the Police in the Investigation of Crime: Is Guided Imagery a Safe Substitute?" *British Journal of Experimental and Clinical Hypnosis* 3 (1985): 25–31; Gisli H. Gudjohnsson, "Discussion, Commentary of 'The Use of Hypnosis by the Police in the Investigation of Crime: Is Guided Imagery a Safe Substitute?'" *British Journal of Experimental and Clinical Hypnosis* 3 (1985): 37–38; Richard J. Ofshe, *Making Monsters* (New York: Simon & Schuster, 1994).

36. Ofshe, *Making Monsters*, pp. 165–75. The story of the Ingram case is well told in Lawrence Wright's *Remembering Satan: A Case of Recovered Memory and the Shattering of an American Family* (New York: Knopf, 1994).

37. Jan Hollingsworth, *Unspeakable Acts* (New York: Congdon and Weed, 1986), p. 175.

38. Carl A. Raschke, *Painted Black* (New York: Harper & Row, 1990), pp. 209–15; John Crewdson, *By Silence Betrayed: Sexual Abuse of Children in America* (Boston: Little, Brown, 1988), pp. 129–31.

39. Gail S. Goodman, Christine Aman, and Jodi Hirschman, "Child Sexual and Physical Abuse: Children's Testimony," in *Children's Eyewitness Memory,* eds. Steven J. Ceci, Michelle P. Toglia, and David F. Ross (New York: Springer-Verlag, 1987), pp. 1–2. Details of the case, including excerpts of children's interviews and much of what follows in this chapter, are available in Debbie Nathan, "Revisiting County Walk," *Issues in Child Abuse Accusations* 5, no. 1 (1983): 1–11; and Debbie Nathan, "Reno Reconsidered," *Miami New Times,* 3–9 March 1993, pp. 12–29. All legal documents cited are available as *State of Florida v. Francisco Fuster Escalona,* No. 84-19728 (Appeal No. 85-2531), at the Dade County records storehouse at 9350 NW 12th Street, Miami. See also Hollingsworth, *Unspeakable Acts.* Hollingsworth's personal and financial ties to the Country Walk prosecution effort are described in Nathan. Her account of the case nevertheless makes reliable use of defense and prosecution discovery and trial documents.

40. Research for the discussion of the Fuster case was done by author Debbie Nathan in 1991 for articles that appeared in Miami's *New Times* (3–9 March 1993) and *Issues in Child Abuse Accusations* 6 (1993). Secondary sources were, mainly, the *Miami Herald* and Hollingsworth, *Unspeakable Acts.* Nathan also spent five days in Miami during August 1991 and reviewed numerous boxes of records in *State of Florida v. Francisco Fuster Escalona,* No. 84-19728 (Appeal No. 85-2531), stored at a Dade County records storehouse at 9350 N.W. 12th Street. The materials included depositions from prosecution as well as defense witnesses. Nathan also interviewed Ileana Fuster's former defense attorney, Michael Von Zamft (Francisco Fuster's trial attorney, Jeffrey Samek, died in the late 1980s). Phone interviews were conducted with psychologist Michael Rappaport and, later, with private investigator Stephen Dinerstein. In addition, Nathan reviewed several hours of videotaped interviews with complaining child witnesses, conducted mainly by Drs. Joseph and Laura Braga. The authors have also reviewed materials presented in Frank Fuster's effort to reopen his case in 1994.

41. Hollingsworth, *Unspeakable Acts,* p. 176.

42. Sworn statement of Stephen M. Dinerstein, *State of Florida v. Francisco Fuster,* in the Circuit Court of the 11th Jud. Cir., in and for Dade County, Case No. 84-19728 A, p. 4.

43. "Statement of Ileana Flores Regarding Florida v. Fuster, *State of Florida v. Francisco Fuster,* In the 11th Judicial Circuit, in and for Dade, Florida, Case No. 84-19728," in *Issues in Child Abuse Accusations* 6 (1994): 8–9.

44. Hollingsworth, *Unspeakable Acts,* pp. 264–65, 343–48.

45. Ibid., pp. 315–16, 321.

46. Letter from Ileana Fuster to Judge Robert H. Newman, 13 February 1987 (in discovery materials for *Florida v. Ileana Fuster* [Dade County, Fla.], no. 84-19728B).

47. Deposition of Shirley Jean Blando, *Florida v. Francisco Fuster Escalona* (Dade County, Fla.) No. 34-19728, 1 August 1985, pp. 53–54.

48. Ibid., p. 43.

49. Ibid., pp. 52–53.

50. Ibid., p. 52.

51. Ibid., pp. 32, 39.

52. Sworn statement of Steven Dinerstein, 29 November 1993, filed in *State of Florida v. Frank Fuster;* Steven Dinerstein, conversation with author, 16 May 1994.

53. Deposition of Shirley Jean Blando, pp. 71–72.

54. Charles B. Mutter, M.D., P.A., telephone interview with author, February 1993.

55. Al Messerschmidt and Jay Ducassi, "Ileana Fuster: Frank Beat Me Soon After Met," *Miami Herald,* 13 September 1985, p. C2.

56. Hollingsworth, *Unspeakable Acts,* p. 332.

57. Dinerstein, *Florida v. Francisco Fuster,* p. 4.

58. Ibid., pp. 4–5.

59. Deposition of Shirley Jean Blando, p. 120.

60. Ibid., p. 121.

61. Deposition of Norman Reichenberg, Ph.D., *Florida v. Ileana Fuster* (Dade County, Fla.), No. 84-19728B, 31 July 1985, p. 52.

62. "Statement of Ileana Flores," p. 9.

63. Hollingsworth, *Unspeakable Acts,* p. 355.

64. Michael Von Zamft, Esq., personal interview with author, July 1991.

65. Ibid.

66. Michael Rappaport, telephone interview with author, August 1991.

67. Ibid., 24 February 1993.

68. Ibid., August 1991.

69. "Statement of Ileana Flores," pp. 9–10, 20.

70. Ibid., p. 20.

71. Ibid., pp. 10–11.

72. Ibid., pp. 10, 15.

73. Ibid., pp. 11, 14, 17, 18.

74. Hollingsworth, *Unspeakable Acts,* p. 424.

75. Ibid., p. 475.

76. Deposition of Ileana Flores Fuster, *Florida v. Ileana Fuster* (Dade County, Fla.) No. 84-19728B, 11 September 1985, p. 138.

77. Ibid., 18 September 1985, p. 19.

78. Ibid., p. 15.

79. Ibid., p. 4.

80. "Statement of Ileana Flores," p. 20.

81. Heather Dewar and Christopher Marquis, "U.S. Deports Country Walk Sex-Abuse Figure," *Miami Herald,* 24 May 1989, p. A1.

82. Robert Rosenthal, telephone interview with author, March 1995. Ileana's deposition and other new evidence are the basis of a legal challenge to Frank Fuster's convictions now before the Dade County court (*State of Florida v. Fuster*).

83. Steven Almond, "Reno Reconsidered: Bob Fijnje," *Miami New Times,* 3–9 March 1993; Peter J. Boyer, "Children of Waco," *The New Yorker,* 15 May 1995, pp.

38–45; Trevor Armbrister, "Justice Gone Crazy," *Reader's Digest*, January 1994, pp. 33–40.

Chapter 9. The Medical Evidence

1. Sanford J. Fox, *Science and Justice: The Massachusetts Witchcraft Trials* (Baltimore: Johns Hopkins University Press, 1968), p. 77.

2. John Winthrop, cited in ibid., pp. 80, 81, 82.

3. Ibid., p. 80.

4. Ibid., p. 81.

5. David Chadwick, introduction to John McCann, "Anatomical Standardization of Normal Prepubertal Children," audiocassette of presentation at Health Science Response to Child Maltreatment Conference, Center for Child Protection Children's Hospital and Health Center, San Diego, Calif., 21–24 January 1988, available from Convention Recorders, San Diego.

6. McCann, "Anatomical Standardization."

7. McCann's findings were published the following year. See John McCann et al., "Genital Findings in Prepubertal Girls Selected for Nonabuse: A Descriptive Study," *Pediatrics* 86, no. 3 (September 1990): 428–39; John McCann et al., "Perianal Findings in Prepubertal Children Selected for Nonabuse: A Descriptive Study," *Child Abuse and Neglect* 13 (1989): 179–93.

8. Roscoe L. Pullen, ed., *Communicable Diseases* (Philadelphia: Lea and Febiger, 1950).

9. H. S. Crossen and R. J. Crossen, *Diseases of Women* (St. Louis: Mosby, 1942), p. 888.

10. Arthur Hale Curtis, *A Textbook in Gynecology*, 3rd ed. (Philadelphia: Sanders, 1940), p. 160.

11. A. W. Root, "Endocrinology of Puberty: 1. Normal Sexual Maturation," *Journal of Pediatrics* 83 (1973): 1–19.

12. *Stedman's Medical Dictionary*, 22nd ed. (Baltimore: Williams and Wilkins, 1972), p. 597

13. McCann et al., "Perianal Findings in Prepubertal Children."

14. Debbie Nathan, "False Evidence: How Bad Science Fueled the Hysteria over Child Abuse," *LA Weekly*, 7–13 April 1989, pp. 15–16, 18–19.

15. Ibid.

16. See Jeffrey M. Masson, *The Assault on Truth: Freud's Suppression of the Seduction Theory* (New York: Farrar, Straus & Giroux, 1984), p. 15.

17. Ibid., pp. 22–25.

18. Arno Karlen, *Sexuality and Homosexuality: A New View* (New York: Norton, 1971), p. 185.

19. Tardieu as cited in Jeffrey Weeks, "Inverts, Perverts, and Mary-Annes: Male Prostitution and the Regulation of Homosexuality in England in the Nineteenth and Early Twentieth Centuries," in *The Gay Past: A Collection of Historical Essays*, ed. Salvatore J. Licata and Robert P. Peterson (New York: Harrington Park Press, 1985), p. 117.

20. Tardieu as cited in Karlen, *Sexuality and Homosexuality*, p. 186.

21. Karlen, *Sexuality and Homosexuality*, p. 196.

22. Testimony of Dr. Bruce Woodling, in *People v. Scott Kniffen et al.*, Kern County, California; Sup. Ct. No. 24208, RT 1802.

23. Bruce Woodling and Peter D. Kossoris, "Sexual Misuse, Rape, Molestation and Incest," *Pediatric Clinics of North America*, 28, no. 2 (1981): 481–99.

24. Wilmes R. G. Teixeira, "Hymenal Colposcopic Examination in Sexual Offenses," *American Journal of Forensic Medicine and Pathology* 2, no. 3 (September 1981): 209–15.

25. Jack Epstein, "Latin American Women Take On Macho Culture," *Pacific News Service*, 18–22 April 1994, p. 5.

26. Teixeira, "Hymenal Colposcopic Examination."

27. Bruce A. Woodling and Astrid Heger, "The Use of the Colposcope in the Diagnosis of Sexual Abuse in the Pediatric Age Group," *Child Abuse and Neglect* 10 (1986): 111–14.

28. Hendrika B. Cantwell, "Vaginal Inspection as It Relates to Child Abuse in Girls Under Thirteen," *Child Abuse and Neglect* 7 (1983): 171–76.

29. See *People v. Pitts,* Kern County, Calif. Sup. Ct. Nos. 28244, 27641, and 27774, RT 5361–5365.

30. *In re Scott and Brenda Kniffen,* Kern County, California, Sup. Ct. No. HC 5092A & B., Exhibit 84A (transcript of interview of Tricia McCuan (pseud.)) and Exhibit 84B, declaration of Tricia McCuan (pseud.).

31. Slip opinion, *People v. Brenda Kniffen, et al.,* California Court of Appeal, Fifth District, No. F004423, pp. 34–36; *People v. Scott Kniffen,* RT 625, 651–52.

32. *People v. Scott Kniffen,* RT 10, 416–17.

33. Ibid., RT 10,402–6; 10,446–49.

34. Ibid., RT 10,422–23, 10,447.

35. Ibid., RT 651–52.

36. Ibid., RT 9,331–32.

37. See *People v. Pitts,* 223 Cal. App. 3d 606 (1989).

38. Ibid., RT 5,373–5,423.

39. See *In re Pitts,* Kern County, California Sup. Ct. Nos. 3676, 3703, et seq., bill of Dr. Bruce Woodling marked paid in full, Exh. 18 (contrast with Woodling's trial testimony that he was paid $150 an hour, or $1,200 a day; see *People v. Pitts,* RT 5,426.)

40. Curriculum vitae, Astrid Heger, M.D. (n.d.) (photocopy in author's possession); Nathan, "False Evidence," p. 16.

41. Kevin Cody, "McMartin Kids' Doctor Says Physical Abuse a Certainty," (Hermosa Beach, Calif.) *Easy Reader,* 14 January 1988.

42. Mary A. Fischer, "A Case of Dominoes?" *Los Angeles Magazine,* October 1989, p. 132.

43. See, for example, "Sexual Abuse Diagnostic Center Medical Evaluation of A.R.," Children's Institute International, 22 February 1984 (photocopy in author's possession).

44. Bruce Woodling and Astrid Heger, "Sexual Abuse of Children—Microscopic and Colposcopic Examination of Suspected Victims of Child Sexual Abuse," presentation at Annenberg Center for Health Sciences, Rancho Mirage, Calif., 1985, available as audiocassette No. 85-15-13-05, Annenberg Center for Health Sciences, Eisenhower Medical Center, Rancho Mirage, Calif.

45. The quote, whose substance is attributed to Tardieu, is taken from Paul Bernard, *Des Attentats à la pudeur sur les petites filles* (Laboratoire de Médecine Légale de Lyon) (Paris: Octave Doin, 1886), p. 139, as cited in Masson, *The Assault on Truth,* p. 27.

46. *Response: Child Sexual Abuse—A Medical View,* film, directed by Astrid Heger, Los Angeles: United Way, 1985.

47. Faye Fiore, "Did Pediatrician Believe McMartin Teacher Innocent?" *Torrance* (California) *Daily Breeze,* 18 December 1985, p. A1.

48. Chris Woodyard, "Court Watches First McMartin Videotape: Defense Tries to Show Interviewer Bias," (Los Angeles) *Herald Examiner,* 15 January 1985, p. A7; Sandra Krebs and Dr. Astrid Heger interview with Sarah D., February 9, 1984, defense version (photocopy in author's possession).

49. *Response: Child Sexual Abuse.*

50. David Johnson, "More Training in Directing Child Sexual Abuse Needed, Expert Says," *Los Angeles Times,* 28 January 1986, p. 3.

51. Nathan, "False Evidence," pp. 15–16, 18–19.

52. Curriculum vitae, Heger.

53. American Medical Association, "AMA Diagnostic and Treatment Guidelines Concerning Abuse and Neglect," *Journal of the American Medical Association* 254, no. 6 (9 August 1985): 796–98.

54. Lawrence S. Neinstein, John Goldenring, and Sarah Carpenter, "Nonsexual Transmission of Sexually Transmitted Diseases: An Infrequent Occurrence," *Pediatrics* 74, no. 1 (July 1984): 67–76.

55. Woodyard, "Court Watches First McMartin Videotape."

56. Quoted in Mary Kinetz, "Physical Evidence of Child Abuse," (Manhattan Beach, Calif.) *Beach Reporter,* 31 October 1985.

57. Carol Berkowitz, "The Medical Evaluation of the Child Sexual Molest Victim," audio-cassette of presentation at Health Science Response to Child Maltreatment Conference, Center for Child Protection Children's Hospital and Health Center, San Diego, Calif., 21–24 January 1988, available from Convention Recorders, San Diego.

58. Debbie Nathan, "Child Abuse Evidence Debated: New Data May Aid in Sex-Crime Cases," *Ms.,* March 1989, pp. 81–82.

59. Video of N. Fuster, 26 November 1985, Exh. P-2, transcribed in *Florida v. Francisco Fuster Escalona,* in 11th Judicial Circuit Court, Dade County, Florida No. 84-19278, 20 September 1985, pp. 450–92, and 21 September 1985, p. 23.

60. Deposition of N.F.G, *N.G. v. Arvida Corporation et al.,* Case No. 91-935656, Circuit Court of the 11th Judicial Circuit in and for Dade County, Florida, 28 October 1992 (photocopy in author's possession).

61. W. L. Whittington et al., "Incorrect Identification of Neisseria Gonorrhoeae from Infants and Children," *Pediatric Infectious Disease Journal* 7, no. 1 (1988): 3–10.

62. Medical report of C.B.F. (1987), by Dr. A. Haroutunian, United Hospitals of Newark (photocopy in authors' possession).

63. *New Jersey v. Margaret Kelly Michaels,* Sup. Ct., New Jersey Appellate Division, No. A-199-88-T1 (15 April 1991), p. 36.

64. Lisa Manshel, *Nap Time* (New York: Morrow, 1990), pp. 90–91.

65. Christopher Hobbs and Jane M. Wynne, "Child Abuse: Buggery in Childhood—A Common Syndrome of Child Abuse," *The Lancet,* 4 October 1986, pp. 792–96.

66. Elizabeth Butler-Sloss, "Report of Inquiry into Child Abuse in Cleveland 1987, Final Revise," presented to Parliament by the secretary of state for social services by command of Her Majesty, July 1988.

67. Beatrix Campbell, "Signs of Crisis: Child Sexual Abuse and the Pro-Family State in Britain," *Radical America* 21, no. 4 (1988): 9–11.

68. Ibid., pp. 10–19; Beatrix Campbell, *Unofficial Secrets* (London: Virago Press, 1988).

69. S. Jean Emans et al., "Genital Findings in Sexually Abused Symptomatic and Asymptomatic Girls," *Pediatrics* 79 (1987): 778–85.

70. Abbey B. Berenson et al., "Appearance of the Hymen in Prepubertal Girls," *Pediatrics* 89 (1992): 387–94.

71. Kevin Cody, "Children's Scars Challenged by Buckey's Lawyer," (Hermosa Beach, Calif.) *Easy Reader,* 12 November 1987.

72. Cody, "Heger Accused of Bullying Children."

Chapter 10. Extraordinary Laws

1. National Symposium on Child Molestation (Washington, D.C.: U. S. Department of Justice, 1984); National Symposium on Child Molestation (Washington, D.C.: U.S. Department of Justice, 1985), p. 91.

2. Ibid.

3. Ibid., p. 93.

4. See *People v. Rincon-Pineda,* 14 Cal. 3d. 864, 877–82 (1975).

5. Susan Estrich, *Real Rape* (Cambridge, Mass.: Harvard University Press, 1987), pp. 41–43; note, "The Resistance Standard in Rape Legislation," *Stanford Law Review* 18 (1966): 682; note, "Forcible and Statutory Rape: An Explanation of the Operation and Objective of the Consent Standard," *Yale Law Journal* 62 (1952): 855.

6. *Ballard v. Superior Court,* 64 Cal. 2d. 159 (1966); Annotation, "Requiring Complaining Witness in Prosecution for Sex Crimes to Submit to Psychiatric Examination," 18 A.L.R. 3d 1433 (1968).

7. See John Wigmore, *Evidence in Trials at Common Law,* vol. 3A, sec. 924 A & B (Boston: Little, Brown, 1970), pp. 736–44.

8. *People v. Rincon-Pineda*; California Penal Code Sections 262 (1979), 1112 (1980), 1127d, and 1127e (1974); Leon Letvin, "'Unchaste Character,' Ideology, and the California Rape Evidence Laws," *Southern California Law Review* 54 (1980): 35.

9. Leigh Bienen, *Rape III—National Developments in Rape Reform Legislation, Women's Rights Law Reporter* 6 (1980): 170.

10. Ann Burgess and Lynda Holmstrom, "Rape Trauma Syndrome," *American Journal of Psychiatry* 131 (1974): 981.

11. Ann Burgess and Lynda Holmstrom, "Crisis and Counseling Requests of Rape Victims," *Nursing Research* 23 (1974): 196, 197.

12. Sara Pearlman, "A Psychotherapist's View of Rape," *New Hampshire Bar Journal* 24 (1983): 89, 91.

13. Barbara Rodabaugh and Melanie Austin, *Sexual Assault* (New York: Garland STPN Press, 1981), pp. 53–57; Thomas McCahill, Linda Meyer, and Arthur Fischman, *The Aftermath of Rape* (Lexington, Mass.: Lexington Books, 1979), pp. 23–24; Sedelle Katz and Mary Ann Mazur, *Understanding the Rape Victim: A Synthesis of Research Findings* (New York: Wiley, 1979), esp. p. 216.

14. Charles Feeney, "Expert Psychological Testimony on Credibility Issues," *Military Law Review* 115 (1987): 121, 128–31.

15. *People v. Bledsoe,* 36 Cal. 3d 236, 247 (1984).

16. Judith Herman, *Father-Daughter Incest,* (Cambridge, Mass.: Harvard University Press, 1981), pp. 172.

17. Leslie Sowers, "Unheard Voices," from "Children: Abuse and the Courts" (series), *Chronicle,* (Houston, Tex.) 12 November 1990, p. 10D. See also Dominic Fote,

"Child Witnesses in Sexual Abuse Criminal Proceedings: Their Capabilities, Special Problems, and Proposals for Reform," *Pepperdine Law Review* 13 (1986): 157.

18. John E. B. Myers, *Evidence in Child Abuse and Neglect Cases,* 2d ed. (New York: Wiley, 1992), sec. 7.46.

19. Comment, "A Comprehensive Approach to Child Hearsay Exceptions," *Columbia Law Review* 83 (1983): 1745, 1749; Note, "Parent-Child Incest: Proof at Trial Without Testimony in Court by the Victim," *University of Michigan Journal of Law Reform* 15 (1981): 131; Jacqueline Y. Parker, "The Rights of Child Witnesses: Is the Court a Protector or Perpetrator?" *New England Law Review* 17 (1982): 643.

20. John H. Langbein, "The German Advantage in Civil Procedure," *University of Chicago Law Review* 52 (1985): 833; John S. Applegate, "Witness Preparation," *Texas Law Review* 68 (1989): 277, 310.

21. See Jacqueline Y. Beckett, "The True Value of the Confrontation Clause: A Study of Child Sexual Abuse Trials," *Georgetown Law Journal* 82 (1994): 1605.

22. Myers, *Evidence in Child Abuse,* sec. 5.16.

23. Ibid., chap. 2; John Spencer and Rhona Flin, *The Evidence of Children: The Law and the Psychology* (London: Blackstone Press, 1990).

24. *Rex v. Brasier,* Leach 199, 168 Eng. Rep. 202 (1770).

25. *Wheeler v. United States,* 159 U.S. 523, 527 (1895).

26. See case compilations in Wigmore, *Evidence in Trials,* vol. 2, sec. 506; Myers, *Evidence in Child Abuse,* sec. 2.1.

27. L. D. Pipes, "Workshop Outline: Preparing Child Abuse Victims for the Courtroom Experience," California Consortium of Child Abuse Councils, 13–14 February 1986, p. 2 (in author's possession).

28. *Commonwealth v. Groff,* 548 A.2d 1237 (Penn., 1988); *People v. Jones,* 51 Cal. 3d 294 (1990).

29. Testimony of Dr. Edward Sperling, *People v. Jesus Torres,* Ind. No. 3486/84 (Bronx County, N.Y.), reporter's transcripts: 792–95, cited in memorandum in support of appellant Jesus Torres's leave application, p. 20.

30. Torres's conviction was subsequently overturned on appeal.

31. See, for example, California's Penal Code Section 288 (d), which directs that "in any arrest or prosecution under this section . . . the court shall consider the needs of the child victim and shall do whatever is necessary . . . to prevent psychological harm to the child victim."

32. *Maryland v. Craig,* 497 U.S. 836, 853, fn.2 (1990).

33. Myers, *Evidence in Child Abuse,* chap. 7.

34. Mario Merola, *Big City D.A.* (New York: Random House, 1988), pp. 217–18.

35. Algarin's convictions was later overturned on appeal.

36. Debbie Nathan, *Women and Other Aliens* (El Paso, Tex.: Cinco Puntos Press, 1991), p. 144.

37. *Felix v. State,* 849 P.2d 220, 224, 232–34 (Nev., 1993).

38. *State v. Wright,* 775 P.2d 1224 (Idaho, 1989); *Idaho v. Wright,* 497 U.S. 805 (1990). The Idaho Supreme Court overturned the convictions against Laura Wright, and this decision was affirmed by the U.S. Supreme Court.

39. *State v. Francisco Fuster,* in the Circuit Court of the 11th Judicial Cir., In and For Dade County, Florida, Case No. 84-19728, reporter's transcript, 5 September 1985: 143–48, esp. 147.

40. Ibid., pp. 149–150, 154.

41. *State v. Fuster*, transcript: testimony of Barbara Goldman, 4 September 1985, and testimony of Doris Stiles, 10 September 1985.

42. Marguerite Rosenthal and James A. Louis, "The Law's Evolving Role in Child Abuse and Neglect," in *The Social Context of Child Abuse and Neglect*, ed. Leroy Pelton (New York: Human Sciences Press, 1981), p. 77.

43. *In Re Gault*, 387 U.S. 1 (1967).

44. Melville Bigelow, *History of Procedure in England from the Norman Conquest* (1880; reprint, Boston: Little, Brown, 1987), pp. 301–8.

45. *Frye v. U.S.*, 293 F. 1013, 1014 (D.C. Cir., 1923).

46. Paul Gianelli, "Forensic Science, *Frye, Daubert*, and the Federal Rules," *Criminal Law Bulletin* (September/October 1993): 428–30.

47. Paul Gianelli, "The Admissibility of Novel Scientific Evidence: *Frye v. United States* a Half-Century Later," *Columbia Law Review* 80 (1981): 1197.

48. David Corwin, "Early Diagnosis of Child Sexual Abuse," in *Lasting Effects of Child Sexual Abuse*, ed. Gail Wyatt and Elizabeth Powell (Newbury Park, Calif.: Sage Publications, 1988), p. 253.

49. Ibid., pp. 259–62.

50. *Daubert v. Merrell Dow Pharmaceutical*, 112 S.Ct. 2786 (1993).

51. *State v. Rimmasch*, 775 P.2d 388, 392 (Utah, 1989). See also *Broderick v. Kingsway Assembly of God Church*, 808 P.2d 1211, 1215 (Ala., 1991); *Townsend v. State*, 734 P.2d 705, 708 (Nev., 1992); *Seering v. Dept. of Social Services*, 194 Cal. App. 3d 298 (Calif., 1987); *Glendening v. State*, 536 So.2d 212, 220 (Fla., 1989). But see cases cited in Myers, *Evidence in Child Abuse*, n. 419.

52. See Note, "The Unreliability of Expert Testimony on the Typical Characteristics of Sex Abuse Victims," *Georgetown Law Review* 74 (1985): 429; David McCord, "Expert Psychological Testimony About Child Complainants in Sexual Abuse Prosecutions: A Foray into the Admissibility of Novel Psychological Evidence," *Journal of Criminal Law and Criminology* 77 (1986): 1; David McCord, "The Admissibility of Nontraditional Psychological Evidence," *Oregon Law Review* 66 (1987): 19.

53. Jon Conte et al., "Evaluating Children's Reports of Sexual Abuse: Results from a Survey of Professionals," *American Journal of Orthopsychiatry* 61 (1991): 428, 433.

54. Michelle D. Leichtman and Stephen J. Ceci, "The Effects of Stereotypes and Suggestions on Preschoolers' Reports," *Developmental Psychology* (in press); Stephen J. Ceci et al., "Repeatedly Thinking About Non-Events," *Consciousness and Cognition* 3 (1994): 388–407; Daniel Goleman, "Studies Reveal Suggestibility of Very Young as Witnesses," *New York Times*, 11 June 1993, pp. A-1, A-9.

55. Roland Summit, "The Child Sex Abuse Accommodation Syndrome," *Child Abuse and Neglect* 7 (1983): 179.

56. Testimony of Roland Summit, *State v. Francisco Fuster Escalona*, in the Circuit Court of the Judicial Circuit, Dade County, Florida, Criminal Division, Case No. 84-19728, 27 September 1985, reporter's transcript: 119–20.

57. Ibid., pp. 90, 108, 111.

58. *People v. Bowker*, 203 Cal. App. 3d 385, 392 (1988).

59. *People v. Duell*, 558 N.Y.S. 2d 395, 396 (1990).

60. Myers, *Evidence in Child Abuse*, sec. 4.33, p. 289.

61. *U.S. v. Gillespie*, 852 F.2d 475, 480–81 (9th Cir., 1988); *In Re Amber B.*, 191 Cal. App. 3d 682 (1987).

62. Paul Realmoto and Sybil Wescoe, "Agreement Among Professionals About a Child's Sexual Abuse Status: Interviews with Sexually Anatomically Correct Dolls as Indicators of Abuse," *Child Abuse and Neglect* 16 (1992): 719–25.

63. *In Re Rinesmith*, 376 N.W. 2d 139, 141–42 (Mich., 1985); *In Re M.E.*, 715 S.W. 2d 572 (Miss., 1985); *State v. Speller*, 404 S.E. 2d 15 (N.C., 1991).

64. *People v. Mendibles*, 199 Cal. App. 3d 1277 (1988).

65. Ibid., p. 1295.

66. Myers *Evidence in Child Abuse*, sec. 4.28.

67. Debbie Nathan, "Victimizer or Victim?: Was Kelly Michaels Unjustly Convicted?" *The Village Voice*, 2 August 1988; Dorothy Rabinowitz, "From the Mouths of Babes to a Jail Cell," *Harper's*, May 1990.

68. John Michaels, Kelly Michaels's father, telephone interview with author, September 1994.

69. *Coy v. Iowa*, 487 U.S. 1012 (1988).

70. *State v. Craig*, 560 A.2d 1120, 1128–29 (Md., 1989).

71. *Maryland v. Craig*, 497 U.S. 836, 853–55 (1990).

72. Ibid., pp. 855, 857.

73. See Motion for Leave to File Brief for Amicus Curiae (American Psychological Association, 1990), p. 3. The brief is available in LEXIS, Genfed library, briefs file.

74. Gail S. Goodman et al., *Testifying in Criminal Court: Emotional Effects on Child Sexual Assault Victims*, Monograph of the Society for Research in Child Development (Chicago: University of Chicago Press, 1993), pp. v., 100.

75. See Ralph Underwager and Hollida Wakefield, "Poor Psychology Produces Poor Law," *Law and Human Behavior* 16, no. 2 (1992): 233–43; Gail Goodman, Murray Levine, and Gary B. Melton, "The Best Evidence Produces the Best Law," *Law and Human Behavior* 16, no. 2 (1992): 244–51.

76. Dan Finneran, personal interview with author, 2 May 1995.

77. Yale Kamisar, "Equal Justice in the Gatehouses and Mansions of American Criminal Procedure," in *Modern Criminal Procedure: Cases-Comments-Questions*, ed. Yale Kamisar, Wayne R. LaFave, and Jerold H. Israel (St. Paul, Minn.: West Publishing Co., 1976), p. 502.

78. *State v. Wright*.

79. *Idaho v. Wright*.

80. *State v. Michaels*, 625 A.2d 489 (N.J., 1993).

81. *State v. Michaels*, 642 A.2d 1372 (N.J., 1994).

Chapter 11. Silences Broken, Silences Made

1. Roland C. Summit, "The Child Sexual Abuse Accommodation Syndrome," *Child Abuse and Neglect* 7 (1983): 181–83.

2. Ibid., pp. 184–85.

3. Ibid., p. 188.

4. Ibid.

5. Ibid.

6. Jan Hollingsworth, *Unspeakable Acts* (New York: Congdon and Weed, 1986); John Crewdson, *By Silence Betrayed: Sexual Abuse of Children in America* (Boston: Little, Brown, 1988).

7. San Diego County Commission on Children and Youth Ritual Abuse Task Force, "Ritual Abuse: Treatment, Intervention and Safety Guidelines," September 1991, p. 20; John Gilmore, "Ritual Child Abuse: Horrible, But True," *San Diego Union-Tribune,* 17 April 1989, p. B1.

8. Jill Waterman et al., *Behind the Playground Walls* (New York: Guilford, 1993).

9. *In Re Donna Sue Hubbard,* Kern County, Calif., Sup. Ct. No. 5.5-2378, petitioner's closing brief, appendix A.

10. Diary of Joan Barton (pseud.) (discovery material, *People v. Ray Buckey et al.;* photocopy in author's possession).

11. See Norman O. Brown, *Life Against Death: The Psychoanalytic Meaning of History* (Middletown, Conn.: Wesleyan University Press, 1985; 1st ed. 1959); Herbert Marcuse, *Eros and Civilization: A Philosophical Inquiry into Freud* (Boston: Beacon Press), 1966.

12. Ann Koedt, "The Myth of the Vaginal Orgasm," in *Voices from Women's Liberation,* ed. Leslie B. Tanner (New York: New American Library, 1971); anonymous, "Sex and Women's Liberation," in Redstockings, *Feminist Revolution: An Abridged Edition with Additional Writings* (New York: Random House, 1975), pp. 141–42; Kathie Sarachild, "Consciousness Raising: A Radical Weapon," Redstockings, pp. 144–50; Anne Forer, "Thoughts on Consciousness Raising," Redstockings, pp. 151–52.

13. Gloria Steinem, "Making the Invisible Visible," audio recording of speech presented at the 11th International Conference on Dissociative States, Chicago, 3 November 1994, tape no. 1B.

14. Testimony of Kee MacFarlane, "Child Sexual Victims in the Courts," Hearings Before the Subcommittee on Juvenile Justice of the Committee on the Judiciary of the United States Senate, 2 and 22 May 1984, p. 88.

15. "After McMartin Who Walks Point?: A Roundtable Discussion of Videotaped Testimony from the Film Transcripts," *Roundtable* (Autumn 1990): 7.

16. William K. Stoller, Bakersfield Task Force, SAS, Department of Justice, State of California, Kern County Child Abuse Investigation, case number 85-0181-01A, interview of Kern County District Attorney Edward R. Jagels, 26 November 1985, p. 9.

17. Letter-Report of Investigator Cheryl Hays of the Criminal Investigative Division of the Shelby County District Attorney's General's Office to Ken Lanning, Special Agent for the Federal Bureau of Investigation re: Georgian Hills Day Care case in Memphis, 5 February 1985, pp. 3–4 (photocopy in author's possession).

18. Lawrence Buser, "Court Voids Child Abuse Conviction of Ballard," (Memphis) *Commercial-Appeal,* 21 February 1991.

19. Debbie Nathan, "Bronx Day-Care Scandals: Justice Awaits," *Village Voice,* 10 July 1990, p. 16.

20. Ibid.

21. Mario Merola, *Big City D.A.* (New York: Random House, 1988), p. 216.

22. Larry McShane, "Wrongly Jailed Man, Mother Unite," *Bakersfield Californian,* 25 November 1994, p. A11.

23. Timothy Martin, personal interview with author, July 1990; *In Re Hubbard*, California Court of Appeal No. F021117, Petition, Exh. D (7/19/90 declaration of Timothy Martin).

24. Memorandum from Glenn Stevens to Lael Rubin, Roger Gunson, and Christine Johnston re: "Day Care Center and Satanic Cult/Sexual Exploitation of Children Seminar," 18–21 February and 22 March 1985, pp. 16–17.

25. National Center for Prosecution of Child Abuse, *Investigation and Prosecution of Child Abuse* (Alexandria, Va.: National District Attorney's Association, 1987).

26. Mary Ann Williams, "Witch Hunt," *Chicago Lawyer* 11 (October 1988): 24; Illinois Department of Children and Family Services, *Summary of JCC Investigation—Psychiatric Opinion* (Springfield, Ill., 26 February 1985).

27. Ibid.; T. M. Spencer and Jim Brosseu, "Presumed Guilty," *Savvy Woman*, October 1990, p. 63.

28. Akiki was tried and acquitted; he later sued the San Diego authorities responsible for prosecuting him, and received an estimated $800,000 in an out-of-court settlement. See Jim Okerblom and Tom Blair, "Deal Near in Suit, Say Sources," *San Diego Union-Tribune*, 4 January 1995, p. a1; Jim Okerblom, " 'It's Time to Heal,' Akiki Says After Lawsuit Is Settled Out of Court," *San Diego Union-Tribune*, 7 January 1995.

29. Anne Krueger, "Invasion-of-Privacy Lawsuit Linked to Akiki Trial Dismissed by Judge," San Diego *Union-Tribune*, 19 June 1993, p. B-3; Leslie Wolf, "Satanism at Issue in Akiki Trial: Frenzy of Rumors at Church Recalled," *San Diego Union-Tribune*, 14 August 1993, p. B1; Jim Okerblom and Mark Sauer, "Detective, Prosecutor Had Doubts About Case," *San Diego Union Tribune*, 27 December 1992, p. A11.

30. Jim Okerblom, "Issues of Ritual Abuse Presented at Trial by Akiki Defense Witness," *San Diego Union-Tribune*, 20 August 1993, p. B3; Jim Okerblom and Mark Sauer, "Trial by Therapy," *National Review*, 6 September 1993, p. 39.

31. Paul and Shirley Eberle, *The Abuse of Innocence: The McMartin Preschool Trial* (Buffalo, N.Y.: Prometheus Books, 1993), pp. 32–34.

32. Steve Weiss, telephone interview with author, July 1988. At the time, Weiss lived in Fitchburg, Massachusetts.

33. *New Jersey v. Margaret Kelly Michaels*, Sup. Ct. of New Jersey, Law Division, Essex County, indictment no. 2464-6-85, 29 July 1987, P.M. session.

34. Hubert H. Humphrey III, *Report of the Attorney General's Office on Scott County Investigations* (State of Minnesota Attorney General's Office, February 1985).

35. Richard Cage, "Problems in Multiple Victim Cases" (audio recording of presentation before the Health Sciences Response to Child Maltreatment Conference, Children's Hospital, San Diego, 17–20 January 1990, tape no. 200-19).

36. Alan Rubenstein, *Report: Investigation into Breezy Point Day School* (Office of the District Attorney for Bucks County, Pennsylvania, March 1990); Karl Stark, "No Charges in Preschool Abuse Probe," *Philadelphia Inquirer*, 23 March 1990, p. 1B, 2B.

37. Stark, "No Charges in Preschool Abuse Probe."

38. See *In Re Pitts, et al.*, Kern County, Calif. Sup. Ct. Nos. 3676, 3703, et seq., testimony and exhibits summarized in Petitioner's Opening Brief; Michael Trihey, " 'None of It's True,' Girl Says of Own Molestation Testimony," *Bakersfield Californian*, 10 May 1987, pp. A1, A6; Michael Trihey, "Attorney Claims Molestation Case Report Concealed," *Bakersfield Californian*, 13 May 1987, pp. A1, A2.

39. *People v. Pitts,* 223 Cal. App. 3d 606 (1990).

40. Kenneth V. Lanning, "Investigator's Guide to Allegations of "Ritual" Child Abuse" (Quantico, Va.: FBI Academy, January 1992).

41. Gail S. Goodman et al., *Characteristics and Sources of Allegations of Ritualistic Child Abuse* (Washington, D.C.: National Clearinghouse on Child Abuse and Neglect Information, 1994).

42. Kevin Marron, *Ritual Abuse: Canada's Most Infamous Trial on Child Abuse* (Toronto: McClelland-Bantam, [1988] 1989); Martyn Kendrick, *Anatomy of a Nightmare: The Failure of Society in Dealing with Child Sexual Abuse* (Toronto: Macmillan of Canada, 1988); John Howse, "The Martensville Scandal," Tom Fennel, "The Satan Factors," Patricia Chisholm, "The Search for Safe Day Care," D'Arcy Jenish, "Every Parent's Nightmare"—all in *Maclean's,* 22 June 1992.

43. Philip Jenkins, *Intimate Enemies: Moral Panics in Contemporary Great Britain* (New York: Aldine de Gruyter, 1992).

44. Ibid., p. 185.

45. Ibid., pp. 187–91.

46. Jean La Fontaine, *The Extent and Nature of Organised and Ritual Abuse: Research Findings* (London: HMSO, 1994), pp. 1–35.

47. Jenny Barnett and Michael Hill, "Satanic Panic in New Zealand," *New Zealand Skeptic,* September 1993, no. 29.

48. "Bjugn-saken," *Hvem hva hvor* (Oslo: Aftenposten, 1995), p. 38.

49. Mary Pride, *The Child Abuse Industry* (Westchester, Ill.: Crossway Publishers, 1986); Paul Eberle and Shirley Eberle, *The Politics of Child Abuse* (New York: Lyle Stuart, 1986).

50. See John E. B. Myers, ed., "The Literature of the Backlash," in *The Backlash: Child Protection Under Fire,* ed. John E. B. Myers (Thousand Oaks, Calif.: Sage Publications, 1994); Paul Eberle, telephone interview with author, March 1995.

51. Ralph Underwager and Hollida Wakefield, *The Real World of Child Interrogations* (Springfield, Ill.: Charles C Thomas, 1990); Hollida Wakefield and Ralph Underwager, *Accusations of Child Sexual Abuse* (Springfield, Ill.: Charles C Thomas, 1988); Hollida Wakefield and Ralph Underwager, *Return of the Furies: An Investigation into Recovered Memory Therapy* (Chicago: Open Court, 1994).

52. "Interview: Hollida Wakefield and Ralph Underwager," *Paidika: The Journal of Pedophilia* 3, no. 1, issue 9 (Winter 1993): 4.

53. Ibid., p. 8.

54. Wakefield and Underwager, *Return of the Furies,* p. 377.

55. Richard A. Gardner, *True and False Allegations of Child Sex Abuse* (Cresskill, N.J.: Creative Therapeutics, 1992).

56. Ibid., sec. 1.

57. See, for example, Alexander Cockburn, "Beat the Devil," *The Nation,* 26 February 1990, p. 263; Dorothy Rabinowitz, "From the Mouths of Babes to a Jail Cell," *Harper's,* May 1990, pp. 52–53.

58. Dorothy Rabinowitz, telephone interview with author, 22 June 1995.

59. Bob Williams, "Picking Up the Pieces" and "For Others, Time Eases the Memories," *Los Angeles Times,* 17 July 1988, part 6, pp. 1, 6; Bob Williams, personal interview with author, 1989; "*Los Angeles Times* Inter-Office Correspondence from Bob Williams to Bob Rawitch re: Resignation," 1 September 1989 (photocopy in

author's possession); Bob Williams, "McMartin Memos" (photocopy in author's possession).

60. See, for example, the NCPCA's praise of the book as the leading source of information about the Michaels trial (*Update*, January/February 1991); Lisa Manshel, *Naptime* (New York: Morrow, 1990).

61. Bernice Manshel, telephone interview with author, October 1994.

62. Debbie Nathan, "Reno Reconsidered (Country Walk)," *Miami New Times*, 3–9 March 1993, p. 18; Hollingsworth, *Unspeakable Acts*.

63. Wakefield and Underwager, *Accusations of Child Sexual Abuse*, p. 57.

64. Ibid., p. 58.

65. Clearinghouse on Child Abuse and Neglect Information, *National Center on Child Abuse and Neglect Compendium of Discretionary Grants: Fiscal Years 1975–1991* (Washington, D.C.: U.S. Department of Health and Human Services, National Center on Child Abuse and Neglect, April 1992).

66. U.S. Justice Department, O.J.J.D.P., Grant Project No. 86-JN-CX-K001, PAL Report, 9 July 1991.

67. Grant Manager's Memorandum: the National Center for the Prosecution of Child Abuse Cases; a Cooperative Agreement, Amount $645,871—17 October 1985; memo to Alfred S. Regnery from Ben Shapiro, Office of Juvenile Justice and Delinquency Prevention (OJJDP) [Federal Assistance Application No. 5-0360-8-VA-JS, Juvenile Justice and Delinquency Prevention—Special Emphasis and Technical Assistance, filed by American Prosecutors Research Institute, 20 September 1985].

68. "Program Narrative," in Federal Assistance Application No. 7-0070-0-VA-JN, American Prosecutors Research Institute to Office of Juvenile Justice and Delinquency Prevention, 12 December 1986 (photocopy in author's possession).

69. NCPCA, Investigation and Prosecution of Child Abuse, p. V-67.

70. NCPCA, "Witness Barred," *Update* 3 (December 1990): 1.

71. Ibid.

72. See Richard Ofshe and Ethan Watters, *Making Monsters:* (New York: Scribner's, 1994); Elizabeth Loftus with Katherine Ketchum, *The Myth of Repressed Memory: False Memories and Allegations of Sexual Abuse* (New York: St. Martin's Press, 1994).

73. Ofshe and Watters, *Making Monsters*.

74. Ibid.

75. Ibid.

76. Ibid., pp. 165–75.

77. Fried, "War of Remembrance."

78. Ibid., passim.

79. Ibid., pp. 154–55.

80. Ibid., pp. 155–56.

81. Linda Meyer Williams, "Recall of Childhood Trauma: A Prospective Study of Women's Memories of Child Sexual Abuse," *Journal of Consulting and Clinical Psychology* 62, no. 6 (1994): 1167–76. Donna Della Femina et al., "Child Abuse: Adolescent Records vs. Adult Recall," *Child Abuse and Neglect* 14 (1990): 227–31; Judith Lewis Herman and Emily Schatzow, "Recovery and Verification of Memories of Childhood Sexual Trauma," *Psychoanalytic Psychology* 4 (1987): 1–14.

82. Mark Pendergrast, *Victims of Memory: Incest Accusations and Shattered Lives* (Hinesburg, Vt.: Upper Access, 1995), pp. 85–125, 362–65.

83. P. G. Ney, T. Fung, and A. R. Wicket, "The Worst Combinations of Child Abuse and Neglect," *Child Abuse & Neglect* 18 (1994): 705–14.

84. False Memory Syndrome Foundation Newsletter, "FMSF Scientific and Professional Advisory Board," 17 January 1994; See also American Family Foundation, "Editorial Advisory Board," *Cultic Studies Journal* 10, no. 1 (1993).

85. American Family Foundation, *Satanism: An Information Packet* (see Catherine Gould, "Symptoms Characterizing Satanic Ritual Abuse Not Usually Seen in Sexual Abuse Cases: Preschool Age Children," unpub. ms., 23 May 1986) (photocopy in author's possession).

86. Elizabeth S. Rose, "The Unbelievable: A First-Person Account of Cult Ritual Abuse, *Ms.*, January/February 1993, pp. 40–45; (American Family Foundation News) *Cult Observer* 10 (1993): 2.

87. John Hochman, "Memory Recovery Therapy: A Subculture of Therapy Cults," *FMS Foundation Newsletter,* 1 February 1995, p. 11.

88. Ibid.

89. Steinem, "Making the Invisible Visible"; Stephanie Salter, "Feminist Treason and Intellectual Fascism," *San Francisco Examiner,* 7 April 1993.

90. Anthony Urquiza, telephone interview with author, 24 November 1993.

91. Gail S. Goodman et al., *Characteristics and Sources of Allegations of Ritualistic Child Abuse* (Washington, D.C.: National Center on Child Abuse and Neglect, 1994).

92. See, for example, David Speigel, "Dissociation, Trauma and the DSM-IV," audiocassette of the plenary session of the Tenth International Conference of the International Society for the Study of Multiple Personality and Dissociation, Chicago, 1993, available from Audio Transcripts, Alexandria, Va.

93. Colin Ross, "CIA Mind Control" (unpublished, n.d, photocopy in author's possession).

94. Colin Ross, audiocassette of informal colloquy at the International Conference Memory and Reality: Reconciliation, co-sponsored by The False Memory Syndrome Foundation and the Johns Hopkins Medical Institutions, Baltimore, December 1994 (audiotape in author's possession).

95. Jean Goodwin, "Sadistic Abuse: Principles of Evaluation and Treatment," presentation at the Mesilla Valley Hospital Fifth Annual Sexual Trauma Conference, Las Cruces, N.M., 29 October 1993.

96. Sally Hill and Jean Goodwin, "Satanism: Similarities Between Patient Accounts and Pre-Inquisition Historical Sources," *Dissociation* 2 (1989): 39–44; Richard Noll, "Satanism, UFO Abductions, Historians and Clinicians: Those Who Do Not Remember the Past . . . ," *Dissociation* 2 (1989): 251–53; Jean Goodwin, "Folkloric Techniques of Exorcism: Application to the Treatment of Ritual Abuse Victims," presentation at the First National Conference on Child Sexual Trauma and Adult Sexual Victimization, Grand Traverse Village, Mich., 14 April 1991.

97. Jean M. Goodwin, "Human Vectors of Trauma: Illustrations from the Marquis de Sade," in *Rediscovering Childhood Trauma: Historical Casebook and Clinical Applications,* ed. Jean M. Goodwin (Washington, D.C.: American Psychiatric Press, 1993), pp. 95–111.

98. Ibid, p. 106.

99. Ibid., p. 107.

100. See, for example, Park E. Dietz, R. R. Hazlewood, and J. Warren, "The Sexually

Sadistic Criminal and His Offenses," *Bulletin of the American Academy of Psychiatry and the Law,* 18 (1990): 163–78; Philip Jenkins, *Using Murder: The Social Construction of Serial Homicide* (New York: Aldine de Gruyter, 1994).

101. Mark Sauer & Jim Okerblom, "Trial by Therapy."

102. Steven R. Churm, "Parents Dig Persistently for Evidence," *Los Angeles Times,* 5 June 1990, p. B1. For evidence of implantation of artifacts, see A. W. Brunetti, "Los Angeles County District Attorney Investigator's Report," File No. 83-P-3874, 28 March 1985, and attached exhibit 83P3874, 25 March 1985 (photocopies in author's possession); Debbie Nathan, "McMartin Preschool Tunnels Claims: Evidence of a Hoax, *FMS* (False Memory Syndrome) *Foundation Newsletter* (Philadelphia), September 1994, pp. 5–6.

103. James Wallace, "Satanic Cults: Ex-FBI Agent Fears for Sources," *Seattle Post-Intelligencer,* 4 May 1989, p. B1. See also Nathan, "McMartin Preschool Tunnel Claims"; idem., "The Devil and Mr. Mattox," *Texas Observer,* 2 June 1989, p. 12.

104. Roland C. Summit, "The Dark Tunnels of McMartin," *Journal of Psychohistory* 21, no. 4 (1994): 397–416.

105. Gary Stickel, *Archaeological Investigations of the McMartin Preschool Site, Manhattan Beach, California* (self-published, 1993), p. 104 (photocopy in author's possession).

106. See Ken Baker, managing editor of *Treating Abuse Today,* letter to the author, 7 February 1995; Stickel, *Archaeological Investigations;* John Earl, "The Dark Truth About the Dark Tunnels of McMartin," *Issues in Child Abuse Accusations* 7, no. 2 (Spring 1995): 76–131; Nathan, "McMartin Preschool Tunnel Claims."

107. Steinem, "Making the Invisible Visible"; Stickel, *Archaeological Investigations,* p. 104.

108. Heidi Vanderbilt, "Incest," *Lear's,* February 1992, pp. 49–76.

109. Dorothy Rabinowitz, "A Darkness in Massachusetts," *Wall Street Journal,* 30 January 1995, p. A20; Charles M. Sennot, "Persistent Interviews," *Boston Globe,* 19 March 1995, metro/region, p. 17.

110. Ann Burgess, "Children's Traumatic Memories: Long-Term Follow-up," audiocassette of presentation at the Eleventh International Conference on Dissociative States, Chicago, November 1987, available from Audio Transcripts, Alexandria, Va.

111. B. J. Palermo, "McMartin Investigators Get State Subcontract," (Los Angeles) *Daily Journal,* 17 November 1994, p. A2.

112. See, for example, Myers, *The Backlash.*

Chapter 12. Toward Real Child Protection

1. Alan Guttmacher Institute, *Sex and America's Teenagers* (New York: Alan Guttmacher Institute, 1994) pp. 42, 53.

2. John Hale, *A Modest Inquiry into the Nature of Witchcraft* (1702), quoted in Marion L. Starkey, *The Devil in Massachusetts* (New York: Anchor Doubleday, 1989), p. 263.

Index

3, 6; of Michelle Smith, 45–46, 50, 76,
82, 85, 89, 113, 130, 147, 236; studies
of, 1, 38, 120–23, 127–33, 279*n*70; sub-
version myth and, 4–5, 31–32, 49–50,
103, 241. *See also* Confessions of defen-
dants; Demonology; Evidence; *specific
cases*
Rivera, Geraldo, 4, 234, 242
Robertson, Pat, 35
Rogers, Martha, 255*n*4
Rogers Park Day Care Center (Chicago),
107, 226
Rosemary's Baby , 33–34
Ross, Colin, 240
Rubenstein, Alan, 229
Rubin, Lael, 166, 227
Russell, Diana, 40, 42, 131, 132
Russian Revolution, 33

Sacramento, Calif., 108
Sadistic abuse, 241–42
Salem witch trials, 2, 4, 147–48, 160,
178–79, 253
Sam Stone experiment, 153, 158
San Diego Children's Hospital, 180,
183–84, 198–99
San Diego County Ritual Abuse Task
Force, 222–23, 227, 244
Santa Clara County Juvenile Probation
Department, 18–19
Satanic Church. *See* Church of Satan
Satz, Wayne, 87–88
SCAN (Suspected Child Abuse and
Neglect) Team (UCLA), 70, 73, 76, 79,
82
Scapegoating, 31–32
Schizoaffective disorder, 66
Schizophrenia, 48, 49, 54, 92
Schocken, Marla (pseud.) (Wee Care case,
N.J.), 228
Seattle, Wash., 25
Secondary gain, 125
Seduction theory of neurosis, 46–47
Serial killers, 241
Sex abuse. *See* Child sex abuse; Incest
Sex education in schools, 35
Sex rings, 135, 156; pornography and,

43–44. *See also* Kern County cases;
McMartin Preschool case
Sexuality: breaking the silence around,
223–24; changing attitudes toward, 4,
34, 35, 110, 249; child, 110–11,
154–55, 252; cross-generational, 250;
female, threat of, 133; homosexuality
and, 5–6, 43–44, 57, 115, 186, 249;
nonconventionality in, 115, 249; witch
trials and, 133
Sexually transmitted diseases, 182, 193–95
Shaw, David, 88
Silence of the Lambs (movie), 130
Sixth Amendment, 205–7, 215–17
60 Minutes, 166
Sizemore, Chris, 48–49
SLAM (Stronger Legislation Against
Molestation), 57, 206
Smith, Michelle, 45–46, 48, 50, 76, 82, 85,
89, 113, 130, 147, 236
Snitches, 5, 164–68
Snow, Barbara, 158
Social desirability, 124–25, 151, 152–53
Social Security Act, Title XX, 14
Sodomy, 2, 186
Something About Amelia (TV movie), 107
South Bay Counseling Center, 84
Spencer Township, Ohio, 108
Spitler, Babette (McMartin Preschool case,
Calif.), 73, 84, 89
Stacey, Judith, 18
Star Chamber and High Commission, 162
Stavis, Morton, 215
Steinem, Gloria, 4, 224, 239, 242–43, 247
Stereotypical inducement, 152–53, 158
Stern, Wilhelm, 149
Stevens, Glenn, 87, 166, 272*n*98
Stevenson, Robert Louis, 148
Subversion myth, 4–5, 31–32, 49–50, 103,
241
Suggestibility: of children, 149–54, 158,
168–69, 201; expert witness warnings
about, 151; stereotypical inducement,
152–53, 158; in trance states, 168–70
Summit, Roland, 131, 134, 158, 200, 244;
and the American Professional Society
on the Abuse of Children (APSAC), 135;

Wilbur, Cornelia, 49

Wilcox, Jenny (Ohio case), 230

Williams, Bob, 234

Williams, Linda Meyer, 243

Wilson, Doug, 119, 120

Wilson, Kathryn Dawn (Little Rascals case, N.C.), 3, 255n6

Wilson, Kim, 119, 120

Winfrey, Oprah, 4

Winthrop, John, 179

Witchcraft. *See* Demonology

Women Against Pornography (N.Y.), 40

Women Against Violence in Pornography in the Media (Calif.), 40, 42

Wong case (Kern County, Calif.), 161

Wooden, Ken, 113

Woodling, Bruce, 65, 78, 81, 85, 97, 129, 135, 185, 186–93, 196, 197, 293n39

Wright, Laura (Idaho case), 209, 217–18, 296n38